HISPANIC PSYCHOLOGY

AMADO M. PADILLA
editor

HISPANIC PSYCHOLOGY
Critical Issues in Theory and Research

SAGE Publications
International Educational and Professional Publisher
Thousand Oaks   London   New Delhi

Copyright © 1995 by Sage Publications, Inc.

All rights reserved. No part of this book may be reproduced or utilized in any form or by any means, electronic or mechanical, including photocopying, recording, or by any information storage and retrieval system, without permission in writing from the publisher.

For information address:

SAGE Publications, Inc.
2455 Teller Road
Thousand Oaks, California 91320

SAGE Publications Ltd.
6 Bonhill Street
London EC2A 4PU
United Kingdom

SAGE Publications India Pvt. Ltd.
M-32 Market
Greater Kailash I
New Delhi 110048 India

Printed in the United States of America

Library of Congress Cataloging-in-Publication Data

Hispanic psychology: Critical issues in theory and research / edited by Amado M. Padilla.
    p. cm.
  Includes bibliographical references and index.
  ISBN 0-8039-5552-9 (cl).—ISBN 0-8039-5553-7 (pb)
  1. Hispanic Americans—Psychology. I. Padilla, Amado M.
E184.S75H5836 1995
155.8'468—dc20   94-33265

96 97 98 99 10 9 8 7 6 5 4 3 2

Sage Production Editor: Diana E. Axelsen

To Kathryn, my wife, and my son Diego
who endure most weekends alone while
I edit the *Hispanic Journal of Behavioral Sciences*

Contents

Introduction to Hispanic Psychology   xi
Amado M. Padilla

Part 1: Acculturation and Adaptation

1. Environmental Influences and Personal Choice: A Humanistic Perspective on Acculturation   3
   Raymond T. Garza and *Placida I. Gallegos*

2. Mexican American Family Functioning and Acculturation: A Family Systems Perspective   15
   Erich J. Rueschenberg and *Raymond Buriel*

3. A Multidimensional Measure of Cultural Identity for Latino and Latina Adolescents   26
   María Félix-Ortiz de la Garza, Michael D. Newcomb, and *Hector F. Myers*

4. Acculturative Stress: Minority Status and Distress   43
   Delia H. Saldaña

Part 2: Ethnic Identity and Behavior

5. Ethnic Identity and Self-Esteem:
   A Review and Integration 57
   Jean S. Phinney

6. Ethnic Identity and Adaptation of Mexican
   American Youths in School Settings 71
   Martha E. Bernal, Delia S. Saenz, and
   George P. Knight

7. Ethnic Identity and Bilingualism Attitudes 89
   Aida Hurtado and *Patricia Gurin*

Part 3: Clinical Research and Services

8. Hispanic Mental Health Research:
   A Case for Cultural Psychiatry 107
   Horacio Fabrega Jr.

9. Cultural Considerations in the Use of *DSM-IV*
   With Hispanic Children and Adolescents 131
   Richard C. Cervantes and *William Arroyo*

10. Clinical Issues in the Treatment
    of Chicano Male Gang Youths 148
    Jerald Belitz and *Diana M. Valdez*

Part 4: Health and AIDS Research

11. Language as a Communication Barrier
    in Medical Care for Hispanic Patients 169
    Rosa Seijo, Henry Gomez, and *Judith Freidenberg*

12. Cultural Differences in Attitudes
    and Expectancies Between Hispanic
    and Non-Hispanic White Smokers 182
    *Gerardo Marín, Barbara VanOss Marín,
    Eliseo J. Pérez-Stable, Fabio Sabogal,*
    and *Regina Otero-Sabogal*

13. Communicating the HIV/AIDS
    Risk to Hispanic Populations:
    A Review and Integration 196
    Gustavo A. Yep

14. Impact of Poverty, Homelessness, and Drugs
    on Hispanic Women at Risk for HIV Infection 213
    Adeline Nyamathi and *Rose Vasquez*

Part 5: Gender Studies Research

15. Hispanic Masculinity: Myth or Psychological
    Schema Meriting Clinical Consideration 231
    *J. Manuel Casas, Burl R. Wagenheim, Robert
    Banchero,* and *Juan Mendoza-Romero*

16. Sex Role Identity Among College Students:
    A Cross-Cultural Analysis 245
    Brunilda De León

17. Hispanic Househusbands 257
    Sharon Kantorowski Davis and *Virginia Chavez*

Part 6: Education and Academic Achievement

18. Theoretical Assumptions and Empirical
    Evidence for Academic Achievement
    in Two Languages 273
    Kathryn J. Lindholm

19. Academic Invulnerability Among Mexican
    American Students: The Importance of
    Protective Resources and Appraisals 288
    Sylvia Alatorre Alva

20. Educational Policy and the Growing Latino
    Student Population: Problems and Prospects 303
    Pedro Reyes and *Richard R. Valencia*

References 326
Index 362
About the Editor 367
About the Contributors 369

Introduction to Hispanic Psychology

AMADO M. PADILLA, Editor

This book brings together under one cover important research in Hispanic psychology. By design, all 20 chapters have appeared previously as articles in the *Hispanic Journal of Behavioral Sciences*.[1] The intent is to provide students, researchers, and practitioners easy access to the major theoretical and empirical issues in the field of Hispanic psychology. The book is divided into six major parts: Acculturation and Adaptation, Ethnic Identity and Behavior, Clinical Research and Services, Health and AIDS Research, Gender Studies Research, and Education and Academic Achievement.

The chapters within each of these topical areas are representative of the major themes in Hispanic psychology today. Obviously, these are not the only areas that are being researched and discussed, but they do provide the reader with a very good sampling of the "burning issues" in Hispanic psychology and how these are currently being addressed by social scientists. Furthermore, even though the readings are divided into six major topics, many chapters cut across areas. For example, acculturation is not only important because it presents theoretical and measurement challenges, as shown by the authors in Part 1, but is important in almost every facet of research with Hispanics, ranging from how health care services are delivered to how children are instructed in school.

The objective in compiling this book was to excite readers, regardless of whether they are students or professionals, about the important psychological research and findings being amassed about Hispanics. What we see emerging from these chapters is an important knowledge base about a significant and growing population in the United States. The scholarship is equal to that found in any other specialty area in psychology in its methodological sophistication and contribution to knowledge. More important, though, is the fact that Hispanic psychology shows what is possible when research is framed from an ethnic perspective.

WHAT IS HISPANIC PSYCHOLOGY?

An important concern to the reader is the definition of what constitutes Hispanic psychology. This is an important question because it determines the content of what we call Hispanic psychology and where the work is headed within the broader field of general psychology. Specifically, Hispanic psychology is that branch of ethnic psychology where the population of interest is of Latin American origin, whether such individuals immigrated to the United States or are native-born U.S. citizens who self-identify under any of several national origin designations (e.g., Mexican American, Puerto Rican, Cuban, Guatemalan) or racial/ethnic group (e.g., Chicano, Latino, *mestizo,* Hispanic).

Hispanic psychology is also related to cross-cultural psychology but is distinct in that it concentrates less on intercultural group differences and more on *intra*cultural group differences. In other words, cross-cultural psychology is concerned with the systematic study of experience and behavior as it occurs in different cultures (e.g., Japan and the United States), whereas Hispanic psychology seeks first and foremost to understand the influence of culture and language on people of Latin American origin who share some cultural similarities but who also differ in such characteristics as nationality (e.g., Mexican or Cuban), acculturation level, generation in the United States, political orientation, region of country, and so on. An additional feature of Hispanic psychology and of the psychologists working in this framework is that often the focus is on understanding how experiences with oppression and racism influence the behavior of Latinos.

Another unique feature of Hispanic psychology is the recognition that universalistic principles of behavior do not always apply when societal structures of dominance and oppression exist that influence a person's experiences and interaction with majority group members and institutions. Thus Eurocentric paradigms that are male, middle class, and majority group oriented are frequently inappropriate when applied in the study of Hispanics. In recent years, we have begun to witness a paradigm shift in Hispanic scholarship, which is evident in many of the chapters in this book. This "new scholarship" is marked by conceptual models that make use of Latino cultural and linguistic information, the development of new instruments to assess culture, and interpretations of findings that draw heavily on the social context in which Hispanics live.

Much of the behavioral research with Hispanics has followed the cross-cultural model. The general approach has been to include Hispanics in a study along with members of other ethnic groups (e.g., African Americans or Whites) to determine whether group differences emerge on some dependent variable (e.g., cooperative behavior). If differences are found, an interpretation is generally put forth that attempts to offer a "cultural" explanation for the group differences. To be sure this cross-cultural approach has produced a great deal of interesting and important information about Hispanics. However, out of this cross-cultural approach has grown a theoretical and methodological interest that specifically moves away from comparisons of Hispanics with non-Hispanics and concentrates on understanding the heterogeneity that underlies the different subgroups of Hispanics. For instance, rather than comparing and contrasting Hispanics with other cultural groups, attention may be given to how third- or fourth-generation Mexican American children differ from Mexican immigrant students on educational achievement measures or on differences between U.S.-born Puerto Ricans and island Puerto Ricans on gender role stereotyping. As a result, theoretical notions that incorporate acculturation and/or ethnic identity as moderator variables have become increasingly important in the research literature over the past two decades.

Theories concerning acculturation and its possible accompanying stressors have generally been based on the assumption that the acculturative process is unidirectional and dependent on varying degrees of *direct* exposure to the dominant society. However, in a complex pluralistic society like that which exists in the United States, such an assumption is overly simplistic. Acculturation in a pluralistic society is a process involving both direct and mediated exposure to new values and different lifestyles, and it may also be bidirectional as both immigrants and members of the same ethnic group born in the United States intimately interact. Attention has also been drawn to the stressors involved in families where the generation gap is magnified because parents are immigrants and their children U.S.-born. The issue of acculturation and the psychological stressors that accompany it have not received sufficient attention in these generation and acculturation gap families nor, for that matter, in families in which the spouses differ in ethnicity and culture, resulting in mixed ethnic heritage children who may share the culture of each of their parents. Research on acculturation will necessitate improved theoretical and empirical indexes of acculturative processes. A start in this direction was begun more than a decade ago (Olmedo, 1979; Padilla, 1980b), and refinements continue as we see in the chapter by María Félix-Ortiz de la Garza and her colleagues. Also, Delia Saldaña's chapter points the reader in important new directions of thinking about acculturation stress and psychological functioning.

WHAT ETHNIC LABEL SHOULD BE USED?

The ethnic label used in the title of this book was deliberate but does not indicate a preference. I have been asked on numerous occasions to explain the meaning of the various ethnic labels used by Hispanics. The question is generally embedded in a context of non-Hispanics seeking the most politically correct term to use with their students or research populations. I have also engaged in extended discussions with Latinos who profess that there are only one or two "truly" correct ethnic labels. We recognize that the ethnic label a person chooses to use to self-identify is extremely important and bounded by numerous contextual factors. Some of the factors that determine the choice of an ethnic label are a person's age, acculturation level, generation in the United States, political consciousness, country of birth, region of country, and socioeconomic status. Also important is whether the individual is in school, at work, or in the company of same ethnic group friends or strangers.

In this book, as is true of the *Hispanic Journal of Behavioral Sciences,* authors were free to use whichever ethnic label they felt comfortable using and that best characterized the ethnic identity of the community they were writing about. Thus the reader will likely find all the ethnic labels used by Hispanics to self-identify.

From the perspective offered here, I believe that the "politics" of the label are less important than whatever psychological implications the label may have on individual behavior. Among younger, U.S.-born, university educated individuals, the term Chicano(a) is preferred over Mexican American or Hispanic. On the other hand, the self-designated ethnic label of Latino(a) is preferred by others of Mexican heritage or other Latin American background. Similarly, Cuban origin persons may much prefer Cuban American over Latino, whereas newcomers from Central America would rather be known by their nationality, such as Guatematecos or Salvadoreños. The really important issue, it seems to me, has to do with acknowledging that the ethnic and social group identity that the person uses is important in understanding the experience and worldview of the person, and this constitutes an important consideration in our study of Latinos. Once we recognize the importance of social identity in a person's life, we are more apt to put the cultural, historical, linguistic, and sociological uniqueness of the informants' background at the forefront of our research methodology rather than as an afterthought, which has generally characterized much of psychological research to date. This is where the new scholarship with its paradigm shift is leading as we explore the readings in this book.

The importance of ethnic identity research is seen in the three chapters found in Part 2, Ethnic Identity and Behavior. In her chapter, Jean Phinney provides the reader with a general overview of ethnic identity and self-esteem. Based on her review of the literature, Phinney concludes that strong ethnic identity when accompanied by a positive mainstream orientation is related to high self-esteem. Conversely, individuals experience problems in self-esteem when they have difficulty in demonstrating at least some adaptation to the mainstream group. Martha Bernal and her colleagues continue the discussion of adaptation but situate it specifically in the school setting. They argue that earlier attempts to explain the poor academic achievement of Mexican Americans by relying only on issues of school adaptation have ignored other significant issues related to identity. As an alternative, Bernal et al. offer a social identity theoretical framework where ethnic identity is just one of numerous social identities. According to these authors, this approach offers a more productive avenue for explaining lower academic achievement of Mexican American students. In a chapter that links ethnic identity to political consciousness, Aida Hurtado and Patricia Gurin discuss how solidarity with an ethnic community (e.g., Chicano culture) leads to attitudes and behaviors that favor a social group position. Using a theoretical model of ethnic identity and political consciousness, these authors show the relationship between these constructs and favorable attitudes toward bilingualism.

WHAT ARE THE IMPORTANT ISSUES IN HISPANIC PSYCHOLOGY?

As an observer of the development of Hispanic psychology over more than two decades (Padilla & Ruiz, 1973), it has been fascinating for me to see the expansion of research and issues in the field. Two of these issues have already been mentioned above: acculturation and ethnic identity. Repeatedly, we see the importance of these constructs in psychological research with Latino populations. However, there are other topics that have generated much discussion over the years and which are reflected in this book. Since the establishment of community mental centers in the 1960s, the question of accessible and culturally appropriate mental health services for Latinos has been of primary concern to practitioners (e.g., Padilla, Ruiz, & Alvarez, 1976). The chapters in Part 3, Clinical Research and Services, expand on earlier discussion of mental health services. In a far-ranging examination of Hispanic mental health research, Horacio Fabrega Jr. synthesizes literature from the diverse fields of social medicine, political economy, and social evolution in his quest to broaden the established paradigms and biases in the field of mental health research and service. His goal is to develop a "truly representative cultural psychiatry," which the reader can expand to "cultural psychology and mental health." Fabrega shows us the vision that we need when we think about Hispanic mental health research and service. In the next chapter in this section, Richard Cervantes and William Arroyo bring the reader up to date on the implications of the revisions to the fourth edition of the *Diagnostic and Statistical Manual of Mental Disorders* (*DSM-IV*). More important, they do this from the perspective of Hispanic children and adolescents who have regrettably been ignored in most discussions in the literature on diagnostic assessment and services. Generally, diagnostic assessment concerns have been approached exclusively with Latino adults in mind. The really interesting aspect of the Cervantes and Arroyo contribution is that they force the reader to think about potential sources of cultural bias when strict adherence is mandated in the use of the *DSM-IV* guidelines. By including this reading, I hope to stir up interest among clinicians who specialize in working with Hispanic youths. To ensure that the pot is stirred on the matter of services for youthful Latino populations, the final chapter in this section is devoted to the serious clinical challenges that present themselves when treating Chicano gang members. Authors Jerald Belitz and Diana Valdez deal intelligently with the troublesome issues that surround the question of how to assist with the increasing problem of gangs in Latino communi-

Introduction to Hispanic Psychology   xvii

ties. Youth violence poses major mental health concerns, especially for Latino youths who live in inner cities. The two case studies found in the Belitz and Valdez chapter are especially interesting because they help to orient our thinking about the multiple problems that many of our youths experience.

A major development in psychology over the past two decades has been the emergence of the specialty field of health psychology. Because of their precarious status in this country, many Hispanics are at risk of suffering greater health-related problems than is the general population. Health statistics bear out this assertion. Consequently, any serious book on the psychology of Latinos must include the topic of health from both a prevention and a research perspective. Part 4 comprises four chapters on health issues. The first chapter by Rosa Seijo, Henry Gomez and Judith Freidenberg discusses an important but frequently overlooked issue in health care: the role of language concordance between patient and health care provider. Seijo and her colleagues demonstrate that when client and provider are able to communicate in the same language the client is able to ask more questions of the provider, has better recall of the health-related information given, and is more likely to comply with the treatment. This should not surprise us, but it does show how more health-related research is needed to improve health care to linguistically excluded patient populations.

Smoking continues as one of the major health concerns in the United States. Gerardo Marín and his collaborators show how attitudes and expectancies toward smoking vary between Hispanic and non-Hispanics. They show that the attitudes and expectancies vary across the groups and that acculturation influences the smoking practices of Hispanics.

Finally, because of the epidemic proportion of AIDS in the Latino community two chapters on AIDS research are presented. The first by Gustavo Yep is a review of how a communication/persuasion model can be extended for use in the prevention of HIV/AIDS among Latino. This chapter serves as a good demonstration of how a general theory of communication can be extended to an ethnic population by bridging culture and safe sex information. Often, women are the hapless victims of HIV infection. The dimensions of the AIDS epidemic are magnified in the chapter by Adeline Nyamathi and Rose Vasquez, who discuss findings from a research project that shows how young poverty-level Hispanic women are disproportionately infected with HIV.

The move toward sensitizing the field of psychology on matters of gender relevance is also clearly a part of Hispanic psychology. Part 5, Gender Studies Research, contains three chapters that point toward a new framework for thinking about gender roles in an evolving Latino culture in the United States. The concept of machismo is a salient part of Hispanic culture that may be undergoing some modification through acculturation and the feminist movement among Latinas. In the first chapter, Manuel Casas and his students explore the concept of Hispanic masculinity and place it within the broader realm of gender schema theory. They then use this framework to offer recommendations for clinical intervention with males who negatively adhere to a rigid traditional male gender role. This is an important work because it points out how gender role relationships between Hispanic men and women must change not only in Latin America but in the United States. It also suggests indirectly that the gender role socialization of children among Latinos needs to change.

The chapter by Brunilda De León addresses issues of sex role identity among a college population of students, including Puerto Ricans. Using the Bem Sex Role Inventory, De León found that Puerto Rican men and women are moving away from the strong gender-prescribed behavioral orientations of hypermasculinity and "super" mother. In an unusual chapter, Sharon Kantorowski Davis and Virginia Chavez present qualitative information about stay-at-home Hispanic males who, generally because of loss of employment, are forced to care for children and home while the wife works. These authors discuss how men confront and possibly transcend their machismo and adjust to becoming a househusband. Although the adjustments that must be made by the men studied are great, the study shows that role reversals are possible. The importance of this contribution is that gender role reversals are becoming more commonplace as many Hispanic women find employment outside the home. Together these chapters show how Latino culture is changing when examined from the perspective of male-female relationships.

The final section of the book, Part 6, Education and Academic Achievement, contains three chapters related to educational psychology. In the history of Hispanic psychology, educational research extends back 70 years (Padilla, 1988). The older literature typically involved IQ and/or achievement test performance and its relationship to bilingualism. The *Hispanic Journal of Behavioral Sciences* has sought to encourage the publication of new perspectives on the education of Hispanic school-aged populations. The three chapters in this section represent a "new look" at the problem of school achievement of Hispanic children. The first, by Kathryn Lindholm, discusses a new instructional program—two-way bilingual immersion—which has as its goal bilingual development of both language minority (Latino) and language majority children. Lindholm presents empirical findings for academic achievement in two languages that support the three critical assumptions that serve as the basis for the bilingual immersion model. Her findings demonstrate the validity of bilingual language instruction and show why such programs are viewed as language enrichment programs for both minority *and* majority group children. The popularity of these programs is growing in the United States.

In the next chapter, Sylvia Alatorre Alva reports on a study of educational resilience among a group of 10th-grade Mexican American students. Considerable media coverage has been given to the low school achievement found among Latino students, particularly those in inner-city schools. However, many students do well in school despite coming from environments that place them at great risk for academic failure. Alatorre Alva uncovers important information on the factors that have the potential for enhancing educational resilience among Latino students. Importantly, this chapter demonstrates that academic success in school is just as important a research topic as is school failure if we are to know how to intervene positively on behalf of Hispanic students.

The final chapter by Pedro Reyes and Richard Valencia is a far-ranging analysis of the educational reform movement and its potential impact on Latino students. As Reyes and Valencia know so well, if schools are going to meet the educational needs of Hispanic students in the 21st century, then the educational reforms currently under way and which are transforming public education must not sacrifice equity for excellence. These authors issue a warning that must be taken seriously by psychologists who do work in the nation's schools and with Latino students in particular. Psychologists must contextualize their educational research within the broader policy fabric of the educational school reform movement and cannot be content to confine themselves to bilingual education or special educational assessment, which have been the traditional topics of study in the area of Hispanic educational research.

HOW WERE CONTRIBUTIONS SELECTED?

The explicit purpose of the *Hispanic Journal of Behavioral Sciences* since its inception in 1979 has been to publish relevant articles on Hispanics that could serve as the catalyst for the in-depth behavioral study of people of Latino origin. To this end, the journal has achieved its stated objective and has now concluded nearly two decades of continuous publication. It remains the only journal dedicated exclusively to the publication of behavioral science research on Hispanics.

To provide some context to the selection process, I reviewed and categorized the 300 articles that have appeared in the journal since its inception. Because the journal is interdisciplinary in scope, only those articles of direct psychological relevance were reviewed for topical relevance and suitability for inclusion here. Articles that had broad thematic generalizability were preferred over empirical studies that were more narrow in scope. However, as the reader will see, some chapters are reports of empirical studies, but their implications are far reaching. Some require that the reader be familiar with statistical techniques, including multivariate analysis and factor analysis. Although the contents may exceed the level of a reader with little research training, overall the chapters are very informative even for the person with little quantitative research background. However, another goal in compiling this volume was that it be a research guide to instruct students in the research methodologies used in Latino psychology.

Once selected, the articles were arranged into six categories that exemplify current and important work in the area of Hispanic psychology. As the reader will see, some chapters naturally cut across more than a single category. For instance, research questions involving the role of acculturation in such areas as health psychology, education, and gender studies are evident in the Hispanic psychological literature generally and specifically in the chapters throughout this book. Similarly, the importance of education in some way cuts across almost every research agenda in the study of Hispanics. Thus the final selection of articles for inclusion here was arrived at following painstaking deliberation over which combination of materials would best exemplify the current state of psychological research and knowledge.

WHAT SHOULD READERS GAIN FROM THIS VOLUME?

Several methodological issues touched on in this introductory discussion merit a little more elaboration. As mentioned earlier, the Hispanic culture is both richly heterogeneous and homogeneous. Moreover, as a population description, too many Hispanics hold unskilled and semi-skilled jobs, occupy the lower echelons of the socioeconomic scale, and possess limited educational backgrounds. Yet there are also Hispanics who are members of the middle and upper middle social class, who are professionals, and who strongly identify as Hispanic or Latino. Although a large proportion of Hispanics speak primarily (or only) Spanish, there are many third- and later-generation Hispanics who have minimal or no linguistic skills in Spanish. Heterogeneity is extremely important for an investigator to recognize in designing studies involving Hispanics. Too often in the past, researchers were not careful in defining the Hispanic population that they studied. This is changing, and the hope is that the readings in this book reflect the change that is going on.

Another problem is that investigators often fail to obtain information on the generational status, preference for Spanish, and self-attributed ethnicity of their respondents. Information on these variables provides critical insights into the acculturative level and/or bicultural disposition of subjects. Unless this type of information is collected, it is entirely conceivable that these studies cannot answer the questions they were "designed" to answer because of lack of care in the selection of the Hispanic sample.

Investigators must often control for such variables as Hispanic subgroup (i.e., Mexican, Puerto Rican, Cuban, El Salvadorian), generation (e.g., immigrant, second, third), employment and occupational status of both spouses (or parents, whichever is applicable), and attained education of both spouses (or parents, whichever is applicable). Only when these and other demographic variables are controlled for, especially in investigations where Hispanics are compared with another ethnic group, can we be certain of our conclusions. The literature is filled with studies where these variables are not taken into account, resulting in possible erroneous conclusions or ambiguous findings.

Equally important and still lacking are carefully worked out strategies for obtaining sensitive research information from Hispanic participants. This problem and related strategies are discussed by Marín and Marín (1991). Thus, although this book is not intended as a guide to research with Hispanics, it was my intent to select materials that both inform the reader and afford an appreciation of the state of psychological knowledge about Hispanics. It is my hope that this book's contents spark a new wave of thinking and study by psychologists interested in knowing and learning more about Latinos.

NOTE

1. The first ten volumes of the *Hispanic Journal of Behavioral Sciences (HJBS)* were published as part of research activities funded by a National Institute of Mental Health Grant titled "The Spanish-National Speaking Mental Health Research Center." Amado M. Padilla served as Principal Investigator of this grant. Beginning with Volume XI, 1989, Sage Publications, Inc., became the copyright holder for *HJSB*. Chapters 1, 7, and 10 of this volume appeared in issues of *HJBS* prior to 1989 and are reprinted by permission of Amada M. Padilla, Publisher. Support for publication of Volumes 1 through 10 of *HJSB* was provided by the UCLA Spanish-Speaking Mental Health Research Center.

PART 1

Acculturation and Adaptation

1 ◆

Environmental Influences and Personal Choice

A Humanistic Perspective on Acculturation

RAYMOND T. GARZA

PLACIDA I. GALLEGOS

A cculturation in its many dimensions and derivatives has been studied extensively from various theoretical perspectives. Past efforts have resulted in the development of several models, each with its own emphasis and level of scientific rigor (Padilla, 1980a). As new concepts are presented and quantified, it becomes increasingly critical that we develop and specify models of sufficient theoretical complexity and usefulness to encompass the total scope of the acculturation phenomenon.

This chapter presents a humanistic interaction model and discusses its application in the study of acculturation. Prior to introducing our model, however, we briefly highlight prominent findings and past efforts to identify relevant factors. Next, we present the theoretical foundations of an interactional model previously introduced (Garza & Lipton,

1982) and suggest how this model places the phenomenon of acculturation in a more humanistic perspective. In closing, we propose the multicultural person as a concept that can direct future acculturation research.

Over the years, theoretical models of acculturation have become increasingly complex and sophisticated. Early formulations, such as Stonequist's (1935) "marginal" person theory, viewed the individual as living in the margins of two cultures, lacking roots in either. If marginality breeds poor adjustment, the only healthy alternative is for the individual to choose one or the other culture and to isolate him- or herself in a monocultural cocoon.

The work by Manuel Ramirez (1977, 1983) and associates (Ramirez & Castañeda, 1974; Ramirez, Cox, & Castañeda, 1977; Ramirez, Garza, & Cox, 1980) has provided important evidence showing that participation in more than one culture need not necessarily produce negative outcomes. Instead, they found high levels of adjustment and positive capabilities (e.g., leadership skills) to be associated with high levels of multiculturalism. These results suggest that multicultural persons can develop adaptive strengths and flexibility. Thus exposure to culturally diverse environments can produce positive consequences in individual adjustment and functioning. The question as to why one person adapts positively to the environment while another is completely overwhelmed and defeated by the same environment is yet unanswered. The model we propose has utility in addressing this critical question by providing insight into the dynamics of personal choice and individual variations.

Turning to previous work dealing specifically with acculturation, some researchers have suggested personality types as an answer to how the contingencies of the culture environment are processed and organized (e.g., Padilla, 1980b; Pierce, Clark, & Kaufman, 1978; Szapocznik & Kurtines, 1980), Padilla's (1980b) notions of cultural awareness and ethnic loyalty involve aspects of preference. In pointing to "the personal factor in acculturation," Padilla cites case studies of individuals who seem to defy classification by refusing to conform to a particular cultural type. It is our contention that the humanistic approach provides a framework that can integrate such anomalies and apparent contradictions.

Other theorists (e.g., Berry & Annis, 1974; Spindler & Spindler, 1967) view acculturation as a reactive adaptation to environmental crises. According to Berry and Annis (1974), different individuals choose to move toward, against, or away from the contact arena. Although helpful in identifying options, such formulations fail to give us an adequate explanation of the individual's role in the selection process. Such a stance also fails to account for positive, non-conflict-motivated behaviors such as choosing to acquaint oneself with aspects of another culture for altruistic or even artistic reasons. In outlining the multidimensional aspects of acculturation, Szapocznik and Kurtines (1980) allude to personal choice factors in relinquishing or retaining one's culture of origin. However, more work is needed to identify the factors influencing the choice to retain or relinquish culture. It is our firm contention that a humanistic approach that incorporates aspects of both person and situation could lead to clearer identification of the choice factors and their subsequent impact on behavior.

Another problem is that most studies of acculturation have not devoted enough attention to the simultaneous contributions of cultural, ecological, and personality variables. Simplistic, unidimensional models that view acculturation as a dichotomous linear construct do not address the multitude of factors that affect the individual in adjusting to a complex multicultural society. In fact, even cross-cultural studies of culture and personality have generally overlooked the impact of biculturalism, let alone multiculturalism. By and large, most cross-cultural work in this area has used the modal personality approach, taking what most people in one culture do and comparing it to the mode of another culture. This entirely ignores subgroup and individual variations. A full understanding of this variability is in fact crucial to the development of a heuristically valid theory of acculturation.

From our point of view, such deviations from the cultural mode may indeed involve free will. It is conceivable for an individual, even when confronted with an overbearing set of culturally specific influences, to *choose* to act in a manner incongruent with these cultural demands. Let us consider the example of the individual whose behavior is perfectly congruent with the demands of a particular culture. In this instance, it makes sense intuitively to infer that free will was not operating but that instead the individual was behaving in a mechanistically determined manner. It must be pointed out, however, that such behavior may have been only coincidentally conformant with the cultural demands and that actually it was a strong manifestation of free will. This example illustrates a central point in the humanistic perspective model; even with a strong deterministic sociocultural force, an individual may choose to act to the contrary, indeed exhibiting free will.

It is our contention that an adequate model of acculturation is necessary to provide Hispanic psychology with a conceptual framework for better understanding the complex phenomena associated with acculturation. More important, simplistic models of acculturation that view cultural change as merely movement toward Anglo culture negate the element of individual choice. Cross-cultural studies of Maori acculturation in New Zealand have identified the serious impact that such linear models can have on policy making at the governmental level (Fitzgerald, 1971). These particular studies are especially interesting in that they stress the distinction between acculturation and assimilation. In resisting cultural assimilation, the Maoris managed to adopt and adapt much of the host culture while retaining their cultural core. Fitzgerald (1971) views acculturation not as a simple linear process of change but as a complex, dynamic process wherein the direction of change can be reversed in any acculturative stage by a wide variety of situational factors. This interactional conceptualization stresses the element of individual choice and displays the complicated process of decision making in multiple social and cultural situations.

At this point, we turn to the conceptual foundation of a theoretical model that provides a humanistic alternative to the study of acculturation. Our model as previously discussed (Garza & Lipton, 1982, 1984) draws from the work of Brunswik (1952), Kelly (1955), and Lewin (1935). The model incorporates two basic yet seemingly divergent metatheoretical assumptions: free will and the inherent probabilistic nature of environmental contingencies.

Although it is rarely applied explicitly to social psychology, we have used Brunswik's (1952) "lens model" in developing the conceptual framework for a Hispanic social psychology (see Garza & Lipton, 1984). According to the lens model, in any given situation an individual is faced with a large number of potential stimuli, each with a varying respective probability of occurrence, along with an associated repertoire of possible behaviors, also with varying probabilities of enactment. This is the essence of Brunswik's (1955) probabilistic functionalism. Putting this into a cultural perspective, as we have discussed earlier (Garza & Lipton, 1982), it can be hypothesized that the cultural environment affects the range of stimuli and experiences available, as well as the repertoire of potential social behaviors and the respective probabilities associated with each specific stimulus and response.

Brunswik's (1952) lens model has much utility for multicultural research because of its comprehensive complexity. Brunswik viewed the goal of the organism as survival and adaptation to the irregularities of the environment. To achieve stable relations in the midst of a chaotic world, the individual makes his or her best bet on the basis of all the probabilities available (Hammond, 1955). The person is constantly striving to solve life's problems as effectively as possible. To do so, he or she assesses alternative ways of responding with the purpose of obtaining the most favorable outcomes.

It is important to note that the environment does not impact on individuals uniformly but, rather, scatters its effects differentially. The environment consists of a much richer texture than mere hard-and-fast, one-to-one relations. As such, it is inappropriate to conclude that a particular cultural environment automatically produces certain behaviors. Brunswik (1952) criticized psychologists for not only restricting themselves to simplistic models of man but also proposing simplistic models of the environment. If Chicano or Hispanic psychology is to avoid these same pitfalls, we must accept the irregularities inherent in both person and situation and concentrate our efforts on describing individuals in relationship to the world from a probabilistic stance.

In our efforts to identify specific environmental factors that affect Chicanos, it is crucial that we avoid oversimplification. An example of this would be the notion of classifying Chicanos according to generation. It is inaccurate to assume that a third- or fourth-generation Chicano is necessarily more acculturated that a first- or second-generation Chicano. Although the factor of generation is a relevant consideration, we should not lose sight of the fact that even given the same or similar external environmental factor, many variations can result. Again, we find ourselves dealing with the issue of personal choice and its impact on the development of the individual.

Although a complete review of the controversial free will-determinism debate is inappropriate here, the role of personal choice requires some mention. As Kelly (1955) astutely pointed out, neither free will nor determinism is an absolute but is relative and can only be assessed in comparison to something else. Kelly went so far as to imply that a person is both free and determined, freely determining one's own behavior. Expanding on this notion, we contend that there is an inverse relationship between the probability of environmental (i.e., cultural) contingencies and the potential for a person's free will. Not to discount either unconscious motivations or the inherent capacity to make choices on purely arbitrary grounds (Rychlak, 1968, 1977), individuals often make conscious choices concerning both their exposure to cultural influences and the adoption of corresponding behaviors. Hence the individual can bear quite a bit of the responsibility for his or her cultural characteristics. A Chicano adult can "choose" whether or not to acculturate into the mainstream Anglo society in the sense of adopting or rejecting Anglo cultural perspectives.

Kelly (1955) considered behavior as anticipatory in nature and viewed the person as attempting to systematize his or her view of the world in order to deal with the contradictions inherent in the environment. His dynamic theory is based on the idea of "personal constructs," which can be seen as working hypotheses used by the individual to structure and anticipate life events. The Hispanic lives in a culturally distinct environment composed of influences form several cultures and, to modify Kelly's notion of personal constructs, is exposed to a wide range of "cultural constructs." As in the case of Kelly's personal constructs, cultural constructs do not exist in an absolute sense. To the contrary, a cultural construct is nothing more than what an individual construes it to be, and different individuals may interpret one cultural construct quite distinctly. A cultural construct, then, has no independent existence in reality but is instead a culturally specific artifact subject to individualistic interpretations. Within this humanistic framework, we argue that cultural constructs have a respective probability of influencing the individual, depending on significance and convenience. Theoretically, this probability may range from 0% to 100%. For example, the probability that a highly Americanized Chicano would be influenced by traditional Mexican cultural constructs might be quite low.

As noted earlier, we argue for the existence of an inverse relationship between environmental probabilism and humanistic free will. Specifically, if a cultural construct is very powerful (e.g., prohibition against eating beef in India), the behavior of the individuals with respect to that construct is highly determined, with a majority conforming to the construct. Of course, in line with Kelly's view of personal constructs, an individual can subsequently choose to modify or even reject a given cultural construct, regardless of original environmental strength or saliency.

Concerning biculturals or multiculturals, the range of cultural constructs available to them is much greater than those of monoculturals (if indeed there is such person). Individuals relatively isolated or separated from contact with other cultures will be exposed to a limited range of cultural diversity. For example, fearing apprehension by immigration authorities and lacking fluency in English, undocumented Mexican workers may experience only minimal contact with Anglo American group members. Their avoidance of mainstream American society leads to limited exposure to Anglo American cultural constructs. Of course, intervening variables, in terms of perceived convenience and significance, concern the level of acculturation and culture dominance of the Chicano. A highly Americanized Chicano, in comparison to a highly Mexicanized Chicano, would have a higher probability of exposure to and hence of adopting Anglo cultural constructs, resulting in behavior congruent with Anglo norms. However, considering Chicanos as a multicultural group receiving influences of varying strengths from many different cultures, including but not restricted to Anglo and Mexican influences, it is very difficult to assess the specific cultural aspects resulting in certain personality and behavioral characteristics.

The meaning of the terms "convenience" and "significance" as they apply to cultural constructs should be further examined. When faced with a simple binary decision, an individual is likely to select the more "convenient" of two alternatives. However, this may not be a manifestation of will but merely a mechanistic "noncognitive" response. However, when the decision is personally "significant" to the individual, this factor tends to override that of convenience. If a cultural construct is important or significant to an individual, he or she is more likely to make a deliberate "cognitive" decision as to the course of action, reflecting the enactment of free will.

Two other characteristics of cultural constructs that we have discussed are very important to the theoretical framework presented here: namely, strength and saliency. The saliency of a cultural construct refers to the inherent probabilism within the environment, specifically the probability of the individual being exposed to and influenced by a given construct. However, as has been mentioned, the individual can willfully alter his or her behavior so as to make the exposure to certain constructs more or less likely, thus altering its environmental saliency. The strength of a construct has its antecedents in the history and cultural heritage of an individual as well as in present socioenvironmental contingencies and refers to the potency of the construct on a particular individual. Of course, the concept of strength is applicable only when it has become salient.

From a multicultural framework, we see that the more flexible the minority person is, the more quickly and easily he or she can adjust to the changing environment. If the individual finds the inconsistencies and contradictions of simultaneously living in two or more cultures overwhelming, he or she can retreat into the security of choosing one set of stimuli and totally rejecting another. In an effort to overcome the anxiety and uncertainty of a dual existence, the person constricts or tightens his or her construct system. Although serving a short-term function of decreasing anxiety and uncertainty, the choice to constrict one's worldview results in along-term damage to the person's psychological health and ability to adapt constructively to a complex environment. The constriction process just described may account for both the overacculturation and underacculturation referred to by Padilla (1980b).

The development of an open and permeable cultural construct system allows for the resolution of contradictions and the formulation of constructs that help make life tolerable for the individual. Such persons should be able to exist and fully function in Anglo society without having to reject their native culture and lifestyle. The individual can then live in both worlds without feeling guilty for betraying one culture for another. The person can see him- or herself as consistent and can recognize his or her freedom to choose the behavior most suitable. As originally noted by Kelly (1955), this "propositional thinker" is constantly open to new evidence and is willing to change his or her frame of reference to increase accurate prediction and control of future events.

Although personal choice is ever present, we recognize limitations imposed by the very nature of the environment. Lewin's (1935) dynamic theory of personality focused special attention on the impact of surroundings on the development of the person. He acknowledged that not all "environmental regions" are accessible to all persons. Whether a person's range of free movement is large or small has profound significance on the individual's behavior. Lewin describes environmental barriers that interfere with the individual's abilities to enter into different regions.

The Chicano faced with a wide variety of environmental barriers must choose his or her behavior accordingly. Lewin holds that actions are the result of positive and negative forces that drive or sustain the person. The relative strengths of these internal factors are naturally very numerous and influence the development of conflict. Psychologically, we can define conflict as opposition in approximately equal field forces. When confronted with forces both positive and negative, the individual may experience the wounding of failure and withdraw either physically or psychically from the field. A tragic example of this reaction to conflict can be when a minority person avoids contact with Anglos and in effect turns inward, fearing rejection or failure. Phrasing this in humanistic terms, the individual in this case determines that the situation is hopeless and despairing, contracts physically and psychically, and attempts to build a protective fortress around him- or herself.

On a more positive note, Lewin points out that the individual who can endure existence in an unresolved conflict situation displays great self-control and will. As such, the minority group member who is not overwhelmed by the inevitably contradictory elements of multiple cultural influences is well equipped to master his or her environment. On the other hand, those individuals who cannot integrate and cope with conflicting aspects of the cultural milieu experience limited options and psychological disorientation.

Prior to discussing the specific components of the interactional model we have developed (see Garza & Lipton, 1982, 1984), it seems appropriate to summarize the theoretical foundations that have influenced our conceptualizations. From Kelly's (1955) personal construct theory we have derived the notion of cultural constructs and have suggested how personal choice influences individual adaptation to the environment. Aspects of Lewin's (1935) field theory were useful in our conceptualization of environmental barriers and the dynamic processes involved in dealing with the inevitable limitations confronted by the individual. We have outlined how certain aspects of Brunswik's (1952) lens model are especially applicable to the study of bicultural and multicultural groups. Certainly, both the range of stimuli and the repertoire of responses of all individuals vary widely as a function of acculturation, socioeconomic background, and geographic region, but we propose that such effects are more pronounced with multicultural populations. Hence we have derived our humanistic interaction model by integrating relevant aspects of each of these theories and contend that this approach may lead to the development of a framework with considerable explanatory power, heuristic value, and external validity.

In our interactional model shown in Figure 1.1, there are five components ranging from socioecological influences to social behavior. While both socioecological and multicultural influences affect family and individual factors, social behavior is not determined exclusively by any of these components but, rather, by a continuous interaction among individual, family, multicultural, and socioecological factors. Also, it should be noted that social behavioral expressions provide feedback effects to both the multicultural and sociocultural components.

In designing the model, we purposely avoided a narrow delineation of each of the components; in this way, it was thought that the model would have maximal utility and flexibility for future research endeavors involving Hispanics. However, it may be useful to briefly elaborate on the components. The "socioecological influences" incorporate socioeconomic and other noncultural environmental factors that directly affect "family influences" (e.g., socialization practices and parental attitudes). The "individual" component includes personality as well as other affective and cognitive components, while "social behavior" refers simply to overt behavioral expressions of individuals. Finally, the socioecological component also interacts with the "multicultural influences," which encompass language and societal sanctions.

A critically important feature of our interactional mode is that it allows for a great deal of within-culture individual variability, much as

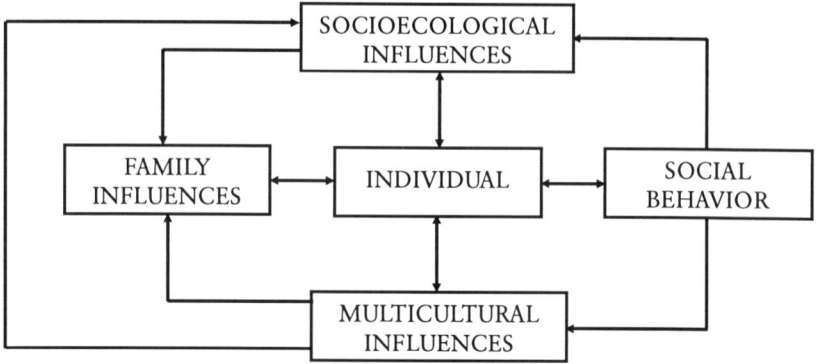

Figure 1.1. A Humanistic Interaction Model
SOURCE: Garza and Lipton (1984). From Garza, R. T., and Lipton, J. P., Foundations for a Chicano social psychology. In Martinez, J. L., Jr., & Mendoza, R. H. (1984). *Chicano psychology*, 2nd ed. New York: Academic Press, pp. 335-336. Reprinted by permission of Academic Press.

may be based on differential perceptions of cultural and other factors. Indeed, as we have noted elsewhere (Garza & Lipton, 1982), the interactional perspective of the model implies that even identical cultural, socialization, and situational factors may lead to totally different social behaviors, depending on individual perceptions of these influences. Conversely, substantially different cultural, socialization, and situational factors may lead to similar behavioral patterns.

While future researchers may use only one portion of the model at a time, the interactional perspective must not be lost. In other words, although the research design need not encompass the entire model, an assessment of the interaction between relevant components should not be ignored. Likewise, the multidimensionality associated with multicultural environments would seem to preempt the use of classical social psychological experimental paradigms. Although such approaches might offer important causal information in a very limited context, nevertheless, given the tremendous potential for subgroup or even individual variability, a highly controlled univariate experimental paradigm is likely to account for only an inconsequential portion of the variance. The study of acculturation requires a multivariate theoretical foundation and research methodology. Such an approach incorporates numerous sociocultural and individual variables. Moreover, a rigorous multivariate approach lessens the likelihood of unjustified overextension or overgeneralization since the relative strength of each cultural construct is readily apparent for the group and can be easily assessed for any subculture or smaller group of individuals.

The uniqueness of the environmental context of multicultural populations requires some additional elucidation at this point. Can the effects of acculturation on personality development and related behaviors be inferred from findings based on the "parent" cultures? An example might help clarify the matter. Even though there is a vast degree of within-group variability due to differential levels of acculturation and assimilation, the Chicano or Mexican American population of the United States has been characterized as a bicultural group. Yet how do their sociocultural influences compare with those of Mexican nationals and those of mainstream Anglos? It is our contention that, in addition to containing qualities characteristically found in "American" and "Mexican" cultures, Chicano culture also contains many unique, hybrid characteristics atypical of either parent culture. This is often the case with so-called bicultural groups (e.g., Jewish Americans, Polish Americans, etc.). In other words, biculturalism entails more than a mere summation of the two cultures involved, essentially the whole being greater than the sum of the parts.

Taking this argument further, the theoretical framework for a truly universal psychology must be expanded to include the concept of multiculturalism. In the final analysis, people in every society are the end product of different sociocultural influences resulting from interactions with family, peers, and other aspects of the external world. In essence, then, everyone is multicultural to some extent. Not only that, but the specific cultural characteristics of each individual are unique, different even from other family members. The crux of this somewhat radical position is "universal multiculturalism." Within this framework, then, Chicanos are a multicultural group of people, with a greater influence from the Mexican and Anglo cultures as well as from a number of other different cultures and subcultures.

In addressing the profound influences of cultural environment on the person, Adler (1974) refers to "a new kind of person," who is both socially and psychologically a product of interwoven cultures. The multicultural person described by Adler has come to grips with the multiplicity of realities with which he or she is confronted. We find this conceptualization consistent with the interactional model in that the multicultural person is characterized by a view of the world as a dynamically moving process and remains constantly open to the myriad of stimuli encountered. While retaining the central sense of self reflected in personal choices, this person is fluid in his/her conceptualizations and free to react in whatever manner deemed most productive in a particular situation.

The concept of a multicultural person is similar to Walsh's (1973) "universal" person and is concerned with a commitment to essential similarities between people everywhere while retaining a strong commitment to their differences. This apparent paradox is resolved by understanding that such a person strives to retain and preserve whatever is most significant and valuable in each culture as a way of preserving the whole.

In summary, it is our overriding concern that the aspect of personal choice has been minimized or ignored in past theoretical developments. By using the humanistic interaction model, we can simultaneously consider the complexity of environmental factors and yet give clear emphasis to the role of individual choice. By taking such an outlook we can begin to develop strategies for developing multicultural skills to deal with the ever-changing, stress-producing society in which we live.

2

♦

Mexican American Family Functioning and Acculturation

A Family Systems Perspective

ERICH J. RUESCHENBERG

RAYMOND BURIEL

Although the Mexican American family has been a subject of inquiry for several decades, the existing literature does not yield an unequivocal picture of this group's characteristics and patterns of functioning. This is due primarily to two factors. First, researchers have come to recognize the extreme diversity in Mexican American families (Andrade, 1982; Grebler, Moore, & Guzman, 1970; Murillo, 1976; Zapata & Jaramillo, 1981). Thus early impressionistic studies that provided general descriptions of the "typical" Mexican American family (Jones, 1948; Lewis, 1949) have been replaced by more recent studies that have been more empirically based and have found higher levels of within-group variability (e.g., Cromwell & Cromwell, 1978; Levine &

Bartz, 1979; Ybarra-Soriano, 1977). The second factor is the diverse nature of the literature itself. Research in this area has varied considerably in terms of conceptualizations, methodologies, design, measures used, and populations sampled (Padilla & Lindholm, 1983; Ramirez & Arce, 1981).

This chapter investigates the relationship of acculturation to family functioning. Family functioning is defined as the pattern of interactions among family members and also the family members' interactions with social systems outside the home. With rare exception, the effects of acculturation on family functioning have been overlooked (Sabogal, Marín, Otero-Sabogal, VanOss Marín, & Pérez, 1987).

Although the impact of social-environmental variables on family functioning has long been supported (Kluckhohn, 1953; Parsons, 1953), most research on the Mexican American family has failed to consider the complex interaction of familial relationships and economic, political, social, and cultural variables.

From a systems perspective (Kaye, 1985) it is possible to view the Mexican American family as an open system with both internal and external aspects of functioning. Internal aspects include the family members' patterns of relationships and interactions and also the structure of the family system. External aspects include the family's interactions with outside social systems including social institutions and the larger context of U.S. society.

Using a family systems framework, Kaye (1985) discusses how the family needs to be viewed as an adapting entity with its own developmental processes. The family unit undergoes its own development that transcends the development of its individual members. From a systems perspective it is possible to view the Mexican American family as capable of adapting to U.S. social systems while retaining many of its internal characteristics that are cultural in nature. There is already some evidence suggesting a "differential" pattern of acculturation within Latino families (Sabogal et al., 1987).

Understanding how acculturation has an impact on family functioning requires examination of how families mediate between society and their individual members and how families equip their members for participation in outside systems. The use of a family systems perspective is helpful for this examination but entails a significant departure from the study of the individual. The essential difference is that within a family systems perspective the family rather than the individual constitutes the main unit of analysis. The family is conceptualized as having its own organization and character that color the behavior of individual family members. That is, the behavior of any family member is at least partially influenced by the total family system.

This chapter attempts to identify selective changes taking place over time within families of Mexican descent. These changes reflect the acculturation process. In general, psychological research on acculturation has neglected family variables, focusing instead on the individual outside this primary social group (Brody, 1970). In their review of research priorities for Hispanics, Padilla and Lindholm (1983) cite a need for in-depth empirical research that takes into account the fact that Hispanic families are in different stages of acculturation. Until recently, acculturation has been viewed primarily from an assimilationist perspective based on the experience of European immigrant families at the turn of this century (Seña-Rivera, 1976). These European families essentially melted into a dominant U.S. society that was phenotypically similar and itself a product of earlier European immigration. The circumstances surrounding immigration of Mexican families, however, are socially, historically, and culturally different. These differences require alternative models that can more adequately describe and explain acculturative processes in Mexican American families (Berry, 1980). Ramirez (1983) argues that the unique acculturation experiences of Mexican American families can produce a bicultural adaptation to U.S. society.

Indeed, the sociohistorical context of the Southwest makes it likely that acculturation of Mexican American families living in this environment will follow a different course than that of European descent families. On the one hand, the pressure to retain Mexican values arises from the fact that the Southwest (a) was once a part of Mexico, (b) is geographically connected to Mexico, and (c) is heavily populated by persons of Mexican descent, many of them recent immigrants. On the other hand, because the dominant institutions in society are largely controlled by Euro-Americans it is necessary for Mexican Americans to adapt their behavior to them in ways different from their behavior in the family and immediate community. The likely outcome, therefore, is some form of biculturalism, with family functioning in the home reflecting a more Mexican orientation and activities outside the home and community reflecting a more Euro-American orientation.

Our study examined three groups of families at different levels of acculturation. Based on the work of Olmedo (1980) and Padilla (1980b), several dimensions of acculturation were considered, including language preference and proficiency, generational status, and recency of migration.

The family systems framework guiding this study predicts that level of acculturation is differentially related to family functioning. Specifically, it was hypothesized that higher levels of acculturation would be positively related to areas of functioning reflecting increased family involvement with external social systems such as school, work, community, and other

U.S. institutions. Conversely, it was also hypothesized that there would be no significant relationship between acculturation and family functioning related to the internal family system and its operations. These include both patterns of intrafamilial relationships that can be described and assessed in terms of the closeness or cohesion among family members, the extent to which family members express themselves to each other, and the extent to which family members are likely to engage in conflictual relations.

The Family Environment Scale (FES) was used to measure family variables related to both internal and external aspects of family functioning. These variables are described in Table 2.1. The FES is appropriate for this study for several reasons. First, it is one of the few family measures available that has both normative data and reliability information. Second, it has been used successfully in research with Mexican American groups (Chavez, 1985). Finally, the FES measures variables related to both the internal family system and the family's involvement and interaction with outside social systems, thus making it well suited for analyses using a family systems framework. The FES contains 10 subscales, 5 of which measure different ways that family members interact with external systems such as work, school, community, and social institutions and ways in which family members are either encouraged or prepared to carry on such interactions. The remaining 5 subscales are related to internal family system mechanisms and relationship patterns. These include the extent to which closeness, expressiveness, and conflict are characteristic of the family and how many organizing and control mechanisms are used to maintain the internal family systems functioning.

METHOD

Subjects

Subjects were 45 husband-wife couples with at least one child living at home. An equal number of couples ($n = 15$) represented three acculturation groups: *unacculturated*—all family members born in Mexico, parents monolingual Spanish-speaking, having immigrated to the United States within the past 5 years; *moderately acculturated*—parents born in Mexico and having resided in the United States at least 10 years, children born in the United States, parents monolingual Spanish-speaking or Spanish-dominant and children with English-speaking ability; and *acculturated*—both parents and children born in the United States, bilingual or English-speaking preference for both parents and children. All

Table 2.1 Family Environment Scale (FES) Variables

Internal family system variables	
Cohesion	Extent to which family members are concerned and committed to the family and the degree to which family members are helpful and supportive of each other
Expressiveness	Extent to which family members are allowed and encouraged to act openly and to express their feelings directly
Conflict	Extent to which the open expression of anger and aggression and generally conflictual interactions are characteristic of the family
Organization	Importance of order and organization in the family in terms of structuring family activities, financial planning, and explicitness and clarity regarding family rules and responsibilities
Control	Extent to which the family is organized in a hierarchical manner, the rigidity of family rules and procedures, and the extent to which family members order each other around
External family system variables	
Independence	Extent to which family members are encouraged to be assertive, self-sufficient, to make their own decisions, and to think things out for themselves
Achievement Orientation	Extent to which different types of activities are cast into an achievement oriented or competitive framework
Intellectual-Cultural Orientation	Extent to which the family is concerned about political, social, intellectual, and cultural activities
Active Recreational Orientation	Extent to which the family participates actively in various kinds of recreational and sporting activities
Moral-Religious Emphasis	Extent to which the family actively discusses and emphasizes ethical and religious issues and values

SOURCE: Adapted from Moos, Insel, & Humphrey (1974).

families fit the following income criteria based on family size: one child in family, less than $9,475 annual income; two children, less than $10,575; three children, less than $13,275; four children, less than $15,975; five children, less than $18,675; six children, less than $21,375; and seven children, less than $24,075.

Families were interviewed in their homes, where each measure was administered to mothers and fathers simultaneously. All items were presented verbally, with each family member giving confidential responses on separate answer sheets. A bilingual-bicultural interviewer was used for all of the families in the unacculturated and moderately acculturated groups and for some of the families in the acculturated group. An English-speaking interviewer conducted the remainder of the interviews. Interviews lasted less than 45 minutes; the average was 25 to 30 minutes per family. Compensation of $10 was offered to each family. Subjects were selected from Head Start families in the San Fernando Valley and San Gabriel Valley areas of Los Angeles County.

Measures

Family Environment Scale (FES)

The FES is a 90-item scale, with 10 subscales representing either internal or external areas of family functioning. Factor analysis of FES items produces two dimensions, relationships and organization, pertaining to internal family functioning and one dimension, personal development, pertaining to external family functioning (Moos, Insel, & Humphrey, 1974). Because our study was concerned exclusively with internal versus external areas of family functioning, subscale scores were analyzed in terms of this dichotomy (see Table 2.1). Chavez (1985) used the FES with a sample of mothers of Mexican descent and found an overall reliability of .75 for U.S.-born mothers and .78 for the foreign-born group. Chavez also obtained subscale coefficients for internal consistency ranging from the mid-40s to the mid-70s.

Sociodemographic Variables

Background information collected from all subjects was used as control data to insure that between-group differences were due to acculturation effects. Background information included parents' education and occupation, urbanicity, reason for migration, and socioeconomic conditions before migration. Information was also obtained regarding whether the family visits friends and relatives in Mexico and whether the family intends to return to live in Mexico. The information on parents' education and occupation was used to obtain an estimate of the family's socioeconomic status using Hollingshead and Redich's (1958) two-factor index.

RESULTS

Analyses

Table 2.2 lists means for the 10 FES subscales. To test hypotheses concerning differential areas of acculturation, a 2 (Parent) × 3 (Acculturation Group) analysis of covariance (ANCOVA) was performed for each of the 10 FES subscales. Sociodemographic variables were used as covariates in each of these analyses to control for extraneous sources of variance possibly related to acculturation and family functioning.

Internal Family System Variables

There were no parent nor acculturation differences involving any of the five internal family system variables. There were also no significant parent by acculturation interactions.

External Family System Variables

The main effect of Parent was significant only for Achievement Orientation. Fathers rated their families as being more achievement oriented than did mothers ($p < .05$).

There were acculturation differences involving all of the external family system variables except Moral-Religious Emphasis. A summary of these main effects is presented in Table 2.3. Between-group comparisons using the Newman-Keuls procedure revealed significant differences between all three acculturation groups for Independence ($p < .05$) and Achievement Orientation ($p < .01$). In each case, the acculturated group scored higher on these two variables than the moderately acculturated group who, in turn, scored higher than the unacculturated group. For both Intellectual-Cultural Orientation and Active Recreational Orientation, the unacculturated group scored lower than either the acculturated ($p < .01$) or the moderately acculturated ($p < .01$) group, who did not differ from each other. Overall, therefore, the pattern is for more acculturated parents to score higher on these four external family systems variables.

There was no significant parent by acculturation interaction.

DISCUSSION

The results provide general support for the stated hypotheses. Level of acculturation was significantly related to four of the five external family system variables: Independence, Achievement Orientation, Intellectual-Cultural Orientation, and Active Recreational Orientation. Conversely, level of acculturation was not related to any of the five internal family system variables.

The significant relationships between acculturation and the external family system variables were all in a positive direction. That is, increasing

Table 2.2 FES Family System Variables: Means for Parent, by Level of Acculturation

Variable	Unacculturated (n = 15)	Moderately Acculturated (n = 15)	Acculturated (n = 15)
Internal family system variables			
Cohesion			
Mother	52.60	50.00	51.60
Father	49.47	47.27	54.80
Total	51.04	48.64	53.20
Expressiveness			
Mother	41.80	44.47	49.47
Father	44.47	45.33	46.73
Total	43.14	44.90	48.10
Conflict			
Mother	45.27	48.20	48.27
Father	44.33	45.80	46.27
Total	44.80	47.00	47.27
Organization			
Mother	54.47	54.53	47.00
Father	52.13	49.60	50.93
Total	53.30	52.07	48.97
Control			
Mother	54.87	53.07	53.00
Father	51.20	53.73	54.40
Total	53.04	53.40	53.70

levels of acculturation were associated with higher scores on these variables. This result indicates that, as families of Mexican descent acculturate, their members become increasingly involved with U.S. social systems and institutions. The nonsignificant results for internal family system variables indicate that the basic internal family system remains relatively unchanged during the acculturation process. In other words, patterns of intrafamilial relationships and interactions do not appear to differ substantially from one generation to the next despite the fact that English becomes the primary language and family members become active participants in U.S. society. Keefe and Padilla (Keefe, 1980; Keefe & Padilla, 1987) obtained similar results with respect to extended family

Table 2.2   *continued*

Variable	Unacculturated (n = 15)	Moderately Acculturated (n = 15)	Acculturated (n = 15)
External family system variables			
Independence			
Mother	29.27	38.73	40.87
Father	36.87	37.47	44.73
Total	33.07	38.20	42.80
Achievement Orientation			
Mother	49.20	51.20	53.20
Father	50.80	54.00	58.40
Total	50.00	52.60	55.80
Intellectual-Cultural Orientation			
Mother	41.00	41.67	46.33
Father	38.67	38.67	47.33
Total	39.84	40.17	46.83
Active Recreational Orientation			
Mother	33.80	35.40	42.60
Father	38.20	31.80	43.40
Total	36.00	33.60	43.00
Moral-Religious Emphasis			
Mother	57.00	57.00	58.13
Father	55.33	56.73	58.47
Total	56.17	56.87	58.30

factors. They found that the Mexican American extended family does not decline despite decreasing cultural awareness and ethnic loyalty.

The only external family system variable that did not change with acculturation was Moral-Religious Emphasis. Although this is an unexpected result, a close inspection of the Moral-Religious Emphasis subscale items suggests that for Mexican American families the variable may really be an internal family system variable. This is consistent with Ramirez and Castañeda (1974), who argue that Mexican Catholicism reinforces and supports other Mexican values and in this way affects many aspects of family and community life.

The overall results of this study support a differential relationship between acculturation and family functioning. As noted earlier, Sabogal

Table 2.3 F Values for Internal and External Family System Variables

Variable	Parent	Acculturation	Parent × Acculturation
Internal family system variables			
Cohesion	.237	2.088	1.232
Expressiveness	.205	1.628	.406
Conflict	1.020	.789	.642
Organization	.368	1.983	2.074
Control	.813	.425	.639
External family system variables			
Independence	1.314	3.592*	.770
Achievement Orientation	4.224*	4.862**	.475
Intellectual-Cultural Orientation	.633	6.308**	.413
Active Recreational Orientation	.687	7.685***	1.302
Moral-Religious Emphasis	.138	.765	.165

*$p < .05$; **$p < .01$; ***$p < .001$.

et al. (1987) also found evidence for differential acculturation. They investigated the relationship between acculturation and three dimensions of attitudinal familism and found that perceived family obligations and the family as referent decreased with acculturation while perceived family support did not. Vega et al. (1986) also found cohesion and adaptability for Mexican Americans to be differentially related to acculturation.

The pattern of findings does not support an assimilationist perspective (Burma, 1967; Glazer, 1985; Stonequist, 1937) for families of Mexican descent. This perspective would predict that as families adapt to life in the United States both internal and external aspects of family functioning should change in the direction of Euro-American culture. The assimilationist model probably accounts for the experience of European descent families in their adaptation to life in the United States. These families seem to have adapted in terms of their interactions with outside social systems as well as becoming increasingly mainstream in their patterns of intrafamilial interactions.

Results of this study suggest that, for families of Mexican descent, acculturation to U.S. society may be better explained by a bicultural model (Ramirez, 1983). This model effectively accounts for differential patterns of acculturation while viewing acculturation as a multidimensional process. Perhaps the more salient question is not whether families change during acculturation but in what areas of family functioning these changes take place.

Different authors have argued about the role of the family in the acculturation process. Heller (1966), for example, states that the Mexican American family hinders acculturation by encouraging overdependence and thereby preventing family members from making a satisfactory integration into U.S. society. M. B. Zinn (1975) views the Mexican American family as serving to protect its members from the negative effects of acculturation, such as prejudice, discrimination, and the imposition of minority status. The present study suggests that acculturation is not an all-or-none phenomenon and that adjustment to U.S. society can take place with the basic integrity of the family remaining intact. This conclusion is consistent with Garza and Gallegos's (1985) view of acculturation as a complex interaction between environmental influences and personal choices.

What happens to families during the process of acculturation has important implications for educators, health and mental health providers, and other agents of social services. Despite this importance, families of Mexican descent continue to be neglected in the research literature. Public policies based on assimilationist perspectives continue to operate, and there is little information to help determine what the relative merits or harmful effects of such policies are for these families. For example, among various groups of human service providers there is the commonly held view that total assimilation into mainstream U.S. society is a necessary prerequisite for successful adaptation to and adjustment for life in the United States. For families of Mexican descent this assimilation entails a rejection of intrafamilial patterns that are closely associated with a cultural heritage. The evidence from this study suggests that assimilation does not occur and is not necessary. Consequently, policies based on alternative perspectives may prove more beneficial.

3
♦

A Multidimensional Measure of Cultural Identity for Latino and Latina Adolescents

MARÍA FÉLIX-ORTIZ DE LA GARZA

MICHAEL D. NEWCOMB

HECTOR F. MYERS

*A*nthropologists and sociologists have looked at acculturation as a behavioral group process (Clark, Kaufman, & Pierce, 1976). Acculturation is the dynamic process that occurs when two autonomous cultural groups are in constant contact with each other, leading to change in one or both cultures depending on the power relationship between them, but this can occur on two levels: at the level of the group and at the level of the individual (Berry, 1980). Psychologists have focused on acculturation as a process in which the individual affiliates and identifies with one or more groups. In measuring acculturation, some investigators have assumed it is the product of a unidirectional and unidimensional process (e.g., Cuellar, Harris, & Jasso, 1980). However, this process can also be conceptualized as an ongoing process that can be assessed at different times and on different dimensions as it interacts with situational variables.

In recent years, considerable interest and attention has been given to this process of acculturation among Latinos(as) both as a construct in its own right (e.g., Cuellar et al., 1980; Keefe & Padilla, 1987) and as a contributor to self-esteem and to a host of functional outcomes in this population (e.g., Mena, Padilla, & Maldonado, 1987; Neff, Hoppe, & Perea, 1987). Although there have been several difficulties in measuring this construct, two recurring problems here emerged in attempts to measure acculturation: the failure to consider multiple domains, including measures of values or attitudes; and inadequate consideration of multi- or bicultural identity. Although many investigators have identified reliable behavioral indicators of this process (language and customs), only recently have psychologists begun to isolate and define attitudinal components of the process. Furthermore, acculturation has typically been conceptualized and operationalized as a unidimensional construct.

DEFINING MULTIPLE DOMAINS

Past research focused largely on single domains, such as language, in attempts to measure acculturation. However, there are several notable exceptions. In an investigation of primarily urban Mexican American adults in the Southwest, Keefe and Padilla (1987) found a factor, Ethnic Loyalty, that was distinguishable from Cultural Awareness, a factor representing acculturation. They emphasized the need for more careful empirical research on each of these concepts represented by multiple domains. Further, they found no clear empirical basis to distinguish between attitudes and behavior, and therefore each factor was represented by indicators from both attitudinal and behavioral domains. In an investigation of Latino(a) college students in a southwestern university, Saldaña (1988, 1994) also found a reliable Ethnic Loyalty factor in addition to reliable scales of Behavioral Preference and Group Participation.

Several investigations have also attempted to identify a hypothesized value domain in acculturation with mixed success. For example, Saldaña (1988, 1994) attempted to measure cultural values by including specific items that measured cultural pride in her acculturation scale but was unable to identify a distinct factor for values. Clark et al. (1976) examined ethnic identity as a dimension of acculturation and, using Kluckhohn and Strodtbeck's (1961) value orientations, also sought to identify an attitudinal component but found no consistent patterns. On the other hand, Szapocznik, Scopetta, Aranalde, and Kurtines (1978) suggested that acculturation has an overt behavioral aspect and a covert value orientation. Their results confirmed this distinction, but the behavior scale was more reliable than the value scale based on Kluckhohn and Strodtbeck's (1961) value orientations.

DEFINING MULTIPLE DIMENSIONS

Although many investigators have recognized that acculturation is a multidimensional construct, many of the measures developed to assess these constructs reflect a unidimensional conceptualization. For example, Cuellar et al. (1980) acknowledge the existence of "true" biculturals yet rely on a single sum score for an acculturation rating. Mendoza's (1989) scale describes an individual on each of four types of cultural orientations yet relies on a single summary score for a general description. The response anchors of these unidimensional scales allow for selecting either *very American,* without any ethnic identification, or *very ethnic,* without any American identification. Biculturals, who may identify as both very ethnic and very American, cannot be adequately assessed on such unidimensional scales. A notable exception is a model developed by Oetting and Beauvais (1990) to measure Native American identity multidimensionally; however, the various domains are somewhat blurred and require further development. Although many investigators maintain that there are multiple dimensions, there are few instruments used consistently by mental health professionals that can adequately present a profile of scores for all of the hypothesized dimensions across multiple domains.

ACCULTURATION RECONCEPTUALIZED

Although the phenomenon of cultural change is recognized as an important process for the individual, the process is less understood than its common descriptor implies. Acculturation is the descriptor used most often in the literature; however, this descriptor is problematic because it implies a unidimensional process. With the emergence of new complex models of cultural change, new descriptors of the process need to be considered. In this chapter, the descriptor "cultural identity" is used to distinguish new conceptualizations of this process from older conceptualizations referred to as acculturation. Cultural identity is a descriptor that allows for a multidimensional conceptualization along various domains and recognizes a distinct process that occurs as part of personality formation versus a process that occurs between groups.

GOALS OF THE STUDY

Our study attempted to identify a multidimensional construct of cultural identity that would effectively assess bicultural as well as monocultural orientations on several dimensions. Specifically, the instrument assesses the individual's sense of familiarity with both American and Latino(a) cultures. This measure of cultural identity also incorporates a specific measure of Latino(a) values/attitudes as well as language and behavioral indicators of cultural identity. We then compare four cultural identity groups (based on the familiarity with cultural scales) on language, behavior, and attitude/value scales.

METHOD

Subjects

A nonprobability sample of 130 college students of Latino(a) descent was recruited from a major urban university on the West Coast. Participation was voluntary and no incentive was offered.

Most of the sample were of Mexican descent (73%) and Salvadorans were the next largest group (9%). The following groups were not represented: Hondurans, Venezuelans, Ecuadorians, Bolivians, Chileans, Uruguayans, and Paraguayans. Although most of the respondents were born in California (62%), a significant plurality (37%) were foreign-born. Approximately 32% of the sample was male, which limited generalizability of this study to females, who comprised 68% of this sample.

Most of the respondents were first- and second-generation Latino(a) Americans (40% and 50%, respectively). Only 11% were third-generation or more, and 13% did not know where their grandparents were born and could not be classified. The majority of the sample had lived in California for most of their lives (92%), and most had attended American schools all their lives (80%). Only 5% had attended school for 6 years or less in the United States. Despite being firmly established as

Table 3.1 Sources of Cultural Identity Scale Items

Source and Brief Description	Cultural Identity Scale
New items	
Familiarity with Latino/a fine art and artists	FL
Familiarity with Latino/a history and politics	FL
Familiarity with Latino/a entertainers	FL
Familiarity with Latino/a legends and symbols	FL
Familiarity with American fine art and artists	FA
Familiarity with American history and politics	FA
Familiarity with American entertainers	FA
Familiarity with American legends and symbols	FA
Language preference for TV	SLP
Language preference for radio	SLP
Language preference for TV with friends	SLP
Language preference for radio with friends	SLP
English speaking capability	EP
English reading capability	EP
English writing capability	EP
Spanish speaking capability	SP
Spanish reading capability	SP
Spanish writing capability	SP
V: Treated unfairly	PD
Years of schooling in the United States	Criterion validity
Number of visits to country of origin	Criterion validity
Hurtado et al. (1989)	
V: Husbands should make all household decisions	F
V: Wife's duty to serve husband	F
V: Only girls should do housework	F
V: Teachers discriminate against Latino/as	PD
V: Perceived discrimination as consumer	PD

U.S. residents or citizens, most had visited their country of origin (78%) at least once, and a substantial number had visited between one and four times (55%).

Thus our study sample can be characterized as primarily second-generation Mexican American females who are well established as U.S. residents but who remain in contact with friends and relatives in their country of origin.

A Measure of Cultural Identity

Table 3.1 *continued*

Source and Brief Description	Cultural Identity Scale
Saldaña (1988)	
Language spoken at home	SP
Involvement in Latino/a political activities	LA
Involvement in minority school activities	LA
Preferred ethnicity of a teacher	LA
Preferred ethnicity of doctor	LA
Preferred ethnicity of future spouse	PLA
Preferred ethnicity of boy/girlfriend	PLA
Preferred ethnicity of boy/girlfriend for relative	PLA
Generation	Criterion validity
Birthplace	Criterion validity
Years of residency in the United States	Criterion validity
Ramirez (1969)	
V: Obey parents	R
V: Obey adults	R
V: Conform to parents	R
Marín et al. (1987)	
Language spoken and read	Criterion validity
Language used as a child	Criterion validity
Language spoken at home	Criterion validity
Language of thought	Criterion validity
Language spoken with friends	Criterion validity

NOTE: V = value/attitude item; PD = Perceived Discrimination; F = Feminism; R = Respeto; LA = Latino/a Activism; PLA = Preferred Latino/a Affiliation; FL = Familiarity With Latino/a Culture; FA = Familiarity With American Culture; SLP = Spanish Language Preference; EP = English Proficiency; SP = Spanish Proficiency.

Measures

Our instrument combined items selected from several existing acculturation scales, supplemented with new items added to provide a multiple dimension assessment of cultural identity (Keefe & Padilla, 1987; Mendoza, 1989; Ramirez, 1969; Saldaña, 1988, 1994; Szapocznik et al., 1978). Table 3.1 presents a brief description of items borrowed from existing scales and descriptions of the criterion scales. Many attitudinal or value items were borrowed from the California Identity Project (Hurtado, Hayes-Bautista, Valdez, & Hernández, 1989). These items were included because of their clarity, relevance, and specificity of content. New items were included to measure familiarity with Latino/a culture and familiarity with American culture as separate dimensions.

RESULTS

Scale Development

Several exploratory maximum likelihood factor analyses with oblique factor rotations were conducted. Oblique factor rotations were chosen because we could not assume orthogonality of any dimensions present. The number of factors chosen was based on interpretability of the eigenvalues, high item loadings, and loadings on one factor. Separate factor analyses were conducted for language (the three-factor solution was chosen that accounted for 63% of the total variance; three eigenvalues were over 1), behavior/familiarity variables (the four-factor solution was selected that accounted for 41% of the total variance; nine eigenvalues were over 1), and value/attitude variables (the four-factor solution was chosen that accounted for 28% of the total variance; 16 eigenvalues were over 1). Items for each factor from the factor analyses were grouped into scales and tested for reliability. Items that poorly correlated with the remaining items were dropped from the scale. The number of items in each scale ranged from three to four.

Table 3.2 presents the Cronbach alpha reliability coefficients for each of the 10 scales obtained. The coefficients ranged from .69 to .91. The largest coefficients were found for the language scales (.87-.91). Coefficients for values/attitudes scales (.72-.81) were comparable to those for behavior/familiarity (.69-.89). One values/attitudes scale was rejected because of a low alpha coefficient.

Scale Intercorrelations

Table 3.3 presents the intercorrelations of 10 scales. There were 15 significant correlations among the scales; however, only 4 exceeded .40 in magnitude.

There was only one significant correlation among the language scales. Spanish Proficiency was positively correlated with Spanish Language Preference ($r = .44$). Spanish Language Preference was also significantly correlated with five other scales; however, most of these correlations fell below .40 in magnitude (only two were above .40). These scales were Preferred Latino(a) Affiliation, Familiarity With Latino(a) Culture, Familiarity With American Culture, Latino(a) Activism, and Perceived

Table 3.2 Reliability Coefficients for the Subscales

Scale	Number of Items	Standardized Alpha Coefficient
Language subscales		
Spanish Proficiency	4	.88
Spanish Language Preference	4	.87
English Proficiency	3	.91
Behavior/familiarity scales		
Familiarity With American Culture	4	.69
Familiarity With Latino/a Culture	4	.77
Latino/a Activism	4	.79
Preferred Latino/a Affiliation	3	.89
Value/attitude scales		
Perceived Discrimination	3	.72
Respeto	3	.77
Feminism	3	.81

Discrimination. Among the behavior/familiarity scales, three significant relationships emerged: Preferred Latino(a) Affiliation was positively correlated with Familiarity With Latino(a) Culture ($r = .34$) and with Latino(a) Activism ($r = .36$), and Familiarity With Latino(a) Culture was positively correlated with Latino(a) Activism ($r = .33$). However, Familiarity With Latino(a) Culture was *not* correlated with Familiarity With American Culture, which confirms the need for two dimensions rather than one. Latino(a) Activism was also correlated with Perceived Discrimination ($r = .53$) and Feminism ($r = .21$), in addition to those listed above.

Among the values/attitudes scales, Feminism was negatively correlated with *Respeto,* a Latino(a) value that embodies respect for one's elders and courtesy to others ($r = -.31$) Feminism was not correlated with indicators of Latino(a) identity or American identity, nor was Respeto correlated with Latino(a) Activism or Perceived Discrimination. Finally, Perceived Discrimination was positively correlated with Preferred Latino(a) Affiliation ($r = .28$).

Validity

Criterion validity was determined in several ways. The 10-factor Cultural Identity Scale was correlated with the Marín, Sabogal, Marín, Otero-Sabogal, and Pérez-Stable (1987) Short Acculturation Scale, generation status, and length of time in the United States. Because of the

Table 3.3 Correlations of Scales

Scale	Spanish Language Preference	Spanish Proficiency	English Proficiency	Preferred Latino/a Affiliation	Familiarity With Latino/a Culture	Familiarity With American Culture	Latino/a Activism	Perceived Discrimination	Feminism
Spanish Proficiency	.44***								
English Proficiency	-.13	-.06							
Preferred Latino/a Affiliation	.40***	.16	.08						
Familiarity With Latino/a Culture	.49***	.42***	.02	.34***					
Familiarity With American Culture	-.36***	-.14	.36***	-.13	.02				
Latino/a Activism	.30**	.06	-.01	.36***	.33***	-.05			
Perceived Discrimination	.24**	.06	-.06	.28***	.10	-.07	.53***		
Feminism	-.05	-.07	.10	-.07	-.04	-.06	.21*	.06	
Respeto	.13	.10	-.12	.11	.10	-.12	-.07	-.09	-.31***

*$p \leq .05$; **$p \leq .01$; ***$p \leq .001$.

small sample we included a probability level of .10. Table 3.4 presents correlations of the 10 cultural identity scales with the 4 criterion variables.

All language scales were significantly correlated with all criterion variables. Of the behavior/familiarity scales, only Familiarity With Latino(a) Culture was significantly correlated with all criteria. Evidence of convergent and divergent validity was also found. Familiarity With American Culture was, as expected, positively correlated with California residency ($r = .21$) and with English proficiency $r = .31$) as measured by the Short Acculturation Scale (Marín et al., 1987). Latino(a) Activism was negatively correlated with California residency ($r = -.15$). Of the attitude/value scales, two were significantly correlated with at least one criterion, but one (i.e., Feminism) was not correlated with any criteria. Perceived Discrimination was negatively correlated with California residency ($r = -.15$) and Respeto was negatively correlated with English proficiency $r = -.17$) as measured by the Short Acculturation Scale (Marín et al., 1987).

Comparison of Four Cultural Identity Groups

A multivariate analysis (MANOVA) was conducted initially using Familiarity With American Culture and Familiarity With Latino(a) Culture as independent variables, each with two levels (high and low as determined by a median split). However, it failed to reveal any interaction, so a one-way MANOVA was used in a second analysis to see if there might be significant differences between the four cultural identity groups.

The groups were created by splitting each familiarity distribution at the median into a range representing high familiarity with a culture and a range representing low familiarity with a culture. Each of the four groups was defined as follows: The bicultural group comprised individuals who scored high on familiarity for both cultures, the Latino(a)-identified group scored high on familiarity with Latino(a) culture but low on American culture, the American-identified group scored high on American culture but low on familiarity with Latino(a) culture, and the low-level bicultural group scored low on familiarity for both cultures. Table 3.5 presents mean comparisons of the four cultural identity groups (highly bicultural identity, Latino(a) identity, American identity, and low-level bicultural identity) on several dependent variables and pairwise post hoc comparisons (Student-Newman-Keuls, $p \leq .05$).

We expected to find some differences among these groups on language use, behavior, and values. We hypothesized that individuals with a strong Latino(a) identity should (a) feel more comfortable using Span-

Table 3.4 Correlations of Scales With Criterion Variables

Scale	California as Place of Longest Residence	Number of Years in School	Generation	Short Acculturation Scale
Spanish Language Preference	−.24**	−.22**	−.31***	−.61***
Spanish Proficiency	−.31***	−.40***	−.66***	−.83***
English Proficiency	.22**	.20*	.18*	.21*
Preferred Latino(a) Affiliation	.00	−.03	−.06	−.27***
Familiarity With Latino(a) Culture	−.39***	−.40***	−.23*	−.45***
Familiarity With American Culture	.20*	.12	.11	.31***
Latino/a Activism	−.15†	−.08	.01	−.13
Perceived Discrimination	−.15†	−.07	−.06	−.07
Feminism	−.06	−.01	.04	.06
Respeto	−.06	−.09	−.04	−.17*

†$p \leq .10$; *$p \leq .05$; **$p \leq .01$; ***$p \leq .001$.

ish over English compared to those with a strong American identity, (b) should be most politically active and prefer the company of other Latino(a) persons, (c) should endorse the values of respeto, and (d) should perceive more discrimination in their environment compared to those identified as American. On the other hand, those with a strong American identity should (a) feel more comfortable using English over Spanish, (b) prefer the company of Anglos, (c) perceive little or no discrimination, and (d) have a feminist orientation. Highly bicultural individuals should have mean scores on the various dependent measures that either fall between the two other cultural identities or, in some way, represent a synthesis of both cultural identities. Low-level biculturals, those who do not identify strongly with either culture, should be least comfortable with Spanish, least politically active, least likely to prefer one ethnic group over another, and least likely to indicate any strong preferences.

Differences between the four cultural identity groups were found on language use and behavior but not on values. Confirming our first hypothesis, Latino(a)-identified individuals were most comfortable using Spanish. Highly bicultural individuals were less comfortable with Spanish than Latino(a)-identified individuals but more comfortable than American-identified individuals. American-identified individuals and low-level biculturals were both equally uncomfortable with Spanish and least com-

Table 3.5   Comparison of Four Cultural Identity Groups on Several Dependent Variables

Dependent Variable	Cultural Identity Group				F Value
	Highly Bicultural	Latino/a	American	Low-Level Bicultural	
Language scales					
Spanish Proficiency	13.3$_{ab}$	14.8$_{acd}$	11.3$_{bc}$	12.3$_d$	7.7***
	(3.5)	(2.1)	(3.2)	(2.4)	
Spanish Language Preference	8.7$_{ab}$	10.5$_{acd}$	5.8$_{bce}$	7.7$_{de}$	16.1***
	(3.0)	(2.5)	(2.1)	(2.7)	
English Proficiency	11.6$_{ab}$	10.7$_a$	11.4	10.7$_b$	4.6**
	(0.9)	(1.3)	(1.2)	(1.6)	
Behavior/familiarity scales					
Latino/a Activism	12.2$_a$	12.2	10.8$_a$	11.2	2.3*
	(3.0)	(2.3)	(2.9)	(2.5)	
Preferred Latino(a) Affiliation	11.5$_{ab}$	11.8$_{cd}$	9.9$_{ac}$	10.5$_{bd}$	6.47***
	(1.9)	(1.7)	(2.1)	(2.0)	
Value/attitude scales					
Perceived Discrimination	9.0	9.6	9.1	8.4	0.64
	(2.9)	(3.0)	(3.2)	(3.0)	
Respeto	13.1	13.1	14.0	13.9	1.52
	(2.6)	(2.4)	(1.7)	(1.7)	
Feminism	6.0	6.9	6.2	6.0	0.93
	(2.3)	(2.3)	(2.7)	(2.3)	

NOTE: A significant difference between groups is indicated by the same subscript letter. Standard deviations appear in parentheses.
*$p \leq .10$; **$p \leq .01$; ***$p \leq .001$.

fortable with Spanish overall ($p < .001$). Similar results were attained on Spanish Language Preference, with the exception that low-level biculturals preferred Spanish more than American-identified individuals ($p \leq .001$). On the other hand, highly bicultural individuals and American-identified individuals were equally comfortable using English, whereas Latino(a)-identified individuals and low-level biculturals were less comfortable with English use ($p < .01$).

Our second hypothesis was partially confirmed. Although there was no difference in political activism between highly bicultural individuals and Latino(a)-identified individuals, highly bicultural individuals were more politically active than American-identified individuals ($p \leq .10$).

Both highly bicultural and Latino(a)-identified individuals were equally likely to prefer interacting with Latinos(as) over Anglos more than American-identified individuals and low-level biculturals were ($p \leq .001$). Surprisingly, the four groups did not differ on the three values/attitudes studied, thus disconfirming our third hypothesis.

DISCUSSION

Our study identified a multidimensional measure of cultural identity that incorporates assessment of language, attitudes/values, behavior, and familiarity with American and Latino(a) cultures. We found 10 reliable scales measuring cultural identity as follows: three language scales, four behavior/familiarity scales, and three values/attitudes scales. Latino-identified individuals, highly bicultural individuals, American-identified individuals, and low-level biculturals differed on measures of language preference, activism, and preferred social affiliations. Although the measures of attitudes were reliable, these measures did not differ across the four cultural identity groups.

Although previous attempts to isolate an attitudinal component of cultural identity met with mixed results, this investigation yielded three reliable measures of attitudes or values. Many past attempts relied on Kluckhohn and Strodtbeck's (1961) values orientations (e.g., Clark et al., 1976; Keefe & Padilla, 1987; Saldaña, 1988, 1994; Szapocznik et al., 1978). Kluckhohn and Strodtbeck (1961) presented a universal system of five value orientations: Human nature (the character of innate human nature), man to nature (subjugation to, harmony with, or mastery over), time, activity ("Being," "Being in Becoming," or "Doing"), and relational (one's relation to others). These five orientations may be too broad to generate measures of cultural identity and may be difficult to translate to decisions in everyday life. Furthermore, the value orientations tend to depict Latinos(as) and other cultures negatively, whereas Americans are rendered favorably. Also, some studies have failed to find differences between Latinos(as) and European Americans on some of these values orientations (e.g., Marín, 1986).

Exploration of how these four different cultural identity groups might differ on language use, behavior, and values revealed interesting differences. Highly bicultural individuals showed the most flexibility with language use, being equally comfortable with English or Spanish, and were politically active. Those with a strong Latino(a) identity were most comfortable with Spanish and preferred the company of Latinos(as). However, the groups did not differ on their endorsement of values. Surprisingly, strongly identified Latinos(as) did not endorse traditional values as opposed to more progressive values. In our study, we used specific values and attitudes regarding respect of elders, sex roles, and perceived discrimination. Although these were reliable and important cultural measures, the values/attitudes measures did not discriminate between the various cultural identity groups. There are several reasons why this may have occurred. First, the sample was drawn from college-bound high school students and college freshmen and sophomores attending a competitive urban university. A highly educated group of Latinos(as) may tend to endorse more progressive values (e.g., feminism) and be more aware of discrimination regardless of their cultural identification. Second, some values may be more indicative of less industrialized and technologically driven cultures in general and less uniquely representative of Latino culture. Third, some values may persist for two or three generations before they are lost and supplanted by new values supported by new traditions. Respeto, for example, may be an important value across many cultures and may persist as an important value within a culture for several generations, rendering it ineffective as a means of distinguishing between cultural identity groups. Finally, the scales only scratch the surface of the Latino value/attitude system. It may be that a more detailed inquiry would yield better discrimination. Although the measures we used were more sensitive than others used in the past, they may yet be too global to capture more specific within-group differences, particularly within a sample of this type that is more homogeneous than the population at large.

Nevertheless, the inclusion of these value/attitudinal scales as part of an assessment of cultural identity is important for several reasons. First, it provides an additional or alternate measure of cultural identity that may be more stable across time and situations than language or behavior. For example, language can be suppressed and lost while participating in the host country's educational system. Behavior can also be context specific. Second, values and attitudes present a potential locus for intervention. Many studies have reported an association between acculturation and drug use, yet they often use language as an indicator of acculturation or ethnic identity (e.g., Amaro, Whitaker, Coffman, & Heeren, 1990; Burnam, Hough, Karno, Escobar, & Telles, 1987). Is the recommendation following from these studies that we change language to change drug use? Obviously not. Then what aspect of cultural identity and its relationship to a target behavior like drug use is amenable to change? Rather than use language as a proxy variable for cultural identity, we need to define multiple dimensions of cultural identity more clearly and to identify how these variables/dimensions covary with other variables of interest on which we can focus interventions. It may be that certain dimensions of cultural identity are risk inducing, whereas others may buffer individuals from undesirable outcomes such as drug use (e.g., Newcomb & Félix-Ortiz, 1992) or are unique to specific groups (Félix-Ortiz & Newcomb, 1992). For example, understanding how different attitudes and values are related to various target behaviors provides a useful focus for the consciousness raising typical of many primary prevention programs and cognitive-behavioral interventions that characterize many psychological treatments.

We assumed that there might be overlap between cultural identity scales suggesting higher-order constructs (e.g., Keefe & Padilla, 1987) so that the cultural identity scales were not forced to be orthogonal. However, only 15 of 45 possible intercorrelations were significant. For example, two of the scales, Familiarity With Latino(a) Culture and Familiarity With American Culture, were designed to test whether cultural identity is unidimensional or multidimensional. Each scale was very reliable, but the scales themselves were *not* significantly correlated with each other. This indicates that American identity is distinct from Latino(a) identity, or, more precisely, multidimensional as opposed to unidimensional. These two scales, each representing a different cultural continuum, more effectively capture the phenomenon of biculturality than earlier scales (e.g., Cuellar et al., 1980). Using the Familiarity scales, it was possible to discriminate between individuals who identify strongly with both cultures (or those who are able to negotiate easily in two cultures) and individuals who strongly identify with only one culture. It is also possible to identify low-level bicultural individuals who do not strongly associate themselves with either culture. These scales were general measures that tapped into self-rated familiarity with different cultural domains. They are different from previous scales that measure knowledge of specific cultural information, which may be biased by what the investigator sees as indicative of cultural knowledge or familiarity (e.g., Clark et al., 1976).

Although this study contributes to our understanding of cultural identity, there are some important limitations that should be noted. The scale structure and pattern of results require verification on a larger, more heterogeneous sample reflecting the Latino community as a whole. This particular sample was restricted in terms of age (young, college age), nationality (mostly of Mexican descent), generational status (mostly second generation), gender (female), and so on. This pattern of results may vary somewhat as a function of age, nationality, generational status, or gender. Furthermore, this sample was not recruited from the community and represents only a small subset of the Latino community who are high functioning, upwardly mobile, and more highly bicultural relative to the larger Latino community. As mentioned earlier here, the progressive, intellectual discourse of the campus environment most probably influenced these results in significant ways and, as a result, limits the generalizability of these results to the larger Latino population. Many studies have found a significant relationship among higher education, cultural identity, and adjustment. For this reason, another sample, larger and predominantly Mexican, has been recruited from the community for further study of these scales (Félix-Ortiz & Newcomb, 1994). Further research is needed to (a) determine cross-cultural discriminant validity of this instrument, (b) identify value differences between majority and immigrant minority cultures, (c) identify other attitudes and values that will discriminate between strongly identified versus less identified Latinos, and (d) determine how these different components of cultural identity are risk inducing or protective factors for certain behaviors, such as drug abuse, psychological distress, or psychological disorders. For example, whereas one behavioral component of Latino(a) cultural identity may be risk inducing for a certain disorder, another value component of Latino(a) cultural identity may be protective. Finally, the interaction of cultural identity and gender should be investigated, particularly when values are being explored.

The importance of having adequate measures of cultural identity should be self-evident. However, many studies of multiethnic populations fail to consider the possible impact of various aspects that reflect this important multidimensional construct. Many existing measures of acculturation and cultural identity are unidimensional or are too restricted in domain. This may lead to misidentification of individuals and faulty conclusions. Short acculturation scales may have higher utility than longer ones, but the gains in efficiency may be achieved at the expense of theoretical and conceptual validity and meaningfulness. Even though language is highly correlated with other indicators of cultural identity, it does not account for all of the variance. For example, many Latinos(as) can no longer speak Spanish fluently, yet retain a strong Latino(a) identity. These individuals would be misclassified on many of the existing scales as "highly acculturated." It would be incorrect to assume that someone who struggles to retain his cultural identity is the same as the individual who abandons her cultural identity in shame. The many differences between these individuals may have implications for mental health and coping. Given the powerful backlash in response to affirmative action programs and the increasingly conservative policies regarding immigration and education of immigrant populations, it behooves investigators to carefully consider the benefits as well as the costs of strong ethnic identification.

4

♦

Acculturative Stress

Minority Status and Distress

DELIA H. SALDAÑA

College can be stressful, especially if a student is Hispanic or other ethnic minority. Hispanics comprise only a small percentage of the total enrollment in higher education and are at risk for higher rates of attrition (McCool, 1984). Further, Hispanic students have experienced poorer academic performance and higher rates of psychological distress when compared to their White peers (Cope & Hannah, 1975; Munoz & Garcia-Bahne, 1978; Powers, 1984; Rugg, 1982; Vasquez, 1978).

Among those reported to be at greatest risk for high levels of stress are Hispanics who are first-generation students (Billson & Terry, 1982), or who have had interruptions in college attendance (Luther & Dukes, 1982). In addition, financial restrictions (Blackwell, 1978; Brown, Rosen, Hill, & Olivas, 1980), being male (Munoz & Garcia-Bahne, 1978), and language difficulties (Brown et al., 1980) have also been associated with negative academic outcomes.

Conceptual and methodological limitations hamper many of the studies done to date. First, most have been based on correlational designs that fail to address the multiple, interactive nature of factors that affect college functioning. Second, many rely on demographic or background variables to predict functioning in the university setting. Relatively little attention has been given to college-related stresses or ways of coping that are more proximal to the university experience and potentially of greater relevance to attrition risk or psychological distress among Hispanic students. Third, little is known about the nature of stresses experienced by Hispanics that are common to all college students versus those that are more relevant to minority status.

Finally, few findings address the heterogeneity of cultural affiliation and class membership among Hispanic university students. Mixed evidence has emerged about the role of ethnic identity that reflects one's level of cultural awareness, group loyalty, and saliency of values perceived as different than those of the dominant group (Clark, Kaufman, & Pierce, 1976; Padilla, 1980a). Although some have asserted that middle-class social and cultural orientation is linked with better academic performance (Oliver, Rodriguez, & Mickelson, 1985), others have reported that bicultural affiliation is associated with less stress and better psychosocial adjustment (Fernández-Barillas & Morrison, 1984). However, little distinction has been made between an individual's ethnicity (particular ethnic group membership) versus potentially stressful aspects of his or her ethnic *identity* in the context of different situations.

Little research has addressed the relationship of ethnic identity to level of acculturation, and these two constructs are often treated synonymously. Yet the literature on acculturation has focused primarily on variables often associated with demographic or social class descriptors (generation level in the United States, language preference, bilingual fluency). In contrast, ethnic identity may more accurately reflect *internal* factors associated with level of acculturation (e.g., cognitive awareness, values, and loyalty to ethnic group membership). Both of these constructs should be separated from realistically based environmental pressures (e.g., within-ethnic group tensions, interactions with nonethnic group tensions, interactions with nonethnic individuals, and real or perceived discrimination) that reflect enduring social *status* marked by minority group membership.

Ongoing stress has been identified as an important determinant of general level of stress (Kanner, Coyne, Schaefer, & Lazarus, 1981; Lazarus & Folkman, 1984; Pearlin, Menaghan, Lieberman, & Mullan, 1981; Pearlin

& Schooler, 1978). Investigations of ongoing stress have identified four major categories: daily hassles, chronic unresolved stress, role strains, and stressful transitions. The persistence and proximity of chronic, unresolved stressors has led to the view that they are powerful predictors of psychological distress. Pearlin, in particular, has elaborated on the manner in which role strains cause stress for the individual by creating tension or conflict between the obligations and expectations associated with one role versus another (Pearlin, 1983; Pearlin & Schooler, 1978). Furthermore, Pearlin (1983) emphasizes a normative influence of stress associated with role strain, referring to this phenomena as "the hardships, challenges, and conflicts . . . that people experience as they engage over time in normal social roles" (p. 8). The concept of role strains is a particularly attractive one because it acknowledges the context in which stress occurs.

The few studies (e.g., Oliver et al., 1985; Patterson, Sedlacek, & Perry, 1984) that compare perceptions and reactions among different groups of minority students indicate that both qualitative and quantitative differences exist. Nevertheless, a clear integrative framework that ties together findings from the various studies has only recently emerged. Prillerman, Myers, and Smedley (1989) proposed a theoretical paradigm that helps account for potential interactions between various individual and situational processes affecting Black students. Their underlying premise is that a person-environment *transaction* is a more appropriate model for an accurate understanding of the functioning of minority students on White campuses than is the traditional emphasis on individual intellective and academic factors associated with success and failure. Others (Cervantes & Castro, 1985; Myers, 1982) have also suggested that a stress, coping, and adaptation model is conceptually suited for research with ethnic minority populations in positions of vulnerability. This study explores the applicability of a multivariate, transactional framework to understand the experiences and outcomes of Hispanic students at a predominantly White university (see Figure 4.1). This task was approached with three main objectives: (a) to delineate factors that enhance the understanding of ethnic identity as it relates to acculturation; (b) to clarify the nature of acculturative stress—that is, stresses that appear more relevant to Hispanic minority status rather than ones that are similar to those experienced by non-Hispanic White students; and (c) to frame the relevance of ethnicity and acculturative stress in terms of their effect on stresses and psychological distress in a university setting.

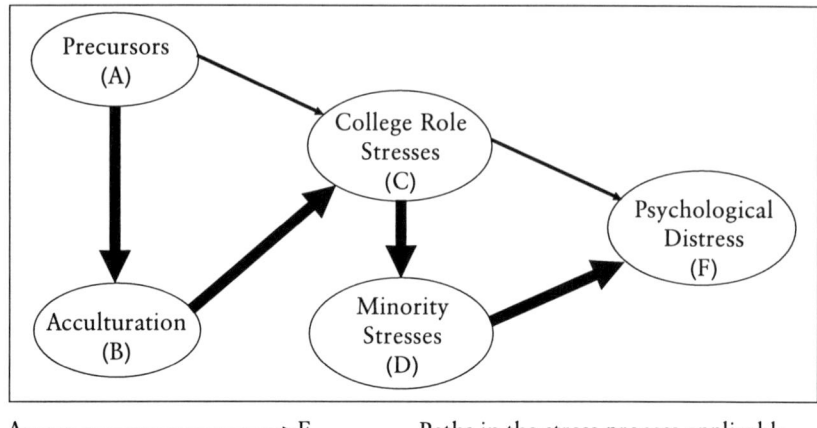

Figure 4.1. Predictive Pathways of Psychological Distress in Hispanic Students at a Predominantly White University

NOTE: Residual arrows have been omitted for visual clarity.

METHOD

Sample

Subjects for this study were a subset ($N = 270$) of respondents to a survey during 1986-1987 of 464 freshmen (102 African Americans, 93 Anglos, 90 Asians, 177 Hispanics, and 3 Native Americans) at a large university in the western United States. Subjects were polled at the beginning and end of their freshman year about college-related stresses and coping behaviors as predictors of psychological and academic outcomes. Subjects were fairly evenly distributed on social class, primarily female (64%-67%), and Hispanic subjects were mostly Chicano (80%) rather than from another Hispanic subgroup.

Measures

Precursor Variables

Information was obtained on social class, gender, and ethnicity. For social class, data was obtained about parents' level of education and occupation, and a socioeconomic status (SES) index was calculated that reflected both components (Hollingshead & Redlich, 1958). Gender was coded for all subjects and entered as a dummy variable for analysis in regression equations. Ethnicity was determined by asking subjects to identify themselves as "Mexican American or Chicano" (1), "Other Latino" (2), "Caucasian" (3), or "Other," which included mixed ethnic background (4). For the purposes of the present analyses, we combined all Hispanic respondents into one category to compare with Anglos and excluded subjects indicating an ethnic status of "Other."

Level of Acculturation

A 23-item Cultural Information Scale (CIS; Saldaña, 1988) was developed to measure transitions in ethnic identity due to demographic and psychological factors. Four items, based on an acculturation scale showing good reliability on other Chicano samples (Cuellar, Harris, & Jasso, 1980), comprised the Demographic Index (DI): generation level in the United States, current language preference, fluency in Spanish, and ethnicity of childhood friends. Psychological Index (PI) items were based on dimensions identified previously in the literature (Clark et al., 1976; Padilla, 1980b) but not incorporated into current measures of acculturation.

Factor-analytic procedures of all items from the DI and PI yielded a four-factor solution that accounted for 58.4% of the variance in level of acculturation. These were Behavioral Preferences, which indicated choice of language for books and magazines, TV programs, and music, and ethnicity of close friends and romantic partners; Cultural Integration, measuring involvement in culturally relevant family observations, community or city cultural celebrations, religious ceremonies, and civic or political activities; Ethnic Loyalty, items rating the personal and familial importance of pride and participation in cultural activities; and Demographic Descriptors, which asked for preferred ethnic identity label, fluency in Spanish, generation level, and language preference. Internal consistency of the scales ranged from .83 to .36 (see Appendix A).

College Role Stresses

Current concerns involved 10 potentially stressful contexts: academics, finances, friendships, family, romance, adjusting to college, health, neighborhood or dormitory life, being a minority, and personal. Specific items were not listed under each context; rather, subjects were simply instructed to rate on a 4-point scale how much of a problem each context was for them, and how important they considered it to be. In addition, each subject identified the most stressful problem area and rated it on a 5-point scale ranging from 5 = *extremely stressful* to 1= *not stressful at all*. The "being a minority" item was deleted for nonethnic students.

Minority Status Stresses

Items in this measure refer to stressful experiences and perceptions of the university that may be particularly relevant to ethnic minority status. A 33-item scale was based on issues identified in previous student stress scales (Edmunds, 1984; Zitzow, 1984). An orthogonal varimax rotated factor matrix yielded five scales that together accounted for 33% of the variance in stress attributed to minority status: academic concerns (46% of shared variance), conflicts between ethnic minority and non-minorities on campus (18%), discrimination (15%), within-ethnic group stresses (12%), and individual preparation concerns (9%). Examples of items were "Maintaining my ethnic identity while attending [university]," "Others lacking respect for people of my ethnic group," "People close to me thinking that I'm acting 'White,' " and "Doubting my ability to succeed in college" (see Appendix B).

Each item was rated on a 6-point scale ranging from 5 = *extremely stressful* to 1 = *not stressful at all* and including 0 = *does not apply to me*. A total score indicating level of stress attributed to minority concerns was obtained as well as individual scores for each of the five domains identified above.

Psychological Distress

The Hopkins Symptom Checklist (Derogatis, Lipman, Rickels, Uhlenhuth, & Covi, 1974) is a 58-item self-report symptom rating scale that identifies the frequency of physical and psychological symptoms experienced over the past 3 months. Ratings were made on a 4-point scale ranging from 1 = *not at all* to 4 = *very often*. This measure has been used extensively in epidemiological studies and is especially relevant to investigations of the relationship between stress and psychological functioning (Burks & Martin, 1985; Cohen et al., 1982). Its advantages include sensitivity to the low levels of symptoms found in normal populations (Uhlenhuth, Lipman, Balter, & Stern, 1974) as well as to changes in symptoms over time (Derogatis et al., 1974). The total score on the index of symptoms was used.

RESULTS

Findings support hypotheses about the importance of including ethnically relevant measures of identity and stress in understanding the psychological functioning of Hispanic students at a White university.

The first set of analyses addressed the independent contribution of precursor variables (SES, ethnicity, gender) to type of stress reported by the subjects. Two stepwise multiple regression analyses were used to test for the independent contribution of each precursor variable on college role strains common to all students and on minority stresses (see Table 4.1). Both SES and ethnicity exerted significant negative effects on college role stresses, indicating that students from lower socioeconomic backgrounds and minority status reported higher levels or role strain stress. SES again evidenced a significant negative effect on minority stresses. However, gender had no significant direct effects on either type of college-related stress.

Second, I examined whether level of acculturation (LA) added significant information to the two types of stress being considered. Two multiple regression analyses using forced entry of sets of variables were used to first test for the effects of LA on college role stress following entry of precursor variables and then for these effects on minority stresses. Table 4.2 illustrates that the psychology index of LA varied somewhat, depending on type of stress studied, being more associated with minority stresses than with college stresses experienced by most students. However, acculturation does not account for a significant proportion of either type of stress, explaining only 4.9% of the variance in college role stress and 1.1% of the variance in minority stresses.

The third area of inquiry addressed the issue of college-related stresses common to all university students (role strains) versus those that were more relevant to Hispanics (minority status stresses). Of special interest was clarifying whether knowledge about minority stresses would significantly increase the amount of explained variance in psychological distress (PD). As seen in Table 4.3, multiple regression analyses using forced entry of sets of variables were used to assess incremental productivity.

The pathway predictive of psychological distress in all students included precursor variables and college role strains in a multiple regression analysis. Although no support for a significant effect of precursor variables on PD was found, the addition of college role strains provided a substantial (27%) increase in the amount of explained variance in PD.

Next, the pathway common to all students was compared to that relevant for Hispanics. Once again, a multiple regression analysis was

Table 4.1 Contribution of Precursors to College Role and Minority Stresses

Variable	Beta	Adjusted R^2	Included in F
Contribution of precursors			
to college role stresses (N = 270)			
SES	−.150	.019	6.14**
Ethnicity	−.137	.030	4.12*
Gender	.061	.030	1.04
Total $R^2 = 7.90$, $F_{(3, 266)} = 3.789$**			
Contribution of precursors			
to minority stresses (N = 176)			
SES	−.191	.031	6.65
Gender	.037	.027	.25
Total $R^2 = 5.80$, $F_{(3, 173)} = 2.280$, n.s.			

*$p = .05$; **$p = .01$.

Table 4.2 Incremental Contribution of Level of Acculturation to Precursors as a Predictor of Stress

Variable	Beta	Adjusted R^2	Included in F
Criterion: College role stress			
(accounts for a total of 4.9% variance)			
SES	−.150		
Gender	−.137	.030	3.71*
Acculturation			
Demographic	−.145	.044	3.61*
Psychological	−.030	.039	.11
Criterion: Minority stresses			
(account for a total of 1.08% variance)			
SES	−.191		
Gender	.037	.038	3.45*
Acculturation			
Demographic	−.177	.051	5.44*
Psychological	−.295	.108	12.00**

*$p = .05$; **$p = .001$.

used to account for the effects of precursors, level of acculturation, college role strains, and minority status stresses on psychological dis-

Table 4.3 Stress and Psychological Distress

Variable	Beta	Adjusted R^2	Included in F
Common to all university students (N = 269)			
Ethnicity			
SES		.007	1.59
Gender			
College role strains	.524	.271	97.50*
Total $R^2 = 27.80$, $F_{(4, 265)} = 26.00*$			
Relevant to Hispanic Students at a White University (N = 176)			
Ethnicity			
SES		.007	1.59
Gender			
Acculturation			
Demographic			
Psychological		.014	1.86
College role strains	.318	.271	97.50*
Minority stresses	.325	.083	19.61*
Total $R^2 = 37.50$, $F_{(6, 170)} = 11.25*$			

*$p = .001$.

tress. Both precursor and acculturation variables failed to exert significant effects on PD. However, minority status stresses significantly increased the amount of explained variance in PD by 8.25%, even after accounting for the substantial effects provided by college role strains.

DISCUSSION

The conceptual model articulated in this chapter provides a promising entry into a more effective understanding of the nature of stresses faced by Hispanic students at a predominantly Anglo university. Previous work in this area was enhanced by clarifying the dimensions of acculturation to include psychological indexes relevant to ethnic identity as well as demographic factors associated with traditional measures of acculturation. This distinction becomes even more important when one considers the relationship of ethnic identity and acculturation level to a stress process that is contextually based (e.g., being a minority college student). This work indicates that the level of acculturation provides important information about the level of minority status stress reported by students but is less relevant in terms of their psychological distress. This preliminary evidence suggests that acculturative stress may be distinct from outcome measures of psychological functioning.

Second, the model proposed addresses the relative association of precursor variables (social class, gender, ethnicity), level of acculturation, stresses common to all students (role strains), and minority status stresses to psychological distress. Delineation of variables into these various sets provides helpful distinctions at different levels. For example, the role of ethnicity and social class can be compared as can the relationship between ethnicity (ethnic group membership) and ethnic identity (psychological factor within level of acculturation). Also, the relevance of these variables to predispose an individual for certain levels of stress can be investigated. Findings indicate that the relevance of social class, ethnicity, and acculturation vary, depending on the criterion selected. In particular, although demographic indexes used in traditional measures of acculturation appear relevant to college role strains common to all students, it is the psychological index associated with increased ethnic identity that seems to be more associated with the levels of *minority status stresses* reported.

Finally, this work suggests benefits of including ethnically relevant factors in predictive models that address the functioning of minority students at a predominantly White university. A substantial increase in accounting for psychological distress was gained by the inclusion of minority status stresses, even after having controlled for the potent effects of college role strains.

The limitations of a cross-sectional design preclude adequate testing of causal relationships in the current study. However, results suggest that a multivariate model, such as that proposed here, may be of special significance in understanding the process of acculturative stress in an undergraduate population. For Hispanics, this implies the relevance of acculturative stress as a dynamic process separate from purely descriptive variables such as ethnicity or social class. Rather, ethnicity, social class, and level of acculturation may serve as risk indexes that mark the Hispanic student's predisposition for higher levels of minority status stresses. This *process* of acculturative stress then appears to be associated with a substantially greater level of psychological distress. These results are expected to serve as an important foundation for future development in this area.

Appendix A Level of Acculturation: Factor Structure

Scale and Item	Factor Loading
Psychological Index:	
(accounts for 52.1% of variance)	
Factor 1: Behavioral Preferences	
(5 items, alpha = .83)	
Books and magazines	.86
Television programs	.78
Music	.75
Dating partner	.68
Close friends	.63
Factor 2: Cultural Integration	
(5 items, alpha = .78)	
Community/citywide celebrations	.78
Family observations	.71
Religious celebrations	.70
Civic or political activities	.61
Peer ethnic preference	.41
Factor 3: Ethnic Loyalty	
(9 items, alpha = .81)	
Importance of identifying cultural heritage	.81
Importance of bilingualism	.64
Importance of cultural pride	.62
Importance of participating in cultural activities	.42
Demographic Index: (accounts for 6.3% of variance)	
(4 items, alpha = .36)	
Ethnic identity label	.76
Fluency in Spanish	.76
Generation level	.58
Language preference	.57

Appendix B Minority Student Stressors Factor Analysis
(factor solution accounts for 33% of the variance)

Scale and Item	Factor Loading
Scale 1: Academic concerns (alpha = .93)	
Not enough professors of my ethnic group	.79
Few students of my ethnic group in my classes	.77
Racist policies and practices of the university	.76

Continued

Appendix B *continued*

Scale and Item	Factor Loading
University lacking concern and support for the needs of students of my ethnic group	.68
Few courses involving issues relevant to my ethnic group	.66
Seeing members of my ethnic group doing low-status jobs and Anglos in high-status jobs	.65
Attitudes/treatment of faculty toward students of my ethnic group	.58
Anglo student and faculty expecting poor academic performance from students of my ethnic group	.56
Tense relationships between Anglos and minorities at this university	.53
Pressure that what "I" do is representative of my ethnic group's abilities, behavior, etc.	.45
Scale 2: Ethnic-nonethnic group concerns (alpha = .84)	
Having Anglo friends	.70
Relationships between different ethnic groups	.69
Anglo-oriented campus culture	.62
Lack of unity/supportiveness among members of my ethnic group this university	.48
Having to live around mostly Anglo people	.48
Having to always be aware of what Anglo people might do	.44
Maintaining my ethnic identity while attending this university	.44
Relationships between males and females of my ethnic group (available dating partners)	.40
Wealthy campus culture	.34
This campus being an unfriendly place	.32
Scale 3: Discrimination concerns (alpha = .86)	
Being treated rudely or unfairly because of my ethnicity	.90
Being discriminated against	.73
Anglo people expecting me to be a certain way because of my ethnicity (stereotyping)	.59
Others lacking respect for people of my ethnic group	.47
Having to "prove" my abilities to others (e.g., work twice as hard)	.36

PART 2

Ethnic Identity and Behavior

5

♦

Ethnic Identity and Self-Esteem

A Review and Integration

JEAN S. PHINNEY

A fundamental question in the study of ethnic identity has been its possible positive or negative impact on the psychological adjustment of minority group members. The issue might be phrased as follows: Is a strong sense of identification with one's ethnic culture likely to act as a positive influence on well-being, by providing a sense of belonging and serving as a buffer against the negative impact of prejudice and discrimination? Or, conversely, might this sense of belonging promote internalization of negative stereotypes and serve to emphasize one's difference from the dominant culture, thus increasing the stress of minority status? This chapter examines theoretical and empirical writing that bears on this question, using self-esteem as the primary indicator of positive psychological adjustment. Although self-esteem is only one of many possible indices of well-being, it has been used widely in research and therefore can serve as a focus in investigating the impact of ethnic identity on psychological well-being.

Most writers concur that ethnic identity is a multidimensional construct, involving ethnic feelings, attitudes, knowledge, and behaviors (Garcia, 1982; Giles, Llado, McKirnan, & Taylor, 1979; Rosenthal & Feldman, 1992; Rosenthal & Hrynevich, 1985; see Phinney, 1990, for a review). Given this multidimensionality, there are several contradictory hypotheses that need to be clarified regarding the relationship of self-esteem and ethnic identity. It could be hypothesized that each component individually contributes to self-esteem; or that some, but not others, make a contribution; or that all the elements taken together underlie adaptation. To begin to untangle these issues, the components need to be clearly defined and distinguished. We can then consider to what degree each may vary in some measurable way that could be related, individually or together, to a measure of self-esteem.

Among the specific components that have been suggested as key elements of ethnic identity are self-identification as a group member; attitudes and evaluations relative to one's group; attitudes about oneself as a group member; extent of ethnic knowledge and commitment; and ethnic behaviors and practices. To examine how these components may contribute in some way to self-esteem, we need to consider them as variables that covary with ethnic identity and that can range from high or positive to low or negative. Table 5.1 presents a graphic representation of these components as variables that define ethnic identity.

When individuals self-identify as group members, evaluate their group positively, prefer or are comfortable with their group membership, are interested in, knowledgeable about, and committed to the group, and are involved in ethnic practices, they may be said to have a high ethnic identity. Alternate terms might be a strong, secure, or an achieved ethnic identity. Conversely, when there is little ethnic interest, knowledge, commitment, or involvement and negative evaluation of the group and of one's membership in the group, then ethnic identity could be called low, weak, or diffuse. According to this model, ethnic identity is seen as a continuum between these two points, and individuals may be located at some point from low to high.

However, the issues are considerably more complex than a simple model suggests. First, for individuals who do not identify themselves as ethnic group members and thus for whom ethnic identity is not a salient or even conscious issue, there is no theoretical reason to hypothesize that ethnic identity would be related to self-esteem. For example, ethnic identity is unlikely to be a meaningful concept or to have an impact on self-esteem among third-generation Polish Americans who are completely assimilated and do not call themselves Polish. In fact, empirical evidence

Table 5.1 Ethnic Identity as a Continuum

High, strong, secure, or achieved ethnic identity:
  Self-identification as group member
  Involvement in ethnic behaviors and practices
  Positive evaluation of the group
  Preference for own group; happy with one's membership
  Interest in and knowledge about the group
  Commitment, sense of belonging to the group

Low, weak, or diffuse ethnic identity:
  Self-identification as group member
  Little involvement in ethnic behaviors
  Negative evaluation of group
  Preference for majority group; unhappy with one's membership
  Little interest in or knowledge about group
  Little commitment or sense of belonging to group

suggests that this is the case for assimilated White Americans (Phinney, 1989; Phinney & Alipuria, 1990). It seems probable that the model applies only to those who self-identify as ethnic group members and for whom ethnicity is a salient issue. Self-identification, then, is not seen as a variable but, rather, as a prerequisite that should be present before ethnic identity is assumed to influence self-esteem. In the model, therefore, ethnic self-identification has been included at both the high and low ends of the continuum.

More important, with regard to this model, we know little about the extent to which the suggested components are interrelated. Studies that measure separately various components of ethnic identity and examine them using factor analysis or similar techniques have shown anywhere from one to six components or factors (e.g., Driedger, 1975, 1976; Garcia & Lega, 1979; Hogg, Abrams, & Patel, 1987), and the structure and definition of the factors vary across ethnic groups and even across ages within the same groups (Rosenthal & Hrynevich, 1985). In addition, there is evidence from studies that look at generational differences (e.g., Keefe & Padilla, 1987; Rosenthal & Feldman, 1992) that while ethnic behaviors and practices decline over time, commitment to one's group may remain high.

These results suggest that the components of ethnic identity vary independently. Someone may identify with a group and have generally positive feelings about it but exhibit few specific ethnic behaviors associated with it. On the other hand, someone may be very involved in the language and culture of the group but have negative feelings about the group or about being a member of the group. If the components vary independently, at least to some extent, then, to understand the relationship of ethnic identity to self-esteem, it is necessary to examine separately the relationships between each component and self-esteem.

The preceding discussion considers ethnic identity as a construct that varies across individuals. However, the same continuum can be thought of as representing the process of ethnic identity formation within an individual. Several models have suggested that there is, or may be, a shift over time from a low or diffuse ethnic identity to a high or achieved one. The Cross (1978) model of Black identity formation, developed during the civil rights era of the late 1960s, proposes an initial state characterized by negative evaluation of Blacks, accompanied by preference for White culture and discomfort in being Black. After an encounter experience that provokes awareness of ethnic issues, the individual becomes immersed in Black culture, thus showing interest and gaining knowledge. The end product is an internalization or acceptance of one's group membership, accompanied by positive evaluation of one's group. A similar model of minority identity formation is described by Atkinson, Morten, and Sue (1983).

A closely related model (Phinney, 1989) has been derived from Erikson's (1968) theory of ego identity formation and Marcia's (1966, 1980) empirical work on ego identity statuses. On the basis of interviews with junior and senior high school students, three stages of ethnic identity formation were identified: an initial stage in which there is little interest or concern with ethnicity, followed by an exploration stage in which there is an effort to learn more about one's ethnicity and its meaning for the individual, which in turn leads to knowledge and ultimately the commitment to one's ethnicity that is characteristic of an achieved identity. Because there has been relatively little research to date on either this model or those of Cross (1978) or Atkinson et al. (1983), it is not clear how many people experience all the stages of this process. Depending on personal or environmental factors, some people may remain in the early or intermediate stages and not achieve internalization or ethnic identity commitment. In any case, these various models emphasize individual differences in the degree to which ethnic issues have been resolved, as well as individual changes in ethnic identity over time. It is possible, as well, that the continuum in Table 5.1 represents fluctuation in aspects of ethnic identity across contexts; that is, an individual's ethnic feelings, attitudes, behaviors and group evaluation may change depending on the circumstances. However, there has been little or no research on this aspect of variation in ethnic identity.

These models have been developed with reference to adolescents and young adults; the issues with regard to children are quite different. Identity, in the sense explored by Erikson (1968), is not salient until adolescence. Because of the cognitive immaturity of children, ethnic identity is qualitatively different for them (Bernal, Knight, Garza, Ocampo, & Cota, 1990); it is less internalized and more influenced by parents and community. Ultimately, the relationship of self-esteem and ethnic identity needs to be examined across all ages, but this chapter focuses on adolescents and adults and does not address the issues in early and middle childhood.

It appears, then, that the elements of ethnic identity and their interrelationships may vary both across individuals and over time and context in the same individual. To understand the impact of ethnic identity on self-esteem, we need to consider the elements individually, with reference to variation both across individuals and over time.

ETHNIC IDENTITY COMPONENTS IN RELATION TO SELF-ESTEEM

Each of the components listed in Table 5.1 might conceivably be related to self-esteem, and evidence for such relationships is considered in the following sections. However, one suggested component, involvement in ethnic behaviors, has not been included. A search of the literature revealed no studies that examined ethnic behaviors as a discrete variable related to self-esteem; rather, global measures that include ethnic behaviors are generally used. Furthermore, it seems likely that the impact of ethnic behaviors and practices on self-esteem would be embedded in the feelings and attitudes that accompany the behaviors. I therefore turned to the remaining aspects of ethnic identity that might influence self-esteem.

Evaluation of the Group

The component of ethnic identity that might be expected both intuitively and theoretically to have the greatest impact on self-esteem is positive versus negative evaluation of one's group. There is substantial theoretical writing on this topic. Tajfel (1981), among others, has pointed out that if one's group has lower status in society or is subjected to prejudice, discrimination, and negative stereotypes, then group members might be expected to have lower self-esteem. Voluminous writing, especially biographical work by minority writers, has documented negative feelings about their own group that were acquired from the pervasive negative images in society (e.g. Du Bois, 1971). However, there is substantial evidence that groups subjected to stereotypes and discrimination do not, in fact, have lower self-esteem (e.g., Crocker & Major, 1989; Gordon, 1980; Rosenberg & Simmons, 1972).

To understand the possible impact of negative evaluation of the group on self-esteem, we need to examine to what extent individuals actually accept negative stereotypes and how they respond to such images of their group. There appears to be little question, first, that minority group members are aware of the images of their group that pervade the media and are evident in their daily life. Ethnic minority high school students who were asked how their group was perceived readily provided a list of stereotypes (Phinney, Alexander, & Chavira, 1991). However, knowledge of the stereotypes is different from acceptance of them. Research that distinguishes stereotypes held by others about one's own group (heterostereotypes) from those held by ingroup members (autostereotypes) shows that autostereotypes are consistently more positive than heterostereotypes (Brigham, 1973; Rickman, 1983; Smedley & Bayton, 1978; Triandis et al., 1982). There appears to be a strong tendency of individuals to think well of their own group.

On the other hand, individuals may accept some negative images of the group but feel that these do not apply to themselves as individuals. In this way, minority individuals can distance themselves from negative images and stereotypes. This strategy was encountered in interviews with minority high school students (Phinney et al., 1991), who acknowledged negative images and stereotypes but added, "They're not talking about me when they say that" and "I'm not like that." It appears that in cases such as these there is a differentiated conception of the ethnic group and recognition that not all members of the group are the same. The individual believes that the stereotype need not refer to him or her personally, and self-esteem is not affected. A similar point is made by

Cross (1987) in distinguishing between reference group orientation and personal identity. As Cross points out, research has seldom assessed self-esteem and group evaluation separately and examined their relationship, although a very limited number of studies have attempted to determine whether acceptance of negative images influences self-esteem.

The measure of Black racial identity developed by Parham and Helms (1981) on the basis of Cross's model has a number of items that reflect negative evaluation of the group: for example, "I believe that large numbers of Blacks are untrustworthy"; "I feel that Black people do not have as much to be proud of as White people do"; and "Most Black people I know are failures." The statements reflecting negative group evaluation are associated with the lowest stage of racial identity, termed preencounter (Cross, 1978). In a study with college students, Parham and Helms (1985) found that their preencounter attitudes were significantly and negatively related to high self-esteem.

Grossman, Wirt, and Davids (1985) also found a relationship between ethnic evaluation and self-esteem. They used a semantic differential method to measure attitudes toward one's own ethnic group among Anglo and Hispanic eighth and ninth graders. The results are complex, but they suggest that individuals with positive ethnic evaluation (termed "ethnic esteem") show higher self-esteem. However, another study with Black college students found that attitudes toward Blacks and Whites were unrelated to two measures of self-esteem (Houston, 1984).

An important and unresolved question in the studies just discussed is the direction of effect. It may be that a positive evaluation of one's group leads to high self-esteem, but it is equally possible that high personal self-esteem results in a more positive group evaluation, or perhaps that a third factor influences both of these variables. Until longitudinal studies are carried out to trace changes in these two variables over time, it is impossible to resolve this issue.

In a further attempt to understand why members of groups that are negatively stereotyped do not have poor self-esteem, Crocker and Major (1989) carried out a detailed review and analysis of the relationship of self-esteem to social stigma (i.e., membership in groups subject to stereotypes and discrimination). Their review deals with groups about which others in society hold negative attitudes, stereotypes, and beliefs, of which minority ethnic groups are just one. They discuss a number of strategies used by stigmatized individuals to protect their self-esteem. Some of these are not directly relevant to the topic of ethnic identity. However, one is central to this issue.

Crocker and Major (1989) provide evidence to suggest that members of stigmatized groups protect their self-esteem by attributing negative experiences and outcomes to their group membership rather than to themselves. For example, if a Black person is treated in a discriminatory or stereotyped way, he or she may assume that it is not a personal insult but, rather, a racial one. The incident then is less likely to affect the self-concept of the victim than would be the case if negative events and images are taken personally.

In summary, some studies suggest that stereotypes and negative evaluation of one's group may be related to low self-esteem, although others do not. It seems clear that holding some negative views of one's group does not necessarily mean lower self-esteem. Those individuals who distance themselves from the negative aspects and relate to the positive characteristics of the group may have high self-esteem. Similarly, those who dismiss negative experiences as being based on stereotypes may not be personally affected.

Feelings About One's Group Membership: Acceptance Versus Rejection

A second component of ethnic identity that may be related to self-esteem is the feeling one has about being a member of the group, particularly the acceptance or rejection of one's ethnicity. The positive side of this feeling is indicated by preference for being a member of one's own group and feeling happy or comfortable being a member. In the Parham and Helms (1981) scale, items of this sort reflect the highest stage in the Cross (1978) model, termed internalization: for example, "I feel good about being Black" and "Being Black just feels natural to me." Similar statements were obtained from interviews with high school students (Phinney et al., 1991): "I accept myself as Mexican" and "I am happy being Black."

The negative side of this feeling is evident in the expressed wish that one were not a member of one's group. The Parham and Helms (1981) scale includes the item "Sometimes I wish I belonged to the White race." In an interview (Phinney et al. 1991), an Asian male said, "If I could have chosen, I would be White." Rosenthal and Hrynevich (1985) had immigrant adolescents assess their similarity to "kids from other countries who try to hide their background."

Although intuitively it seems that sentiments such as this would imply low self-esteem, direct empirical evidence is weak. A study of Black early adolescents by Paul and Fischer (1980) found that acceptance of racial identity was positively related to self-concept. However, it is not clear exactly what is meant by racial acceptance, as the scale is not provided in the article.

A study of Israeli high school students by Tzuriel and Klein (1977) used a measure of ethnic acceptance: "If you could be born again, would you choose to be born as a member of your own ethnic group?" A scale assessing ego identity resolution was used as an indicator of psychological well-being. Although self-esteem was not measured, it has been shown in other studies to be associated with an achieved ego identity (Waterman, 1984). In my study, ego identity resolution was found to be related to high racial acceptance.

In spite of the results of these two studies, others (e.g., White & Burke, 1987) have found no relationship between ethnic acceptance and self-esteem. Similarly, in a 1985 study by Parham and Helms, positive attitudes toward being Black (the "internalization" stage) showed no relationship to self-esteem. Overall, the evidence is weak; until further studies are carried out, no definitive statement can be made about the role of ethnic acceptance or rejection in self-esteem.

Interest in and Knowledge About One's Ethnic Group

Interest in and knowledge about one's ethnic group can be envisioned in several ways. In children, it may reflect instruction by parents and teachers or involvement in a strong ethnic community that provides many opportunities for learning about one's culture. This might be termed passive interest in ethnicity; information is presented to the individual without any particular effort. In contrast, there is the active search for knowledge that is characteristic of the immersion stage in the Cross (1978) model or the exploration stage in models based on Erikson (Phinney, 1989). In questionnaire studies (e.g., Phinney & Alipuria, 1990), this active search for ethnic understanding has been tapped by items such as "I have spent time trying to find out more about my own ethnic group, such as its history, traditions, and customs" and "I have often talked to other people in order to learn more about my ethnic background." Although these questions do not assess specific knowledge, they have the advantage of not involving specific items of information that would be applicable only to specific groups, and thus they can be used across groups.

In a study of college students from four ethnic groups (Asian American, Black, Mexican American, and White), Phinney and Alipuria (1990) examined several aspects of ethnic identity in relation to self-esteem, using the Rosenberg (1979) Self-Esteem Scale. The results showed a significant positive relationship between ethnic identity search and self-esteem for Black males, a somewhat weaker relationship for Mexican American females, and no relationship for Asian Americans and Whites. The results suggest that self-esteem, at least for members of some disadvantaged groups, may be influenced by active learning about one's culture. The actual knowledge that one has about one's culture was not assessed, so no conclusion can be drawn about the relationship of cultural knowledge and self-esteem.

Commitment

The final and perhaps central component of ethnic identity to be discussed is a sense of commitment to one's group. The concept of commitment is derived from Erikson's (1968) discussion of ego identity formation; according to Erikson, adolescents face the critical task of integrating childhood identifications, together with personal inclinations and societal pressures, so as to make a commitment to who they are and what they will become. In his work on ego identity, Marcia (1966, 1980) distinguishes between two types of commitment. A foreclosed identity is based on a commitment that has not been preceded by a search, so that one's views are based on ideas derived from parents or other significant figures; an achieved identity reflects a commitment that has followed a personal search and is based on one's own independent decision.

With reference to ethnicity, commitment involves a clear sense of one's ethnic background and its meaning for one's life. Conceptually, the same distinction between foreclosure and identity achievement can be made with regard to ethnic identity. A foreclosed identity might be characteristic of the individuals who have learned to assert ethnic pride but who have not thought deeply about their ethnicity and resolved for themselves possible conflicts or contradictions associated with being a member of a minority group in society. An achieved ethnic identity, in contrast, implies an internalized sense of oneself as an ethnic group member.

In their study of college students, Phinney and Alipuria (1990) used four items (two positive and two negative) to assess commitment: for example, "I have a clear sense of my ethnic background and what it means for me" and "I am not very clear about the role of my ethnicity in my life." Commitment as measured by these items showed a highly significant relationship to self-esteem (using the Rosenberg, 1979, scale) for the sample as a whole and for Blacks and Mexican Americans. The relationship was significant but weaker for the Asian American and White subjects.

However, these four items do not capture the full complexity of ethnic identity commitment as it applies in the case of an achieved ethnic identity because it does not include the search component. Furthermore, commitment is closely connected with all the other aspects of ethnic identity; specifically, a committed (achieved) ethnic identity is likely to include acceptance, knowledge, and positive evaluation of one's ethnicity. When comprehensive measures of ethnic identity are used, the results regarding self-esteem are conflicting.

In recent work, Phinney (1991) developed a 14-item comprehensive questionnaire measure that taps ethnic identity achievement (including both search and commitment), positive attitudes and sense of belonging, and ethnic behaviors, with items worded in general terms that can be applied across groups. In a study with Asian American, Black, Mexican American, and White adolescents and young adults (417 high school students and 136 college students), highly significant correlations were obtained between high ethnic identity scores on this composite measure and the Rosenberg Self-Esteem Scale for the minority subjects but not generally for the White subjects. This result supports the point made earlier that the relationship is not likely to hold with those for whom ethnicity is not salient, as is generally the case for White students. An exceptional finding reinforces the point. In the high school sample, White students were a small minority (12 of 417); for these students, for whom ethnicity is likely to be highly salient, ethnic identity scores were significantly related to self-esteem. In contrast to these results, studies with Arab-Israeli college students (Zak, 1976) and with Italian Australians (Rosenthal & Cichello, 1986) found no relationship between comprehensive measures of ethnic identity and various indices of self-esteem.

As with the other components that have been considered, the findings are conflicting regarding the relationship between self-esteem and ethnic identity commitment or a more global conception of ethnic identity. Furthermore, the salience of ethnicity for individuals is likely to influence this relationship. As noted earlier, even where a relationship has been demonstrated, the direction of effect is not clear. However, another variable that may be essential in understanding the relationship is the way in which individuals relate to the mainstream culture.

ETHNIC IDENTITY AND MAINSTREAM ACCULTURATION

Awareness of one's ethnic identity results primarily from contact with other ethnic groups; in a homogeneous setting, one's identity as a group member is likely to have little salience. Research on ethnic identity has focused on the individual's orientation toward his or her own group, but the relationship to one's own group is only half of the picture. Good adjustment among minority group members is likely to be a factor of one's relationship to both the ethnic culture and the mainstream. Thus ethnic attitudes, knowledge, and behaviors cannot be considered in isolation. An individual can have a high ethnic identity and be either closely integrated into the mainstream culture or separated from it.

The work of Berry and his colleagues (e.g., Berry, Kim, Minde, & Mok, 1987; Berry, Kim, Power, Young, & Bujaki, 1989) defines four modes of acculturation, depending on the extent to which ethnic group members identify with both their own and the majority culture: A strong identification with both groups is indicative of integration or biculturalism; a strong identification only with the dominant culture reflects assimilation; with only the ethnic group, separation; and with neither group, marginalization.

A recent review (Phinney, Lochner, & Murphy, 1990) of the mental health implications of these four modes of acculturation emphasizes the complexity of the issues. It seems clear that marginalization is the least adaptive mode. This mode is seen among American Indians whose native traditions have been lost and who have not become part of the mainstream. Lacking a clear identity as either Indian or American, many have become the victims of hopelessness, alcoholism, and suicide (Berlin, 1987). Similarly, for many inner-city Blacks, the Black community no longer provides a positive source of identification and the White community provides little opportunity for integration, leaving the individual isolated and at risk (Blackwell & Hart, 1982). Although no studies have specifically addressed marginalization and self-esteem, it seems likely that an individual with both low ethnic identity and little integration into the mainstream would experience low self-esteem.

The separated individual, typically living in a ghetto situation, may derive a secure self-esteem from a supportive ethnic community. Crocker and Major (1989) point out that one method by which stigmatized groups protect their self-esteem is by making comparisons within their own group; such a strategy is obviously facilitated in a ghetto situation, where contact with the dominant culture is minimalized. For example, Black children in segregated schools have higher self-esteem than those in integrated schools (Rosenberg & Simmons, 1972). However, such separation is likely to leave the individual unprepared to move into integrated settings. Szapocznik and Kurtines (1980) suggest that ethnic group members who remain monocultural may suffer adjustment problems due to their failure to learn to adapt to the mainstream. Thus close identification with one's ethnic group, in the absence of adaptation to the majority culture, may present problems that affect self-esteem, at least when the individual interacts in mainstream settings. There are, however, no data that specifically address this question.

The assimilated individual has a primary identification with the mainstream culture and little or none with the ethnic culture. As noted earlier, if ethnicity is not salient, as in the case of European immigrants in America, no impact on self-esteem would be expected. However, for clearly identifiable minorities, such as Blacks, Asians, and many Hispanics, attempts at assimilation may be met with prejudice and discrimination (Dovidio & Gaertner, 1986). Furthermore, such attempts may provoke negative sanctions from their own ethnic group members who feel the individual is betraying his or her group (Steele, 1990). The way in which the assimilated individual deals with these conflicting pressures may be a factor in self-esteem, but little research has been done on this issue.

Finally, integration involves a combined identification with one's own ethnic group and with mainstream culture. A number of empirical studies indicate that this mode of adaptation is related to better psychological outcomes than the other alternatives (Berry et al., 1987; Szapocznik & Kurtines, 1980). Among Hispanic subjects, Lang, Munoz, Bernal, and Sorenson (1982) found that those with a bicultural orientation, as opposed to a monocultural Hispanic (separated) or Anglo (assimilated) orientation, showed better psychological adjustment. Phinney, Williamson, and Chavira (1990) assessed self-esteem and attitudes toward assimilation, separation, and integration in large samples of ethnically diverse high school students ($N = 417$) and college students ($N = 223$). In both samples, the results showed small but significant correlations between self-esteem and endorsement of integration attitudes, whereas assimilation attitudes were negatively related to self-esteem, and separation attitudes were unrelated.

Because of the relative paucity of research on acculturation and self-esteem, the results reviewed are not definitive. However, there are some data suggesting that a high ethnic identity when accompanied by a positive mainstream orientation is related to high self-esteem, whereas ethnic identity without at least some adaptation to the dominant culture may be problematic. A low ethnic identity may be particularly detrimental to the self-esteem of the marginal or isolated individual; for the assimilated person, the low salience of ethnicity may mean that self-esteem is unrelated to ethnic identity.

SUMMARY AND CONCLUSIONS

Although theoretical writing stresses the importance of ethnic identity as a factor in self-esteem, findings of empirical research on the subject are inconclusive. Existing research that examines various components of ethnic identity in relation to self-esteem yields conflicting results. A few studies have reported positive correlations of self-esteem with positive ethnic evaluation and ethnic identity commitment, but a number of studies have found no relationship between self-esteem and various measures of ethnic identity. The general weakness of these results may be accounted for by the fact that these studies do not assess identification with the majority or mainstream culture. Studies that examine modes of acculturation suggest that identification with both one's own group and the mainstream is predictive of the best psychological outcome.

Research indicates that the relationship between ethnic identity and self-esteem only holds among those who identify themselves as ethnic group members and for whom ethnicity is salient. Salience may, of course, be deliberately chosen by some; for others, however, it is thrust upon them by a society that labels anyone who is different from the norm, whether in appearance, language, or customs.

Clearly, additional research is needed to examine the relationship of ethnic identity and self-esteem in greater detail. Such studies need to consider the various components of ethnic identity and take into account orientation toward the mainstream culture. It is important to consider differences and similarities across different ethnic groups; it may be that positive ethnic attitudes influence self-esteem more among the more stigmatized groups. In addition, the relationship might be expected to change over age, as ethnic group members move from homogeneous communities and elementary schools into more diverse educational and work settings; cross-sectional and longitudinal studies would be useful to examine these changes. The relationship also may be influenced by contextual variables, such as the prevailing societal attitudes toward particular ethnic groups. As research begins to sort out these various factors, we should get a clearer picture of the role of ethnic identity in the self-esteem of minority group members.

6
♦

Ethnic Identity and Adaptation of Mexican American Youths in School Settings

MARTHA E. BERNAL

DELIA S. SAENZ

GEORGE P. KNIGHT

In this chapter we review the research on school performance and attrition in Mexican American youths, emphasizing the manner in which their socialization as ethnic minority group members affects their psychological adaptation in schools. The aim of the review is not simply to address how Mexican Americans do in comparison to other groups but, rather, to examine how their membership as Americans of Mexican descent contributes to their adaptation in U.S. schools. The central questions of this review are the following: How is ethnic identity related to the adaptation of Mexican American youths in educational settings? How do the social, cultural, and political contexts within which they go to school affect the adaptations of Mexican American youths? What are the theoretical frameworks that characterize the relationship between sociocultural variables and school achievement in Mexican American youths? Of particular interest for this review were theoretical and research works examining the relationship between school achievement and ethnic, racial, and cultural variables in ethnic minority, and, specifically, Mexican American students.

ORGANIZATION OF THIS REVIEW

In this review, we (a) briefly summarize the empirical literature on the prediction and correlates of school dropout relative to Mexican Americans to provide an understanding of the factors that are correlated with school failure and success, (b) present theoretical views that have bearing on factors believed to cause school failure and on the experience of Mexican American youths in school settings, and (c) discuss a social identity theoretical framework that relates ethnic identity, a key cultural variable, and minority status to the adaptation of Mexican American youths to the dominant society. Previous research and theory are reconceptualized within this framework, and its implications as well as relevant developmental considerations for the adaptation of minority students are highlighted.

Before proceeding, definitions of the terms "adaptation" and "ethnic identity" are in order, especially because there is a general lack of specificity about the meaning of these terms.

Adaptation refers to behavioral or attitudinal changes in response to cultural, social, and interpersonal demands. Adaptation does not imply either positively or negatively valued outcomes; it simply means that individuals make some kind of functional modification in response to demands for change. In educational contexts, students respond in numerous ways to demands for compliance with school rules, peer interaction, and learning tasks and may or may not consequently gain access to their primary objective: an education. Ethnic minority individuals may adapt to the conflict and demands generated by contact with members of the dominant society in a number of ways, including taking on, or rejecting, the other group's cultural values, language, customs, and behaviors.

Ethnic identity is a psychological construct that addresses the important question "Who am I?" It is a set of self-ideas about one's own ethnic group membership and thus is part of the self-concept. These self-ideas are multidimensional, and there is great variability in the relative strengths of these dimensions among Mexican Americans. Individuals must self-identify as members, have some information about the cultural characteristics of their group, and have developed some feelings about their ethnic group membership that are expressed as preferences or nonpreferences for ethnic values and about family, among other things.

THE MAGNITUDE OF THE PROBLEM

A recent report from the National Center for Education Statistics (1989) estimates that national status dropout rates (the number of individuals who are dropouts at any given point in time, regardless of when they left school) stand at 36% for Hispanics, 15% for Blacks, and 13% for Whites, and in the West, where Mexican Americans are concentrated, the Hispanic dropout rate increases to 58%. Problems created by the undereducation of Hispanics are magnified by a rapidly increasing population growth rate, which stems from both a high birth rate and rising immigration (Arias, 1986).

For the individual, the costs of failure to complete school consist of limited economic and occupational opportunities, loss of substantial personal income over a lifetime, and disenfranchisement from society and its institutions (Steinberg, Blinde, & Chan, 1984). For society, the costs of failure to educate ethnic minority youths as contributing citizens are also great (Felice, 1981). For example, Mann (1986) estimates that, across the working careers of dropouts and a continuation of a 25% dropout rate (a low estimate), $7 billion worth of social security benefits will be lost to the nation. One key to attenuating these costs may lie in increasing our understanding of the psychological consequences for Mexican American youths of the social context of their school settings. We turn now to the empirical literature on school dropout.

EMPIRICAL STUDIES OF THE PREDICTION AND CORRELATES OF DROPOUT

To date, the research on the prediction and correlates of school achievement has been relatively atheoretical, and synthesis of results has been problematic because the studies have varied along several methodological dimensions. Nevertheless, certain patterns have emerged.

Early work on the prediction of the academic achievement of children did not focus on Hispanics, but it did underscore the relationship between dropout rates and the combination of three factors: low socioeconomic family background, early academic failure, and race/ethnicity (e.g., Ekstrom, Goertz, Pollack, & Rock, 1986). Moreover, this work suggested that educational problems could be identified as early as the first to third grades on the basis of grade point average, IQ, and math and reading achievement test scores (Lloyd, 1978).

Subsequent investigators focused on the school failure of language minority youngsters, that is, those who are national origin minorities by birth and who speak, in varying degrees, languages other than English (reviewed in Steinberg et al., 1984). Of special interest was the finding that language minority youths of Hispanic background drop out at a higher rate than their counterparts from non-Hispanic backgrounds. Several hypotheses have been offered for this finding, including the possibility that Hispanic students are more likely to come from a lower socioeconomic status (SES) background and that the strong desire of Hispanic families to maintain the dominant Spanish language, as compared to families of other ethnic groups, presents an impediment to their children's school adaptation. Canadian survey data, however, have revealed large achievement differences between groups whose primary languages were Portuguese, Italian, or Chinese even though there were small SES differences between these minority groups (Cummins, 1984, p. 99). Furthermore, other non-English-speaking groups, such as Asians, also strive for maintenance of their native language and cultural identity, and their children do not experience academic deficiencies.

Some factors have been found to influence dropout differentially among ethnic groups. For example, 14-year-old Hispanics were much more likely to drop out if they had recently resided outside the United States than if they were longtime U.S. residents (Rumberger, 1983). Generally, however, in the few studies in which separate data on Hispanics were collected, information about respondents' Hispanic group membership, generation of migration to the United States, and English language competence were unavailable.

More recently, Velez (1989), using the high school and beyond 1980 data set, found that factors predicting dropout differed with Hispanic groups. Among Mexican-descent students, cutting classes, suspensions, heavy dating, being older, and being female increased the odds of dropping out, whereas among Cuban students the factor most predictive of dropout was suspensions. In Puerto Rican students, confrontation, being female, and being older predicted dropout. Among Cubans, students with two parents and from higher SES homes and those who were relatively recent immigrants were significantly less likely to drop out. Recent immigrants of Mexican and Puerto Rican descent, in contrast, were more likely to drop out. Factors related to dropout, however, are not causes per se. A number of theories have been proposed to explain the causes of dropout in ethnic minority students.

THEORIES ABOUT CAUSES OF DROPOUT IN MEXICAN AMERICAN YOUTHS

Two major types of contemporary theories guide research on the school performance of minority students; both emphasize external causes residing in the social ecology of the student. Other theories dwell on endemic causes, especially the deficits of students and their families in explaining dropout (Carter, 1979; Jensen, 1962; Riesman, 1962), and are not discussed here.

Primary Cultural Discontinuities or Mismatch Between Home and School

The cultural mismatch theories emphasize microlevel sociological variables, including disparities between home and school environments as causes of underachievement. Ogbu (1987) has referred to these disparities as primary cultural discontinuities that are generated from preexisting differences between immigrant and host societies. Primary cultural discontinuities cause conflict between students and schools and lead to academic failure. These conflicts are a result of differences between minority and Anglo cultures in nonverbal and verbal communication, cognitive styles, cultural values, and behaviors. Neither students nor teachers and school staff are held to blame for these unfortunate cultural incompatibilities, but their explanations of what they perceive as strange in each other are not cultural. Thus teachers and students may make attributions about the others' internal traits and perceived deficiencies rather than viewing their mutual behavior as interactional phenomena based on cultural differences.

Such interactions, attributions, and labeling on the part of both school staff and students result in disruptions of the teaching and learning process. These disruptions, moreover, lead to students' rejection of the cultural values and academic demands of the schools and, consequently, to academic failure in ethnic minority children. Related to these cultural mismatches is the fact that low-status minority students often experience inferior instruction and discrimination in classrooms because of White teachers' racial and ethnic biases (Cummins, 1984; Laosa, 1977).

The primary evidence for cultural mismatch theory comes from findings that academic achievement is lower and dropout rates higher in language minorities as compared to minorities with an English language background (Steinberg et al., 1984) and that youths migrating in their teens have more academic problems than those migrating earlier in life (e.g., Rumberger, 1983). These two groups, language minorities and immigrant minority youths, would be expected to experience greater culture conflict. Additional evidence supporting this theory comes from research demonstrating (a) the existence of significant cultural discontinuities between home and school in terms of rules that govern patterns of interaction (e.g., Au, 1980; Kagan, 1984; Phillips, 1972; Wong-Fillmore, 1983) and (b) the effectiveness of interventions designed to reduce cultural disparities in the classroom and improve ethnic-minority school achievement (e.g., Goldman & Trueba, 1987; Slavin, 1983; Tharp & Gallimore, 1989; Tharp et al., 1984).

Secondary Cultural Discontinuity/ Cultural Ecological Theory

This theoretical approach emphasizes the influence of macrolevel sociological variables, such as political, economic, and educational institutional structures, on minority school failure. According to Ogbu (1987), its most vocal proponent, there are different types of minorities. Being a member of a "castelike or involuntary minority" is associated with poor school performance as well as with low income, discrimination, depreciation, and exploitation. Castelike minorities are groups that were incorporated into U.S. society involuntarily through slavery, conquest, or colonization. Black, Native American, Puerto Rican, and Mexican American groups qualify as castelike minorities, as distinct from immigrant minorities such as Japanese, Vietnamese, or Nicaraguans who originally came to the United States voluntarily. On initial contact between the White and castelike minority group members, only primary cultural differences in the content of their cultures exist. Secondary cultural differences develop as contact between them continues, such as when children of the two groups go through their school years and have to adapt to each other in various ways. These secondary cultural discontinuities represent a new kind of cultural difference that consists of reactions or response styles by minority children to their treatment by the dominant group. Their reactions include ways of feeling, perceiving, understanding, and coping with their condition in U.S. society and their relationship to Whites. In other words, given a history of the experience of being second-class citizens, children develop new and different cultural patterns or adaptations, and these are the secondary cultural discontinuities to which Ogbu refers.

The kinds of adaptations that involuntary minority group members make to their minority status vary and include changes in communication and interaction styles, stronger ethnic ties, and rejection and distrust of the culture and customs of the dominant group. Most important for their schooling is their increasing disbelief that their chances of obtaining a good education equal those of Whites coupled with their belief that, for them, formal education is not the way to make it socioeconomically. In reaction to such realization of barriers to socioeconomic mobility, minority youths behave in ways that result in school failure. Their resulting behavioral styles have at least two main features: cultural inversion and an oppositional social identity.

Cultural inversion is the tendency of a minority group to see behaviors, events, meanings, and symbols of the dominant group as inappropriate for them and as a means of repudiating the derogatory images placed on them by Whites (Ogbu, 1987). Cultural inversion can result in the development of a cultural framework of opposition wherein psychological pressures are brought to bear on minority members to avoid acting in accordance with the dominant group's frame of references—for example, working for good grades—because they are viewed as White behaviors. Thus involuntary minority youths "develop a new sense of social identity in opposition to the social identity of the dominant group" (Ogbu, 1987, p. 323). This new social identity promotes behavior patterns that result in school failure.

The evidence supporting the secondary discontinuity hypothesis is primarily based on two kinds of demonstrations. The first demonstration is that immigrant versus indigenous minority status and not SES accounts for the differences in school achievement found between immigrant and nonimmigrant minorities. Immigrant minorities in many parts of the world have been found to be academically successful. Results of ethnographic research suggest that this greater academic success is not restricted to students of middle-class background and thus that SES cannot account for the greater achievement of immigrant minority youths (Gibson, 1987).

The second demonstration in support of the secondary discontinuity hypothesis is that involuntary minorities experience school difficulties and dropout to a greater degree than immigrant minorities. If primary cultural differences were the cause of school resistance and failure, immigrant children, who experience the most cultural disparity between home and school, would be more likely to fail. However, since they have not had the sociohistorical experience of discrimination, denigration, and realization of the economic worthlessness of education, immigrant youths should be striving to succeed in school. Involuntary minorities, on the other hand, have given up the attempt to succeed and have adapted by rejecting the educational system and its practices. Involuntary minority groups such as Mexican Americans and Puerto Ricans, for example, are reported to demonstrate poor school performance in comparison to immigrant minorities, including Asian Americans, other Hispanic immigrant groups such as Cubans, Nicaraguans, and Central Americans (Suarez-Orozco, 1987), and even immigrant Mexican-descent youths (Matute-Bianchi, 1986).

Secondary cultural discontinuity theory is also supported by the results of recent ethnographic research conducted in a California high school by Matute-Bianchi (1986, 1989). Her retrospective data showed that limited-English-proficient (LEP) Mexican-descent high school students had a higher graduation rate compared to the rate for all Mexican-descent students. On the basis of interview data, the Mexican-descent students were categorized into five groups based on self-classification: recent Mexican immigrant, Mexican oriented, Mexican American, Chicano, and *cholo*. Each of these groups was described as having certain characteristics, ranging from those of Mexicano or Mexican orientation who were recent immigrants, Spanish speaking, and academically and socially integrated in the school to those of Chicano and *cholo*/low rider subcultural orientations who were nonimmigrants, held in low esteem by the more Mexican-oriented students and the school, and alienated both socially and academically from the school. In keeping with Ogbu's (1987) theory, the more academically successful Mexican-oriented students, who were either immigrants or children of immigrants, linked their academic success to higher-status adult occupations, whereas the unsuccessful Chicano or *cholo*-oriented students did not make this connection.

Matute-Bianchi's (1986, 1989) work suggests that the cultural and other social identity patterns of the youths had formed as part of the adaptational processes influenced by the youths' sociohistorical experiences as immigrants or nonimmigrants. Furthermore, these social identity patterns were related to the youths' academic motivation and performance. This suggestion makes a compelling case for research on the differential experiences of immigrants and nonimmigrant youths on the processes they encounter in their school careers, on their coping patterns and resources, and on their social identities.

The ethnographic research results supporting secondary discontinuity theory must be viewed as suggestive, however, because of problems due to small sample size, the representativeness of the samples, possible experimenter bias, and the confounding of SES levels with ethnic group and other variables. Furthermore, ethnographic investigators fail to provide even the most elementary descriptive data. Nevertheless, this theory offers some important suggestions regarding the role of culture, ethnic identity, and adaptation of immigrant minority youths to dominant culture school settings.

CRITIQUE OF PRIMARY AND SECONDARY CULTURAL DISCONTINUITY THEORIES

Primary Cultural Discontinuity Theory

We now discuss criticisms of these two theories. There are several key criticisms of cultural mismatch theory. The first and most obvious contention is that immigrant language minorities, whose primary cultural discontinuities with the dominant group schools are greatest, have been found, in some instances, to have greater school success than nonimmigrant language minorities (reviewed in Ogbu, 1987). Second, it remains unclear how much of the home culture schools must reproduce to reduce cultural differences sufficiently to promote achievement. Third, and most important, is the argument that demonstration of the effectiveness of cultural educational interventions does not explain why children fail or succeed in school; that is, it does not address the *process* leading to failure or success.

Secondary Cultural Discontinuity Theory

There are several criticisms, as well, of secondary cultural discontinuity theory. For example, it does not explain how some involuntary minorities become academically successful (Jordan & Jacob, 1987) or how they can gain a higher social class as they become rapidly assimilated (Jordan & Jacob, 1987; Trueba, 1988). In addition, this perspective does not explain why involuntary minority students respond to microlevel sociocultural school interventions that merely change aspects of the classroom culture (Vogt, Jordan, & Tharp, 1987). Most important, however, is Ogbu's (1978, 1982, 1983, 1987) apparent failure to elaborate either the educational or societal interventions that should be taken to eliminate the underachievement in involuntary minority youths. In his theory, these youths are doomed to present and future academic failure.

In summary, many interventions have been found to be effective in the promotion of academic achievement by those who adhere to a cultural mismatch theory, but the success of these interventions does not identify the causes of underachievement. The theory of secondary cultural discontinuity, on the other hand, seeks to identify causes of underachievement but fails to offer interventions. Neither theory has led to investigation of the processes leading to school failure. We know something about the factors that are correlated with or predict dropout but not much about how they act on youths' lives. Finally, in the case of both theories, the constructs implicated in school failure are located in the environment, and internal causes are not examined.

ACADEMIC FAILURE OF MINORITY YOUTH: AN ALTERNATIVE APPROACH

The range of factors implicated within each of the two theories addressing cultural variables in school achievement has been relatively broad; however, there has been no attempt to examine the interaction of ecological factors with individual factors in explaining the pervasive academic difficulties of minority youths (Jordan & Jacob, 1987). Social identity theory is a theoretical approach that might provide an initial basis for integrating the views of these traditional theories and for guiding future work. This theory, originally formulated by Tajfel (1978b, 1982), and later elaborated by Turner (1982), considers the roles of both the individual's internal self-concept and the external social context. We describe the basic postulates of this theory next and then apply it to understanding the academic achievement of Mexican American youths.

A Social Identity Approach

Social identity theory is a framework for understanding how group membership influences our behavior and relations with members of our own and other groups. The theory rests on three basic assumptions:

1. We categorize our social world into units comprised of similar others (ingroups) and units comprised of dissimilar others (outgroups).
2. We strive for a positive self-concept that is derived, in part, from our membership in the ingroup.

3. The positive or negative valence of our self-concept is partly dependent on how we evaluate the ingroup relative to outgroups.

According to Tajfel (1982), our social identity represents a major portion of our self-conception and provides a central definition of and evaluation for the self. Social identity also guides our behavior, particularly in instances of intergroup relations. In this review, we conceptualize the self-concept as composed of multiple social identities (e.g., ethnic, racial, gender, and academic), each possessing numerous components (e.g., self-identification, knowledge, preferences, and values). Moreover, we believe that personal identities, which are categorizations based on interpersonal attributes (e.g., "I am smart" and "I am popular"), may have similar effects on the individual as do group-derived social identities.

Categorization and Social Comparison in Social Identity Theory

According to the theory, two basic processes—categorization and social comparison—play a major role in determining how we come to develop views of ourselves and others in the social environment. Categorization involves both assignment of individuals to groups and designation of the attributes associated with each group. Consequently, categorization of persons into groups (e.g., Mexican American, student, sister, and friend) serves to define their position within a given social matrix and allows us to draw inferences about individuals based on their group membership.

Once categorization occurs, we engage in social comparison as a means of determining our self-evaluations or self-worth (Festinger, 1954). That is, we derive the value of our group by comparing it to other groups. Thus, if we are members of relatively privileged groups, we compare our group favorably to outgroups and consequently derive a positive self-concept from our category membership. In contrast, if we are members of disadvantaged or devalued groups—including minorities—we might have difficulty achieving a positive self-concept as a function of the valence associated with our group.

Behavioral Effects of Social Identities

In addition to providing information about the relevant attributes and evaluations associated with group membership, each of our social identities has a set of rules and appropriate behaviors that guide our actions. These elements may promote different interaction patterns with members of the ingroup and the outgroup (Brewer, 1979; Tajfel, 1982). For example, their ethnic identity can lead Mexican American students to interact in certain ways with ethnic peers (warmer, more open, trusting) and in a different way with Anglo peers. These different behavior patterns may result from the amount of shared knowledge between individuals and/or from the relative preference for the ingroup over the outgroup.

In summary, the basic premises of social identity theory are that we are social creatures who strive for positive self-concepts, we categorize ourselves and those around us into ingroups and outgroups, and we are responsive to the evaluations and expectations of the social groups to which we belong. Social identity theory lends itself to the analysis of complex intergroup relations and is especially useful in understanding the effects of minority group status. In the sections that follow, we use a social identity framework to reconceptualize primary and secondary cultural discontinuity perspectives.

Cultural Discontinuities and Ethnic Identity

Primary Cultural Discontinuity Theory and Ethnic Identity

Cultural mismatch theory suggests that, in adapting to culturally dissonant school settings, Mexican American students may not have the cultural requisites for academic achievement because they are unassimilated; this incongruity leads to conflict and ultimately school failure. Reconceptualization in terms of social identity theory requires consideration of two propositions. First, the social identity adopted by a student in a classroom (what we call the "prevailing social identity") will contain a specified set of rules and behaviors, and second, there are joint effects on the youths' adaptation of internal social identity and external social-contextual factors.

In applying social identity theory to the task of understanding the performance of youths in culturally disparate school settings, it is useful first to determine which of a youth's many social identities (Mexican American, student, or boy) will prevail in the academic situation. This helps assess the compatibility of situational requirements and the rules and behaviors associated with the prevailing social identity. One possibility is that a youth's prevailing social identity may be based on a "master status," which is a relatively robust self-categorization that pervades most of an individual's social interactions (Goffman, 1963). Alternatively, the prevailing social identity may be due to less stable situational factors. Ethnic identity or gender identity, for example, might become salient if the individual is numerically distinctive (e.g., a token) along one of these identity dimensions in the immediate social environment (McGuire, McGuire, Child, & Fujioka, 1978; Saenz, 1990; Saenz & Lord, 1989). Whatever social identity prevails in the classroom (be it situationally induced or based on a master status) will consequently shape the youth's behavior.

Ethnic identity in Mexican American youths may be the prevailing social identity either because it serves as a master status or because ethnicity is numerically salient (i.e., the child is one of a few Mexican Americans in the classroom). In either case, the elicitation of the youth's ethnic identity may result in the exacerbation of the differences between behavior patterns associated, respectively, with home and school environments, resulting in cultural discontinuity. In short, Mexican American youths whose ethnically based behaviors and/or attitudes are incompatible with the requirements of school tasks may be less likely to respond to the demands of the immediate social environment. Under these conditions, attributes such as their traditional Mexican cooperativeness, respectfulness, and unassertiveness may result in processes that lead to academic failure. In contrast, if the social identity "student" prevails and its contents include appropriate classroom behaviors, the youth may be more responsive to environmental demands and consequently more successful.

Adaptation, however, is not strictly determined by internal social identity factors. It is also important to consider the effects of outgroup members' responses to the youths' group membership. That is, members of the dominant society—including Anglo teachers and peers—may be influenced by their perceptions of the minority status of Mexican American students. Because members of the dominant society may associate minority groups with subordinate status, discriminatory practices on their part might be common. In the classroom, these practices might take the form of low ability expectations, inferior teaching, or denigration of Mexican American individuals and their culture. Over a period of time, these practices might present an impediment to the full participation of Mexican American students in school settings. Thus ethnic identity might not only influence the individual directly but also indirectly through the responses of outgroup members.

It is interesting to note that successful interventions designed to reduce minority student difficulties address the potentially negative responses toward minority youths of the dominant outgroup. Such interventions feature instruction that has been culturally contextualized, fosters cultural pride for minority youths, and communicates positive recognition of the ethnic students' category membership (Tharp, 1989). Accordingly, to the extent that social contexts can be made friendlier, compatible, and more responsive to minority youths' social identities, academic achievement can be improved.

In summary, a social identity approach can encompass the cultural mismatch perspective and expand our consideration of relevant factors to include both the social context and the individual. By identifying the prevailing social identities of students (including associated expectations and behaviors) and assessing their compatibility with environmental demands, we can be better informed about minority youths' adaptation to the classroom environment.

Secondary Cultural Discontinuity Theory and Ethnic Identity

Secondary cultural discontinuity theory suggests that the relative disadvantages of minority members—across economic, political, and social domains—promote patterns of interaction between dominant culture and minority group members that convey a second-class status on the latter. These patterns coupled with the perceived lack of a relationship between education and success for minority group members may lead to cultural inversion and, consequently, academic failure.

In examining this process from a social identity approach, it is necessary to consider that an essential component of our social identities is an assessment of self-worth. According to the theory, individuals both strive for a positive self-concept and derive meaning from the valence associated with their group membership. For minority group members, striving for a positive self-concept may arouse conflict and low self-esteem if the individual recognizes that the ingroup is devalued relative to the outgroup. Mexican American students, for example, might realize from a relative comparison of their ethnic group to the dominant group that the ingroup is devalued not only in the classroom but also in society at large. Minority youths may be faced with the difficult task of trying to derive a positive self-concept from their ethnic identity despite their membership in a disparaged group (Tajfel, 1978b).

A social identity approach suggests several courses of action that might be taken by individuals faced with the circumstances described above. One possibility is that individuals may choose to leave their own group and join the outgroup. This option, however, is not feasible when group membership is based on a nonmalleable attribute, as is the case with ethnicity. Another possibility is that minority youths may incorporate their groups' devaluation and internalize feelings of inadequacy into their ethnic identity. Minority members might also withdraw from membership in their own group and thus become marginal or alienated altogether. Also, minority members may choose to reject externally based evaluations of the ingroup. In short, they may establish their own standards and repudiate those of the dominant outgroup. These last two options, in combination, might yield a state akin to Ogbu's (1987) cultural inversion concept. Finally, members of a disparaged group may reinterpret the reasons for their low status (make situational attributions rather than implicate internal causes) and/or engage in social action that leads to desirable outcomes for the ingroup.

In applying these conceptual responses to the circumstances faced by Mexican American youths, one can outline predictable behavior patterns. For example, incorporating negative self-views into their ethnic identities would probably diminish Mexican American youths' morale and achievement behavior in the classroom, possibly leading to adaptations of withdrawal and alienation. Similarly, Mexican American youths might choose to repudiate institutions and values associated with the Anglo culture, including the motivation for success in school. These outcomes, as well as those cited in the previous paragraph, might occur as a function of the incompatibility of ethnic identity behaviors and the demands of the classroom situation. However, these negative outcomes need not occur.

Positive Adaptive Outcomes

Positive adaptive outcomes, that is, incompatibility, may not always result when the prevailing social identity is ethnic identity. Instead, ethnic identity may produce a variety of adaptations that have positive educational outcomes in Mexican American youths. Such outcomes are likely if ethnic identities do not preclude self-categorization as a good student. Similarly, rejection of the host culture and its ways does not necessarily mean rejection of education. Matute-Bianchi (1989) describes a subgroup of Mexican American students who label themselves "Mexicanos" and maintain the values of their culture of origin. Among these values, there is a desire to achieve in school. As one would expect, compatibility between their ethnic identity and classroom requisites in this subgroup of Mexican American youths typically results in academic success. She also describes the adaptation of a sample of high-achieving Japanese Americans in terms of "accommodation without assimilation," that is, cultural maintenance along with willingness to accommodate to the academic demands of the dominant culture schools.

In short, when academic success is a value embedded within a minority student's ethnic identity, behavior that promotes success is likely, even in instances where cultural disparities exist between home and school environments. This idea is supported by work demonstrating that the school achievement of immigrant minorities (who more closely identify with their ethnic group) is better than that of nonimmigrant minorities (who experience fewer disparities). Immigrant minorities, it is suggested, maintain the education-related values of their culture of origin, and this social identity overrides external pressures.

Ethnic identity may also promote academic achievement by buffering the psychological stress experienced by minority youths in dominant school settings. This buffering effect may occur because of the existence of a support network composed of similar others who promote acceptance and pride in one's ethnic culture. In this case, the ingroup defines social reality for the individual and the views of sources outside the central reference group are less important (Matute-Bianchi, 1989). Also, buffering might arise out of one's ethnic identity if a positive affective evaluation is associated with it. In this situation, ethnic identity would promote a positive self-view that encourages achievement.

A social identity approach thus can account for the detrimental effects due to secondary cultural discontinuity; it can also account for instances in which Mexican American youths succeed. Moreover, this approach outlines the psychological processes underlying success and failure. In examining the academic achievement of Mexican American youths it is important to first determine the evaluative content of their social identities and of the cognitive, affective, and behavioral patterns driven by such content. Then, it is necessary to isolate some of the factors in the social environment that communicate negative evaluations. Such an analysis can suggest whether interventions should focus on individual factors or on the environment. It is likely that the degree of amenability to intervention of environmental factors will be a function of their proximity in the youths' social ecology. For example, classrooms, peers, teachers, school administrators, and textbooks may be more easily accessed for intervention than prevailing social attitudes embedded in public institutions. Nevertheless, even when institutional racism is a prominent and relatively unchanging factor, other intervention alternatives exist within a social identity framework.

THE ROLE OF DEVELOPMENTAL PROCESSES

Any intervention designed to correct or prevent minority underachievement may need to consider the developmental state of the individuals involved and the manner in which that developmental state may place the individual at risk. Although some of the work on ethnic minority achievement considers developmental issues (e.g., Tharp, 1989), a vast majority of this research has not incorporated these issues. Thus it is imperative for researchers focusing on the role of social identities in ethnic minority achievement to investigate the manner in which developmental processes affect social identities and, in turn, achievement.

Developmental changes, for example, may have an impact on the relationship between a youth's social identities, particularly ethnic identity, and academic performance. Harter (1983) describes the self-concept as changing from self-definitions couched in terms of specific, observable physical attributes and behaviors during early childhood to abstractions composed of overgeneralized psychological traits regarding affects, motivations, and cognitions during adolescence and adulthood. Bernal, Knight, Garza, Ocampo, and Cota (1990) have demonstrated developmental shifts within the ethnic identities of Mexican American children. The increasing complexity of social identities and the shifting salience of different social identities with age may affect, in turn, the environmental contexts and persons most influential on the individual. In addition, developmental changes in social comparison processes (e.g., Ruble, 1983) or causal attribution processes (e.g., Costanzo & Dix, 1983) may influence the individual's interpretations of and responses to situations. As psychological and social dimensions become more salient aspects of the self, evaluations deriving from school rather than home and from interactions with peers rather than family members may gain importance.

This shifting salience of identities may lead to considerable conflict, for example, during late childhood and early adolescence because ethnic identity, which is largely composed of psychological dimensions, may become increasingly salient at a time when peers also have more impact on self-evaluation. Resolution of these conflicts may take many forms, ranging from subjugating one social identity in favor of another, developing contextually specific hierarchies for one's social identities, or abandoning earlier social identities in favor of a newly developed social identity that creates a new support group (e.g., a gang member). Furthermore, the manner in which Mexican American children resolve this conflict may have bearing on subsequent academic performance depending on whether conflict resolution leads to a hierarchy of social identities that value or do not value academic achievement.

These developmental shifts in social identities and the hierarchical organization of the identities have implications for evaluating the previous evidence regarding the cause of achievement problems among minorities. It may be that cultural mismatches have more impact on the education of younger minority children because of their susceptibility to microlevel classroom variables, as suggested by Erickson (1987). In contrast, secondary cultural discontinuities may be more influential on older children and adolescents because of their increasing self-definition as ethnic minorities and their greater awareness of the social consequences of their ethnic group membership with its sociopolitical and economic realities. The ethnic identity of young Mexican American children is very concrete and relatively unsophisticated regarding the implications of ethnic group membership. In contrast, older children and adolescents are more likely to be trying to resolve who they are by prioritizing their various social identities, including their ethnic identity, and at the same time self-defining in terms of social group memberships. Thus secondary cultural discontinuities along with the enhanced influence of peers may lead these older children and adolescents to respond to the derogatory messages of the dominant culture by becoming involved with and strengthening a marginal identity and oppositional culture (i.e., a culture different from that of the family and different from that of the dominant society).

In conclusion, the extant theory and research concerning cultural influences in the adaptation of Mexican American youths to school settings have failed to adequately account for underachievement among these youths. This literature also has failed to adequately attend to factors indicating differences within the population of Mexican American youths, such as ethnic identity, generation of migration, and language competence. We suggest that a social identity theoretical framework may represent a means of more adequately explaining the underachievement of ethnic minority youths. Finally, the potential for development shifts in social identities suggests that investigators need to consider and investigate the developmental mechanisms that may influence the way in which the social identities of Mexican American youths affect their adaptation to schools.

7

♦

Ethnic Identity and Bilingualism Attitudes

AIDA HURTADO
PATRICIA GURIN

*L*anguage is an obvious differentiator among ethnic groups (Giles & Powesland, 1975), one that fosters the political, economic, and cultural dominance of the majority group and the solidarity of the minority group (Fishman, 1986). Its political significance is evident in current efforts by the dominant U.S. English-speaking majority, reacting against the new, larger immigration and especially the growing size of the Spanish-speaking minority, to make English the official language of the land. The successful passage of California Proposition 63, declaring English the official language of the state, verifies the vehemence of reactions to language and ethnics. In 1979, there were 18 million people in the United States who spoke a language other than English at home and half spoke Spanish. No language other than English can claim as many speakers as Spanish (U.S. Bureau of the Census, 1982). This chapter explores the extent to which attitudes toward bilingualism reflect ethnic identity and political consciousness for persons of Mexican descent in the United States.

Approval of bilingualism is defined as the desire to preserve competency in Spanish as proficiency in English is achieved (and should not be confused with nationalism, which sometimes rejects the dominant language). Our survey tested a set of relationships where a childhood linguistic environment and an adult structural integration influence ethnic identity and, in turn, affect attitudes toward bilingualism and political consciousness.

THE SIGNIFICANCE OF LANGUAGE ATTITUDES

The debate over bilingualism in the United States is waged both between Anglos and Chicanos and among Chicanos themselves. The term *Chicanos* is reserved here to indicate people of Mexican descent who were born in the United States or Mexico but were *raised* in the United States and as such are a native minority. *Mexican descendants* is a more inclusive term and applies to Chicanos as well as to recent immigrants from Mexico. Some Mexican descendants support bilingualism, feeling strong loyalty to Spanish, especially as a medium for discussing cultural matters, for emotional expression, and for intragroup interaction (Sole, 1977); others believe that retaining Spanish is either unimportant or may inhibit success in an English-dominant country. Some Chicano parents with a limited command of English nevertheless will speak only English to their children in the hope that their children will not acquire Spanish accents (Krear, 1969). In addition to these feelings, Mexican descents often battle with the pressures placed on them by the dominant English-speaking group to assimilate culturally and linguistically.

Why do people of Mexican descent disagree about bilingualism? The history of immigration and of language acculturation in the United States has produced strong pressures for becoming monolingual in English. Americans of European descent and representatives of institutions that deal with Spanish-speaking groups are baffled because the Spanish-speaking Americans have not followed the rapid linguistic assimilation that characterized European immigrants. Cross-cultural contacts in the United States inevitably involve the expectation that English is the appropriate language for discourse. However, members of the U.S.'s majority culture are beginning to recognize that the growth and size of the Spanish-speaking population, due to a consistently high fertility rate of Mexican descendants and the large influx of people from Cuba, Puerto Rico,

Mexico, and other Latin American countries, may force bilingualism into social life in many regions of the United States. Living in a country with this history understandably produces ambivalent language attitudes among Spanish-language groups.

Within this historical context, other factors also influence attitudes toward maintaining Spanish, among them variations in the structural positions and childhood linguistic environments of Mexican-descent population, ethnic identity, and political consciousness.

SOCIAL PSYCHOLOGICAL INFLUENCES

Structural integration, represented by education and a secure economic status, may influence bilingualism attitudes because the more integrated have felt directly the pressures to drop Spanish (Fishman, 1972). Many institutions make success dependent on English ability. For example, in San Antonio, Texas, de la Zerda and Hopper (1979) found that placement decisions of employment interviewers were influenced by a prospective employee's degree of Spanish accentedness. Applicants with no noticeable accent were favored for supervisory positions and those with Spanish accents for semiskilled positions. This also influences the evaluations that native Spanish-speakers themselves draw of English and Spanish. Those who have achieved success may overvalue English and see little use in retaining competence in Spanish. Control of Puerto Rican commercial activities by English-dominant mainland companies has produced a preference for English among upwardly mobile island Puerto Ricans (Angle, 1976).

Childhood socialization in a predominantly Spanish-speaking environment should have a positive effect on loyalty to the Spanish language. Adults who had early, consistent exposure to Spanish would have been fluent Spanish speakers as children and likely to have found retention easier than adults who grew up where English was more dominant. A Spanish childhood linguistic environment should also increase appreciation for language as a cultural expression.

Language attitudes may also emanate from *ethnic identity*. Individuals form social identities by distinguishing their group from another. Because language is such an obvious marker of ingroup and outgroup differences, it is a social construction readily available for group identification (Giles, 1977; Williams, 1979). Major differences between languages are highlighted, minor ones magnified, and some manufactured in the push for distinctiveness (Fishman, 1968).

Many studies in different sociohistorical context confirm a close connection between ethnic identity and language attitudes. There are many instances where language is critical to nationalism and/or ethnic identity: Fishman (1968) provides evidence from West Africa, the Swahili region of Central and East Africa, new Guinea, Scandinavia, and Southeast Asia; Giles and Powesland (1975) from the French Canadians, the Welsh and Scots in Great Britain, the Bretons in France, and the Basques in France and Spain; and Mercer, Mercer, and Mears (1979) from Indian immigrants in England.

Similar results have been found for the Mexican-origin population in the United States. In their study of a Mexican sample from San Antonio, Texas, de la Zerda and Hopper (1975) found that variation in ethnic identity was systematically related to evaluations of accented English and Chicano dialect. People who thought of themselves as American or Latin American downgraded these speech styles and favored standard English. People who considered themselves Mexican or Mexican American accepted the minority speech styles but still favored standard English. In contrast, people who identified as Chicano downgraded standard English and favored Chicano dialect.

Although most research on Mexican-origin people has treated ethnic self-labeling as just another background variable not unlike gender or age, the social constructions of ethnic labels must be examined to explain why some but not other ethnic labels are implicated in language attitudes. A full examination of identity requires distinguishing personal/attributive from social/categorical aspects of identity. As one type of social identity, ethnic identity derives from awareness and acceptance of one's ethnic membership as part of the self. For Chicanos, ethnic identity is not simple or unidimensional but potentially involves several dimensions, among them national origin, culture and language, race and color, and minority status. We examine four dimensions of ethnic identity.

The first involves thinking of one's self in ethnic terms that became highly politicized during the Chicano movement of the late 1960s and 1970s—*pocho/pocha, Indian, cholo/chola, Chicano/Chicana, raza, mestizo/mestiza*. The movement reinterpreted these terms, several of which had derogatory connotations, to symbolize pride. Applying these terms to the self signifies a new political ethnic identity that includes commitment to language as a basis for solidarity in the Chicano community. The second dimension involves thinking of one's self in traditional cultural terms as Mexican and Spanish speaker, which implies a cultural identity. In contrast, the other two dimensions of ethnic identity—thinking of one's self as having American instead of foreign nationality and thinking of one's self as Hispanic or Latin (terms associated with Mexican descendants aspiring to upper mobility)—should be negatively related or, at best, irrelevant to bilingualism attitudes. Approval of bilingualism is thus conceived here as a reflection not of *stronger* ethnic identity but of *particular* meanings that ethnicity has assumed for Mexican-origin people.

How does ethnic identity become politicized for individuals? Tajfel (1978a) asserts that *political consciousness* emerges naturally from social identity because identity is rarely or never secure. For dominant groups, superiority must be preserved. Signs, symbols, and political ideology that justify differentiation must be constructed and carefully perpetuated to insure identity. For subordinate groups, positive distinctiveness must be achieved despite denigration by the dominant group. When mobility is blocked or when the values or primordial ties of members preclude leaving the group, political consciousness arises as members reinterpret and affirm the previously denigrated identity. This new consciousness also provides motivation for collective action to change group inequalities. This process, discussed by writers from a variety of perspectives with language idiosyncratic to each as "decolonization" (Fanon, 1963; Memmi, 1968), "identity transformation" (Hall, Cross, & Freedle, 1972), and "disassimilation" (Hayes-Bautista, 1974), involves new ways of thinking about the relationship between subordinate and dominant groups. Despite concern with different target groups, nearly identical concepts have been suggested in these various models of political consciousness.

We emphasize three interrelated aspects of political consciousness: (a) power discontent, a sense of grievance over the relative lack of power and influence of Mexican-origin persons; (b) rejection of legitimacy, the belief that the economic, social, and political status of Chicanos is illegitimate, the result more of structural constraints than of deficiencies of Chicanos themselves; and (c) collective orientation, the conviction that collective political action is needed to improve the status of the Mexican-descent population.

Some types of ethnic identity are more likely than others to produce politically conscious appraisals of the intergroup situation of Chicanos and Anglos. The social meanings attributed to ethnicity and thus to the ethnic labels that members apply to themselves represent different types of adaptations to subordination. Thinking of one's self as American or as an upwardly mobile Hispanic implies acceptance of the stratification system and belief that individuals should deal with their own ethnicity through individual solutions, not by collective mobilization. In contrast, thinking of one's self as part of *la raza*—a member of a solidarity community as an Indian or mestizo minority, a Chicano *in* but not *of* the American scene—signifies that the individual has embarked on the path to becoming politically conscious. It is this kind of identity that initiates and is then reinforced by what we are calling political consciousness. Other identities, just as ethnic, are either conservative in the sense of accepting intergroup differentials or are simply irrelevant to political consciousness, as we predict cultural identity is likely to be. Thus, while social differentiation and awareness of ethnicity potentially set the stage for political consciousness, the social construction of ethnicity determines when discontent, withdrawal of legitimacy, and collectivism are apt to emerge.

METHOD

Sample and Procedure

The data come from the 1979 Chicano Survey conducted by the Institute for Social Research at the University of Michigan. Participants were from the five southwestern states of California, New Mexico, Arizona, Texas, and Colorado and the Chicago metropolitan area. Face-to-face interviews, which lasted an average of 3 hours and 20 minutes, were conducted by bilingual/bicultural interviewers in urban as well as rural areas. Of the 991 completed interviews, 464 were in English and 527 in Spanish, conducted according to the respondent's language preference. The probability sample covered approximately 90% of the adults of Mexican descent identified by the 1970 U.S. Census. Eligible respondents were heads of households or their spouses and of at least half-Mexican ancestry. When only one adult was eligible, that person was interviewed; when both were eligible, one was randomly selected. A more detailed definition of the population and sampling design and procedures can be found in Arce and Santos (1981).

The main objective of the survey was to examine the mental health implications of ethnic identification and political consciousness among persons of Mexican origin (Arce, Gurin, Gurin, & Estrada, 1976). Mental health was broadly defined to include labor force participation, language issues, cultural preference, social identity, and family-related issues. The analyses reported here focus on the data on language, political consciousness, and social identification.

For two reasons we analyzed only the data collected from the 429 U.S.-born, English-dominant speakers who elected to take the interview in English. Because retaining Spanish fluency becomes difficult when English proficiency is achieved, language attitudes are more closely tied to ethnic identity among individuals who are dominant in English (Carranza & Ryan, 1979). Also, the historical development of the Chicano population since the U.S. conquest of Mexican land in 1948 (Alvarez, 1973) has caused a wide variety of ethnic identity expression among U.S.-born English speakers. Accordingly, most previous work on ethnic self-identification (Dworkin, 1965; Rodriguez-Scheel & Arce, 1981) Hurtado & Arce, in press) has documented it primarily among this group of Mexican descents.

Sample Characteristics

The sample was relatively young, with the average age being 35.71 years (SD = 11.4 years). Respondents' average income was $14,084 ($SD$ = $8,176). Average years of education was 11.4 (SD = 2.9). Two thirds of the respondents were female, and the majority were married (77%), with the rest either separated, divorced, or widowed (17%) or never married (5%). The majority of the respondents' parents were born in the United States (61% of fathers and 74% of mothers).

Measures

Structural integration was measured by achieved educational level and the preceding year's family income (with 16 income categories, ranging from less than $2,000 to more than $30,000). Age was also included in the analysis.

The respondent's *childhood linguistic environment* was measured by an index of two questions: which language was spoken most in the home and which language the parents preferred the respondent to speak when the respondent was a child. A high score indicates exposure mostly to Spanish and a low score, mostly to English.

Ethnic identity measures were derived from factor-analyzing 31 labels that respondents selected or rejected as self-descriptive. Each label appeared on a card that the interviewer handed to respondents, asking them to keep it if it "describes how you think about yourself" and give it back if "you don't think of yourself that way." The labels referred to ethnicity, gender, class, work, and family roles.

Using the OSIRIS computer package, we conducted principal component and common factor analyses to determine the appropriate number of factors to maintain and make initial exploration of the underlying data structure. These analyses were performed on Pearson correlation coefficients. We used the Kaiser criterion, which extracts for rotation the number of factors with eigenvalues of 1 or higher, to determine how many factors should be retained. A common factor analysis, specifying orthogonal (varimax) rotation and a six-factor solution, yielded factors that reflected interpretive conceptual distinctions.[1]

The six-factor solution provides a social identity measure that gives a person a score on each of six dimensions. Four of the six are ethnic terms and were used in the study as a measure of ethnic identity (see Table 7.1). These four ethnic dimensions give a more complex measure of ethnic identity than is usual in studies of ethnicity because this multidimensional approach does not force respondents to make artificial, mutually exclusive choices of ethnic labels. Instead, a respondent has a score on *all four* dimensions.[2] Of course, these ethnic dimensions are not entirely independent. For example, thinking of one's self in Ethno-Political terms also means a greater likelihood of applying Mexican Traditional terms to one's self (both dimensions were significantly correlated +.32). However, our interest was in discerning the *independent effect* of each type of ethnic identity after adjusting for the shared variance among the four dimensions. Unit-weighted measures were formed from selecting labels that loaded highly on each of the four ethnic factors. The scores on each range from 10 to 40, with the higher score indicating a greater number of labels on that dimension accepted by the respondent as self-descriptive.

Mexican-Traditional identity involved thinking of one's self as Mexican and as a Spanish speaker. The second factor, American/Foreigner identity, is a continuum contrasting American at one end with foreign at the other and had eight labels: foreigner, immigrant, Mexican American, American of Mexican descent, United States citizen, English speaker, United States native, and American. The loadings of foreigner and immigrant had opposite signs from the rest of the labels on the factor, which indicates that seeing one's self as a Mexican American or English speaker meant *not* being a foreigner or immigrant. The third factor, Ethno-Political identity, uses terms the Chicano movement projected as part of Chicanismo, such as pocho/pocha, Indian, Cholo/Chola, Chicano/Chicana, raza, mestizo/mestiza. The fourth, Upwardly Mobile Ethnicity, used terms that reflected mobility both in social class terms (working class and middle class) and in ethnic terms (Hispanic, Latin[3]). The ethnic labels on this factor make no reference to being of Mexican descent and represent designations implying high status in most of the Spanish-language

Table 7.1 Rotated Factor Loadings for Social Identity Scales

Social Identity Label	Mexican Traditional	American Foreigner	Ethno-Political	Upwardly Mobile Ethnicity
1. Mexican	−.49			
2. Spanish speaker	−.48			
3. Foreigner		.43		
4. Immigrant		.57		
5. American of Mexican descent		−.70		
6. Mexican American		−.63		
7. American		−.70		
8. U.S. citizen		−.81		
9. English speaker		−.71		
10. U.S. native		−.77		
11. Pocha/o			−.61	
12. Indian			−.43	
13. Chola/o			−.62	
14. Chicana/o			−.54	
15. Raza			−.51	
16. Mestiza/o			−.48	
17. Middle class				.36
18. Hispanic				.68
19. Latin				.60
20. Working class				.49
Percentage total variance	.85	13.5	6.5	7.8

communities in the United States. (It should be noted that while both working class and middle class loaded positively on this factor, poor loaded negatively. In this sample, working class was similar in meaning to middle class.)

Three dimensions of political consciousness were measured following procedures originally developed in studies of gender, race, class, and age consciousness (Gurin, Miller, & Gurin, 1980). All of the indexes for this study were derived by the same factor analyses procedures used for the ethnic identity measures.

Power discontent was measured by asking respondents whether various groups have too much, about the right amount, or too little influence in American life and politics. Factor analysis of responses to 14 groups produced three indexes; the one used here measured discontent over the power to dominant groups (Whites, businessmen, and policemen).

Rejection of legitimacy was measured by two indexes. One assessed the respondent's awareness of discrimination against people of Mexican descent—for example, that "Anglo children get more help and attention from teachers than children of Mexican descent"—and contained nine items. The second explicitly measured explanations for disparities between persons of Mexican descent and Anglos. Respondents were asked to choose between two explanations for disparities: one that attributes them to systemic problems, such as discrimination, labor market forces, poor schooling, or lack of opportunity, and the other to personal deficiencies, such as lack of motivation, talent, or inappropriate values and behavior. This index contained five items.

Collective orientation was measured by two indexes. One tapped attitudes toward traditional political action, such as participating in electoral politics and advocating changes in the law. The other included nontraditional actions and targets outside electoral politics, such as pressuring employers to hire more people of Mexican descent. There were three items in each of these indexes. The scores for all the political consciousness indexes range from 10 to 50, with the higher score indicating a higher degree of political awareness.

Bilingualism attitudes were measured by an index consisting of responses, on a 4-point scale, showing extent of agreement from *strongly agree* to *strongly disagree* to the following statements: "People of Mexican descent should know two languages"; "Children of Mexican descent should learn to read and write in both Spanish and English"; "All school subjects should be taught in both Spanish and English"; "A person who speaks more than one language gets along better with different kinds of people." This index is based on one of the factors derived from analyzing 15 normative statements about English and minority languages (e.g., Spanish, Chinese) in the United States. The scores for this index range from 10 to 50, with a higher score indicating the respondent's approval of Spanish/English bilingualism.

Correctional techniques were used to test the hypothesized direct and indirect effects of the three sets of predictors. All measures were intercorrelated and used in an ordinary least squares regression to predict variations in approval of bilingualism. Those measures that did not have significant direct effects in the initial regression were eliminated. These were American/not foreigner identity, individual-system blame, traditional and nontraditional action ideologies. A reduced-form regression was then performed, the results of which are presented below.

Table 7.2 Regression Coefficients of the Independent Variables on Bilingualism Attitudes

Predictor	Beta
Background variables	
Age	.06
Income	−.07
Education	.02
Language of origin	.07
Ethnic identity	
Mexican-Traditional	.10*
Ethno-Political	.11*
Upwardly Mobile Ethnicity	−.13*
Political consciousness	
Power of discontent	.11*
Dominant group's legitimacy: Mexican discrimination	.21*

NOTE: Percentage variance in bilingualism attitudes explained by the independent variables is 14%.
*$p \leq .05$.

RESULTS

Direct Effects

Table 7.2 presents standardized coefficients for predictors in the reduced-form regression. Only 14%, a moderate amount of variance in bilingualism attitudes, was explained by the proposed model. In general, however, the results provide support for the major sets of hypothesized relationships.

Ethnic identity and political consciousness both significantly influenced bilingualism attitudes. The major way in which the direct effects departed from our expectations was the irrelevance of the social background variables in explaining bilingualism attitudes.

Three of the four ethnic identity measures had significant effects. Thinking of one's self in Mexican Traditional cultural terms and in Ethno-Political terms was associated with approval of bilingualism, whereas Upwardly Mobile Ethnicity was associated with disapproval.

Two political consciousness measures influenced attitudes toward bilingualism. People who were aware that discrimination operates in the lives of the Mexican population and were discontented over the power of dominant groups were more approving of bilingualism than others.

Indirect Effects

Although the multivariate results did not show a direct effect of structural integration or childhood linguistic environment, they could operate indirectly through identity and political consciousness. Two additional regressions were run to examine this possibility. In the first, the multivariate effects of the background variables on identity were assessed; in the second, the joint effects of background and identity variables on political consciousness were examined. These effects are depicted in Figure 7.1.

The background variables did influence both ethnic identity and political consciousness. Age was significantly associated with the Mexican-Traditional dimension of identity, after controlling for age as younger persons were less likely to have grown up in Spanish-language environments, which promoted thinking of the self in traditional cultural terms. Younger persons expressed their ethnicity especially in identities based on being Mexican and Spanish speakers but also on political bases as Chicano and as part of *la raza*. Because these two aspects of identity influenced language attitudes, age and childhood linguistic environment did indirectly affect approval of bilingualism.

Structural integration, represented by attainment of higher income and at least high school education, influenced the other aspects of identity. Having higher income and education was associated with thinking of the self as Hispanic and Latin, terms viewed by Chicanos as indicative of upward mobility. This Upwardly Mobile Ethnicity was *negatively* related to bilingualism. Structural integration thus discourage maintenance of Spanish not directly but in the ways that structurally assimilated Chicanos have come to think of themselves.

The additional regressions also show that ethnic identity had both direct and indirect effects on bilingualism attitudes. Indirectly, these politically conscious people perceived systemic discrimination against Mexicans—they felt the dominant group was too powerful and the disparities in social conditions between Mexicans and Anglos were illegitimate—and thus developed positive attitudes toward Spanish. Coming to think of one's self as Chicano was important because it facilitated these political attitudes and fostered approval of bilingualism.

Thinking of one's self in traditional terms, which directly encouraged positive views of bilingualism, also operated indirectly through political consciousness. But here the impact was negative. A Mexican-Traditional identity resulted in acceptance of power differentials, and the more politically contented disapproved of bilingualism.

Ethnic Identity and Bilingualism Attitudes

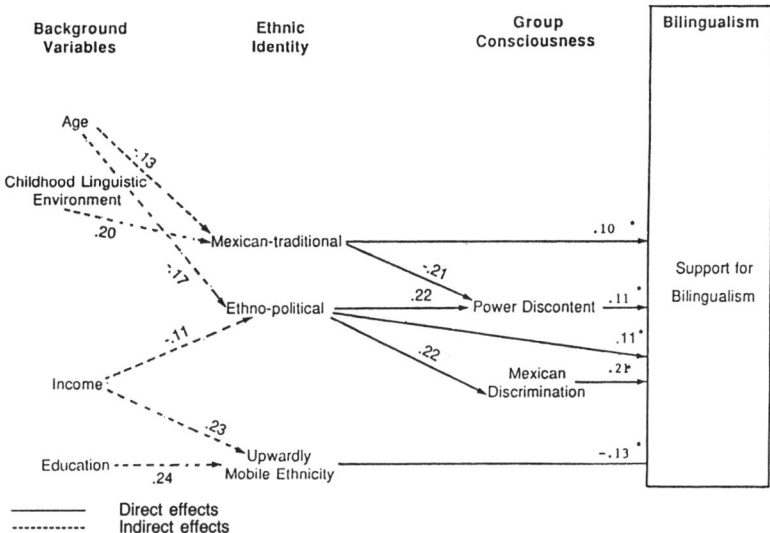

Figure 7.1. Statistically Significant Direct and Indirect Effects (standardized regression coefficients)
NOTE: All of these effects are significant at less or equal to .05.

DISCUSSION

These results indicate that positive views of bilingualism among persons of Mexican descent may be brought about in two different ways, both of which implicate ethnic identity. They also show that social experiences, represented by childhood linguistic environment and structural integration, operated primarily through effects on ethnic identity.

One way that Mexican descendant support bilingualism is through their cultural identities as Mexicans and as Spanish speakers. Those persons who were culturally identified were more supportive of maintaining Spanish and considered speaking two languages desirable. This Mexican-Traditional identity was found in two groups: the young and those who grew up in predominantly Spanish-speaking environments. However, this path is not without complexity, even contradiction. People with a strong Mexican-Traditional identity also expressed conservative views of power differentials in the United States. They believed that dominant groups should have the power they currently hold. This conservatism mutes the positive impact that their culturally based identities have on language attitudes.

A second, less complicated path applies particularly to the young who have come to think of themselves in ethnic terms politicized by the Chicano movement. They not only described themselves as Chicanos/Chicanas but also accepted racial designations (Indian, mestizo/mestiza, and la raza) as self-descriptive. In these ways, they asserted pride in being different from the dominant majority. They also applied previously degrading terms to themselves, evidence they had turned pocho, traditionally used to designate people who spoke corrupted Castilian Spanish or were "Mexican slobs with pretensions of being gringos" (Madrid-Barela, 1977), and cholo, originally coined for zoot-suiters and later applied broadly to gang members, into positive affirmations of the Chicano experience. In part, their support of bilingualism followed directly from this sense of self as politically ethnic and, in part, was fostered by the political views simultaneously involved with this sense of self. This clearly shows that ethnic identity can represent a set of politically conscious beliefs, which include disapproval of the current distribution of power in society and causal attributions that hold structural barriers, not Chicanos, responsible for Anglo-Chicano status disparities.

Does structural integration discourage support for bilingualism as the assimilation literature suggests it will? The results give a mixed answer. Attaining higher income and more schooling neither discouraged nor encouraged the Ethno-Political identity, which promotes the political consciousness in which bilingualism attitudes are embedded. However, structural integration fostered self-conceptions as Hispanic and Latin, which discouraged acceptance of bilingualism. Thus the impact of structural integration depends on the way the structurally integrated think of themselves. The better educated and more affluent are disposed to think of themselves in upwardly mobile ethnic terms, which devalue the importance of maintaining Spanish for themselves and their children, whereas the structurally integrated who do not describe themselves as Hispanic and Latin are as supportive of preserving Spanish as other persons of Mexican descent. It is not the fact of structural attainment but the meaning it may assume, influencing self-conceptions and political attitudes, that threatens support for bilingualism.

NOTES

1. Kim and Rabjohn (1980), Kim, Nie, and Verba (1977) and others have recommended use of tetrachoric r coefficients in the analysis of dichotomous data. The benefit of the tetrachoric is that it adjusts for the marginal frequencies of the variables it correlates. Use of this r is sometimes problematic, however, in that it sometimes overinflates correlations to values of +1.0. Several such values were obtained for this data. To eliminate these correlations, three variables had to be dropped from the factor analyses. The resulting factor solutions based on 28 variable tetrachoric matrixes did not make satisfactory conceptual sense. However, we were assured that the Pearson r and tetrachoric r solutions yielded very similar results when we repeated the Pearson r analysis on the same 28 items. This demonstrates that while tetrachoric r values can be quite different from Pearson r values the relationships *among* those values *can* be quite similar. Moreover, because the solution based on Pearson rs could include all variables and made more conceptual sense, we concluded that the Pearson matrix was the appropriate choice for our analyses.

2. Of course, this means that we are not excluding any respondents by ignoring the two nonethnic factors as all respondents are scored on *all six* dimensions.

3. Latin can also be construed as denoting solidarity with people from Latin American countries. However, the label Latin loaded with the label middle class. Also, respondents who identified with Upwardly Mobile Ethnicity were more educated and had higher incomes. Therefore, we argue that Latin in this particular sample is associated with higher structural integration rather than an indication of solidarity with Latin Americans.

PART 3

Clinical Research and Services

8

♦

Hispanic Mental Health Research

A Case for Cultural Psychiatry

HORACIO FABREGA JR.

This chapter examines the mental health problems of Hispanics from the standpoint of cultural psychiatry, the field of study that addresses relations between culture and psychiatric illness. In the present context, it involves analyzing the influence of Hispanic culture on psychiatric illness problems of Hispanics—for example, the distribution, causes, manifestations, diagnosis, course, and treatment of such illness problems. These topics need to be examined in light of the fact that Hispanics constitute a large segment of a complexly stratified population of a pluralistic society. The way in which this society defines and handles psychiatric illness of Hispanics, viewed in relation to the way it defines and handles illnesses of other segments of the population, is a topic that cultural psychiatry should address. The mental health problems of Hispanics and the way that such problems are conceptualized and handled in a society, the dialectical interplay between illness phenomena and established categories of disorders, are integral to cultural psychiatry. Both sets of phenomena are seen as cultural in nature and as having political, economic, and sociological consequences.

In examining Hispanic mental health research it is useful to introduce the idea of an "establishment psychiatry." This constitutes the dominant professional perspective about mental health problems and is seen to reflect a universalist focus and a biological determinism. In establishment psychiatry, genetic and neurobiological structures are the real and important loci of psychiatric illness problems. The form of illness and distress that these structures give rise to are described as relatively fixed and common to *homo sapiens*. This means that the nosology celebrated in the catechism of establishment psychiatry, namely, the American Psychiatric Association's *Diagnostic and Statistical Manual of Mental Disorders* (3rd edition, revised) (*DSM-III-R*) is accurate, relatively unproblematic, and capable of refinement and improvement as to details but beyond the need of structural alteration. A model of psychiatric disorders is reflected in establishment psychiatry: Underlying psychiatric disease processes surface as illness problems in their pristine natural form and are shunted to clinical research treatment establishments where they can be accurately identified, entered into suitable research protocols, and eventually treated by means of the latest technologically refined practices that double-blind studies have established as efficacious. It is instructive to examine how this "establishment" model of mental health problems conforms to realities as described for Hispanic populations.

THE MEANING OF HISPANIC CULTURE
IN HISPANIC MENTAL HEALTH RESEARCH

This section reviews how researchers in the Hispanic mental health field appear to be using the concept of culture. One view seems to be that of a population trait, much like the standard demographic variables of age, gender, and social class (Lopez, 1989; Lubin, Natalicio, & Seever, 1985; McLaughlin & Balch, 1980; Randolph, Escobar, Paz, & Forsythe, 1985). Hispanic culture is referenced by surname, place of birth, or that of parents, or physical characteristics, or simply by the subject's endorsement of "ethnic" preference. The role of culture in affecting such things as bias vis-à-vis diagnosis or treatment is all-important, and a researcher attempts to show statistical relationships between Hispanic identity and ways that diagnoses are made and treatment modalities structured. Important characteristics of Hispanics are either not addressed (simply the fact of differences vs. a reference group is important) or if addressed are often not spelled out ahead of time. The richness of the concept of culture and Hispanic culture in particular appears to be bleached out of these studies, which rely merely on trait features of clients or clinicians.

In studies of psychiatric epidemiology in Puerto Rico (Canino, Bird, Shrout et al., 1987; Helzer et al., 1990) culture appears to mean national (Helzer & Canino, 1989). Contemporary nations share a number of characteristics, such as political and economic structures, social stratification systems, beliefs regarding science and secular rationality, and the desirability of Western education. There is power left in the concept of culture when differences are examined between Puerto Rico and St. Louis and especially Taiwan, but it is not clear that this is tapped in view of the rationale of these epidemiologic studies. For example, much of the potential variability of cultural effects is weakened when purely quantitative aspects of drinking technologically processed forms of alcohol and when abstractly stipulated behavioral complications of heavy sustained drinking in modern societies operate as "effects" of culture and alcoholism. The studies by the Puerto Rico group are models of psychiatric epidemiologic research and rigorously attempt to examine cultural variation. However, their work is based on a preestablished model of alcoholism as a "disorder" and does not seek to understand cultural variations in the way that alcohol is used, how excess drinking is conceptualized and handled, and how all of this fits in with distress and impairment as culturally grounded. In short, that "alcoholism" must also be viewed in relation to Hispanic cultural traditions needs to be appreciated.

The article by Zippin and Hough (1985) more deeply considers culture. They based their study on the alleged importance among Hispanics (Mexican and Mexican Americans) of the family and significant others as natural support systems in the maintenance of self-function. The role of perceived difference between self and others with respect to life events was analyzed in relation to mental health. The authors predicted that Hispanics would be more affected by these differences than Anglos because of self-family integration differences stemming from cultural traditions. They found some support for their hypotheses. The report of this study is difficult to understand fully, and the study itself seemed to have problems. However, it is an example of a study in which the content of Hispanic culture is more thoroughly considered.

A more elaborate analysis of the content of Hispanic culture is found in studies that concentrate on folk disorders and their meanings in both rural and urban populations. Some of these studies are descriptive and, of course, can entertain extended aspects of native beliefs and theories

(Rubel, 1960; Tousignant, 1984). Other researchers operate through more controlled data collection methods (Jenkins, 1988a, 1988b; Low, 1981, 1985). These studies are able to enhance one's appreciation of how culture affects responses and interpretations of psychiatric illness because of their empirically controlled methods, their focus on identified families of patients carefully diagnosed, and the rich and sensitive use they make of cultural traditions.

A more cautious approach is shown in the articles by Lopez and Hernandez (1986, 1987), who studied how mental health clinicians used the concept of culture in their work with clients. The authors analyzed summaries provided by clinicians of cases in which the clinicians judged that culture had been used in diagnosis and treatment. In a somewhat reductionistic way, Lopez and Hernandez seem to struggle to uncover basic elements of culture that are used by clinicians in their attempts to diagnose and treat actual patients identified because "cultural factors" loomed important. The authors' restraint with respect to their claim that culture affects the manifestations and nature of clinical psychopathology in Hispanics is notable and surprising.

Differences in the way culture is used analytically reflect several things. The most obvious one is the strategy and general orientation of the researcher. Empirically oriented, quantitative, and quasi-experimental studies require an abstract and static conceptualization of culture, whereas ethnographic descriptive studies can luxuriate in symbols and semantic networks. Of course, psychologists, social workers, sociologists, and anthropologists have long traditions of research behind their efforts. Moreover, there are real philosophical problems in trying to "pin down" basic elements of culture, many seeing the attempt as flawed and missing the distinction between explanation and interpretation. Finally, because Hispanic culture is invariably seen in relation to Anglo culture and both are integral to complex nation states, the quandary of cultural homogeneity versus pluralism is also an issue. Factors such as these pose scientific dilemmas complicating the understanding of how cultural factors influence Hispanic mental health problems. Given the conventions that need to be followed so as to provide knowledge that will affect policy (e.g., what constitutes a disorder, how a cultural influence needs to be documented), quandaries that make difficult the full explication of cultural influences can be seen as retarding and/or blunting the efforts to promote a full appreciation of Hispanic mental health problems.

One disappointment about the way the concept of culture is used involves the relative neglect of the specifics versus the varieties of Hispanic culture. In some respects, Hispanics are handled as all alike, a factor that approximates how the concept of Black ethnicity is used (Fabrega, Mezzich, & Ulrich, 1989). There is a glossing over of the distinctness of the various regional traditions that contribute to "Hispanicity" (e.g., Caribbean vs. native Indian vs. Iberian) and sometimes of associated social variables (e.g., social class). Very often, Hispanicity is taken into account more deeply but only with respect to degree of difference or alleged "movement" toward the Anglo culture. A variety of scales of acculturation have been developed for Mexican Americans, Cubans, and Puerto Ricans (Cuellar, Harris, & Jasso, 1980; Szapocznik & Kurtines, 1980; Torros-Matrullo, 1980). This raises the question of what they might have in common and whether, in relation to mainstream Anglo culture, the concept of a generic Hispanic culture has any power. It would be instructive to attempt to evaluate whether, and if so, how, acculturation scales overlap. Can different types of Hispanics (e.g., Mexican Americans) be distinguished from others (e.g., Puerto Ricans) on these acculturation scales? What power is there, in fact, in the idea that there is a set of Hispanic cultural traits that transcend regional origins and social class? These questions are intrinsic to a cultural psychiatric approach. When answered in relation to mental health problems, they would clarify understanding of the way that cultural factors impact on psychiatric illness and whether service providers and reimbursers accommodate or fail to accommodate to Hispanic realities.

HISPANIC MENTAL HEALTH RESEARCH

Hispanic Beliefs, Attitudes, Illness Pictures, and Systems of Care

In studies conducted in East Los Angeles, Karno and Edgerton (Edgerton & Karno, 1971; Karno & Edgerton, 1969) reported a general similarity among Anglo and Mexican Americans regarding concepts of illness. In addition, they pointed to the importance of language orientation in relation to attitudes and beliefs about psychiatric illness. Parra and Yiu-Cheong So (1983) conducted a study also involving attitudes and understanding about mental illness among Mexican Americans. This study was much less controlled than that of Karno and Edgerton. Parra found no support for an acculturation hypothesis and showed that younger Chicanos perceive mental illness differently and in a narrower way. In a report concentrating on attitudes toward the mentally ill, Parra (1985) showed that age and gender of the Mexican American were influential but that in general few overall differences were obtained between Anglos and Mexican Americans. A classic topic of community-centered study involves simply the description of folk illnesses among Hispanics (see Rubel, 1960; Tousignant, 1984).

The study of lay systems of care is a favorite topic in medical anthropology and health services research. Alegria, Guerra, Martinez, and Meyer (1977) describe and analyze some of the properties of the lay treatment centers available to Mexican Americans of San Antonio, Texas. The study is conservative in posture, drawing attention to the separateness between establishment versus folk/lay systems of care. In contrast, Kreisman (1975) reports on the creative integration of folk and establishment traditions in the treatment of two Hispanic psychotic patients. Hohman, Richeport, and Marriott (1990) have documented the extent to which spiritualism appears to be used as an adjunct support system in Puerto Rico. Building on insights of medical anthropologists (Garrison, 1977; Harwood, 1977), they relied on data gathered in an epidemiological study and showed that selected social characteristics, reported use of mental health professionals, and subdiagnosable symptoms of depression were related in a logistic regression model with resort to spiritualists. Hohman et al. (1990) concluded that spiritualists did not appear to be major participants in the treatment of mental health problems in Puerto Rico. They point to the need for prospective studies to better establish (a) when persons turn to spiritualists and (b) the interplay between the resort to these lay versus establishment "clinicians." The covert pattern of use of spiritualists in Puerto Rico compared with Brazil, for example, is a factor that limits the validity and generalization ability of this study. The extent of reliance on spiritualists is likely to be underreported.

Low (1981) showed the diverse components of the lay syndrome *nervios* (nerves) in patients of medical and psychiatric clinics. The social cultural origin of perceived sources of nervios is underscored. In her cultural interpretation of this symptom complex, Low showed that it signals family difficulties and a sense of personal dyscontrol but does not endanger a sense of social identity as does the concept of mental illness. Elsewhere, Low (1985) compared the nervios symptom complex in widely discrepant Hispanic and non-Hispanic settings, arguing against the view that it constitutes a culture-bound disorder. Jenkins (1988a) studied native conceptions and attitudes about psychiatric illness among the relatives of Mexican American schizophrenics. This study provides insight into how family members use the concept of nerves to cope with the burden of psychiatric illness and, in particular, to lessen stigma and maintain solidarity. In another study, Jenkins (1988b) compared the concept of nerves among Anglos and Mexican Americans. This study challenges an important dictum of establishment psychiatry: namely, that schizophrenic illness tends to be viewed similarly across cultures. Jenkins also discussed possible reasons for and functions of a concept of schizophrenia versus nerves to explain disturbing symptoms involving cognition and emotion. These studies offer a Hispanic picture of the meaning of terms and concepts used by establishment psychiatry. The concept of nerves, for example, is anchored deep in native Hispanic cultural traditions. Important questions arise about establishment concepts and practices viewed as cultural versus biomedical phenomena. In other words, how do Hispanic consumers view the material addressed by the establishment, how are they affected by its conceptualizations, and how do they integrate native and establishment knowledge?

The theoretical locus of these studies is far away from the setting where paradigms of establishment psychiatry operate. Hence the information they produce does not directly challenge but simply sensitizes establishment psychiatry to alternative models. They warn that underneath and around the methodological tentacles that psychiatric epidemiologists thrust into the community, there exists a plethora of real-life mental health problems and ways of conceptualizing and handling them that elude the epidemiologic reach. All of the latter problems mark the culturally authentic nature of psychiatric illness viewed in its cultural richness versus biomedical abstractness.

Psychiatric Epidemiologic Studies Involving Hispanics

The field of psychiatric epidemiology, generally speaking, is anchored in establishment paradigms. Drawing on establishment concepts, it seeks to establish prevalence and incidence figures. Besides informing on these traditional measures, it can point to unusual clinically relevant facts and distribution patterns about a population. A number of such studies have increased awareness of distinctive clinical pictures and profiles of Hispanics.

There is a long-standing controversy about the level of psychological distress among Hispanics, with much evidence suggesting mental health problems and some indicating artifacts produced by response style (e.g., Dohrenwend, 1966; Krause & Carr, 1978). Roberts (1980) reviewed the literature pertaining to this problem and on the basis of a controlled study involving Mexican Americans of Alameda County, California found support for increased distress compared to Anglos. Many of the reports pointing to increased distress of Hispanics are a consequence of the scales used and the Hispanic's alleged tendency to somatize problems. Escobar and coworkers (Escobar, 1987; Escobar et al., 1986; Escobar, Burnam, Karno, Forsythe, & Golding, 1987; Escobar, Randolph, & Hill, 1986; Escobar, Rubio-Stipec, Canino, & Carno, 1989) have emphasized the high prevalence of somatization problems among Mexican Americans. Angel and Guarnaccia (1989) have reported similar patterns among Puerto Ricans. Their study included a general explanation of the role of affective states, conceptions of self, and social context in shaping psychological distress toward a somatization mode. It would appear that Hispanics, perhaps preferentially those of lower social class, express and show distress and maladaptation in a phenomenologically different mold than does the contrastive Anglo (i.e., White, non-Hispanic) group. Similar results involving somatization as an idiom for the expression of psychological distress of Hispanics have been found in Latin America (Escobar, Gómez, & Tuason, 1983; Mezzich & Rabb, 1980). These studies point to high levels of psychological and somatic distress in Hispanics and are to be distinguished from controlled psychiatric epidemiologic studies that aim to measure levels of disorders using establishment psychiatry criteria and rationales. A somatization content to the Hispanic's idiom of distress is tantalizing and compels interdisciplinary efforts aimed at clarifying the interplay between culture, emotion, and the self.

In studies aimed at measuring levels of organic disorders, Escobar, Randolph, and Hill (1986) pointed out the fallacies of using the Mini Mental State Examination as a measure of organic impairment among Hispanics. They argue that language and educational levels can contribute to spuriously high levels of cognitive impairment as measured by the Follstein battery. Bird, Canino, Rubio-Stipec, and Shrout (1987) produced comparable results in Puerto Rico. The study by Canino, Bird, Shrout et al. (1987), of quintessential establishment psychiatry vintage, has underlined the similarity in epidemiologic profile with regard to selected psychiatric disorders between people of Puerto Rico and selected U.S. communities except for the former's higher measures of somatization and cognitive impairment (explained in large part as others mentioned earlier). Garcia and Marks (1989) reported on the prevalence of depression among Mexican Americans of Los Angeles using the CES-D scale. A higher level of endorsement of certain items of the CES-D was observed among Mexican Americans than among Anglos of Los Angeles, but the meaning of this is not clear because matters involving semantics and culture could be an explanation. However, the study lected U.S. communities except for the former's higher measures of somatization and cognitive impairment (explained in large part as others mentioned earlier). Garcia and Marks (1989) reported on the prevalence of depression among Mexican Americans of Los Angeles using the CES-D scale. A higher level of endorsement of certain items of the CES-D was observed among Mexican Americans than among Anglos of Los Angeles, but the meaning of this is not clear because matters involving semantics and culture could be an explanation. However, the study questions whether depression may be realized differently in Hispanics and Anglos and not just involving somatization. They also pointed to differences in the factor structure of depression symptoms among less adapted and younger Mexican Americans. In a similar vein, using epidemiologic data from Puerto Rico, Rubio-Stipec, Shrout, Bird, Canino, and Bravo (1989) conducted factor analyses on the symptoms of the Diagnostic Interview Schedule (DIS) that enter into the diagnosis of four types of disorders. They compared results with those obtained in the same way and using the same instrument for Mexican Americans and Anglos of Los Angeles. They were able to produce similar profiles for alcoholism and affective disorder but not phobic or psychotic disorders. Thus, even though the same parent set of symptoms and logic of evaluation were used, the symptom profiles of these latter two disorders failed to show concordance across ethnic groups. The results, in general, support the ideas of commonality and difference in the way that symptoms cluster in Hispanics and Anglos.

In an illuminating study using data collected by means of the DIS in Puerto Rico, Guarnaccia, Rubio-Stipec, and Canino (1989) showed how the native syndrome *ataques de nervios* can elude the diagnostic reach of the epidemiologists. Many of the "somatic-anxiety" symptoms of this syndrome happen to be picked up by the DIS, and through an analyses of these and from results of extra probes added to the study, they were able to show that probable ataque "patients" (compared to non-*ataque* "patients") were more likely to (a) receive certain DIS diagnoses (e.g., depressive disorder, anxiety-panic disorders) and (b) use health care services (including spiritualists). Guarnaccia et al. suggest that ataques can be considered a cultural idiom of distress that describes a cluster of symptoms similar to a panic attack. In contrast to the latter, however, it does not "come out of the blue" but follows culturally relevant social stresses. Their study thus raises questions about the cross-cultural validity of panic disorder as a nosologic syndrome, although it does tend to support the cross-cultural validity of key somatic symptoms of distress.

(b) can be correlated with certain DIS disorders, and (c) can modify and cloud the clinical picture of still other disorders. A limitation of this study is that it tends to stop short of stipulating, or at least commenting on, whether, and if so, when, a cultural idiom of distress constitutes an illness or medical problem in the native Hispanic system and the differences between such problems in the two systems of medicine (i.e., Hispanic and establishment).

In summary, studies of the type reviewed in this section can challenge establishment psychiatry but only weakly since they rest on its paradigms. They emphasize that establishment rubrics tend to constrain and shape the nature of the psychopathology they uncover. Despite this bias, important differences in the structure and interpretation of symptoms among Hispanics are still manifest. In some instances, establishment categories appear to capture bona fide native mental health problems; in others, they inappropriately label modes of communicating distress. The studies, then, perpetuate the echo raised by community descriptive studies considered earlier as to the cultural uniqueness of Hispanics vis-à-vis mental health pictures: An imperfect fit is obtained between establishment and Hispanic models of mental health problems. Most important, the echo is sounded even when establishment psychiatry's instruments are used: Its categories and its logic are used to compel attention to cultural distinctiveness and to possible limitations of the establishment paradigms.

Establishment Conventions in Diagnosis and Treatment of Hispanics

One of the strongest challenges to the way the establishment deals with the mental health problems of Hispanics is offered by those who concentrate on the dynamics of mental health care. This is a probing challenge insofar as it clarifies the lack of sensitivity in establishment diagnostic categories and treatment practices.

The articles by Del Castillo (1970) and Sabin (1975) are classic statements of the earnest concern of clinicians about the problem of underestimating psychopathology in Hispanic patients when the mother tongue is not used. In contrast, studies by Marcos and coworkers (Marcos, 1976; Marcos, Alpert, Urcuyo, & Kesselman, 1973; Marcos, Urcuyo, Kesselman, & Alpert, 1973) have disclosed that schizophrenics can actually appear more compromised and disturbed when interviewed in English. The study by Lubin et al. (1985), however, reports that the picture of disability painted by bilingual subjects when they complete the Depression Adjective Checklist is essentially the same in Spanish or

English; furthermore, male bilinguals did not differ from females. Because this study did not identify who the subjects were (e.g., patients or nonpatients; acculturated or nonacculturated), it is not possible to learn whether psychopathology per se is colored by language and/or culture, and because general descriptions of mood were employed, it is not possible to specify whether significant aspects of illness problems that therapists must deal with are influenced by these same variables. Marcos (1976) analyzed the effects on and implications for psychotherapy of relying on a patient's second language. McLaughlin and Balch (1980) found that the ethnicity of the clinician made little difference in the way that clinical vignettes involving Anglos and Chicanos were rated with respect to several clinical parameters. They, of course, relied on general hypothetical decisions involving idealized pictures of illness and did not probe in a realistic way either patient psychopathology or clinician practices. The study by Skilbeck, Acosta, Yamamoto, and Evans (1984) documents that Hispanics seeking outpatient psychotherapy self-report symptoms more prominently than Blacks and that clinicians' estimates of Hispanics' severity of disorder parallel the Hispanics' self-reports. In this study, then, Hispanics were shown to differ from Blacks in the way they self-reported and were diagnosed, but Hispanics did not differ from Whites. The study deals with a self-selected group of individuals presumably sufficiently acculturated to seek establishment care, which may partially account for their similarity to Whites.

The review analyses and empirical studies of Lopez and coworkers (Lopez, 1989; Lopez & Hernandez, 1986, 1987; Lopez & Nuñez, 1987) address the general problem of the effect of cultural background on diagnosis and treatment. Considerable emphasis is given to Hispanics, but other ethnic minorities are also included. Lopez's work constitutes a sober and critical look at how Hispanics might fare badly as a result of possible cultural biases inherent in establishment practices. Far from accepting the popular dictum that culture affects psychopathology and invariably leads to biases, he is concerned with documenting empirically whether, and if so, how, interview schedules and clinicians might deal with the potential problems of cultural differences. His studies can be consulted for details and analyses of findings of sources for bias. The study by Baskin, Bluestone, and Nelson (1981) addressed Hispanics (and also Blacks) and documented the association between ethnicity and psychiatric diagnosis and the influences of clinician ethnicity in all of this.

Canino, Bird, Rubio-Stipec, et al. (1987) showed that two Hispanic clinicians achieved acceptable reliability when offering multiaxial ratings of Puerto Rican children, but they did not consider any notions pertaining to family and social class background that might influence a "cultural" orientation. In effect, this study emphasizes that establishment criteria can be reliably applied to Puerto Rican children but leaves unexamined the questions of whether differences in cultural orientation might affect ease and/or relevance of diagnosis in terms of establishment paradigms. In other words, are there differences in the way that disorders are manifest and/or in the applicability of diagnostic categories among Puerto Rican children? Are all Puerto Rican children the same from a cultural standpoint simply because they live on the same island and speak Spanish, or might there exist differences in beliefs, attitudes, and behavioral styles that might affect the structure and content of psychopathology? Is the idea of modernization versus traditionalism a viable one to apply to the cultural orientation of Puerto Rican children? What is distinctly "Puerto Rican," and how does it vary in relation to social class? Or, could it be that the researchers are examining psychopathology in subjects before adult cultural differences become realized (i.e., enculturated; see Shweder, 1985, for a review)? Finally, how might all of this differ among "mainland" Puerto Rican children? These questions can, of course, be applied to Hispanics from other nations. Besides touching on the topic of when or whether cultural differences become manifest, the questions raise the problem of cultural homogeneity versus cultural pluralism and the quandaries of measuring cultural orientation in a socially stratified society.

Rogler and coworkers (Rogler, 1989; Rogler, Malgady, & Costantino, 1987; Rogler, Malgady, & Rodriguez, 1990) have underscored the ubiquity of the influence of culture in evaluation and treatment. They point to the vigilance that staff need to adopt with respect to the implementation of establishment concerns regarding care delivery and the beneficial consequences that can result from rendering services responsive to cultural identity. An interesting question, never directly formulated by them, is whether culturally sensitive services constitute Hispanic mental health care versus suitably modified establishment psychiatry care and/or whether any meaningful difference can be said to exist between these two posited categories. Olmedo's (1981) review deals with the question of testing linguistic minorities and points to the important influence of bilingualism, acculturation, and explanatory framework. This review exclusively addresses psychological assessment and is not central to issues of mental health per se. However, the controversy about IQ testing of minorities invokes the same reasoning as that involving the differences between culturally authentic procedures for assessing psychiatric disorders.

Studies of the genre considered in this section are penetrating insofar as they point to insensitivities (if not misguided efforts) of relying narrowly on establishment methods, procedures, and theories. Despite their critical and challenging nature, they are limited to the extent that they do not force a true reexamination and/or reformulation of establishment rationales. The studies beg the following sorts of questions: Can or should a culturally sensitive approach to the problems of mental health of Hispanics rely on rationales developed using culturally distinctive epistemologies and paradigms? Should not establishment psychiatry paradigms be modified or reformulated so as to authentically reflect the realities of Hispanics' mental health problems?

Realization of Psychiatric Disorders in Hispanics

Studies that examine the symptom patterns of "bona fide" psychiatric disorders among Hispanics aim to document differences. Such findings may merely attempt to point to variability associated with ethnicity. However, because they can potentially uncover unique patterns of variability in Hispanics they raise the question of the suitability of establishment conventions, if not stereotypes, with respect to specification of disorders. They thus pose a potential challenge to establishment psychiatry. Because the studies rely on abstract criteria for disorders, they tend to wash away cultural differences. Thus should such studies uncover differences they are seen as exposing more deeply embedded cultural biases (Fabrega, 1989).

The study by Velasquez and Gimenez (1987) dealt with three separate categories of psychiatric inpatients and was aimed at clarifying whether the Minnesota Multiphasic Personality Inventory (MMPI) could produce differences in symptom patterns that allowed distinctions based on diagnosis. The study adds to the literature that underscores the disparities between what the MMPI produces as compared to the *DSM-III-R*. Because the study did not rely on a protocol of evaluation that took culture into account in a significant way, it cannot be expected to weaken the claim that establishment psychiatry categories as realized in the *DSM-III-R* are in any way distorted or inappropriate. Furthermore, the fact that the study dealt with a highly special group of patients who were not culturally or linguistically specified (inpatients committed to a maximum security facility) further limits what can be made of its results. The study by Randolph et al. (1985) compared the way in which Hispanic and Anglo schizophrenics reported symptoms. The rate of false positive diagnosis of schizophrenics based on the DIS was the same in both groups, and no association between DIS diagnoses and ethnicity was found, leading the investigators to conclude in a preliminary way that the DIS was associated with little cultural bias. Furthermore, ethnicity was not associated with differences in DIS subscales or ratings based on other structured clinical instruments. However, ethnic differences resulted in the way that DIS-negative subjects handled reports of illness in a face-to-face interview, with Hispanics consistently underreporting symptoms compared with Anglos who, in an open-ended setting, came forth with symptoms. In a subsequent report of the same study, Escobar, Randolph, & Hill (1986) emphasized again the similarity between Anglo and Hispanic symptoms but indicated that Hispanics reported a later age of onset, more somatization, and less time in hospitals. Because somatic symptoms are not criteria of schizophrenia in establishment psychiatry, the observed difference in clinical phenomenology of schizophrenia among Hispanics and Anglos is given little weight by the investigators. A limitation of the study is that it involved only Hispanic males who were relatively well acculturated. In a study focusing on symptoms of depression and anxiety among Mexican Americans of El Paso, Ross and Mirowsky (1984) emphasized the importance of a belief in external control. They judged that Mexican culture, through an emphasis on external control and fatalism, produces opposed effects on anxiety versus depression. Finally, the study by Rubio-Stipec et al. (1989), reviewed above, pointed to differences in the way that phobic and psychotic disorders were realized among Puerto Ricans, Anglos, and Mexican Americans. Concordance was shown, however, with respect to alcoholism and affective disorders.

In summary, these studies rely on establishment categories of disorder and establishment measures of psychopathology, and all seem to support the view that within this version of psychiatry Hispanics and Anglos in general present similar clinical pictures in some classes of disorders. The studies do not address whether establishment rationales and formulations regarding the indicators of disorders might exclude, disregard, or simply be insensitive to aspects of psychopathology that may naturally inhere in behavior patterns shaped by Hispanic cultural traditions. As indicated above, this was documented to be the case in Puerto Rico with respect to the symptoms associated with ataques de nervios (Guarnaccia et al., 1989).

Research on Evaluation Instruments

Given the awareness of the importance of language and culture in rendering mental health diagnosis and treatment sensitive to Hispanics, one can anticipate that a large effort has been mounted in the area of translation of instruments. If diagnosis of psychiatric illness were entirely an anatomical or physicochemical affair, this would be unnecessary, but given its behavioral basis and the dependence of accurate description on language, the emphasis on semantical and syntactical efforts becomes obvious. The study by Mahard (1988) involved assessing the value of the CES-D as a measure of depressive mood in an elderly Puerto Rican population. The alleged validity of this instrument was emphasized. Interviews were conducted in Spanish, but it is not clear whether the instrument itself was translated or completed by the interviewer or the patient subject.

The work of the Los Angeles and Puerto Rico groups (Bravo, Canino, & Bird, 1987; Bravo, Canino, & Rubio-Stipec, 1991; Burnam, Karno, Hough, Escobar, & Forsythe, 1983; Canino, Bird, Rubio-Stipec, et al., 1987) is an example of the effort to render establishment instruments suitable. The two Spanish versions of the DIS that they have produced are in most respects identical in language, although some modifications were introduced by the Puerto Rican group. In particular, they (a) attempted to formally assess whether reports of unusual beliefs (e.g., involving spirits) constituted psychopathology or purely cultural perspectives and (b) related reports of potential psychopathology to social and psychological functioning. The problems of disentangling psychopathology from cultural material and establishing that reports of behavioral difficulties constitute true pathology have been squarely faced and resolved to the researchers' satisfaction. Interestingly, the Puerto Rican group drew attention to the differences between cultural conceptions and experiences of time in Los Angeles and their homeland. Most important, in a number of publications the two groups of researchers have largely replicated profiles of reliability, validity, and concordance of instruments and prevalence of disorders in mainland U.S. community settings.

In reading these articles one gets the impression that the researchers want to establish commonality of methods of procedure by equating the "standardized" measures of the DIS obtained in non-Hispanics with those of Hispanics and by obtaining epidemiologic measures that either match or not too strongly deviate from those obtained on the U.S. majority. In other words, the logic of *DSM-III-R,* which is the parental authority for the English and Spanish DIS, is handled as authoritative and nonproblematic. It appears to be assumed that behavioral problems well-connected to native cultural traditions, such as those involving folk illnesses, are adequately captured by existing categories in the catechism of *DSM-III-R.* This perspective is consistent with that of most psychiatric epidemiologists, and its cultural implications need to be appreciated: An epidemiological study points to what establishment psychiatry deems a bona fide psychiatric disorder. Its results stipulate the kinds of community mental health problems worthy of study and legitimately entitled to treatment. As implied earlier, discrepancies between establishment cultural categories of disorder and Hispanic cultural categories of illness (or "distress") constitute important raw data for a truly cultural analysis of how Anglo-American psychiatry operates in contemporary society.

Viewed in light of the science of psychiatric epidemiology, workers involved in the translation of the DIS have performed a service to Hispanic mental health research by broadening the efficacy of a key assessment instrument. Problems in the validity of this instrument and in the community assessment of psychopathology remain, to be sure, but they are integral to establishment rationales and paradigms and cannot be covered here.

Hispanic Research Involving Psychiatric Theory

Research directed at the validity of diagnostic categories, at systems of diagnosis, and at clinical facts regarding the cause, course, and treatment of psychiatric disorders has the potential of questioning basic structures of psychiatric knowledge. It is pertinent to examine whether, and if so, how, mental health research involving Hispanics is contributing to this type of challenge to establishment psychiatry. The problem of genesis or precipitants of mental health problems are not discussed because this has been amply covered in the literature. For example, the review analysis of Cervantes and Castro (1985) involving the applicability to Mexican Americans of a stress-mediation-outcome model can be consulted as an example of an attempt to examine the relevance of establishment etiology concepts for this group. The studies by Roberts (1987) and Ramirez (1987) are also germane.

Alarcon (1983) has provided an eloquent critique of the *DSM-III-R* from the standpoint of Latin American psychiatry. He draws attention to the need for psychocultural categories of behavior and culturally sensitive criteria of definition to facilitate application of the basic rubrics of psychopathology. In a more specific sense, the bulk of his criticisms involve the questionable appropriateness of *DSM-III-R* Axis II categories for Latin Americans and the necessity of modifying Axes IV (stressors) and V (adaptive functioning) so as to render them appropriate to the Latin American social setting. Mezzich (1989) provided a general statement about the contributions that have and can be made to worldwide classification systems by researchers and clinicians knowledgeable of Latin American psychiatric problems. His report lucidly outlines the purposes and rationale of classification in psychiatry and persuasively points to the need for taking into account Latin American psychiatric realities. Alarcon and Mezzich, then, both implicitly underscore the centrality of diagnosis and classification in constituting a scientific psychiatry and stress that such systems of codification should address the needs of diverse cultural groups. Their writings constitute an urging and exhortation to Hispanic mental health researchers. Neither Mezzich nor Alarcon, however, directly asserts that establishment classification systems might be biased or that they might selectively ignore, overinclude, or misrepresent Hispanic realities, but this is certainly suggested.

The studies conducted by the Los Angeles group (Jenkins, Karno, Selva, & Santana, 1986; Karno et al., 1987; Magaña et al., 1986) on the course of schizophrenia constitute another locus of scientific/academic activity that is centered on a critical pillar of establishment psychiatry. Like other studies focused on Hispanics, theirs attempted to replicate establishment "facts," in this instance, the role of expressed emotion (EE) among relatives of schizophrenic patients on the latter's course of illness. Their results to date tend to support generalizations drawn from British and Anglo American subjects. The relatively lower levels of EE among Hispanics compared with Anglos was related to traditional notions of the family in Mexican culture. The potential buffering effect of high-contact families with respect to high EE among some relatives was hypothesized. In other words, high-contact, high-EE Hispanic family members may very well contribute stress to the patient, but high contact with low-EE members that is available because of Hispanics' larger families may mitigate this effect. One anticipates that as these researchers continue to analyze in a more elaborated but still controlled way the effects of family interaction in Hispanic families of schizophrenics, facts about the course of schizophrenia will come to reflect in a compelling way insights generated from the study of Hispanic culture. In this sense, establishment facts could be seen as truly Hispanicized.

The brief review in this section has questioned what can be construed as an establishment fact about mental health research and practice and what would constitute a Hispanicized establishment fact in this knowledge paradigm. One can extend this line of inquiry and rhetorically ask what would constitute a fact in a truly Hispanic psychiatry, and what is the likelihood of a universal establishment science of psychiatry that transcends cultures?

POLITICAL-ECONOMIC IMPLICATIONS OF HISPANIC MENTAL HEALTH RESEARCH

A theme within medical anthropology focuses on a critical examination of theory and practice of biomedical psychiatry (Schepper-Hughes & Lock, 1986; Singer, Baer, & Lazarus, 1990). In this light, it is instructive to examine in a general way the kinds of questions pertaining to Hispanic mental health research that a critical medical anthropology could address.

A critical evaluation of how Hispanic mental health research fits in to establishment psychiatric knowledge and policies would begin by first describing the size, distribution, and social composition of the Hispanic population, including its age and marital structures and its religious, economic, educational, and occupational profile. The amount and kinds of mental health problems of Hispanics, those receiving and not receiving treatment, would need to be estimated. Information about levels of disorders as stipulated by establishment criteria and levels of distress as realized in Hispanic populations would be needed. The social characteristics of disordered and distressed Hispanics need to be computed. This would be followed by a comparison of Hispanic parameters with those of other ethnic minorities, such as Asians, Blacks, American Indians, and native Alaskans.

How Hispanics in need of mental health care actually receive treatment is not at all easy to establish. Community studies could provide estimates of the kinds of persons seen and institutions/clinics/hospitals visited by Hispanics. A picture should ideally be developed of a putative Hispanic mental health system. Data on the number and types of Hispanic mental health practitioners, and their distribution and mode of practice, would need to be collected and analyzed in relation to the size and characteristics of the population they service. Information pertaining to the social and ethnic composition of the clients of Hispanic mental health workers and institutions would need to be collected and analyzed to get a picture of who is being serviced in this "Hispanic mental health system." In areas where Hispanics constitute a sizable population segment, details of the ethnic composition of the clients serviced by non-Hispanic mental health workers and institutions would also be needed. The languages spoken naturally by clients/patients and service providers would need to be assessed. Finally, the picture that results would be compared to that painted of other ethnic/minority mental health workers and clients.

The obvious aim of analyses such as these is to describe the mental health problems of Hispanics, how and from whom they currently receive mental health care, and the consequences of all of this. To estimate the need for and adequacy of coverage of mental health services, the quality of care received needs to be ascertained. This is an enormously difficult problem in the health services field generally. Assessing quality of care in the *mental* health field constitutes a no less formidable problem, and ascertaining all of this in *Hispanics,* considering the special and complex role that culture and language play in mental health care and social adaptation generally, can be expected to complicate the problem even further. Nevertheless, such estimates and others that can easily be surmised are needed if one intends to examine Hispanic mental health problems in relation to how effectively establishment psychiatry is currently dealing with them.

Despite the fact that one could conclude that establishment psychiatric science has been significantly broadened and sensitized by knowledge drawn from Hispanic mental health research (Rogler et al., 1987, 1990), it is not at all clear that establishment psychiatric knowledge structures and practice directives have in fact accommodated the need for services that this research underscores. How extensively and how well are Hispanic mental health needs being met, and how does this picture compare with that of other minorities? Are a sufficient number of Hispanic mental health researchers and clinicians being trained in comparison to the size and needs of other ethnic/minority groups? Is establishment psychiatric policy regarding the research and treatment of mental health problems sufficiently sensitive to cultural factors? Are administrators and funding agency representatives of establishment psychiatry adequately responding to the mental health needs of Hispanics, and how does this compare with policies, decisions, and subsidies affecting other ethnic/minority groups?

Such questions are problematic and amenable to scientific inquiry. A broad picture of cultural psychiatry takes into account the relationship between medical system characteristics (e.g., conceptualization and theories of disorders) and community mental health problems as culturally and sociopsychologically contextualized. This relationship is studied across types of societies. A more direct concern is how the social and medical institutions of a society describe, respond to, and treat psychiatric illness problems, however these may be defined in the society. Cultural psychiatry is concerned with dialectics that involve such polarized entities as (a) biology and culture, (b) existing "real world" psychiatric problems and conceptual paradigms about them, (c) knowledge of cause and systems of practice, and (d) objectives of treatment and end products of treatment efforts. A cultural psychiatry should address such dialectics as (a) assimilation and acculturation of cultural minorities to mainstream society and (b) assimilation and acculturation of knowledge about minority mental health problems to mainstream or establishment psychiatric knowledge, practice, and policy.

The following are illustrations of questions that can serve to orient a culturally sensitive approach to Hispanic mental health research:

1. Why should biologically validated "disorders" be the only analytic units in psychiatric epidemiology or assessment of need of mental health services? Are there indigenous syndromes of disability that are not in the *DSM-III-R* categories but should be? Should the formal requirements for the diagnosis of *DSM-III-R* entities be modified to accommodate Hispanic realities?

2. Is the complexity of the clinical condition of Hispanics (clinical condition equals the total clinical facts about a patient) greater than that of Anglos? How easily are Hispanics' disorders diagnosed? Does clinical complexity (e.g., pattern of comorbidity, ease of diagnosis, recourse to rule out diagnoses) differ in relation to degree of acculturation? Or, is there something intrinsic to the biocultural nature of Hispanicity that renders a clinical condition more or less complex in light of establishment psychiatry conventions (see Fabrega et al., 1989; Fabrega, Pilkonis, Mezzich, Ahn, & Shea, 1990)?

3. Given the complexity of migration/acculturation experience with respect to social and psychological adjustment, is it possible to identify syndromes or disorders triggered by it that are not but need to be included in a psychiatric nosology? Does the concept of an adjustment disorder sufficiently account for migration/acculturation problems? If it does, should not Hispanic academicians be arguing for its legitimacy and authenticity as an entity in the nosology (Fabrega, Mezzich, & Ulrich, 1988)?

4. What correspondences can be drawn between mental health problems (including bona fide psychiatric disorders) among native Hispanics of Latin America and migrant Hispanics in the United States? Does resorting to spiritual release through altered states of consciousness constitute a normalized pattern of behavior that promotes mental or physical health adjustment in Latin American settings, and is the ease of resorting to these experiences curtailed in the United States, rendering migrants more vulnerable to mental and physical health problems? Is the community/society of the United States more secularized than that of Latin America? If so, what losses or gains are accrued, from a mental health standpoint, as a result of migration?

5. What benefits and or deficits accrue to Hispanics by resorting to indigenous healing traditions? Are there mental health problems for which in-

digenous healing traditions surpass establishment ones? Even if establishment mental health services are rendered culturally sensitive, can a valid and useful calculus be created for measuring the benefits and losses incurred to a hypothetical Hispanic patient as a result of receiving such services with reference to specific psychiatric disorders? Is the loss associated with establishment treatment of a particular disorder greater or smaller than that associated with indigenous treatment? What parameters of a disorder compel establishment treatment versus indigenous treatment?

6. A psychiatric diagnostic system should provide a mental health clinician something of clinical value for understanding and managing a patient's condition. Could one develop an axis that takes into account a Hispanic person's ability to constructively make use of psychiatric treatment and profit from it? This might include such things as (a) reading/speaking/writing skills in English; (b) awareness and acceptance of establishment models of psychiatric illness and treatment; and (c) level of stigma accorded psychiatric illness by persons and significant others. Alternatively, a person's capacity to integrate and participate in mainstream society could be assessed and measured. This might include such things as level of educational attainment, acquired working skills and habits, level of social skills, availability of support groups, and degree of opportunities and/or ambitions for assimilating into mainstream society. It is obvious that the phenomena considered in this axis of a psychiatric diagnostic system blend with phenomena subsumed by the concepts of assimilation and acculturation. Hispanic mental health researchers, with other ethnic minority groups, could usefully be engaged in developing such an axis to render the catechism of establishment psychiatry (e.g., *DSM-III-R*) truly responsive to Hispanic needs.

7. What would constitute a valid psychiatric treatment outcome measure for Hispanics? What areas of behavior as formulated in terms of Hispanic traditions constitute a return of function among Hispanics? Are the rationales and instruments used in the field of psychiatric rehabilitation sensitive to behavior and adaptation modes of Hispanics?

HISPANIC MENTAL HEALTH RESEARCH KNOWLEDGE, SOCIAL CHANGE, AND CULTURAL EVOLUTION

Hispanic Americans constitute a relatively large minority of the population. Consequently, their mental health problems are not an inconsiderable part of what the science and practice of establishment psychiatry should address. Moreover, because Hispanics are a large minority and growing, their problems of mental health, when properly defined and understood, should in theory contribute to the production of establishment psychiatric knowledge itself. Furthermore, because Hispanic Americans and their native language and culture are linked directly to that of a large portion of the western hemisphere and the Iberian peninsula of the European continent, Hispanicity constitutes an important influence in molding the social and psychological behavior of a large segment of the world's population. In other words, even though one must concede great variability, it is still the case that Hispanic cultural traditions involving conceptions of self and other, styles of emotional experience and expression, patterns of social relations, and general attitudes and values about life, to name but a few, are social-psychological parameters that share basic structures and content among a large number of people of the world. To the extent that aspects of mental health problems reflect these and related cultural themes, one must assume that cultural parameters of a Hispanic psychopathology are important elements that the theory and practice of a truly representative psychiatry should address. Finally, the premises and knowledge structures of any truly representative psychiatric science should ideally reflect insights about psychiatric illness deriving from the study of the mental health problems among Hispanics.

The preceding constitutes a general rationale for the incorporation of research knowledge about Hispanic mental health problems in a representative science of psychiatry. To look critically at how establishment psychiatry operates in relation to Hispanics (or Blacks, Asians, Native Americans, and Eskimos) is to adopt a cultural psychiatric and historical/evolutionary approach. This is the case because in this approach the concepts of culture and that of societal/historical change are all-important. They are used to understand (a) what constitutes a Hispanic psychiatric illness (i.e., what consumers of mental health services need and want); (b) what service systems controlled by establishment psychiatry are able and willing to offer and why; (c) the discrepancies and inconsistencies regarding definition of problems and structure of care; and (d) the processes of social and historical change that are set in motion when these differences are made public through research. All of this is seen as integral to political-economic factors operating in the society and on establishment psychiatry and to sociological factors promoting historical change.

Researchers interested in the problem of cultural evolution as well as problems of acculturation/assimilation viewed in a historical framework have a test case in the field of ethnic minority mental health research. The impetus for and the nature and consequences of ethnic minority research reflect the process of acculturation/assimilation viewed in a cultural evolutionary frame of reference. Ethnic minority research may be conceptualized as a component of the adaptive response of the ethnic minority group itself. Viewed generically, an ethnic minority group encounters adaptive problems and challenges in the parent society and responds with a mixture of negative and positive adaptive changes. Research involving the mental health problems of the ethnic minority group is one such potentially positive response because it is often produced by minority/ethnic researchers, is prompted by deficiencies or puzzles found in the established mental health practice and knowledge structure of the society, and is at least partially geared to changing, modifying, or sensitizing them. Ethnic minority groups differ with respect to how actively they become involved in producing research knowledge about the social conditions (among others) that contribute to mental health problems. The Hispanic group's social conditions, mental health problems, and adaptive research responses must be assumed to differ from those of Blacks, Asians, and Native Americans. In short, if one adopts a large-scale cultural evolutionary view of minority mental health research, a number of interesting questions emerge:

1. What is the relationship between the social characteristics of the ethnic minority population and the kinds of mental health research questions it generates, is able to solve, and in fact attempts to solve? How does all of this contribute to the plight of the ethnic minority group? Are there differences across ethnic minorities, and how is one to explain these differences?
2. In a proximal sense, what promotes minority research? Is it to be viewed as an affirmation of the minority's "spirit," as stemming from policy requirements of administrative agencies and personnel, or is it simply a result of interests posed by the problem itself—a purely cognitive scientific matter involving curiosity?
3. How do the cultural, historical, and political economic conditions of an ethnic group contribute to its social adaptation in the larger "parent" society, and are the distinctive mental health problems that result properly represented in research? What are the generic conditions that attend the adaptation of ethnic groups versus the culturally distinctive ones? What are the mental health correlates of these two types of conditions, and which ones are favored by researchers and policy-setting representatives of funding agencies? How are the results of research on ethnic minority groups used in the parent society? Do the insights and knowledge structures produced by ethnic minority researchers make an impact on administrators such that the social conditions and associated mental health problems are adequately studied, modified, or confronted differently? How do these factors differ across ethnic groups and why?

4. To what extent is ethnic minority mental health research a spearhead for social and political change? To what extent does it merely follow or reflect social and political changes taking place in the society at large?

SUMMARY AND CONCLUSIONS

Some of the research literature pertaining to mental health problems of Hispanics was reviewed. An underlying emphasis of this chapter is that contemporary mainstream perspectives on mental health problems are governed by definitions, rationales, and imperatives that are positivistic and strongly influenced by biological factors. Because knowledge and practice conventions are integral to colleges and universities, research institutes, research funding agencies, public as well as private institutions that pay for mental health services, and the underlying theory behind these directives is certified by the state, the dominant perspective was termed establishment psychiatry. In effect, social policy regarding mental health research and services provision is set by establishment psychiatry. Research involving mental health problems of Hispanics was examined in terms of how it relates to establishment psychiatry. In general, the research broadens the knowledge base of establishment psychiatry. Psychiatric epidemiologic knowledge, in particular, has been extended to cover Hispanic populations, and the study of the course of schizophrenia has been sharpened and deepened through work involving Mexican Americans. Much research has pointed to biases in diagnosis and to differences between establishment paradigms of disorders and Hispanic models of psychiatric illness and distress. Although some have suggested that Hispanic cultural realities in the area of psychiatric illness need to be included in establishment conventions, few have actually challenged in a direct way the validity of such conventions. I have implicitly and explicitly attempted to point out how Hispanic realities might be used to render establishment psychiatric conventions more representative and valid. Hispanic mental health research knowledge was also examined from the standpoint of political economic factors and the change and evolution that inevitably affect social and medical systems.

9

Cultural Considerations in the Use of *DSM-IV* With Hispanic Children and Adolescents

RICHARD C. CERVANTES

WILLIAM ARROYO

The fourth edition of the *Diagnostic and Statistical Manual of Mental Disorders* (*DSM-IV*) was issued in 1994. This publication will be used by a wide array of professionals who have an interest in mental health and, in particular, symptoms of mental disorders. These professionals have diverse training backgrounds, espouse diverse theoretical orientations, and, given recent Census Bureau data, will use this diagnostic system on more children and adults of various ethnic, cultural, and racial backgrounds.

This diagnostic classification system, like its predecessors, is the primary tool used in the United States to diagnose mental disorders by clinicians who work in all levels of care, in consultation, and in the general community. Reimbursement for mental health services is also affected. Statistical data are generated to be used by social science researchers as well as policymakers, whereas epidemiologists might use the *DSM-IV* to assess community prevalence rates of mental disorders.

The cultural diversity of populations found in the United States underscores the importance of using a diagnostic system that is widely applicable and culturally relevant. Hispanic groups in the United States account for a significant portion of the recent population growth in the United States; also, this population tends to be younger than other segments of the population and is estimated to be the fastest growing population of youths (Chapa & Valencia, 1993). A diagnostic classification system that is based on clinical research with Hispanic populations has more clinical utility than one that does not. Related issues in regard to the *DSM-IV*'s predecessors and other diagnostic criteria and their use with Hispanic populations have been addressed in numerous articles (e.g., Alarcon, 1983; Leon, 1990).

The efforts to publish the *DSM-IV* were directly related to the preparation of the 10th revision of the *International Classification of Diseases* (*ICD-10*) by the World Health Organization (1992). Official U.S. diagnostic systems must be compatible with *ICD* by international treaty (Frances, 1990). Although there was considerable interchange between the two efforts, differences remain between the two diagnostic systems, although certainly less than was evident in prior editions. Several Hispanic psychiatric associations were consulted during the development of the *ICD*'s 10th edition. They recommended that cultural aspects be addressed, that the multiaxial system be used, and that effective international collaboration be promoted (Mezzich, 1987).

A number of significant changes were made for *DSM-IV*. The criteria for change included historical tradition (*DSM-III* and *DSM-III-R*), literature reviews, unpublished data, field trials, and consensus of mental health professions as well as *ICD-10* compatibility. The threshold for making revisions was set higher than that given prior editions (American Psychiatric Association, 1991).

The incorporation of criteria for disorders that first present in children and adolescents essentially began with the publication of *DSM-III* (American Psychiatric Association, 1980) and was continued in the fourth edition. Although there are various changes of diagnostic criteria that address developmental issues, aspects of culture that affect diagnostic decisions are rarely mentioned in the *DSM-IV*. Our intent here is to provide the reader with issues to consider as related to the use of *DSM-IV* with Hispanic children and adolescents. These issues are raised from the perspective of current trends in research for Hispanic children as well as from our own clinical experiences in providing mental health services to Hispanic families in a large university-based outpatient clinic in Los Angeles.

CULTURE, MENTAL HEALTH, AND DIAGNOSIS

Clinical diagnosis in the mental health professions might best be viewed as a process for categorizing the symptom experiences of persons identified as suffering from internally or externally induced psychological distress. The process of categorization and diagnosis of these symptom clusters can occur in one of two distinct fashions: direct interview on the part of a trained clinician or client self-report instruments. This process of categorization becomes progressively more difficult in younger age groups, where children are less able to clearly articulate their feelings and emotions and such psychological states can only be inferred from adult reports or observable behaviors. Self-report symptom inventories for children are few and are heavily dependent on reading and abstraction abilities. To complicate the diagnostic process even more, there are issues of language proficiency of the clinician, the parent, and the child as well as cultural beliefs surrounding the causes of and cures for psychological problems (Cervantes & Acosta, 1992; Sue & Sue, 1987).

With respect to the actual consideration of cultural factors in the diagnostic process, López and Hernandez (1986) conducted a survey of 118 mental health professionals and found that the vast majority (83%) considered culture for most or all of their culturally diverse clients. These investigators found that culture was considered by the sampled clinicians at various stages in the treatment process, including the initial evaluation phase (13%), the clinical judgment phase (21%), the process of making a clinical diagnosis (23%), and the treatment process itself (36%). What is important here is the fact that the majority of clinicians surveyed did not consider culture when arriving at clinical diagnoses.

The literature remains quite disparate and there continues to be little agreement on how clinical diagnoses should be viewed or researched, particularly in relation to the Hispanic client. Padilla and Ruiz (1975) suggested that misdiagnosis of the Hispanic client often led to treatment approaches that were potentially inappropriate. In reviewing literature addressing culture and diagnosis, issues of validity and reliability of current diagnostic systems continue to surface, although not necessarily from purely a Hispanic perspective or from the perspective of children and adolescents.

Validity

Spitzer, Endicott, and Robins (1975) note the different types of validity that should be distinguished when the validity of a classification system is under consideration. There are face validity or descriptive validity, predictive validity, and construct validity. The identification of a diagnostic category first involves face validity. This generally involves descriptions from experienced clinicians about what they think the essential features of a particular disorder should be. Some argue that many of the child diagnostic categories of *DSM-III-R* have only face validity. When the category has descriptive validity, it justifies the assumption that this represents a distinct behavioral syndrome rather than a random collection of symptoms or clinical features.

There were 12 *DSM-IV* field trials (American Psychiatric Association, 1993) sponsored by the National Institute of Mental Health (NIMH) in collaboration with the National Institute of Drug Abuse (NIDA) and the National Institute on Alcohol Abuse and Alcoholism (NIAAA). *DSM-III*, *DSM-III-R*, *ICD-10*, and *DSM-IV* criteria were compared in 5 to 10 different sites; each site had approximately 100 subjects. Representative groups of subjects from various sociocultural and ethnic backgrounds were chosen to ensure generalizability of the field trial results. However, all instruments and interviews were conducted in English. More than 70 sites and 6,000 subjects were involved in the 12 field trials. Reliability and performance characteristics of each criteria set as a whole, as well as the specific items within each criteria set, were compared. Unfortunately, the *DSM-IV* provides no details on specific subject selection criteria or actual numbers of Hispanic children or adult participants. Furthermore, there is no indication that the variables of acculturation and English proficiency were controlled.

The issue of validity in clinical diagnosis for culturally diverse populations must first be discussed in terms of "omissions" of psychological symptoms or syndromes, which are prominent in some cultural, racial, or ethnic groups but not in others. Such omissions from existing or new nosologic systems such as the *DSM-IV* raise concern with the use of these systems for culturally diverse clinical groups or research participants. As an example, Prince and Tcheng-Laroche (1987) argue that there are, in fact, a number of "culture bound syndromes" (CBS) that fall outside current diagnostic systems. These authors also recommend that an international (mental) disease classification be developed or incorporated into existing systems. Such CBSs have been described for the Japanese culture, *taijin kyofuscho* (Kirmayer, 1991), Korean culture, *Hwa-Byung*

(Lin et al., 1992), and many other distinct cultural groups. Alarcon (1983) referred to such CBSs as "psycho-cultural syndromes" in providing a Latin American perspective on *DSM-III*.

Within the Hispanic population, several CBSs have been described and articulated by clinicians for several years (*mal de ojo, susto, ataques de nervios*), yet no rigorous attempts have been made to understand such syndromes within the context of modern psychiatric epidemiology for adults or children. Some of these categories are included in *DSM-IV* in Appendix I of culturally bound syndromes.

In an attempt to address the impact of cultural definitions and meanings of certain categories of symptoms, Acculturation Problem is a new subcategory of disorders in *DSM-IV*, labeled Other Conditions That May Be a Focus of Clinical Attention, although no systematic field studies were conducted for this new syndrome and no specific diagnostic criteria have been articulated.

The text description of most diagnostic categories contains a section entitled Specific Culture, Age, and Gender Features, which includes descriptions of preferred idiomatic descriptions of distress, culturally specific symptom patterns, and available information regarding age and gender.

Validity problems in many diagnostic systems can also be associated with the inclusion of nonrelevant or potentially biased diagnostic categories and might pose additional problems for the *DSM-IV*. This is a critical issue, particularly with regard to the diagnosis of Hispanic children and adolescents where educational and treatment decisions hinge on accurate diagnosis. Various problems related to the applicability of current diagnostic categories to Hispanic populations have been discussed in the psychiatric and psychological literature. Questions regarding their validity, and therefore the continued use of these diagnostic categories, have been raised by several authors (Adams, Dworkin, & Rosenberg, 1984; Alarcon, 1983; Boxer & Garvey, 1985; Malgady, Rogler, & Costantino, 1987; President's Commission on Mental Health, 1978).

Studies of adult Hispanics have generally shown that cultural and social factors affect critical aspects of diagnostic rates (Baskin, Bluestone, & Nelson, 1981), self-reported psychiatric symptoms (Skilbeck, Acosta, Yamamoto, & Evans, 1984), and diagnoses of community mental health clients (Flaskerud, 1986). In terms of the Hispanic client, however, findings are difficult to integrate, given the varied research methodologies used. For example, Skilbeck et al. (1984) found that Hispanic clients who sought outpatient mental health services reported their symptoms as more numerous and more intense when compared to African

American clients. Hispanic clients were found to score highest on 8 of the 11 Symptom Checklist 90-R scales, although they were generally very similar to Anglo clients in their self-reported symptoms. Hispanic clients were also found to show a significant relationship between self-reported symptoms and therapist-reported diagnoses. The authors conclude that the SCL-90-R is a relatively good overall measure of psychiatric symptoms across ethnic groups, but they recommend caution in use of the self-report measure with African American clients.

In a similar study using the SCL-90-R, Randolph, Escobar, Paz, and Forsythe (1985) found clinical diagnoses of schizophrenia to concur with diagnoses obtained through the use of the NIMH Diagnostic Interview Schedule (DIS). In this study, ethnicity was not found to affect the rate of false negative DIS schizophrenic diagnoses. There was no significant difference in the concordance rates found for Anglo clients when compared to Hispanic clients. Finally, Hispanic clients who were found to be schizophrenic based on *DSM-III-R* clinical interviews and DIS ratings also tended to score in the direction of more symptoms when completing the self-report SCL-90-R. Whether such studies are conclusive in terms of the validity of *DSM-IV* diagnostic categories for use with Hispanics is not clear. Without systematic validity studies conducted separately for Hispanic groups, current and proposed categories of symptom clusters might not be relevant for all Hispanic groups, particularly as acculturation has been shown to be an important mediator of self-reported symptoms for this population (Montgomery & Orozco, 1985).

Baskin (1984) found a great degree of variability in specific diagnostic categories given by international mental health professionals in response to a set of four clinical vignettes. In a study of 20 countries and 93 representative mental health professionals, Baskin concludes that there is wide variation in the use of a preferred nosologic system but that there are significant cultural variations attributed to specific symptom clusters. That study again highlights the need for diagnostic systems that include valid cultural syndromes.

Reliability

The issues involved in obtaining reliable diagnostic information for culturally distinct groups have been articulated recently by Guarnaccia, Good, and Kleinman (1990). Potential reliability problems include diagnosticians' degree of knowledge of the patient's culture, the language used in the clinical evaluation, and the usefulness of existing diagnostic instruments from which clinical diagnoses can be derived. Canino, Bird,

Rubio-Stipec, et al. (1987) found a very high rate of agreement (interrater reliability) between trained Puerto Rican child psychiatrists when using the structured Diagnostic Interview Schedule for Children (DIS-C) (see Costello, Edelbrock, Dulcan, Kalas, & Klaric, 1984). Ethnic and language match between the children tested in the study and the diagnosticians no doubt played an important role in achieving high interrater reliability estimates for many of the *DSM-III-R* disorders of childhood and adolescence. Although it appears from the clinical literature that existing diagnostic instruments such as the SCL-90-R, DIS, DIS-C, and others might be reliable measures of various clinical symptom clusters, the question remains whether these instruments capture the entire phenomenology of psychological distress among Hispanic clients.

PSYCHIATRIC DIAGNOSES WITH HISPANIC CHILDREN AND ADOLESCENTS

The diagnostic categories in DSM-III-R and its predecessors have been applied to patients of different ages, socioeconomic groups, races, ethnic groups, religious backgrounds, and linguistic abilities since 1952. The assumption that these diagnostic categories have universal validity might, in part, be responsible for the continued use of such nosology systems despite the fact that no specific validation studies with Hispanic groups exist.

The field of research with regard to psychiatric diagnoses of children and adolescents is very limited when compared to the work with adults, in particular with respect to validity and reliability issues (Arroyo & Cervantes, in press; Cantwell, 1980). This general lack of research into diagnostic issues related to children's mental health is likely the result of a variety of factors. First, the number of diagnostic categories in the first two editions of the *DSM* were very few, compared to the diagnostic categories present in the *DSM-III-R* and *DSM-IV*. Well-specified diagnostic classifications for children and adolescents were simply not recognized. Another factor is that there is less reluctance, as well as more knowledge, among mental health professionals to diagnose psychopathology in children and adolescents than there was one or two decades ago. For example, an examination of the children's mental health literature reveals an increase in the study of childhood depression (Kovacs, 1985; Puig-Antich, 1982; Welner, 1978). Despite the fact that diagnostic criteria for depression in children and adolescents have been lacking, there now exists much more agreement on the application of adult criteria of dysthymia and major depression for use with younger populations (Poznanski, 1985).

Although it might be argued that there is a small but growing body of literature that addresses the issue of diagnosis of children and adolescents in general, similar literature for Hispanic children and adolescents is nearly nonexistent. Only a handful of studies address the matter of diagnostic categories (Canino, Bird, Rubio-Stipec, et al., 1987; Canino, Gould, Prupis, & Shaffer, 1986; Costantino, 1982; Padilla, Cervantes, & Maldonado, 1988).

In a study by O'Donnell, Stein, Machabanski, and Cress (1982), which examined dimensions of behavioral problems (and not diagnoses per se) in Mexican American preschoolers, the investigators concluded that diagnostic classification systems should incorporate "culturally relevant patterns" so as to achieve cross-cultural applicability and diagnostic accuracy. As mentioned in the review of diagnostic issues of Hispanic adults, it seems that the modest literature available on Hispanic children and adolescents argues for inclusion of cultural considerations in any diagnostic system used with Hispanic children or adolescents.

The areas of concern in studies involving Hispanic adults (e.g., validity, reliability) also apply to research with the younger Hispanic populations. However, the aspect of developmental issues must be added in studies of these younger age groups. The ideal standard with which to compare Hispanic youngsters would be the developmental norms for the particular Hispanic group to be studied. However, this matter is further complicated by the fact that acculturation would probably also affect such developmental norms. It is also recommended (Krener & Sabin, 1985) that when minority youngsters are studied or diagnosed, information on normative data regarding child rearing and socialization practices can greatly influence the course of treatment by mental health professionals.

OVERVIEW OF *DSM-IV* DIAGNOSTIC CLASSIFICATIONS: IMPLICATIONS FOR HISPANIC CHILDREN AND ADOLESCENTS

In 1991, the *DSM-IV* task force issued *DSM-IV Options* (American Psychiatric Association, 1991), which described the various options for revisions of the *DSM-III-R*. Two years later, the *DSM-IV* Draft (American Psychiatric Association, 1993) was issued, and finally the *DSM-IV* was released in 1994.

Three unifying principles underlie the organizational scheme adopted by the *DSM* manuals. At times these principles have conflicted. In *DSM-*

III-R, for example, the diagnostic categories were based on (a) phenomenologic similarity to help facilitate differential diagnosis (e.g., Mood and Anxiety sections), (b) etiology (e.g., Organic and Substance Use sections), and (c) age of onset (e.g., Disorders Usually First Evident in Infancy, Childhood, or Adolescence). The organizing principle chosen to categorize a particular diagnosis was dependent on various factors: the level of knowledge regarding etiology, historical continuity, importance of differential diagnosis, and attempts to improve the user friendliness of the classification (American Psychiatric Association, 1991).

The *DSM-IV* has 16 major diagnostic categories and 1 additional section, Other Conditions That May Be a Focus of Clinical Attention. These major diagnostic categories are similar to those in *DSM-III-R*, with some modifications (e.g., Cognitive Disorders, in part, replaced the Organic Mental Syndromes and Disorders section). Many of the minor subcategories also changed (e.g., Learning Disorders replaced part of Specific Developmental Disorders), and a few of the minor subcategories were converted to major categories (e.g., Sexual and Gender Identity Disorder). There are also many new suggested minor classes (e.g., Childhood Disintegrative Disorder and Mixed Anxiety-Depressive Disorder).

Historically, *DSM-II* contained few diagnostic categories for children and adolescents. However, 44 subtypes were introduced in *DSM-III* in a special section, Disorders Usually First Diagnosed in Infancy, Childhood or Adolescence. This section was expanded to 46 subtypes in *DSM-III-R*. There are 42 in *DSM-IV*. The organizational scheme for *DSM-IV* maintains a similar section to that in *DSM-III-R* with some modifications; for example, some categories have been removed (e.g., Eating Disorders). In addition, except for Mental Retardation, all developmental disorders are to be coded on Axis I. A separate section of diagnostic categories for youths, however, has its drawbacks (Rutter & Schaffer, 1980). Clinicians who work primarily with children and adolescents tend to overlook the diagnoses that are in other major diagnostic categories. Another problem is that many of the other diagnostic categories often have their onset during childhood or adolescence.

Cultural aspects of mental disorders have been much more slowly incorporated into the *DSM* system for either children or adults (Fabrega, Ahn, Boster, & Mezzich, 1990). The reason for this is unclear, despite the fact that since the publication of the first *DSM* in 1952, the growth of the population of culturally diverse groups in the United States has increased dramatically. The introduction in *DSM-III-R* (American Psychiatric Association, 1987) cautioned its users in the application of *DSM-III-R* to people from other ethnic or cultural backgrounds. It advised that the use of the manual be culturally valid. Specific recommendations regarding cultural aspects in the appropriate use of diagnostic criteria were very limited. In the Introduction of *DSM-IV,* there is a section on Ethnic and Cultural Considerations that describes the three types of culturally relevant information to be found in the manual: a discussion in the text of cultural variations in *DSM-IV* classifications, a description of culture bound syndromes, and an outline for cultural formulation. Unfortunately, this information on cultural considerations has been omitted from the Quick Reference to the Diagnostic Criteria From *DSM-IV* (American Psychiatric Association, 1994).

The *DSM-IV* task force recruited advisers who are international experts to ensure that the revisions would be cross-culturally applicable. One effort to ensure cultural relevance of the *DSM-IV* was sponsored by NIMH in the formation of a team of experts in the field of cross-cultural mental health. The charge of this Committee on Culture and Diagnosis was to make recommendations to the task force so as to enhance the cultural validity of the *DSM-IV.* (One of the authors, William Arroyo, served on a subcommittee that focused on the diagnostic categories used with children and adolescents.) The outcome by the Group on Culture and Diagnosis (1993) is a compendium of proposals and supporting papers submitted to the *DSM-IV* task force. The committee's recommendations included changes in criteria, changes in the text, and the addition of a Cultural Formulation. The Cultural Formulation, included in an appendix, provides the cultural context for each person for whom a diagnosis was determined.

POTENTIAL SOURCES OF CULTURAL BIAS IN THE USE OF *DSM-IV* FOR HISPANIC CHILDREN AND ADOLESCENTS

Table 9.1 presents a number of diagnostic categories considered to be most susceptible to bias given the cultural (including linguistic) differences found among many Hispanic children and adolescents.

There are several diagnostic categories that must rely on data obtained from intellectual and cognitive tests. Reliance on such tests, where little if any normative data are available for Hispanic youths, represents a major source of bias and potential inaccurate diagnosis. These categories include mental retardation, reading disorder, mathematics disorder, disorder of written expression, autistic disorder, Rett's disorder, expressive language disorder, and mixed receptive expressive language disorder. Other notable facets of diagnostic assessment in relation to these categories are language fluency and literacy. Prior to the determination of any of these diagnoses, a clinician should assess these elements of each child (and often the parent) in regard to both English and Spanish. The level of fluency and literacy will often vary among family members. The level of fluency would be meaningful if the assessment tool required the clinician to read the test; the level of literacy would be important if the assessment tool were to be read by the child or parent. In some areas of the United States, Hispanic families speak a mixture of English and Spanish; such language use might be very functional for them and therefore challenge the clinician in an effort to determine fluency. Fluency is particularly important in the determination of the presence of psychotic thought processes. Those clinicians who have difficulty understanding the speech pattern of a limited English speaker might mistakenly infer a thought disorder.

Some of the diagnostic categories rely on the assessment of socialization, including communication. These include mental retardation, autistic disorder, Rett's disorder, childhood disintegrative disorder, conduct disorder, separation anxiety disorder, selective mutism, reactive attachment disorder, and substance abuse disorder. Socialization is strongly culturally determined. The elements of socialization and modes of communication will also be influenced by the level of acculturation that a youngster might have undergone. Children who do not make eye contact might not do so out of respect for an authority figure; they do not necessarily have socialization difficulties. Children from families in which interdependence is highly valued by their culture might be erroneously thought to have a serious problem with separation from family members. Children and youths who engage in antisocial behaviors might do so primarily because this is the norm of their neighborhood; the neighborhood rules might be more significant to a child than rules of the broader society. Therefore, it is important that clinicians have an understanding of the local cultural norms.

Other categories are related etiologically to the stress that immigrant families have undergone. These might include separation anxiety disorder, posttraumatic stress disorder, conversion disorder, and somatization disorder. Some of the syndromes might be so-called culturally bound and might not be acknowledged by Western mental health professionals.

Text continued on page 146

Table 9.1 *DSM-IV* Diagnoses Most Likely to Be Culturally Biased

Disorder	Potential Sources of Bias	Recommendations for Use
Mental retardation	An individually administered IQ test is required to make a diagnosis of mental retardation; neither the person's English language proficiency (ELP) nor language preference (LP) are addressed in the criteria. A presumption is that any standardized IQ test will suffice, which, of course, is inaccurate given the lack of normative test data available for Hispanic youth. The criterion for adaptive functioning does call for comparison to members of the person's cultural group.	Where possible use IQ measures normed on Hispanic populations or use nonverbal IQ measures. Where significant discrepancies between verbal and performance, discuss meaning of discrepancies.
Reading disorder	Standardized test of reading and measured intelligence are elements of the criteria. There is no reference to linguistic diversity. Limited English Program (LEP) immigrants will have a disadvantage.	Clinicians should consider degree of ELP, LP, and migration history. Also, see recommendations under mental retardation.
Mathematics disorder	A standardized math test is required. Directions and word problems in English place an LEP person at a disadvantage.	Clinicians should consider degree of ELP, LP, and migration history. Also, see recommendations under mental retardation.
Disorder of written expression	A standardized writing skills test is required. Language of the test is not addressed. Recent Hispanic immigrants will perform poorly on such a test.	Clinicians should consider degree of ELP, LP, and migration history. Also, see recommendations under mental retardation.
Autistic disorder	Impairments in social interaction and communication including language are elements of criteria. Although it may not make a difference in those persons with severe or profound mental retardation, it may in others with more intelligence. Social interaction and communication styles are strongly influenced by culture.	Clinicians should understand culturally relevant standards of social interaction and communication and consider the context of the evaluation or treatment.
Rett's disorder	Impairment in expressive and receptive language are included in the criteria. There is no reference to ELP or LP.	Do not base language assessment solely on standardized language tests.

Table 9.1 *continued*

Disorder	Potential Sources of Bias	Recommendations for Use
Childhood disintegrative disorder	Communication, social relationships, play, and adaptive behavior are elements of criteria. All of these are strongly culturally influenced. Some Hispanic children may be judged as being impaired if comparing above behaviors to non-Hispanic behavioral norms.	Clinicians should understand culturally relevant standards of social interaction and communication.
Attention-deficit hyperactivity disorder	Not paying close attention, not sustaining attention, and not listening are elements of criteria. These elements are often a function of being able to comprehend language and other aspects of communication. Newly arrived Hispanic immigrants who are non-ELP may have comprehension difficulty and be falsely diagnosed.	Clinician must ensure that attentional problems are not related to English language comprehension or that anxiety is not related to adjustment issues/acculturation.
Conduct disorder	A violation of major societal rules is part of the criteria. Inner city Hispanic youth may abide by gang-infested neighborhood norms or rules that may be quite different than that of societal norms, thereby increasing the likelihood of falsely making a diagnosis. Many Latin American youngsters who have emigrated from war-torn countries have engaged in many antisocial activities prior to arriving in the United States through their membership in one of the warring factions. This has been their sociopolitical reality. Children migrating from very impoverished Latin American countries may have learned survival behaviors considered antisocial.	Determine the neighborhood norms and conditions in homeland prior to emigrating. Also, clinician should assess all environmental influences that shape delinquent behaviors.

continued

Table 9.1 *continued*

Disorder	Potential Sources of Bias	Recommendations for Use
Separation anxiety disorder	Anxiety as well as symptoms of posttraumatic stress disorder are often observed in refugee or immigrant children who have been forcefully and suddenly separated from loved ones and who may have also suffered traumatic experiences such as the homicide of family members. Some Hispanic cultures strongly value interdependence among family members; separation from family members via immigration or other means is normally stressful for these families. Recently immigrated Hispanic children, who are placed in a school environment where only English is spoken, may develop similar anxious symptoms as a normal reaction to multiple separations.	Determine the neighborhood norms, conditions in homeland prior to emigrating, and cultural values of family. Clinician should assess the number of separation events and severity of these events for immigrant children. Assess child's exposure to community violence or separation anxiety due to neighborhood violence/gang involvement.
Pica	Involves a reference to culturally sanctioned practice.	Determine culturally sanctioned practices.
Expressive language disorder	Standardized measures of both receptive and expressive language will be used to determine diagnosis. There is no reference to ELP or LP. Newly arrived Hispanic youth will likely have difficulty with instruments that are not linguistically relevant.	Clinicians should consider degree of ELP, LP, and migration history. Also, see recommendations under mental retardation.
Mixed receptive	See expressive language disorder.	See expressive language disorder.
Phonological disorders	Expected speech and speech sound production are elements of criteria. There is no reference to non-English-speaking people. Hispanic children have a higher likelihood of being falsely diagnosed.	Use linguistically appropriate measures.
Stuttering	Normal fluency is a criterion. There is no reference to language proficiency. Newly arrived Hispanics who are assessed in English skills will be at a disadvantage.	Assess in linguistically relevant fashion.

Cultural Considerations and the DSM-IV

Table 9.1 *continued*

Disorder	Potential Sources of Bias	Recommendations for Use
Selective mutism	Immigrant and refugee children, who speak a language other than that one used in the new host country, may not speak to strangers in their new environment. This may be encouraged and condoned by the parents who themselves are fearful of the new and hostile environment, who also do not have the facility of the new language, and who no longer have a supportive environment.	Determine language proficiency and language predominantly spoken in social context (i.e., school, etc.). Clinician should consider ELP and LP as well as migration history.
Reactive attachment disorder	These behaviors may be common among children in some inner city neighborhoods and rural areas where the child experiences severe isolation, lack of stimulation, and deprivation. Immigrant children are often prohibited by their parents from socializing beyond the household out of fear for child's safety. These may be children from neighborhoods where community violence occurs.	Determine neighborhood conditions. Assess child's ability to establish attachment and bonding with close family members.
Conversion disorder	A reference to culture is made in criteria. This is an often misused diagnosis for Hispanics who exhibit symptoms of culture-bound syndromes.	Determine country of origin and common culture-bound syndromes in country of origin. Seek consultation.
Somatization disorder	This disorder as well as other somatoform disorders are commonly misused in lieu of a mood disorder for Hispanics.	Consider a mood disorder in differential diagnosis.
Substance-related disorder	Social impairment is an element of the criteria. Socialization is strongly culturally influenced. Some substance-use patterns, especially alcohol-use patterns, may be culturally sanctioned and condoned among Latino cultures.	Determine culturally relevant standards and practices.

continued

Table 9.1 *continued*

Disorder	Potential Sources of Bias	Recommendations for Use
Schizophrenia and other psychotic disorders	Various proposed changes of criteria do not include any reference to cultural factors. Symptoms such as mutism, marked social isolation, magical thinking, impairment in role functioning as wage earner, and poverty of speech can be readily applicable to many Hispanics and certainly many who are immigrants and have limited English proficiency.	Determine language fluency and acculturation. Seek consultation from bilingual expert. Refer for bilingual school evaluation.

AXIS IV AND OTHER RELEVANT ISSUES FOR HISPANIC CHILDREN

Mezzich (1987) and others (e.g., Alarcon, 1983) have argued that a variety of important psychocultural variables are not part of existing nosologic systems and that these systems might not capture the true clinical phenomenology of the Hispanic client. Along a similar line, Cervantes, Padilla, and Salgado de Snyder (1991) and Vargas and Cervantes (1987) suggest that psychosocial stressors, including language barriers, discrimination, and value conflicts, are critical diagnostic variables that must always be assessed in the initial phase of treatment with the Hispanic client. Acosta (1979) suggests that the lack of sensitivity to these psychosocial factors limits the therapists' understanding of the Hispanic client, which in turn might result in lower use of service rates and/or early termination from treatment.

Axis IV in the multiaxial *DSM* has been reserved for a clinical rating of the degree of psychosocial stressors affecting an individual patient. In the *DSM-III* and *DSM-III-R,* there was little mention of the need for clinicians to rate those psychosocial stressors associated with culture or the process of acculturation. Early proposals for changes in Axis IV, which were included in the *DSM-IV* options manual, were promising from the standpoint of cultural relevance. A Personal Resources Scale was proposed, which asked the clinician to rate an individual's social support and environmental resources. Ratings would be provided along a continuum ranging from adequate support/resources to deficient support. Clear examples were provided, giving the rating scale internal consistency.

A second proposal was also made for Axis IV, which would have required the clinician to provide a brief qualitative description of significant life stress events. Unfortunately, neither of the proposed changes were made, and a rather simplistic listing of Psychosocial and Environmental Problems is now included in the *DSM-IV*. No mention of cultural factors or stressors is made in the revised Axis IV.

CONCLUSION

By all accounts, the Hispanic population is one of the youngest and fastest growing ethnic minority groups in the United States. In Los Angeles County alone, over 60% of the 600,000 students attending public schools are Hispanic, with a large proportion of these children being non-English speaking (Los Angeles Unified School District, 1993). The size and youthfulness of the population has important implications for health care, education, and social service providers as well as for behavioral science researchers.

In this chapter, we have attempted to highlight the importance of having a diagnostic system that is valid and reliable for Hispanic youths. Currently, only a small number of research studies have examined issues of validity and reliability of the *DSM*, and our search of the literature revealed no diagnostic field studies of Hispanic children or adolescents.

As so many authors have argued, inattention to cultural factors in the diagnostic process can lead to misdiagnosis and subsequent errors in the treatment of Hispanic youths. We have provided some very general guidelines in the use of the *DSM-IV*, with an emphasis on the impact of culture on the diagnostic process for Hispanic children. We hope that our comments and suggestions will stimulate further thought and care in the use of the *DSM-IV* for Hispanic and other culturally diverse groups of youths.

A# 10

♦

Clinical Issues in the Treatment of Chicano Male Gang Youths

JERALD BELITZ

DIANA M. VALDEZ

In the past several years, the problem of gangs and community violence has presented a threat to the well-being of minority children. Gabarino, Kostelny, and Dubrow (1991) describe the urban environments in which many of these children live as "war zones." In these war zones, children are frequently exposed to gangs and the violence often associated with gang activity. Although there has been community concern with the increase in gang violence and the recruitment of minority youths into gangs, the mental health literature has given little attention to the assessment and treatment of Chicano gang-involved youths.

Statistics show an overrepresentation of minority youth in juvenile detention and correctional facilities (Schwartz, 1989). Typically, gang-involved youths are seen in correctional settings rather than in mental health settings. Gang youths are often viewed as being so ingrained in an antisocial lifestyle that they are not considered amenable to mental health treatment. Morales (1992) points to the growing public apathy toward the needs of inner-city youths, particularly the urban youth gang. He advocates for the mental health treatment of gang-involved youths, particularly because mental health treatment needs that go unmet will facilitate a youth's involvement in a gang.

This chapter examines those psychosocial factors related to the understanding and treatment of Chicano gang-involved youths. Treatment issues are described from adolescent developmental and family systems models. Two case studies are presented that highlight factors relevant to these models as well as treatment modality issues. The perspectives and observations presented here are derived from our work in a juvenile justice setting and a community mental health program for children and families. Because of the high percentage of gang-involved males seen in both of these settings, we focus only on Chicano males who have adopted a tough and violent street persona known as the *vato loco*.

DYNAMICS OF GANG PARTICIPATION

Family Systems Dynamics

Many of the Chicano youths who are involved in gangs come from families experiencing economic, psychological, and cultural conflicts (Adler, Ovando, & Hocevar, 1984). Recent literature has related family environmental variables with participation in Chicano youth gangs. Specific variables cited are single-parent families, which are "female centered," inadequate parenting or supervision of children, domestic violence, family members with histories of alcoholism and drug addiction, poverty and inadequate housing, and pressures of acculturation and discrimination (Adler et al., 1984; Morales, 1992; Vigil, 1988a, 1988b).

In their study on the family correlates of gang membership, Adler et al. (1984) showed that when compared to non-gang-member families, gang-member families differed in terms of the quality of family interaction, supervision and discipline, family affection patterns, and maternal attitudes toward males. Non-gang-member families were more likely to go out together, be consistent in their discipline, and display their feelings more openly in the family. The mothers of gang members described their husbands as rarely involved in the family's activities. They also had more negative attitudes toward their husbands.

In our work with Chicano gang youths, specific family variables were observed to underlie the violent and aggressive behaviors exhibited by some youths. These youths, who are often more disturbed, also experience intense feelings of isolation and marginality within their families, culture, and other systems in which they participate (i.e., school, community, church). Although many of these youths come from families that are female centered, they are not necessarily female dominated because often an aggressive male father figure has impacted the family's history and, more specifically, the youth's psychosocial development. This parental male is perceived as the most powerful member of the family system, who gratifies his needs through the use of aggression or intimidation. Many of these youths have been physically abused by this male adult and also have witnessed their mothers and/or siblings being battered. If the male figure is no longer in the home, his presence survives in the form of fantasy or family mythology long after his departure.

Because of their own experiences of victimization from male figures, the mothers are too fearful to protect either themselves or their children from this violence. Adler et al. (1984) found that the mothers in their study were characterized as being afraid of their husbands, dissatisfied with their lives, and feeling trapped by life's circumstances. The boys look to their mothers for protection and support and are unable to comprehend their mothers' inertia. Feeling abandoned and betrayed, they experience their mothers as passive and uncaring and, in some instances, as hostile. The boys begin to experience ambivalent feelings toward their mothers, which are too painful for the boys to tolerate.

Alcohol and drugs are a potent part of the dynamics. Much of the family violence occurs while the male adults are intoxicated. The abusive behavior is a function of the abuser's state of mind or intoxication and occurs independently of the youth's behavior or emotional status. The boys experience a pervasive sense of helplessness and powerlessness in an environment that is unpredictable and violent.

To defend themselves against the intense feelings of abandonment and powerlessness, and to mobilize their rage, the boys identify with the abusive father. They learn that aggressiveness brings power and control and can effectively prevent further victimization. As the boys approach adolescence, they more closely resemble their aggressive models as they attempt to exert their will on the family. The mothers often relinquish their adult authority and provide their sons with an inappropriate and disproportionate sense of control. This further validates and strengthens the youths' identification with the aggressor. Many mothers then displace the rage they feel toward their own abusers onto their sons, which causes conflict between mother and son.

As the family system becomes less capable of satisfying the youths' psychological needs, the boys search for replacement families to fulfill their dependency needs. The street gang functions as a "surrogate family" (Morales, 1992), providing nourishment for the boys' emotional needs. Morales (1992) writes, "The gang member receives affection, understanding, recognition, loyalty, and emotional and physical protection" (p. 137). These are the basic human needs that a family is expected to gratify (Erickson, 1968). Virtually all of the members refer to their particular gang as *mi familia* and to each other as "homeboy," *carnales,* "cuz," or "bro."

Once a youth is accorded membership into the gang, he is fully accepted as a family member. New members are provided with a nickname or "tag" to make more explicit that youth's inclusion in the family. The nickname reflects a personality trait that is unique to that individual and typically connotes recognition and acceptance of that member's strengths and deficits. Many boys report that they are willing to die or kill for their gang, expressing their ultimate love and loyalty to their *familia.*

Adolescent Identity Issues

The essential task of adolescence is the formation of an independent adult identity, which requires the adolescent to become less dependent on the parents, develop a sexual identity, develop peer relationships, and derive security from one's growing mastery of the self and the environment (Slaff, 1979). Offer and Offer (1975) concluded that most adolescents master the developmental tasks of the stage but that this is a particularly stressful period for the individual with a history of long-standing problems or a disrupted developmental pattern.

Vigil (1988a, 1988b) described the identity crisis experienced by Chicano adolescents who are drawn to gangs, with particular emphasis on their confusion about their masculine identity. Due to the disorganized family environments of gang-involved youths, their psychosocial needs have been ignored or poorly sated. The youths have limited involvement with community resources (e.g., church activities, community centers) and minimal opportunity to interact with more positive role models. Vigil (1988a) observed that these youths have been exposed to street life since early childhood, leading to continuous experiences of "street socialization and acculturation" (p. 426). Older gang members, *veteranos,* serve as role models for the latency and preadolescent youths. Thus the behaviors, attitudes, and values of known gang members are adopted and internalized by these youths. This is occurring concomitantly with the consolidation of the youths' identification with the aggressor at home and with their increasingly conflictive relationship with their mothers.

Membership in the gang allows for separation from the family of origin and serves as a functional means of resolving the identity crisis. Gang members are counterparts who validate and legitimatize each other's experientially and culturally determined concepts of masculinity. Affiliation with the gang provides the youths with a reference group, which allows them to integrate the negative aspects of themselves into a newly constructed self-identity. The ranking-in ritual, whereby the youth joins a gang, is a rite of passage that confirms the youth's self-identity as a man and gang member.

Emotional Disturbance

Gang members are generally viewed as criminals and consequently receive psychiatric diagnoses such as conduct disorder or antisocial personality. However, for many of these youths, their hostility and aggression masks an underlying depression and/or posttraumatic stress disorder, which are experienced in response to emotional or physical abuse, losses, or deprivation. Because of the youths' identification with the aggressive male in his life, the anger is not directed against the adult who inflicted the pain. Instead, it is displaced onto people and property in the community. In his investigation of masked depression in adolescence, Glaser (1981) determined that the more typical symptoms of depression exist beneath the array of aggressive and hostile behaviors. The youths' sense of powerlessness, vulnerability, and self-hatred is masked, yet expressed by their aggression.

The aggression is most often directed against rival Chicano gang members. These rivals are mirror images of each other in terms of their sociocultural histories. The only differences that separate the gangs from each other are the barrios in which they live. Rivals function as projective identifications for each other, whereby they project onto one another the negative qualities they have masked or incorporated into their identities as gang members. The youths are seeking to destroy what they hate about themselves. In extreme cases, they are willing to commit homicide as a means to express their intense rage or commit a symbolic suicide. Others act out suicidal impulses by provoking rival gang members or engaging in gang banging with the implicit intent of being killed. One gang member, who connected his gang activity with his suicidal impulses, fantasized about forming an antigang gang named the Lost Chicano Tribe because, as he stated, "We're destroying ourselves."

Substance abuse, a common recreational activity among gang members, has been identified as a symptom of depression in adolescence (Glaser, 1981; Robbins & Alessi, 1985) and as a correlate of psychological stress in urban Hispanic youth (Schinke, Moncher, Palleja, Zoyas, & Schilling, 1988). The verbal expression of sadness or depression is not sanctioned by the gang; it is viewed as a sign of weakness not consistent with their construct of what is masculine. Consequently, the adolescents cope with their painful emotional states in ways sanctioned by the gang culture. They either blunt their pain with alcohol and drugs or act it out in violent behaviors.

Issues of Mastery and Competence

Just as aggressive and dangerous behaviors mask depression, they also serve to protect the gang member from experiencing the affective states of fear and anxiety. As young children, many of these gang members lived in powerless fear as they endured their paternal figures' unpredictable violence and abuse and their mothers' inability to protect them. As described earlier, they identified with the aggressor to feel powerful and to master their feelings of vulnerability and fear. When these youths are exposed to the threats of the streets without benefit of parental protection, their feelings of fear and powerlessness are further activated. Again, the youths look to powerful male figures from whom they can learn how to control their emotions and adapt to the threatening demands of the street. Frequently, they identify with the *vatos locos,* who are perceived as fearless, powerful, and invulnerable.

This phenomenon of adopting a tough street persona is referred to as *locura* (Moore, 1988; Vigil, 1988a, 1988b). Vigil details a state of mind that uses daring, dangerous, and unpredictable behaviors as a means of managing one's aggression, anxiety, and fear. Loco attitudes and behaviors operate as a counterphobic defense. By acting loco, the youth both denies and confronts his worst fears, physical and psychological destruction. The loco behavior is driven by the gang member's struggle to achieve mastery over his external environment and his own destructive impulses toward others and himself.

Membership in a gang also provides these youths with a sense of competency and purpose. These youths have failed to gain competency in the tasks typically assigned to children. They do not experience success in school, athletic or recreational organizations, or church groups and are unable to imagine themselves functioning in the world beyond the barrio streets. Also, these youths have experienced the pain and rejection of prejudice and discrimination. Invariably, they have been informed that they are ethnically inferior and inadequate. Consequently, the outside world is seen as culturally alien, threatening, and impenetrable. Gang members will travel into other barrios, but they phobically avoid nonbarrio environments. Behind their bravado, they view themselves as ill-equipped to succeed in what they experience as a hostile and rejecting Anglo world. Instead, they become expert *vatos locos* and learn to master the streets. Insulated from the outside world, they give their life purpose and meaning through their gang endeavors.

TREATMENT MODALITIES

Individual Therapy Issues

Because a history of emotional and/or physical trauma and its subsequent emotional disturbances is often associated with gang involvement, the psychological consequences of abuse must be processed in therapy. The therapy relationship provides a safe environment in which the youth can identify and explore the overwhelming and frightening feelings associated with abuse. As trust develops, the adolescent can verbalize and understand such feelings as powerlessness, fear, guilt, depression, and rage without the threat of being devalued as a male or rejected for acknowledging vulnerability. The therapist's tolerance of the material and acceptance of the youth validates both the adolescent's experiences and existence. It is critical for the therapist to establish a therapeutic alliance before facilitating the exploration of this material. By not recognizing the issue of trust as core to the youths' psychosocial development and current level of functioning, the therapist will inadvertently sabotage treatment.

Through the therapeutic relationship, with emphasis on both the positive and negative transferences, the youth can explore his intense and often ambivalent feelings toward his mother and father figure(s). This allows the adolescent to explore his identification with the aggressor and ambivalent attachment to his mother. It is essential for the therapist to tolerate this material and reframe it as a developmentally appropriate response to a traumatic history so that the youth experiences the therapist as an adult who is powerful, attentive, and caring without being abusive or controlling. Within this therapeutic context, the adolescent can learn to identify and manage a wider range of emotions and to differentiate between emotional states and behavioral actions. This helps the youth gain self-acceptance of his feelings and integrate negative affects into a more complex whole self.

Much of the therapy focuses on identifying how the youth's needs are being met by gang participation. This entails exploration of the youth's yearning for a family to provide for his dependency needs and his quest to establish a congruent psychological and cultural identity. Because the youths feel empty without the support and self-definition of the gang, encouraging them to leave the gang is tantamount to asking them to commit psychological suicide. Also, ranking out of a gang is physically dangerous. Typically, the youth must endure a brutal assault by gang members, and then he is left vulnerable and unprotected in an environment populated by rival and hostile gang members.

Therapy enables the youth to develop more adaptive ways of meeting his needs and functioning in the larger world so that gang involvement can progressively recede in importance. This involves working at such issues as career choices, sexual relationships, social interactions with peers, and the use of alcohol and drugs. It is imperative to facilitate the youth's expansion of his identity as a Chicano beyond being a gang member or *vato loco*. The therapist encourages the boys to maintain positive elements previously associated with gang membership, such as being strong, loyal, willing to take risks, and being a survivor. These qualities can be reframed as adaptive attributes that can be used by more positive endeavors that are consistent with the newly developing construct of what it means to be a Chicano male.

Finally, the therapy relationship can promote philosophical examinations of the meaning of life and death, importance of morality, and the human capacity for good and evil. If the therapist is able to be nonjudgmental yet clear and consistent about the value of nonabusive and responsible behavior, this process can be of major therapeutic importance. This cognitive processing helps youths understand and tolerate their confusing affective states and to more critically question the meaning of their gang involvement.

Family Therapy Issues

Family therapy is an integral component of treatment. Because family dysfunction has been identified as a correlate to gang involvement, the underlying family problems need to be openly and directly addressed.

It is not unusual for the therapist to act in the capacity of a case manager, helping the family access and negotiate various agencies such as the Department of Human Services, Juvenile Justice System, and Housing Authority. This must be done in a manner that respects and empowers a family.

Much of therapy focuses on the family history of violence, abuse, and neglect. Family secrets, which concealed or denied the violence, need to be disclosed so that the honest communication of feelings and perceptions can be achieved. This involves exposing the family mythology about the abusive father figures who typically no longer live with the family. Exploration of each member's feelings about his or her family history provides the family with more accurate reality testing and validates their experiences. By understanding the youth's emotional responses to the family's traumas, the family can better comprehend the context and meaning of his gang participation and violent behaviors.

A primary goal is to assist the family in their ability to verbally express and listen to strong affects without becoming aggressive or punitive. This allows the youth to communicate his rage, sadness, and sense of rejection to the abuser and/or to those who failed to protect him. Furthermore, this permits the nonprotecting parent or other family members to process their traumatic family experiences, thus giving context and meaning to their inability to either protect the youth or satisfy his psychosocial needs. Healing is more difficult when the abusing and/or nonprotecting parent refuses to accept responsibility for his or her behavior and for his or her contribution to the family disorganization.

The youth's role in the family needs to be explored and redefined. For example, the boy's gang-related violence can be reframed as learned abusive behavior resulting from the identification with the aggressor. Their mothers can be helped to see their sons as children poorly equipped to negotiate the developmental demands of adolescence rather than as replicas of their aggressive husbands and/or significant male partners. This might release the youth from continuously enacting his gang-reinforced role of the man of the house and instead allow him to have more of his own developmental psychosocial needs met within his family system.

The sociocultural stressors that impact on the family and family patterns of relating to one another need to be explored. Such discussions provide a fuller context for understanding the family problems and the youth gang participation. Extended family members with positive Chicano identities can be brought into the family system or even into the therapy sessions. Often this helps the family identify their cultural strengths and integrate them into more positive individual and family identities.

Concurrently, parents need to be empowered as the decision-making adults in the family. Parents are responsible for establishing the family rules for what is appropriate and permissible in the home. Understanding and accepting the expression of feelings does not equate to tolerating abusive behavior. Family therapy facilitates the implementation of developmentally appropriate expectations, guidelines, and consequences for the children's behaviors. Ideally, the family will create a mechanism for resolving conflict that includes respect for each other and respect for their family.

Group Therapy Issues

Group therapy, especially as an adjunct treatment, is a powerful agent of change for many gang members. Members from rival gangs are invited to join the group as long as they voluntarily commit to follow the group rules, which focus on creating a safe and respectful environment. Specific rules include maintaining the building and property where the group is held as neutral territory, no tagging or graffiti on the property, no wearing of clothes that will knowingly provoke or agitate other group members, showing respect for others by not being verbally or physically aggressive toward or threatening others, allowing everyone an opportunity to participate, and attending on a voluntary basis even if the adolescent is court ordered to receive treatment. The adolescents participate in an all-male group so that they can comfortably and honestly explore issues of abuse, sexuality, and masculine identity.

By participating in a group, the youths are afforded the opportunity to affiliate with another reference group. Within the group setting, the boys can learn to trust others enough to verbally explore and discuss their family histories and their emotional responses to their family trauma. Frequently, it is startling and reassuring for the boys to discover that others share consubstantial life stories. Consequently, the youths receive further validation for their feelings and experiences. This also helps the youths break down the artificial barriers that separate them from rival gang members and reduces the alienation they feel when outside their own barrio.

A major group theme is the exploration of identity issues. Members examine their self-identity and sense of masculinity vis-à-vis their gang membership. These discussions center on how and what the boys learned from their male role models. Through the work, the boys typically disclose their histories of abuse and process with each other how they identified with aggressive males in their efforts to be powerful and masculine. They begin to understand that their aggressive behaviors mask their vulnerability and enhance their value and acceptance in the gang. When they can accept their peers' vulnerability and uncertainty, they can begin to loosen their own rigid self-definition. At this point, the youths can expand their construct of masculinity to include a wider range of attitudes, feelings, and behaviors. They also begin to see themselves as having an identity beyond that of being a gang member.

Identity issues are also processed within a sociocultural context. As they struggle with defining their self-identity, they invariably explore their culture, sense of being a Chicano, and how gang membership reinforces their Chicano identity. Such discussions lead to examining the messages they received about their ethnic identity from their families, churches, schools, neighbors in their barrio, the media, and various representatives from the social agencies with which they interacted. The youths endeavor to differentiate the positive and negative qualities they associate with being Chicano and thus labor to synthesize these qualities into a more complex and complete Chicano identity. This process of identity development further involves searching for role models who have strong ethnic identities but who are not gang involved or abusive.

The group facilitates the learning of new social skills, including the ability to provide and receive feedback, be assertive in a nonaggressive manner, provide and receive emotional support, and relate to females in a mutually respectful manner. Through the interaction with the group members, each individual learns about his interactional patterns and his impact on others in his world. With feedback and support from the group, the youths can experiment with new behaviors within the group, within their barrio, and within the larger community. Essentially, they are helping each other to look to a more promising future with and without the gang.

Case Study 1: Gang as Surrogate Family

The first case presentation shows how family dynamics and the need to promote one's cultural identity contribute to gang participation.

Benito is a 17-year-old male who was adopted at birth by a Mexican American couple who had no children of their own. His adoptive parents and their extended families had lived in the same barrio for three generations. His mother stayed at home performing all of the household chores and the father worked for the state government. Both parents were active in the Catholic church, with the father being recognized as a community leader.

The father was an authoritarian man who used physical and verbal aggression to dominate and control his family. Benito, rather than watch his father beat his mother, would provoke his father into redirecting his aggression toward him. His father would discipline him by whipping him, beating him, or destroying his personal belongings. His mother would never act to protect him because of her own fear of the father's abuse.

Benito, fueled by his rage and sense of powerlessness, became increasingly hostile and oppositional toward his father. He felt love and loyalty to his mother because of her role as mother, but he disregarded any limits she set on his behavior and showed her little respect. He resented his father's positive standing in the community and desired to reveal the family secret of his father's abuse. Benito viewed his father as an Anglo "wanna-be" who hated his Chicano culture and roots.

At the age of 13, he was ranked into his barrio gang and was tattooed with gang-related symbols. Although he was of small stature, he was quickly tagged as loco and was seen as an invaluable gang banger. By this time, Benito had multiple contacts with the juvenile justice system and several failed attempts of psychological treatment.

Benito was court ordered into treatment at age 14 because he planned to kill his father and himself. He also had fantasies of killing the parish priest and the Pope. This occurred shortly after his mother finally asserted herself and separated from his father. When he entered treatment, he had disowned his family and regarded his gang as *mi familia*. He referred to his mother as his legal guardian and refused to have any contact with his father. At this time Benito said, "I'm not living, I'm surviving."

Benito was seen in inpatient and outpatient treatment by the same psychotherapist over a 3-year period. Initially, Benito did not trust his therapist, whom he viewed as another authoritarian adult who was going to control, dominate, and punish him. He also questioned whether the therapist could understand a Chicano youth from the barrio. His ability to verbalize his mistrust and apprehension actively engaged him in the therapeutic process.

Therapy focused on Benito's relationship with his father, with particular emphasis on his identification with the aggressor. He expressed his rage at his father for adopting him and then violating his commitment to love and protect him. He also fantasized about torturing and killing his father to pay him back. He hated feeling powerless and vulnerable and identified with his father's violence and aggression to psychologically defend himself. He also internalized his father's portrait of him as an evil delinquent destined for prison. Exploration of this revealed Benito's efforts to recapitulate his abuse history. He would go to the *pinta* as an adolescent who would be victimized by the older inmates while the prison guards turned a blind eye. Then, as he grew stronger and more psychologically adroit, he would abuse and victimize the newer and weaker prisoners.

Much therapy time was devoted to exploring his gang affiliation and identity. Benito talked about being rejected twice, once by his biological mother and then by his adoptive parents. The gang functioned as *mi familia*, which would never betray or reject him. He spoke fondly of having his own family, where he was accepted and valued because he was a *vato loco*. Benito felt that the only way to express his Chicano identity was to be a gang member who claimed his barrio.

Adults, such as his father, who had successful jobs in the world beyond the barrio were discounted as hypocrites. He identified with his father's aggressive power but rejected his father's other values and qualities. He identified with the *veteranos* on the streets. His construct of a Chicano male was of a man who abused drugs and alcohol and who aggressively defended himself, his family (his gang), and his barrio against real or perceived threats.

As Benito became increasingly capable of exploring these issues and verbalizing his anger, he was better able to access his depression. He talked about how his rage protected him from experiencing his sadness, with the realization that his suicidal impulses resulted from his intense feelings of powerlessness and loneliness. He further talked about feeling empty inside. His rage against the world kept his fear and sadness out of his conscious awareness. Gang membership served to partially fill this void and to help him defend himself against his depression. He described how he had bricks of rage built all around him and that inside the wall was a baby crying and screaming: "I'm a tiny baby and my father is going to kill me. My mother is watching."

Family therapy with his mother allowed Benito to confront his mother about her complicity in his abuse. She described her fear and sense of powerlessness but was able to accept responsibility for not protecting him. She reassured Benito that she loved him regardless of how he felt or behaved. She also asserted her parental role and established limits for what she would and would not allow in her home in terms of how he behaved.

Throughout treatment there were philosophical explorations of such topics as morality, the meaning of life, life after death, and the ability of an individual to change his fate. These discussions improved Benito's abstract critical thinking, which facilitated his ability to analyze his gang involvement and his identity development.

Benito's relationship with the therapist was an instrumental component of treatment. Consequently, through both the positive and negative transferences, he was better able to experience, tolerate, and express his ambivalent feelings toward others and was better able to see himself in a more integrated manner with a broader range of affect. With the assistance of psychotherapy, Benito was able to project a future for himself that went beyond his gang. He talked of creating his own family, having children, and working to support them. He was able to visualize the little boy growing up to be a man.

Case Study 2: Confronting the Gang—
A Multimodal Treatment Approach

The second case example highlights the importance of using a multimodal treatment approach to address family dynamics, intrapsychic conflicts that result from childhood sexual abuse and neglect, and peer support of the adolescent's gang identity.

Chris is a 17-year-old Mexican American adolescent who was born to an unwed adolescent mother. Chris and his mother lived with his maternal grandparents, Mexican Americans who spoke Spanish at home and treated Chris as if he was their son. When Chris was 4 years old, he and his mother moved into their own residence with the mother's boyfriend. His mother and "stepfather" soon began abusing alcohol and drugs, neglecting Chris's emotional needs. During the times when his mother was either too intoxicated or away from the home working, his stepfather sexually abused Chris in a sadistic and ritualistic manner. This abuse occurred for 4 years until his mother separated from the stepfather because of his emotional abuse of her. Chris and his mother then returned to live with his grandparents.

By then, he was an angry, oppositional, withdrawn boy. Chris had often attempted to communicate his abuse to his family but never felt heard or protected. He was enraged at his mother for her failure to parent him and at the grandparents for their inability to hear his half-spoken pleas for help. Feeling powerless and unloved and filled with murderous hate, he rejected his family, his church, and his education.

Chris was ranked into the gang at the age of 12. He had multiple tattoos, each one representing a loss or significant trauma in his life. He regarded this gang as *familia* and boasted that he would die or kill for his *familia*. Despite frequent arrests and the threat of being sent to a boys' detention facility, he maintained his intense gang activity. When he was 15 years old, his girlfriend became pregnant. Because of ongoing conflict in their relationship, his girlfriend would frequently break up with him. During one of these breakups, Chris felt so rejected and depressed that he threatened to kill her. To control his rage, he made a suicide attempt.

After a brief psychiatric hospitalization for alcohol and drug detoxification and to determine his suicidal status, Chris was transitioned to outpatient therapy. He has since been in individual, family, and group psychotherapy for the past 2 years. Because of the severity of his problems and the family problems, a male and female cotherapy team was selected to work with him.

From the onset, Chris was eager to ventilate his feelings, particularly his rage against his mother and stepfather. He quickly established a positive transference with the female therapist but tested the character of his male therapist before trusting him. He eventually felt validated and reassured that he would not be rejected or punished by the male therapist for disclosing his feelings or revealing his past aggressive actions.

Much of his individual therapy focused on helping Chris identify, express, and tolerate his emotional responses to the abuse, abuser, and his mother. With the benefit of artwork, guided imagery, and the safety he felt within a therapeutic relationship, Chris was able to access his memories and process his painful experiences. Furthermore, he was able to associate these emotions as causal factors related to his substance abuse, gang membership, gang violence, and suicidal and homicidal impulses. He understood how he identified with the aggressor and defended himself against feeling powerless by victimizing those weaker than himself. It was at this point that Chris began to show remorse for his own aggression toward others.

Individual therapy also allowed Chris to process his conflicting feelings toward his mother. He desperately wanted her to love him and parent him, but he so mistrusted her that he rejected any of her overtures to heal the relationship. His rage was always present, and he continued to threaten and verbally abuse her at home. As he gained the capacity to tolerate his intense ambivalent feelings, he was encouraged to process them with his mother in family therapy.

Family therapy included extended family members with close emotional ties to Chris. These relatives served to reconstruct his family history in a more realistic manner and to help Chris and his mother communicate and relate in a manner that was less aggressive and more consistent with the family's Chicano history and identity. In the family therapy, Chris was able to verbalize his past and current emotions to his mother. His mother was able to acknowledge Chris's pain, offer him comfort, and apologize for her role in his abuse and neglect. She communicated her fear, anger, and anxiety concerning his violence toward her and his gang activities. The extended family members supported and validated his mother, thus allowing Chris to accept this feedback and make changes in his behavior.

For several months, Chris also participated in group therapy. The group, composed of other gang members, helped Chris explore his identity as an adolescent, gang banger, and Chicano. Chris and the other group members processed how they used their gang membership to define themselves as *cholos* and to master their fears and anxieties. With the support of the group, Chris looked at his male role models and how he learned to be a *vato loco*. He was encouraged to experience ambivalence toward these models and to differentiate the positive and negative attributes he valued. He was further encouraged to identify other Chicano males who had a positive influence on his life and who could function as resources and/or current role models.

The group also facilitated increased social and interpersonal skills. Chris learned the difference between aggressive and assertive communication and behaviors. He learned that other gang members and peers would accept and value him if he stepped outside his *vato loco* role. With the support of the group, Chris was able to see himself as sober, owning his own property, living with his girlfriend and children, and working to support his family. Although he continued to identify himself as a member of this gang, he gave himself permission to move away from his gang activities to take care of his family and of himself.

In this example, the importance of involving the extended family in the adolescent's treatment was critical in bolstering the adolescent's and mother's familial and cultural identities. The decision to use a male-female therapist team was also important in addressing issues related to the boy's conflict with his mother and his identification with the male aggressive models in his life.

DISCUSSION

This chapter has examined family and adolescent developmental variables that play a critical role in the behavior of Chicano gang youths.

Although gang membership can be explained in terms of certain developmental tasks pertinent to adolescence, including identity formation, mastery and control, and independence, family characteristics also interact with gang membership to produce certain kinds of gang behavior.

Our clinical experience suggests that severe abuse and rejection by a father figure and a mother who cannot protect her children from such abuse underlie the aggressive and violent behaviors that are seen in the more seriously disturbed *vato loco*. This finding is consistent with research that shows that inadequate fathering and mothering play a significant role in the etiology of male violence (Miedzian, 1991; Moore & Vigil, 1987).

Although families in minority communities experience considerable stress from poverty, discrimination, and the pressures of acculturation, factors which have been correlated with gang involvement, not all of the children from these families become involved in gangs. Furthermore, not all gang members engage in violent behaviors. Critical factors that contribute to gang membership and violence are family disintegration, cultural dissolution, abusive family relationships, and histories of interpersonal violence. Violence becomes reinforced both within the family context and within the gang and is socially reinforced in the development of masculine identity (Miedzian, 1991).

As noted by Morales (1992), the mental health needs of Chicano gang youths continue to be ignored. The media continue to portray an image of these youths as antisocial and criminally motivated. The sensationalism around the gang culture among Chicano youths promotes the inaccurate perception that gang behavior is simply an extension of the Latino culture. Although certain negative family characteristics have been described that contribute to gang membership and violent behavior, these characteristics are not found in all Latino families. Further research, however, is important to identify family patterns in non-gang-member families that divert their children from the socialization of the streets. Our experiences indicate that a focus on cultural identity, with its prosocial and nonviolent implications, is an important component of any gang diversion program.

Advocacy for gang-involved youths in the courts is necessary to prevent further criminalization of Chicano youths. Frequently, minority status is automatically associated with gang membership, which serves to create negative stereotypes and expectations by those systems (i.e., school and juvenile justice in which Chicano youths are involved). Mental health professionals play a key role in providing the court with a context for the behaviors of these youths and making appropriate mental health referrals.

Treatment resources must exist in the community to meet the multiple treatment needs of this population. Specialized services for gang-involved youths by professionals who have training in the treatment of minority group children and knowledge of the gang subculture cannot be overemphasized. The typical gang prevention or intervention programs that exist within the juvenile justice system are limited in their ability to explore complex and volatile family issues that play a significant role in the maintenance of gang behavior. These programs are important, however, because they provide important monitoring and prevention of the adolescent's delinquent activities in the community.

Although a discussion of community intervention models for gang-involved youths is beyond the scope of this chapter, greater collaboration between the various community agencies in which the child is involved is necessary. The legal system can assist the mental health professional in the treatment of these families because treatment can be mandated as a special condition of a child's probation. Finally, special intervention programs are necessary to keep these youths in school because children are at risk for dropping out during their middle school or high school years.

In summary, the problems of gang violence pose a significant threat to the mental health of Chicano children. As mental health professionals, we must continue to advocate for the needs of these disenfranchised children who are often victims and perpetrators of violence in their communities.

PART 4

Health and AIDS Research

11

♦

Language as a Communication Barrier in Medical Care for Hispanic Patients

ROSA SEIJO

HENRY GOMEZ

JUDITH FREIDENBERG

The language barrier can be a major problem in communication when physicians and patients do not share the same language. This problem is manifested when attempting to communicate medical information from one party to the other. This chapter evaluates whether having a bilingual or monolingual (English-speaking) physician affects recall of information and question-asking behavior by Hispanic patients. We report mainly on elderly patients who have resided in the United States for many years and differ in their English language proficiency. This is an important issue in the doctor-patient interaction that ultimately has an impact on health care delivery and use.

Many studies (Ley & Spelman, 1965; Shapiro & Saltzer, 1981; Stoeckle & Waitzkin, 1972, 1976) have attempted to understand the intricacies of the doctor-patient interaction. Patient question-asking behavior during the encounter and patient information recall after the encounter are two parameters that have been used to assess the success of the doctor-patient interaction (Bertakis, 1977; Brody, 1979). However, studies have not shown how language discordance between physician and patient can affect patient information recall and question-asking behavior with its possible implications for Hispanic health care. We combined these factors in an attempt to show that language differences between physician and patient can affect the doctor-patient encounter and might help to explain why Hispanic patients underuse health care in the United States.

Language differences between physician and patient have been studied as possible sources of misunderstanding and miscommunication between the two parties (Alpert, Kesselman, Marcos, & Urcuyo, 1973; Baxter & Bucci, 1981; Gozzi, Korsch, & Francis, 1968; Korsch, Negrete, Freemon, & Davis, 1971; Manson, 1988). These language differences have also been viewed as counterproductive in the use of health care by Hispanic patients (Cox, 1986; Falvo & Tippy, 1988). An important area where language discordance between physician and patient becomes apparent is in the doctor-patient encounter where the necessity to convey information by the two parties is essential in understanding the patient's illness and its manifestation.

Several studies in the mental health literature have looked at how doctor-patient interactions can be affected by differences in language spoken by patient and provider. Poma (1983) reviewed how language differences can alter the physician-patient relationship in Hispanics. Poma noted that use of mental health facilities and gratefulness from patients improved when they can use their maternal language to communicate problems. He also believed that the language used as a child continues to be the language used as an adult to communicate emotions. If health is viewed as an emotional issue, then Poma suggested that the patient will communicate more effectively with someone who understands his or her native language. An article by Quesada (1976) also explored language as a communication barrier to health delivery in Hispanic patients. Like Poma, he believed that the language spoken shapes the cognitive structure of the individual who speaks that language. Quesada also mentioned studies that show decreased referrals when doctor and patient do not share the same native language.

Our study is not only about language but about communication and culture and how all these factors can become integrated in the complex social interaction between a doctor and a patient. Speaking the same language is hardly synonymous with sharing the same culture. For example, the culture of a Spaniard in Madrid, a Dominican in New York City, and a Puerto Rican on the Island cannot be more different, yet the same language—Spanish—is being spoken in all three instances. In our study, in addition to language spoken during the visit, the physician and the patient groups differed by national origin, ethnic identity, gender, and social class status, all markers of inequality in our society. Yet certain underlying similarities, partially historically determined, made communication more fluid among the bilingual physicians and the patients. Given cultural diversity among Hispanics in the United States (Bean & Tienda, 1987; Moore & Pachon, 1985), one could hardly argue that there is such a thing as a "Hispanic culture," yet it must be some specific aspect of culture—in our study, language—that influenced our findings that patients seen by bilingual physicians had better recall and asked more questions than those seen by English-speaking physicians. What is the role of language when the physician is monolingual and translators have to be employed?

Poma (1983) looked at the problems of using translators in the Hispanic patient-English speaking physician interaction. He felt that translations are often literal and do not express the original speaker's thoughts. Translations can also lead to confusing and misleading information for both parties. Poma also noted that no two translators report a physician-patient interaction identically. Finally, Poma stated that a translation implies a personal interpretation of facts and that the translator's beliefs will influence what he or she hears and tells the patient. Similar problems were encountered in psychiatric settings by Alpert et al. (1973) and Baxter and Bucci (1981), where lack of communication between physician and patient due to language differences could lead to (a) viewing patients as "more pathological" when Hispanic patients are interviewed in English than when interviewed in their native language or (b) Hispanic patients leaving the hospital due to their inability to communicate in English.

Several studies have gone beyond simple observations to analyze how the doctor-patient encounter is affected by language discordance between patient and provider. A study by Shapiro and Saltzer (1981) examined English- and Spanish-speaking patients' patterns of communication with White Anglo physicians. Shapiro and Saltzer found that physicians established significantly better rapport with English-speaking patients than with Spanish-speaking patients, English-speaking patients were given a better explanation of their therapeutic regimen than were Spanish-speaking patients, and physicians were able to elicit patient feedback significantly better from the English-speaking patients than from the

Spanish-speaking patients. Finally, Shapiro and Saltzer also noted that the interaction factors of language, translator, and ethnicity appeared to influence whether medication instructions were understood by the patient. An interesting study by Manson (1988) looked at the effects of language concordance between physician and patient as determinants of patient compliance. Manson found that the language discordant group was more likely than the language concordant group to be noncompliant with their medications. Moreover, patients in the language discordant group were more likely to miss an appointment and more likely to make an emergency room visit.

All these studies showed that language discordance between patient and physician is of great importance in affecting the doctor-patient encounter and its outcome. However, when exploring the complex issue of language and communication, the sociocultural aspects of the population studied must be kept in mind. Both Quesada (1976) and Poma (1983) described cultural aspects of Hispanics that can affect their relationship with the physician. They believe that Hispanic patients look for an "authoritarian-paternalistic" relationship with their doctors. Hispanic patients want doctors to tell them what to do without much discussion of the disease. According to Poma and Quesada, Hispanic patients view a doctor who asks many questions as being incompetent. Even though these cultural factors are not considered in this chapter, they must be kept in mind when exploring the relationship between Hispanic patients and doctors.

Language discordance affects patient recall as measured by information transferal and patient question-asking behavior. Shapiro and Saltzer (1981) briefly explored patient recall and how it can be affected by language. However, their methods did not allow them to explore this topic in sufficient depth. We used the methodology found in the literature that assesses communication of information to the patient and patient recall to analyze the effects of language differences between patient and provider. An important determinant of the success of the doctor-patient interaction is the communication of information during the interaction and the amount of information recalled by the patient. Several studies have explored these issues. A classic study by Ley and Spelman (1965) looked at communication of information during the physician-patient encounter and its effects on patient recall. Their findings suggest that communication of information from doctor to patient can be affected by the nature and complexity of the information given. A study by Brody (1979) took Ley and Spelman's (1965) model a step further by looking at specific patient characteristics that can affect patient recall. He found that inaccurate-recall patients were older and lived alone. He also noted that inaccurate-recall patients had lower comfort and activity levels, were given more complex treatment plans, and were less satisfied with their physician. Brody's study demonstrated the important effect of various patient characteristics on how much information a patient acquires during the doctor-patient encounter.

Several studies directly observed or taped the doctor-patient encounter, thus affording a better assessment of information transferal to the patient (Bertakis, 1977; Falvo & Tippy, 1988; Korsch et al., 1971). These methods can be used to directly quantify and record information given to the patient by the physician, eliminating indirect measures such as questionnaires or chart reviews. Bertakis (1977) studied physician-patient encounters by audiotaping them. Results showed how the doctor-patient interaction and patient recall can be improved by allowing the doctor and patient to explore sources of mutual misunderstanding and information gaps. In addition, the Bertakis study demonstrated how taping the interaction allows for a more objective and reliable way of approaching the information transfer between physician and patient.

Patient question-asking behavior and its relationship to the physician-patient encounter has been addressed by several studies. Korsch et al. (1971) studied 287 doctor-patient encounters in a pediatric walk-in clinic. They found that 37% of the patients asked 0 to 2 questions throughout the encounter. Similarly, a study by Boreham and Gibson (1978) found that patients asked few questions and that the physician provided most of the information during the interaction. Several explanations have been offered for this type of patient behavior. Boreham and Gibson believed that physicians establish a dominant role in the doctor-patient encounter by discouraging patient question asking. Cox (1986) believed that patients do not ask questions because this implies a lack of confidence in the physician's judgment. Bochner and Pendleton (1980) also suggested that patients from low socioeconomic classes tend not to ask many questions. Few studies have investigated question-asking behavior in Hispanic patients. Poma (1983) and Quesada (1976) suggested that because of their cultural beliefs Hispanic patients will not ask many questions. However, the literature has failed to address the important issue of whether language of provider affects question-asking behavior in Hispanic patients.

METHOD

Setting and Population

Approximately 87% of Latinos live in urban areas including New York City (Perez-Stable, 1987), where one neighborhood, East Harlem, has a high concentration of Hispanics (45% are Puerto Rican), as noted by Deuschle and Diaz (1981). Because the majority of the Hispanic population in the United States is relatively young, the aged have only recently begun to receive attention (Applewhite, 1989; Becerra & Shaw, 1984; Maldonado, 1985; Torres-Gil, 1986). The elderly constituted 10% of the population of East Harlem in 1980, of which 31% had incomes below the poverty level (Community Service Society of New York, 1987) and 39% lived alone. Mortality and morbidity rates are higher in East Harlem than in other health districts in the city (Fisher & Julius, 1987; Mulvihill & Skovron, 1982); the constraints inherent in an uncoordinated service delivery system translate into barriers for the East Harlem Hispanic elderly (Deuschle & Diaz, 1981).

As in many Hispanic communities, the cultural and linguistic differences between the minority group and the majority group influence health care. Yet among the health care problems encountered in East Harlem is the low availability of Hispanic health care workers and physicians. In Mount Sinai, one of the major hospitals serving East Harlem, only 2% of its physicians and 3% of its nurses are Hispanic (Deuschle & Diaz, 1981) This gap between the number of Hispanic patients and the low availability of Hispanic physicians and other health care workers can lead to cultural and communication barriers that might affect the patient-doctor interaction and the adequate delivery of health care.

Internal Medicine Associates (IMA) was selected as a site to explore issues of health care in Hispanics because a variety of bilingual and English-speaking physicians with different backgrounds provide medical care to a predominantly Hispanic population. IMA is the general medicine clinic for Mount Sinai Hospital. It is staffed by 10 to 15 faculty physicians and approximately 100 residents who provide care for 5,000 to 6,000 patients every year (M. Rexach, personal communication, May 4, 1990). The patient population is approximately 75% female, with 60% to 65% over 50 years of age; it is 65% Hispanic, 40% of which reside in East Harlem and do not have easy access to medical care (M. Rexach, personal communication, May 4, 1990). Most of the population suffer from chronic illnesses such as diabetes, asthma, and heart disease. The goals of the clinic are to provide continuity of care, long-term treatment, and education for these patients.

Subjects

The study population of 51 patients was broken down into two groups: those who interacted with a bilingual physician ($n = 24$) and those who interacted with a monolingual physician ($n = 27$). Of those in the monolingual physician group, 15 interacted in English, 9 interacted with a translator present, and 3 interacted in Spanish. The patients who interacted in Spanish with English-speaking physicians did so mainly with nonverbal cues and one- or two-word descriptions. For example, a patient would point to the right side of his or her abdomen and say *dolor*, which meant right-sided abdominal pain to the physician.

Hispanic patients were selected from appointment lists given to the faculty physicians at each session. Whether a patient was Hispanic or not was decided by the person's name and/or surname and from discussion with the physician who knew the patient. The majority (88%) of the study population was born in Puerto Rico, and 12% were from Colombia, Cuba, Peru, and the Dominican Republic. Mean age was 62 years, 78% were female, and 92% were unemployed, primarily due to retirement. Formal educational level was low, with 12% never attending any type of school and 41% having completed some elementary grades. Of the sample, 78% had some proficiency in English, ranging from fair to poor, and had lived in the United States an average of 36 years. The sample self-reported an average of five visits to the IMA clinic in the past year. There were no major differences in age, educational level, proficiency in English, years in the United States, employment status, number of visits to the clinic in the past year, and the number of information items given between the patients seen by the bilingual physicians and those seen by the monolingual (English-speaking) physicians.

Procedures

The study was divided into two parts. The first part consisted of observing the physician-patient encounter as it occurred. The second part consisted of a direct interview with the patient immediately following the encounter. Of the 54 patients approached to participate in the study, 3 refused after being informed of the study, which resulted in a study sample of 51.

Four bilingual and 5 monolingual faculty physicians participated in the study. The bilingual/monolingual status of each physician was determined by using a self-rating 5-point scale denoting proficiency in Spanish, where 1 = *excellent* and 5 = *poor* (monolingual physicians were classified as 4 or 5).

All 9 physicians were associated with IMA; 56% were male, and 44% were bilingual. The 4 bilingual physicians had excellent self-rated proficiency in Spanish and all were born in Latin American countries. The 5 English-speaking physicians had poor self-rated proficiency in Spanish and all were from the United States, except for 1, who was from Canada.

Data were collected by the two senior authors, with one author doing all the observing before the other author did all the interviewing alone with the patient. This procedure was done to ensure greater reliability and minimize potential bias. The fact that both observer and interviewer completed a systematic data sheet on every encounter made subjective factors less likely to play a major role in the direction of finding the desired results.

During the doctor-patient conference, the observer could not avoid being in full view of the patient due to the characteristics of the locale; however, every effort was made not to compromise the doctor-patient conference in any way.

Before the physician-patient encounter began, the physician was asked to self-rate proficiency in speaking Spanish and to provide country of origin. During the interaction, the observer recorded the number of questions asked by the patient and classified it into the areas of information, opinion, instructions, or miscellaneous. Finally, the observer recorded the content of information given by the physician on the Observational Worksheet and classified it into the areas of diagnosis, laboratory information, treatment, recommendations, or social/personal aspects. Details of each area were also included.

A direct interview was conducted immediately following the doctor-patient encounter and was conducted in Spanish. The Patient Interview Schedule consisted of two parts. The first part was a series of eight questions concerning patient characteristics, number of years in the United States, self-rated proficiency in speaking English, and number of prior visits to the IMA clinic in the past year. The second part consisted of questions related to the areas of diagnosis, laboratory information, treatment, recommendations, and social/personal aspects covered during the interaction.

The information given by the physician during the encounter was compared to the information recalled by the patient following the encounter.

This was done by calculating the ratio of information recalled by the patient and the amount of information given by the physician. For example, if the patient recalled two out of four specific items of information, the recall score was 50%. Perfect recall was scored as 100%. Patients were given credit for answers if they were similar to what the doctor said. No credit was given for information volunteered by the patient that was not given by the physician. Also, no credit was given if only part of an information item was mentioned. Overall scores were obtained for the population as a whole and for the monolingual and bilingual physician groups. Overall scores were also obtained in the five categories of information for the population as a whole and for the monolingual and bilingual physician groups. Patient question-asking behavior was divided into three groups: no questions asked, one question asked, or more than one question asked between the monolingual and bilingual physician groups.

RESULTS

The primary intention of this study was to analyze the differences in patient recall and patient question-asking behavior for the Hispanic patients seen by bilingual physicians in comparison with those seen by monolingual physicians.

Patient Information Recall

The study found that language differences between physician and patient had an effect on patient information recall. The Hispanic patients seen by the bilingual physicians had a higher statistically significant patient information recall than did those seen by the monolingual physicians (72.7% vs. 54.0%) based on t-test analysis ($t = 3.14$, $df = 49$, $p < .05$, two-tailed test).

The content of information recalled by the patient was broken down into five categories consisting of diagnosis, laboratory information, treatment, recommendations, and social/personal aspects to assess in which areas gaps of information recall occurred. Overall, the mean information recall was higher for the patients seen by bilingual physicians in all five categories. The greatest differences occurred in the categories of laboratory information, treatment, and social/personal aspects (see Table 11.1). No major difference was found between the overall mean amount of information given by bilingual physicians compared to monolingual physicians.

Table 11.1 Patient Recall, by Categories of Information Provided by Physician (in percentages)

		Patient Recall	
Information Category	Overall	Bilingual Physician Group	Monolingual Physician Group
Diagnosis	70.3	73.8	64.5
Laboratory	80.1	88.6	73.7
Treatment	43.5	50.2	38.0
Recommendations	82.5	84.1	80.9
Social/personal	59.1	90.0	33.3

Further findings on patient recall were discovered when assessing the monolingual physician subgroups. It was found that when a translator was present, recall was lower (43.1%) than when a translator was not present and both physician and patient spoke in English (58.4% recall) or Spanish (64.3% recall). An additional point is that the proficiency in English was poor among most of the Hispanic patients studied, even those who saw an English-speaking physician. However, recall was higher in the monolingual physician subgroup where the interaction was carried out in English, indicating that the communication difficulty was more serious when using translators. This points to the fact that although language, communication, and culture are certainly interrelated, they can and do operate in quite distinct domains.

We subscribe here to the anthropological notion of culture that stresses the dynamic interplay between the individual and the environment both in a general sense and as more specifically related to the circumstances of daily existence. Culture is not a "thing" but a process that is socially constructed during the course of interaction. The patients who reported better recall when interacting with physicians using the same language clearly subscribe to a view of their own identity and that of the service providers' that suspends, at least for the period of contact, all major markers of difference between the two. Thus culture, rather than a given, is what people communicate about in an appropriate way, and appropriateness depends on the setting.

Patient Question-Asking Behavior

Overall, the number of questions asked per visit ranged from 0 to 4, with a mean of 0.8 questions. Of the questions asked, 41.5% referred to information, 41.5% to opinion, and 17% to miscellaneous issues; none referred to instructions. In this study, 14 of 24 patients seen by bilingual physicians asked one or more questions per visit as compared to 11 of 27 patients seen by monolingual physicians. This was statistically significant based on chi-square analysis ($\chi^2 = 7.63$, $df = 2$, $p < .05$).

DISCUSSION

The recall rate in the bilingual physician group was 72.7% compared to 54% in the monolingual physician group. Studies by Shapiro and Saltzer (1981) and Manson (1988) implicated language discordance in affecting explanation of therapeutic regimens and influencing understanding by the patient. Our study went a step further by assessing the possible effects of language discordance on patient recall. In addition, confounding variables mentioned in the Results section did not contribute to differences in recall between the patients seen by bilingual physicians and those seen by monolingual physicians. This strengthened the argument that the recall difference was due more to language discordance than to other factors. However, other issues relating to communication difficulties should not be excluded from causing differences in recall. Such issues include cultural influences and beliefs from both patient and physician, social factors involved in the interaction, nonverbal communication patterns, and technicality of the language used (Chrisman & Kleinman, 1983; Stoeckle & Waitzkin, 1976).

Overall recall results in the categories of diagnosis, laboratory information, treatment, recommendations, and social/personal issues indicated that those patients seen by bilingual physicians had a higher recall in each category than those seen by monolingual physicians. The largest differences occurred in the categories of treatment and social/personal issues. These results parallel Baxter and Bucci's (1981) study, where Hispanic patients recalled less concerning their therapeutic regimens and also imply that Hispanic patients are more apt to discuss emotionally laden topics with physicians who understand their native tongue. Differences in treatment recall between the two groups can also be explained by the observation that this category had more information items to recall. This was due to a high incidence of multiple illnesses in this elderly sample requiring complex medical treatment regimens.

Another significant result was that Hispanic patients who saw bilingual doctors asked more questions than did those who saw English-speaking doctors. However, it is difficult to interpret the meaning of this finding because all the patients asked few questions regardless of the language spoken by their physicians. There are two ways to interpret this finding from the perspective of culture: One is that patients feel encouraged to present not only provider-validated notions of "disease" but their own experience of "illness" (Kleinman, 1979), thus placing their medical conditions within the economic, social, and political domains that provide the former with meaning. The other interpretation is that the patients might not view it appropriate to ask questions not only because of power differentials with the physicians but because they believe physicians should be voluntarily telling them what is wrong. In a study conducted by the third author on health-seeking behavior among Hispanic elderly in East Harlem, who constitute 40% of the IMA patient population, it was found that physicians are one among alternative providers consulted with the goal of determining what caused the condition (*uno va buscando la causa*). It was expected that physicians will know what is wrong and what to do about it, so in this respect the patient need not ask questions.

Most of the patients seen at the IMA clinic are from a low socioeconomic background, which has also been found in the literature to be associated with decreased patient question-asking behavior (Bochner & Pendleton, 1980). The nature of Hispanic question-asking behavior, regardless of cause, makes it difficult for the physician to decipher the patient's needs or to assess whether the patient has really understood the physician's instructions. These issues can lead to inadequate physician-patient communication and suboptimal patient care.

CONCLUSION

Our study demonstrated that language discordance between physician and patient can have an effect on the interaction of these two parties and its outcome by leading to decreased patient information recall of the encounter and decreased patient question-asking behavior during it. It is important for physicians to be aware of this because less informed patients will feel less satisfied with the encounter and may have decreased compliance. Furthermore, patients who do not recall well the instructions given by the physician will be more likely to make mistakes in following the doctor's treatment which can lead to inadequate patient care. Physicians should also be aware of the importance of establishing an adequate emotional relationship with their patients. As seen in this study, patients were less likely to discuss their personal problems with physicians who did not speak their native language. This factor may imply that patients communicate emotionally better in their own language and that English-speaking physicians should be aware of this when interacting with Hispanic patients to avoid frustrations on both sides.

Although one possible limitation of this study might reside on experimental bias, we believe the results have important implications for the training of practitioners, patient care, and policy guidelines.

Future studies should be designed to ensure experimental blindness in the interviewers and/or the raters. They should also explore the structure of verbal communication between physician and patient. Technicality of physician's language, type of questions asked by physicians, and emotional verbal tones employed by physician and patient are other types of verbal communication that influence the physician-patient encounter and affect its outcome. It would also be interesting to conduct a longitudinal analysis of patients' compliance with their treatment plans.

What are the contributions of this study for Hispanic patients and physicians that deal with them? First, this study emphasized an awareness of how language can have important effects on the physician-patient interaction and showed that miscommunication due to language discordance goes beyond a simple misunderstanding of words. It affects the emotional and cultural components of the interaction and leaves both physician and patient feeling uneasy and questioning whether the interaction achieved its purpose—adequate patient care. Beside leaving readers with the feeling that more bilingual physicians are needed, this study, above all, emphasized that speaking a different language often increases the perception of social distance. Therefore, it is important that all health care workers dealing with patients who speak a different language establish an emotional rapport, a type of "formal friendliness" that will generate respect and understanding between the Hispanic patient and the physician or health care worker.

12

♦

Cultural Differences in Attitudes and Expectancies Between Hispanic and Non-Hispanic White Smokers

GERARDO MARÍN

BARBARA VANOSS MARÍN

ELISEO J. PÉREZ-STABLE

FABIO SABOGAL

REGINA OTERO-SABOGAL

Current approaches (Ajzen & Fishbein, 1980; Petty & Cacioppo, 1986) to social persuasion and behavior change emphasize the need to understand the attitudes and expectancies of a given population prior to developing targeted intervention strategies. The exploration of attitudes and expectancies becomes even more important whenever different ethnic groups are involved, as cultural traditions influence not only behavior patterns but also attitudes and values (Triandis, 1972).

Although cigarette smoking is the single most important preventable cause of death and disability in the United States, little has been done to develop culturally appropriate interventions for ethnic minority groups, and particularly for Hispanics. Nevertheless, there is evidence (e.g., Escobedo & Remington, 1989; Marcus & Crane, 1985; Marín, Pérez-Stable, & Marín, 1989; Remington et al., 1985) that the prevalence of cigarette smoking among Hispanics should be a cause of concern for health officials. For example, data from the 1985 National Health Interview Survey (Centers for Disease Control, 1987a; Shopland & Brown, 1987) show that among men approximately 31% of Hispanics and 32% of non-Hispanic Whites smoked cigarettes. The corresponding figures for women were 21% among Hispanics and 28% among non-Hispanic Whites. These regional and national studies with adults as well as those conducted with adolescents (e.g., Greenberg, Wiggins, Kutvirt, & Samet, 1987) have shown that differences exist between Hispanics and non-Hispanic Whites not only in terms of current smoking prevalence but also in the mean number of cigarettes smoked per day (Humble, Samet, Pathak, & Skipper, 1987; Marín, Pérez-Stable, Marín, Sabogal, & Otero-Sabogal, 1990).

Given the differences in cultural characteristics (e.g., Marín & Triandis, 1985; Triandis, Marín, Lisansky, & Betancourt, 1984) that have been identified between Hispanics and non-Hispanic Whites, we hypothesized that there are significant differences in the attitudes and expectancies related to cigarette smoking held by smokers of these two ethnic groups. These differences, when identified, should become the basis for developing culturally appropriate smoking cessation interventions. In fact, our research has shown, for example, that Hispanic smokers differ from non-Hispanic White smokers in the stereotypes they hold of people who smoke cigarettes (Marín, Pérez-Stable, Otero-Sabogal, Sabogal, & Marín, 1989).

The presence of ethnic-specific differences among smokers is a tenable hypothesis given that differences in knowledge and behaviors toward other cardiovascular risk factors (Hazuda, Stern, Gaskill, Haffner, & Gardner, 1983) and cancer prevention (Coreil, 1984) have been previously found between Hispanics and non-Hispanic Whites. This study sought to identify those cultural differences that may exist in the attitudes and expectancies of Hispanic and non-Hispanic White smokers. These differences could then be used to aid in the development of culturally appropriate smoking prevention and cessation programs for Hispanics.

METHOD

Subjects

Respondents were 263 Hispanics and 150 non-Hispanic Whites who were currently smoking cigarettes and residing in the metropolitan area of San Francisco, California. The participants were recruited solely for this study through street posters and public service announcements on the radio and through face-to-face contact in waiting rooms in hospital-based and community clinics and from churches, schools, colleges, and community organizations from the counties of San Francisco, Alameda, and San Mateo. Efforts were made to recruit equal numbers of non-Hispanic Whites, English-speaking Hispanics, and Spanish-speaking Hispanics from each of the types of sites and from each of the counties. Each respondent was paid $10 for participation in the interview, which took approximately 60 minutes. The study was presented to the respondents as a survey of health practices and attitudes and anonymity was guaranteed.

Table 12.1 shows the demographic characteristics and smoking behavior of the Hispanic and non-Hispanic White respondents. Both samples were fairly similar in terms of their mean age, income, and level of education.

Of the total Hispanic sample, 71% were foreign-born and 55% preferred to answer the questionnaire in Spanish. In terms of ancestry, 39% were of Mexican origin, 34% belonged to families that came from a Central American country, 8% were of South American background, and 4% came from Puerto Rico; the rest (15%) did not specify a country of family origin.

Instruments

The interview schedule was derived following Triandis's (1972) suggestions for studies of the subjective culture of a given ethnic group. First, intensive, open-ended interviews of approximately 60 minutes were conducted with Hispanic and non-Hispanic White smokers, former smokers, and nonsmokers of both genders (15 in each group). Items dealt with the values, attitudes, norms, and expectancies of smokers. Responses were then content analyzed and were used to develop the closed-ended stems and response categories contained in the structured interview schedule.

Most items in the structured interview were Likert-type with either 4- or 5-point response categories where the highest point indicated agreement with or acceptance of the statement. Standard sociodemographic

Table 12.1 Demographic Characteristics and Smoking Behavior of Samples

	Hispanics (N = 263)	Non-Hispanic Whites (N = 150)
Percentage male	58	50
Age (years)		
Mean (*SD*)	31.9 (11.2)	34.7 (13.7)
Range	17-70	16-75
Level of education (years)		
Mean (*SD*)	13.3 (3.9)	13.9 (2.8)
Range	0-20	3-20
Income level		
Mean	$300-$400	$300-$400
Range	$100-$1,000	$100-$1,000
Time living in U.S. (years)		
Mean (*SD*)	15.0 (15.0)	N/A
Range	< 1-58	
Percentage foreign born	71	N/A
Number of cigarettes/day		
Mean (*SD*)	12.0 (11.7)	21.5 (13.1)
Range	1-80	1-65
Age started smoking (years)		
Mean (*SD*)	16.8 (4.6)	16.8 (4.2)
Range	7-51	8-44
Number of years smoking		
Mean (*SD*)	12.8 (10.5)	16.8 (12.7)
Range	1-53	1-54
Percentage smoking filter cigarettes	95	91

NOTE: Numbers in parentheses denote standard deviations.

items and a number of questions dealing with smoking behavior were also included. A valid and reliable short scale (Marín, Sabogal, Marín, Otero-Sabogal, & Pérez-Stable, 1987) to measure level of acculturation was applied to Hispanic respondents. This scale measures the amount of cultural learning (primarily in terms of language use and preference) that has taken place in Hispanics due to their contact with non-Hispanics in the United States. Analyses with this acculturation scale have shown that it is appropriate for the Hispanic subgroups studied here. Individuals who scored between 1 and 2.99 on the acculturation scale were considered to be low in acculturation to the U.S. culture while those with higher scores (between 3 and 5) were considered to be highly acculturated (36%).

Items were developed in either English or Spanish and were then decentered (Werner & Campbell, 1970) and translated into the other language through the double-translation procedure (Brislin, Lonner, & Thorndike, 1973) with the help of two translators.

RESULTS

In evaluating the sociopsychological constructs related to cigarette smoking we used separate (by ethnicity) factor analyses to identify common structures across both ethnic groups. When we found factor structures among Hispanics that differed from those found among non-Hispanic Whites, comparisons between the two ethnic groups were made only on the common factor scales, as is recommended in cross-cultural research (Brislin et al., 1973). Furthermore, initial analyses contrasted the responses given by Mexican American and Central American subjects since they constituted the two largest Hispanic subgroups in the sample. Because no statistically significant differences were identified, the responses of all Hispanic respondents are considered as a group independent of ancestry.

Smoking Behavior

As shown in Table 12.1, non-Hispanic Whites reported smoking more cigarettes ($M = 21.5$) per day than Hispanics ($M = 12.0$), $F(1, 403) = 61.75$, $p < .001$. Among the Hispanic respondents, 52% ($n = 136$) reported smoking fewer than 10 cigarettes per day ("light smokers"), 24% ($n = 64$) reported smoking between 10 and 19 cigarettes per day ("moderate smokers"), and 24% ($n = 63$) reported smoking 20 or more cigarettes per day ("heavy smokers"). The smoking patterns for the non-Hispanic Whites were different: 16% were light smokers, 24% were moderate smokers, and 60% were heavy smokers.

Generalized Attitudes Toward Smoking and Quitting

Respondents were asked to rate on separate 4-point scales how pleasant, satisfying, and enjoyable it would be for them to continue smoking in the 30 days following the interview. The results suggested that smoking implies greater pleasure among non-Hispanic Whites than among Hispanics, particularly in terms of being enjoyable ($M = 3.2$ for non-Hispanics vs. $M = 2.9$ for Hispanics), $F(1, 404) = 9.00$, $p < .01$, and pleasant ($M = 3.0$ for non-Hispanics vs. $M = 2.6$ for Hispanics), $F(1, 407) = 9.09$, $p < .01$.

Hispanic females ($M = 3.1$) reported enjoying continued smoking to a greater extent than Hispanic males ($M = 2.8$), $F(1, 258) = 6.48$, $p < .01$, but no other differences in attitudes were found in terms of gender. The type of smoker (i.e., light, moderate, or heavy) also failed to produce statistically significant differences in the respondents' attitudes toward smoking within each ethnic group. The level of acculturation of the Hispanic respondents had no significant effect on their generalized attitudes toward smoking within the 30 days following the interview.

Perceived Situational Antecedents of Smoking

Respondents were given a list of places and situations that may lead an individual to smoke cigarettes. Table 12.2 presents those situational antecedents that were perceived to be very likely to lead to smoking (a mean of 2.5 or higher on a 5-point scale) as well as those cases where there were statistically significant differences between Hispanics and non-Hispanic Whites.

There are a number of events (e.g., being at a party or in the company of other smokers) and psychological or emotional conditions (e.g., when nervous or worried) that are perceived by both ethnic groups as likely antecedents of smoking. Significantly, there were a number of antecedents that Hispanics rated as less likely to move them to smoke in comparison to the ratings made by non-Hispanics. Most of these situational antecedents seem to be related to habitual behaviors (e.g., while driving a car) and to some negative emotional states (e.g., when bored).

Principal components factor analyses with varimax rotations (15 iterations) of the responses to the 27 antecedents showed four common (across ethnic groups) factors with eigenvalues greater than 1.0. The first factor was labeled *Home Relaxation* and included items related to smoking at home, before falling asleep, or while watching television or reading a book. The second factor was labeled *With Meals* and included items about smoking while drinking coffee or at a restaurant. The third factor, *Emotional Smoking,* was made up of items dealing with smoking while feeling worried, nervous, or angry. The fourth factor was named *Social Smoking* and included items referring to smoking while at a party or in the company of friends.

Table 12.2 Antecedents of Smoking Perceived as Most Likely

Antecedent	Hispanics	Non-Hispanic Whites
At a party	4.3	4.2
Drinking alcoholic beverages	4.1	4.3
With other smokers	4.1	4.3
When nervous/tense	4.0	4.2
When worried	4.0	4.0
With friends	3.9	3.9
At a bar	3.9	4.4 **
After meals	3.7	4.2 **
Waiting for someone	3.5	3.7 *
When angry	3.4	3.8 *
When bored	3.4	3.7 *
When feeling happy	3.3	3.4
At a restaurant	3.3	3.6
Inside their home	3.1	3.8 **
While drinking coffee	3.0	3.9 **
Watching television	3.0	3.4 **
Before going to bed	2.9	3.3 *
Driving a car	2.9	3.3 **
On phone	2.5	3.3 **

NOTE: Ordered by importance for Hispanics. (When answering a question "How often do you smoke when . . . " 1 = never; 2 = almost never; 3 = sometimes; 4 = almost always; 5 = always.)
*$p < .01$; **$p < .001$.

A comparison of the means of these four factors across ethnic groups showed that Hispanics considered their smoking as less frequently motivated by events related to the Home Relaxation factor ($M = 2.87$), $F(1, 322) = 14.38, p < .001$, and to the With Meals factor ($M = 3.23$), $F(1, 322) = 19.57, p < .001$, than the non-Hispanic Whites ($M = 3.26$ and 3.81, respectively). However, both ethnic groups considered the factors Emotional Smoking (means of 3.79 for Hispanics and 4.00 for non-Hispanics) and Social Smoking (means of 4.09 for Hispanics and 4.07 for non-Hispanics) as equally likely to promote smoking.

Neither the gender nor the acculturation level of the Hispanic respondents affected their ratings of the likelihood of smoking under the conditions depicted by the four factor scales. But as could be expected, heavy smokers felt that they would be more likely to smoke under more circumstances than light or moderate smokers (Table 12.3). Heavy Hispanic smokers felt that they would be more likely to smoke than the lighter Hispanic smokers when faced with the events making up each of the four factors: Home Relaxation, $F(2, 241) = 37.0$, $p < .001$; With Meals, $F(2, 228) = 3.69$, $p < .001$; Emotional Smoking, $F(2, 259) = 16.84$, $p < .001$; and Social Smoking, $F(2, 254) = 15.0$, $p < .001$.

Perceived Consequences of Smoking

A number of possible consequences or results of continued smoking were presented to respondents, and they were asked to estimate their likelihood on a 4-point Likert-type scale. Both ethnic groups (see Table 12.4) felt that there were two likely consequences related to continued smoking: harming one's own health and having bad breath. In addition, Hispanics were more certain than non-Hispanic Whites that smoking harmed the health of one's own children, $F(1, 239) = 15.9$, $p < .001$. Non-Hispanics, however felt more strongly that continued smoking would make the respondent feel controlled by a habit, $F(1, 409) = 19.9$, $p < .001$, and that smoking would result in having holes in one's clothes, $F(1, 411) = 12.8$, $p < .001$.

Separate principal components factor analyses with varimax rotation (15 iterations) were conducted for the data from both ethnic groups. Three common factors with eigenvalues greater than 1.0 were identified. The first factor was named *Damaged Health/Appearance* and included items dealing with smoking harming one's health or producing bad breath, wrinkles, and bad-smelling clothes. The second factor, *Social Presentation*, was made up of two items dealing with being more popular and feeling more attractive or elegant. The third factor was labeled Damaged Clothes because its one item dealt with burning holes in one's clothes when smoking. There were no statistically significant differences in the answers to the three factor scales between Hispanics and non-Hispanic Whites except for the one-item Damaged Clothes factor and where differences have already been identified (Table 12.4).

The gender of the respondents was unrelated to these ratings within both ethnic groups. Analyses by the number of cigarettes smoked within each ethnic group produced only two statistically significant differences: Heavier Hispanic smokers perceived Damaged Clothes as more likely ($M = 1.6$) than lighter smokers ($M = 1.3$), $F(2, 265) = 7.81$, $p < .01$, and heavy non-Hispanic smokers perceived Damaged Health/Appearance as more likely ($M = 2.9$) than lighter non-Hispanic smokers ($M = 2.5$), $F(2, 145) = 4.73$, $p < .01$.

Table 12.3 Mean Perceived Significance of Smoking Antecedents, by Smoker Type

Antecedent	Hispanics			Non-Hispanic Whites		
	Light Smokers	Moderate Smokers	Heavy Smokers	Light Smokers	Moderate Smokers	Heavy Smokers
Home relaxation	2.5	2.9	3.7*	2.2	3.0	3.6*
Meals	2.8	3.2	4.2*	2.8	3.6*	4.1*
Emotional smoking	3.5	3.8	4.3*	3.2	4.0	4.2*
Social smoking	3.9	4.1	4.6*	3.6	4.1	4.2*

*All scales statistically significant at $p < .001$ within each ethnic group.

Hispanics with low levels of acculturation ($M = 3.1$) felt more certain that the items included in the Damaged Health/Appearance factor would occur if they continued smoking than did the highly acculturated ($M = 2.7$), $F(1, 249) = 12.4$, $p < .001$. The acculturation level of the respondents did not affect their responses to the other two dimensions.

Perceived Consequences of Quitting

Respondents were asked to rate on a 4-point Likert-type scale the likelihood of 12 consequences that could be expected if they quit smoking within the 30 days following the interview. As noted in Table 12.5, giving a better example to one's children was perceived as the most likely consequence of quitting smoking by Hispanics and non-Hispanic Whites alike. Hispanics felt more certain than non-Hispanics that quitting smoking would be associated with having a better taste in one's mouth, $F(1, 404) = 11.45$, $p < .001$, improved family relations, $F(1, 249) = 17.25$, $p < .001$, and providing a better example for their children, $F(1, 231) = 12.3$, $p < .001$. Non-Hispanic Whites reported being more certain than Hispanics that quitting smoking would make them feel that they accomplished something difficult, $F(1, 411) = 18.9$, $p < .001$, make them feel more nervous, $F(1, 409) = 30.3$, $p < .001$, and make it difficult for them to concentrate, $F(1, 410) = 13.9$, $p < .001$.

Separate principal components factor analyses with varimax rotation (15 iterations) were also conducted. Two common factors were identified. One factor, *Withdrawal Symptoms,* was made up of four items dealing with the likelihood that quitting smoking would result in more headaches, feeling dizzy, becoming more nervous, and having difficulty con-

Table 12.4 Perceived Likelihood of Consequences of Smoking

Consequence	Hispanics	Non-Hispanic Whites
Harm your own health	3.4	3.3
Have bad breath	3.2	3.0
Harm health of others	2.7	2.5
Clothing smell bad	2.8	2.9
Harm health of your children	2.7	2.0 *
Get more wrinkles	2.5	2.2
Feel controlled by habit	2.5	3.0 *
Better control your nerves	2.3	2.3
Your family criticizes you	2.2	1.9
Feel more attractive	1.7	1.7
Be more popular with friends	1.7	1.7
Burn holes in clothes	1.4	1.8 *

NOTE: Answers on a 4-point scale (1 = no; 2 = probably no; 3 = probably yes; 4 = yes) to the question "If you continue smoking in the next 30 days, will you...."
*$p < .001$.

centrating. The second factor was named *Gains From Quitting* and included four items dealing with breathing more easily, having a better taste in one's mouth, being a better example for children, and feeling that something difficult was accomplished. Non-Hispanic Whites were more certain ($M = 2.2$) than Hispanics ($M = 1.9$) that quitting smoking could bring Withdrawal Symptoms, $F(1, 403) = 17.6$, $p < .001$, but there were no ethnic differences on the Gains From Quitting factor. Likewise, gender or the acculturation level of the Hispanic respondents did not influence the way the items making up the two factorially derived dimensions were rated.

The number of cigarettes smoked did, however, produce some important differences. Among Hispanics, heavy smokers ($M = 2.2$) were more likely to perceive Withdrawal Symptoms, $F(2, 257) = 8.59$, $p < .001$, and Gains From Quitting ($M = 3.6$), $F(2, 159) = 4.53$, $p < .01$, as probable than lighter smokers ($M = 1.7$ and 3.3, respectively). Similarly, non-Hispanic White heavy smokers were also more likely ($M = 2.3$) to expect Withdrawal Symptoms as a consequence of quitting smoking in the 30 days following the interview, $F(2, 142) = 7.80$, $p < .001$, than lighter smokers ($M = 1.8$). There were no differences in the perceptions of the likelihood of the items included in the Gains From Quitting factor for the non-Hispanic respondents.

Table 12.5 Perceived Likelihood of Consequences of Quitting

Consequence	Hispanic	Non-Hispanic Whites
Provide a better example for your children	3.8	3.5*
Have better taste in mouth	3.5	3.2*
Become more physically healthy	3.4	3.5
Spend less money	3.4	3.4
Feel you accomplished something difficult	3.3	3.7*
Breathe more easily	3.3	3.2*
Improve relationships with family	2.8	2.2*
Gain weight	2.5	2.8
Become more nervous	2.2	3.0*
Have difficulty in concentrating	1.9	2.3*
Get more headaches	1.7	1.9
Feel dizzy	1.6	1.8

NOTE: Answers on a 4-point scale (1 = no; 2 = probably no; 3 = probably yes; 4 = yes) to the question "If you stop smoking in the next 30 days, will you. . . . "
*$p < .001$.

DISCUSSION

Our study identified some important cultural differences between Hispanic and non-Hispanic White smokers. Differences were found in the antecedents of smoking (e.g., the lower significance ascribed to smoking as relaxation or habit among Hispanics), the consequences of smoking (e.g., Hispanics' concern for harming the health of their children), the consequences of quitting (e.g., the Hispanic expectancy of providing a better example for their children by quitting), and in the generalized attitudes toward smoking. Hispanic smokers were more positive about quitting, perceived stronger reasons to do it, and were less concerned about the negative physical consequences than non-Hispanic Whites.

By the same token, similarities across ethnic groups were found in all of the measured constructs. Hispanic and non-Hispanic White smokers, for example, agreed on the fact that social situations and emotional states act as important antecedents of smoking. Likewise, smokers from both ethnic groups agreed that cigarette smoking harmed their health and produced bad breath and that by quitting they would be providing a good example for their children. In addition, both groups of smokers felt that cigarette smoking did not enhance their social presentation.

Although our data show that Hispanic and non-Hispanic White smokers share a number of expectations regarding their habit, the identification of ethnic differences in attitudes and expectancies of smokers is essential for the development of culturally appropriate smoking cessation programs. By taking into consideration these culture-specific characteristics of the members of an ethnic group, either because they are unique to the group or because they are perceived as particularly important by the members of the group, the interventions can properly address the concerns of the targeted individuals. Based on our findings, a cessation intervention targeting Hispanic smokers should emphasize techniques that deal with smoking in social situations and when under emotional stress because these were perceived as particularly important. Likewise, our data suggest that being a good example for children by quitting would be an important motivator for Hispanic smokers. An additional significant motivator that should be emphasized in a targeted intervention for Hispanics is the fact that by smoking cigarettes a smoker is damaging the health of children. While some of these expectations are also shared by non-Hispanic Whites, a targeted intervention must concentrate on those expectations that differentiate Hispanics from non-Hispanics as well as on those attitudes and perceptions that are particularly important for Hispanics.

Our results were also consistent in showing that Hispanics seem to give special significance to smoking as a social phenomenon carried out among friends. Despite their light smoking behavior, Hispanics were as likely as non-Hispanic Whites to report smoking for social and emotional reasons. Antismoking interventions with Hispanics will need to address these normative considerations and reduce the social acceptability of smoking in order to be maximally effective.

The lack of important gender differences in the various measures indicates that these attitudes and expectancies may only be moderated to a minimal extent by gender differences in socialization. Although most studies (e.g., Marcus & Crane, 1985; Marín, Pérez-Stable, & Marín, 1989) show that a substantially greater proportion of Hispanic men smoke compared to women, the attitudes and norms among smokers, at least as measured in this study, seem to be fairly similar. This finding would imply that similar prevention and cessation interventions can be designed for both genders, at least in terms of the psychosocial constructs studied here.

The number of cigarettes smoked per day was an important modifier of the attitudes and expectancies held by the two ethnic groups. The heavier smoker tended to respond to all of the measures in a way indicating higher frequency of smoking cigarettes in response to a larger number of antecedents, expecting more of the various consequences of smoking, and perceiving the negative consequences of quitting as more likely than those who smoked less. These results are probably explained by the greater level of addiction to nicotine that would be expected of heavier smokers. The need to target heavy smokers with strategies that are different from those directed at lighter smokers is reinforced by these data. It is expected that while culturally appropriate low-contact interventions (e.g., self-help manuals, media-based clinics) that incorporate the findings reported here would be useful with Hispanic light smokers, heavier smokers will need more intensive interventions (e.g., cessation clinics or one-to-one consultations) that provide behavioral techniques to change the stronger culture-specific expectations that may be held by them.

The role of acculturation in the responses of the Hispanic smokers is also of interest here. In some antecedents and consequences, the more highly acculturated provided responses that were not only different from those of the less acculturated but that were similar to the ones reported by non-Hispanic Whites. These findings support the hypothesis that as part of the cultural learning implied in acculturation, Hispanics change their smoking behaviors (e.g., more acculturated Hispanics smoke more cigarettes per day; Marín, Pérez-Stable, & Marín, 1989). In addition, acculturation affects smoking-related attitudes so that, for example, the more acculturated Hispanics have stereotypes of smokers that resemble those of the non-Hispanic Whites (Marín, Marín, Otero-Sabogal, Sabogal, & Pérez-Stable, 1989; Marín, Pérez-Stable, Otero-Sabogal, Sabogal, & Marín, 1989).

This study, although an initial and somewhat limited effort, shows that culture or ethnicity does indeed modify the attitudes and expectancies of individuals regarding cigarette smoking. The results also imply that smoking prevention and cessation interventions with Hispanics need to consider these differences in order to be more effective and culturally appropriate. Larger and more complex and more representative studies should be able to identify additional differences between Hispanics and non-Hispanic Whites in a clearer way and in turn help achieve the national public health goals of reducing the proportion of smokers. In the meantime, we have developed a self-help manual (*Guía para Dejar de Fumar*, NIH Publication No. 88-3001)[1] that incorporates the findings mentioned here. Preliminary evaluations of this self-help manual show that it is well received by Hispanic smokers and that it is effective in motivating and teaching Hispanic smokers to quit.

The observed group-specific differences and the conclusions that can be drawn from our study must be considered in the context of its limitations. First, we used a volunteer, convenient sample that is not representative of a broader population. Thus, even though the demographic characteristics of our sample do not differ substantially from those of San Francisco's Hispanics, the generalizability of the study is limited. Second, our conclusions may not be generalizable to Puerto Ricans and Cubans who may differ from Mexican American and Central American Hispanics in their smoking behavior. Future studies with other Hispanic subgroups using a similar methodology are needed. Third, we did not validate any of the respondents' reported attitudes and expectancies with actual observations of behavior. This, of course, is a limitation inherent in most social science research of this type.

NOTE

1. Free copies can be obtained by calling 1-800-4-CANCER.

13

♦

Communicating the HIV / AIDS Risk to Hispanic Populations

A Review and Integration

GUSTAVO A. YEP

In Latinos and AIDS: A National Strategy Symposium, Hahn and Castro (1989) succinctly summarized the devastating effects of the HIV/AIDS epidemic on Hispanics:[1] AIDS has disproportionately affected Latino communities in this country. Statistics from the Centers for Disease Control (1991) validate such an assertion: As of June 30, 1991, 29,586 of the 182,834 documented cases of AIDS reported in the United States were Hispanics. In other words, approximately 16% of the reported AIDS cases are Hispanic even though they only represent about 8% of the population (U.S. Bureau of the Census, 1984) or, more simply stated, Hispanics are twice as likely to be affected by HIV than the general population. Such disproportion would be even more extreme if gay and bisexual men with AIDS were excluded: The AIDS case incidence ratio of Hispanics to non-Hispanic Whites is 9.3 to 1 (Centers for Disease

Control, 1987b). For example, Hispanic women are approximately 9 times more likely than non-Hispanic White women to contract HIV (Mays, Cochran, & Roberts, 1988). Marín (1989) described the severity of the HIV/AIDS problem among Hispanics: "The statistics imply an urgent need for massive prevention campaigns in order to lower infection rates in this group, which is already markedly underserved by health services" (p. 412).

The spread of HIV in Hispanic populations has been reported to occur through both documented modes of transmission: exchange of bodily fluids through unprotected sexual intercourse and needle sharing (Hahn & Castro, 1989). Because transmission of the virus can be controlled by specific changes in behavior, prevention has become the key (Albee, 1989; Becker & Joseph, 1988). Primary prevention involves proactive actions to reduce or eliminate the transmission of HIV in unaffected populations through risk reduction in high-risk groups (Albee, 1989). Former Surgeon General C. Everett Koop (1987) also noted that everyone can reduce their risk of exposure to HIV by adopting simple and effective preventive measures.

Unfortunately, HIV/AIDS prevention campaigns have encountered difficulties with cultural appropriateness in relation to their target population. In *Primary Prevention of AIDS: Psychological Approaches,* Mays (1989) describes an example of how cultural insensitivity actually damaged future HIV/AIDS prevention efforts:

> An outreach project of a predominately White gay male organization targeted to the Hispanic community openly advocated condom use as a prevention strategy for HIV infection for Hispanics. This led to a confrontation with the Catholic church. As a result of the confrontation that occurred, the church issued an official statement against the use of condoms. While AIDS education had previously been conducted through church groups and on church property used by community groups, after the public statement neither the parish priests nor the church members were willing to violate openly the recommendations issued by the church. Hispanics AIDS educators felt they lost a great deal of ground with individual churches after this cultural blunder. (pp. 272-273)

To avoid such cultural misunderstandings, HIV/AIDS education and prevention programs need to take into account cultural perceptions of the target audience (B. Marín & Marín, 1990a; Peterson & Marín, 1988). In terms of HIV prevention for Hispanics, B. Marín and Marín (1990a) observed the urgent need to develop culturally appropriate programs.

In her review of contemporary theories and models of persuasion, Reardon (1991) identified several theoretical formulations including Bandura's (1977) social learning theory, Petty and Cacioppo's (1981) elaboration likelihood model, and McGuire's (1989) communication/persuasion model. Although social learning theory demonstrates how patterns of behavior are acquired through internal and external sources of influence (Bandura, 1977) and the elaboration likelihood model shows why certain components of a persuasive message are more influential in producing behavioral changes (Petty & Cacioppo, 1981), McGuire's (1989) communication/persuasion model presents the most comprehensive description of the relevant variables affecting the outcome of a persuasive communication situation. Specifically, McGuire's model demonstrates how source, message, channel, receiver, and destination factors come together to create persuasive effects.

Using McGuire's comprehensive model as a framework, this chapter reviews and synthesizes past research on communication factors affecting HIV/AIDS prevention among Hispanics so that culturally appropriate messages may be designed for this population. This study has two main objectives: (a) to review research on input variables related to HIV/AIDS preventive behaviors in Hispanic populations, in particular, analyzing past empirical research investigating source, message, channel, and receiver factors associated with HIV prevention, and (b) to address the implications of the findings on output variables, including design, implementation, and evaluation of culturally appropriate HIV/AIDS prevention programs for Hispanic populations.

MCGUIRE'S COMMUNICATION/PERSUASION MODEL

McGuire (1989) presented a communication and persuasion matrix for the analysis and design of public communication campaigns. This matrix consists of two sets of variables: input (communication) variables and output variables. Input variables are the basic components that are used to construct persuasive communication. In other words, they formulate the communication process in terms of who says what, to whom, through what medium, and directed at what kind of target audience. Specifically, they focus on source (e.g., credibility, attractiveness), message (e.g., type of appeal, type of information), channel (e.g., modality, directness), receiver (e.g., lifestyle and skills of target audience), and destination factors (e.g., immediate/long-term change, prevention/

cessation of behavior). Output variables refer to the various outcomes of the persuasive process. They range from exposure to the message to comprehension, acceptance, behavioral change, and subsequent behavioral reinforcement and maintenance.

This chapter review past research on HIV/AIDS prevention with Hispanic populations in terms of (a) source, (b) message, (c) channel, and (d) receiver factors. Furthermore, it addresses the implications of the findings on the design, implementation, and evaluation of HIV/AIDS prevention campaigns for Hispanics. Finally, it discusses directions for future research.

Source Factors

In the communication/persuasion model, source factors pertain to features and characteristics of the perceived communicator (i.e., the persuader) to whom the message is attributed. This category includes to whom urban Hispanic youths talk about HIV/AIDS and condoms (Ford & Norris, 1991) and sources of information about AIDS among Hispanic adolescents and adults (G. Marín & Marín, 1990).

Interviewing a community group of 30 Hispanic males and females in Detroit, Ford and Norris (1991) asked their respondents two basic questions: "Who do you talk with about AIDS?" and "What do they say?" To the first research question, most respondents (87%) replied that they do talk to someone about HIV/AIDS. Friends, siblings, and classmates were the most preferred (50%) sources of communication, followed by parents, teachers, and counselors. In terms of the content of their communication, the second research question, most respondents received messages of concern about their vulnerability to HIV/AIDS (58%), followed by messages containing factual information about AIDS and advice about the selection of safe-sex partners. The findings from the study seem to indicate that Hispanic youths prefer to talk to peers— friends, siblings, classmates—about HIV/AIDS to address their feelings of concern and worry about contracting the deadly virus.

Investigating a random sample of 460 Hispanics residing in the San Francisco Bay Area, G. Marín and Marín (1990) interviewed their respondents over the telephone regarding the credibility of 16 possible sources of information about AIDS: 4 from the entertainment world (a television or movie actor, a popular recording artist, a well-known sports personality, and a popular radio announcer), 3 from the United States government (a politician, the surgeon general, and a government official), 4 from well-recognized professions (a teacher, a priest, a well-recognized union leader, and a medical doctor), 2 from the community dealing with the epidemic (a counselor at a clinic and a person with AIDS), and 3 from the respondent's interpersonal network (a friend, a relative, and the spouse or significant other). The majority of the respondents rated sources directly involved in the epidemic as the most credible: a medical doctor (96%), a clinic counselor (94%), and a person with AIDS (92%). The surgeon general and a teacher presenting a message about AIDS were also perceived to be highly credible, and a politician talking about AIDS was viewed as the least credible source of HIV information.

Message Factors

Message factors in the persuasive communication model include linguistic styles, organization of arguments and ideas, types of appeals, and length and relevance of message. In the present review, the studies focused on a variety of message characteristics including analysis of the difficulties involved in the direct translation of HIV/AIDS preventive messages from English to Spanish (Marín, Marín, & Juarez, 1988; Pino, 1989), the degree of comprehension of HIV prevention terminology (Marín et al., 1988) and readability of condom instructions (Richwald, Schneider-Munoz, & Valdez, 1989), the recognition of Hispanic cultural values (Marín, 1989; Marín et al., 1988), and the teaching of cognitive-behavioral skills in HIV prevention messages (Schinke, Botvin, Orlandi, Schilling, & Gordon, 1990).

Based on their past experiences, Marín et al. (1988) cautioned against the direct translation of HIV prevention materials originally written in English for several reasons: (a) They often tend to be difficult to understand, (b) they are sometimes insulting, and (c) they can confuse and mislead readers. In order to develop effective preventive messages for Hispanics, Marín et al. (1988) proposed the use of carefully stated educational objectives in Spanish and the pretesting of all messages before they are widely disseminated to detect difficulties with reception, comprehension, and clarity. The recommendations from the National Strategy Symposium for Latinos and AIDS concurred with this position. Summarizing the sentiments and advice of her colleagues, Pino (1989) recommended the use and adaptation of HIV prevention materials and models that are spiritually, culturally, and socially relevant to Latinos. In short, there is a need to create and develop appropriate culture-specific messages in HIV prevention efforts.

In their recommendations for enhancing the cultural appropriateness of HIV/AIDS prevention messages for Hispanics, Marín et al. (1988) pointed out the existence of HIV-related terminology that has created considerable confusion among Hispanic readers. Based on their research on such readers, they concluded that (a) the term *infecciones* (the Spanish word for infections) should be replaced by *enfermedades* (diseases) because *infecciones* exclusively refers to an infected wound rather than other potential diseases; (b) the phrase *vida sexual activa* (an active sexual life) should be substituted by *relaciones sexuales* (sexual relations) because *vida sexual activa* connotes prostitution and daily sex; (c) the phrase *estar infectado* (to be infected) should be replaced by *es portador(a) del virus* (to be a carrier of the virus) to avoid confusion between HIV infection and having AIDS; and (d) the term *farmaceuticos* (pharmaceuticals) should be changed to *medicinas* (medicines) because the former tends to be confused with the term pharmacist in Spanish. Finally, Marín et al. (1988) noted that the Spanish terms for vaginal, anal, and oral intercourse carry a high degree of social undesirability.

Because use of condoms has assumed a critical role in HIV prevention, Richwald et al. (1989) examined the degree of readability of condom instructions in Spanish. For the study, 25 brands of condoms were selected. Fifty-two percent of the condom manufacturers included instructions in Spanish and seven different Spanish texts were identified from this group. Readability tests were performed and the findings indicated that such texts pose difficulties in comprehension for any person whose reading skill level was below the ninth grade. Because a significant number of Hispanics are not literate in English or Spanish, the research findings suggest that written materials provided with condoms are not effectively promoting HIV prevention among some Hispanics. To increase the efficacy of written instructions in Spanish, the authors recommended the use of (a) standard Spanish vocabulary, (b) short and simple communication messages, (c) factual and straightforward information, and (d) graphic and pictorial instructions to enhance comprehension and recall.

To develop effective HIV/AIDS prevention strategies for Hispanics, basic core cultural values must be taken into account. Marín and Marín (1991) identified several basic Hispanic cultural values: allocentrism, *simpatia,* familialism, *respeto,* and machismo. Allocentrism, or collectivism, is a cultural trait associated with the preference for interpersonal relationships in ingroups that are nurturing, empathetic, loving, intimate, respectful, and willing to sacrifice for the welfare of the group.

Simpatia is a Hispanic cultural script that emphasizes the need for promoting and maintaining harmonious and pleasant interpersonal relationships. Familialism is a key Hispanic cultural value that stresses the importance of the family in the individual's life including strong feelings of identification, attachment, dependence, loyalty, reciprocity, and solidarity among members of the family unit. *Respeto,* a construct from high-power, high-distance cultures, accentuates the importance of deference or respect for individuals who occupy roles of higher prestige, recognition, and power in society. Machismo, a Hispanic gender role behavior, alludes to the assumed cultural expectation for men to be dominant in social relationships. Marín (1989) endorsed the incorporation of such core cultural values into HIV/AIDS prevention message strategies for Hispanic populations.

In their discussion of strategies for preventing HIV infection among Hispanic adolescents in New York City, Schinke et al. (1990) proposed intervention messages based on social learning theory. Their prevention curriculum was composed of messages combining elements of cognitive-behavioral skills for problem solving, coping, and interpersonal communication with emphasis on ethnic pride and HIV facts. The first element of the prevention curriculum is problem solving. It is a skills-intervention program consisting of five steps: stop, options, decide, act, and self-praise. Stop, the first step, teaches adolescents to pause when confronted with a problem associated with HIV infection risk, define the nature of the problem, and clarify their role in solving it. Options, the second step, instructs adolescents to consider alternative solutions to the identified problem by using brainstorming techniques. Decide, the third step, trains adolescents to systematically select the best possible solution based on costs, benefits, and feasibility. Act, the fourth step, coaches youngsters to plan and rehearse their solution that culminates with the verbalization of their response to the situation in the form of a message strategy. Self-praise, the final step, conditions adolescents to reward themselves for their efforts in problem solving in high-risk situations. The second component of the program developed by Schinke et al. (1990) is coping. This element of the intervention assists adolescents in the acquisition of skills for coping with tensions that may provoke HIV risk-taking behavior, for example, intravenous drug use and unsafe sexual encounters. Such intervention uses cognitive-behavioral strategies to teach adolescents to adaptively manage interpersonal —for example, peer pressure and negative modeling—and intrapersonal stress—for example, temptations and urges—and to properly reward themselves for handling risk-taking situations successfully. The third element of the prevention curriculum is interpersonal communication. This communication skills acquisition component uses videotaped vignettes in which youths view other Hispanic adolescents successfully managing high-risk situations. Through imitation learning and behavioral rehearsal, adolescents learn communication skills that will enable them to gain confidence and maintain positive interpersonal relationships through adaptive HIV risk management. Finally, the HIV intervention curriculum also emphasizes ethnic pride and HIV facts. Messages exemplifying ethnic pride are materials that recognize the achievements of the culture through the use of Hispanic literature, poetry, and inspirational discourse. Messages containing HIV facts present information about AIDS, HIV infection, high-risk behaviors, and prevention methods. Although promising, the cognitive-behavioral skills model for HIV/AIDS prevention developed by Schinke et al. (1990) has not yet been empirically tested. Caution must, therefore, be exercised regarding the efficacy of such a program until more conclusive research data become available.

Channel Factors

In the communication/persuasion model, channel factors pertain to the medium for disseminating persuasive messages. Although it is based on an artificial dichotomy (see, e.g., Reardon & Rogers, 1988), the channel in public communication and education campaigns has been typically divided into two categories: mediated and interpersonal. Research focusing on channel variables examined the actual channels Hispanics used to learn about HIV/AIDS (Hu, Keller, & Fleming, 1989), the perceived credibility of mediated channels disseminating information about HIV/AIDS (G. Marín & Marín, 1990), and the differences between Hispanics and non-Hispanics in terms of their willingness to provide interpersonal HIV/AIDS prevention advice (Marín, Marín, & Juarez, 1990).

Exploring the actual sources of HIV/AIDS information acquisition, Hu et al. (1989) examined a group of 216 Hispanics from three clinics in Oregon. Their respondents, who ranged in age from 15 to 73 years, reported acquiring more information about HIV/AIDS from the broadcast media—for example, radio commercial, television program—than the print media—for example, pamphlets, newspaper article. Furthermore, their research findings indicated that monolingual Spanish (or those whose identified primary language is Spanish) respondents reported having fewer sources of HIV information and a greater tendency to rely on broadcast media channels than their bilingual counterparts.

Assessing the credibility that Hispanics assign to various channels for the acquisition of information about HIV/AIDS, G. Marín and Marín (1990) interviewed a random sample of adults in San Francisco. Respondents were asked to rate the credibility of information about HIV/AIDS presented through 10 different channels of communication: 3 were from the electronic media (a radio commercial, a television commercial, and a soap opera on television), 5 from the printed media (a newspaper essay, a pamphlet, a book, a poster, and a *fotonovela*—a photo-illustrated novel), and 2 from other mediated channels (a lecture at a group meeting and an AIDS hotline). The majority of the respondents perceived an AIDS hotline to be highly believable (85%), followed by a book (82%), a pamphlet (76%), and a newspaper article (70%). On the other hand, the least credible channels of HIV/AIDS information were the television soap opera and the *fotonovela*. Research findings indicate that nontelevision channels are perceived as more credible than television channels with regard to HIV/AIDS information for Hispanics.

Interviewing a sample of Hispanic and non-Hispanic White adults in San Francisco, Marín et al. (1990) investigated the potential utility of the interpersonal channel of communication in HIV/AIDS prevention. The study explored respondents' reactions to the hypothetical situation of having an intravenous drug-using family member who is placing himself and his wife at risk for HIV infection. Hispanic respondents were more willing than their non-Hispanic counterparts to provide HIV/AIDS prevention advice. In particular, Hispanics were more willing to discuss various methods of preventing HIV infection, more strongly believed that the drug-using family member would comply with their advice, believed that they would be less embarrassed to discuss such prevention methods, and were more convinced that their advice would protect the hypothetical drug user's spouse from HIV infection. Hispanics were also more likely to suggest that an older family member was the most appropriate person to talk to a relative about HIV/AIDS prevention. These results indicate that the interpersonal channel can be a powerful medium for the dissemination of informative as well as persuasive messages related to HIV prevention among Hispanics.

Receiver Factors

In McGuire's (1989) communication campaign model, receiver factors are composed of characteristics of the recipients of persuasion or the target audience. In HIV/AIDS prevention campaigns, such audience characteristics include (a) knowledge of HIV/AIDS (Crawford & Robinson,

1990; DiClemente, Boyer, & Morales, 1988; Flaskerud & Nyamathi, 1989; B. Marín & Marín, 1990b; National Center for Health Statistics, 1989; Strunin, 1991); (b) attitudes toward condoms, drug use, sexuality, and homosexuality (Ford & Norris, 1991; Jue, 1987; Morales, 1990); and (c) current risk behaviors among Hispanics (Harrison et al., 1991; Sufian et al., 1990).

The first receiver factor is knowledge of HIV/AIDS among Hispanics. Although the National Health Interview Survey has examined knowledge and attitudes about HIV infection and AIDS since 1987, only provisional data from 1988 on Hispanics have been documented (National Center for Health Statistics, 1989). The research findings revealed that Hispanic adults were less knowledgeable than non-Hispanic White adults about AIDS, HIV transmission, and methods of prevention. Because the survey was conducted in English, the results only provide information about English-speaking Hispanics. The level of HIV knowledge of monolingual Hispanic adults was not assessed.

Investigating minority students' knowledge, attitudes, and misconceptions, DiClemente et al. (1988) administered the AIDS Information Survey to 628 subjects (261 White, 226 Black, and 141 Latino). The instrument was composed of three subscales measuring the following research variables: (a) knowledge of HIV/AIDS, (b) perceived susceptibility, and (c) misconceptions about casual contagion of HIV. In terms of knowledge of the cause, transmission, and prevention of HIV/AIDS, ethnic differences were identified. Specifically, White respondents were more knowledgeable than their Black counterparts, and Black students were more knowledgeable than their Latino peers. With respect to the second variable, perceived susceptibility, a relationship between ethnicity and knowledge level emerged. In particular, Black and Latino respondents were more likely to be found in the lower AIDS knowledge group, and lower level of knowledge was associated with a higher level of perceived susceptibility to HIV/AIDS. Simply put, results indicated that less knowledge about HIV/AIDS was correlated with greater levels of perceived risk of contracting the virus. Finally, Black and Latino respondents were approximately twice as likely as White subjects to have misconceptions about the casual transmission of HIV, for example, "You can get AIDS by using someone's personal belongings" or "You can get AIDS by shaking hands with someone who has the disease."

Examining adolescents' perceptions and knowledge of HIV in Massachusetts, Strunin (1991) confirmed earlier findings in two separate studies. Results from both studies indicated that Hispanics are less knowledgeable about casual, sexual, and drug use transmission of HIV than are White or Black adolescents. Hispanic and Asian adolescents expressed the most worry about acquiring HIV. Although a number of Hispanic youngsters indicated changes in their sexual behavior, they were using less effective methods—for example, "being more careful with sexual partners" as opposed to "abstaining from sex"—than were Asians, Blacks, or Whites.

Several other empirical investigations concurred with previous research findings. In a study of male high school seniors, Crawford and Robinson (1990) found Latino students to be less knowledgeable about HIV than their African American and Caucasian peers. Similarly, Flaskerud and Nyamathi (1989), in their assessment of HIV knowledge, attitudes, and practices in Black and Latina women, concluded that Latinas (aged 16-71 years) were less informed than their Black (aged 16-52 years) counterparts.

Interviewing a random sample of 460 San Francisco Hispanic adults, B. Marín and Marín (1990b) examined the relationship between acculturation and knowledge about HIV/AIDS. Their results indicated that most of the respondents demonstrated good knowledge of the true modes of HIV transmission. However, many expressed incorrect beliefs about the casual transmission of the virus; that is, they erroneously believed that one can contract HIV through public toilets, mosquitoes, or being coughed on by someone who is infected. As expected, degree of acculturation was significantly and positively correlated to levels of HIV/AIDS knowledge. For example, lower levels of acculturation were associated with lower knowledge. More specifically, the less acculturated respondents generally had more erroneous beliefs about HIV transmission through casual contact as well as being less aware that HIV-infected persons do not necessarily look ill. Because acculturation differences persisted even after controlling for educational level, the research findings indicate the need to correctly inform the less acculturated Spanish-speaking Hispanics by providing them with specific transmission knowledge in HIV/AIDS prevention campaigns.

The second receiver factor deals with attitudes toward condoms, drug use, sexuality, and homosexuality among Hispanics. Based on her extensive experience with people with HIV at AIDS Project Los Angeles (APLA), Jue (1987) notes that Hispanics tend to view AIDS as a White American problem. Jue also observed that Hispanics are culturally Roman Catholics; therefore, the attitudes of the Church regarding sexuality, birth control, abortion, homosexuality, and family life are important factors in the planning and delivery of services to Hispanic communities.

Elaborating on Jue's (1987) observations, Morales (1990) examined the psychosocial reality of Hispanic gay and bisexual men. He noted that these men often live three different lives among three distinct communities: the gay and lesbian community, the Hispanic community, and the predominantly heterosexual non-Hispanic White mainstream community. Because such communities have different cultural expectations, norms, and rules, a Hispanic gay/bisexual person has to constantly balance conflicting values and behaviors. For instance, Hispanic gay/bisexual men may experience a double stigma—being a member of an ethnic minority and a sexual minority at the same time. For some, such increased stress may be manifested in the form of substance abuse. Others may experience discrimination and prejudice. Therefore, HIV/AIDS prevention efforts, for this population, must address not only medical and psychological factors related to HIV/AIDS but also the complex psychosocial world of this high-risk target group.

Examining a different set of attitudes relevant to HIV prevention, Ford and Norris (1991) explored Hispanic attitudes and beliefs about condoms. In their qualitative study, they asked their respondents two open-ended questions: "Tell me what's good about condoms" and "Tell me what's bad about condoms." Hispanic men reported fewer positive attitudes and beliefs than Hispanic women. In particular, the majority of Hispanic men (60%) only reported one positive belief about condoms: They prevent pregnancy. On the other hand, the majority of Hispanic women reported positive beliefs about condoms in several areas: (a) They prevent pregnancy (78%), (b) they protect from STDs (78%), and (c) they protect from AIDS (62%). The negative attitudes and beliefs about condoms were much more diverse: They break, they are uncomfortable, and they decrease pleasure. The research findings seem to indicate that Hispanic men have more negative attitudes toward condoms that must be addressed in HIV prevention messages.

The final receiver variable deals with current-risk behaviors identified in the target population. Although there is documented evidence for high-risk sexual and drug-using behaviors among Hispanics (e.g., Marín, 1989; Mata & Jorquez, 1989; Rogers & Williams, 1987), such behavioral risk factors vary by gender, age, and region. Hahn and Castro (1989) provided a summary of behavioral risk factors associated with HIV among men, women, and children: (a) Adult Hispanic men are generally infected through sexual contact with other men or intravenous (IV) drug use; (b) women are usually infected through sexual relations with IV drug users or by their own use of IV drugs; and (c) the majority of Hispanic children with HIV infection are born to mothers who have been directly or indirectly involved with IV drug use.

Using a sample of 599 IV drug users in New York City, Sufian and her associates (1990) assessed the behaviors of these individuals in terms of risk for HIV infection. Through their observations, the researchers concluded that Puerto Rican IV drug users are at substantial risk for HIV/AIDS both through their drug use and their sexual behaviors. Two main high-risk behaviors were identified: the sharing of possibly contaminated needles and the enactment of unsafe sexual activities with intimate partners. More specifically, they found that 72% of the Puerto Rican IV drug users shared needles at least once in the 6 months prior to data collection. Furthermore, the subjects continued to put their partners at risk for HIV infection through unprotected sexual encounters, that is, sex without a condom.

Investigating a sample of 620 adult women from South Florida, Harrison et al. (1991) explored the prevalence of risk behaviors, AIDS knowledge, and perceived vulnerability in this group. They discovered a consistent incidence of unprotected sexual activity across the four racial/ethnic groups (Hispanic, White, Black, and Haitian) in their study. For example, the majority of the Hispanic women (65.1%) reported having unprotected sexual intercourse with their main partner. In addition, a substantial number of Hispanic women (44.8%)—the highest among the four ethnic groups—indicated that they would not use condoms with an HIV-positive partner. Others stated that they would have unprotected sex with "johns" (28.9%) and with a bisexual main partner (23.3%).

Implications for HIV/AIDS Prevention for Hispanics

Past research related to HIV/AIDS prevention in Hispanic populations provide social scientists, campaign planners, service providers, and health educators with useful data for designing, implementing, and evaluating HIV/AIDS information and education programs. In addition, McGuire's (1989) communication/persuasion model serves as a useful framework for synthesizing and applying such research findings to HIV/AIDS prevention campaigns.

In terms of source factors, it appears that Hispanics prefer to discuss their personal anxieties and concerns about HIV with their peers—friends and siblings—and prefer to discuss HIV facts with professionals who are directly involved with the epidemic, such as medical doctors and clinic counselors. With respect to message factors, HIV/AIDS prevention messages are more effective if they are not directly translated from English materials, include Spanish HIV-related terminologies that are conceptually equivalent to their English terms, incorporate fundamental Hispanic cultural values, and possibly instruct their audience to enact some specific cognitive-behavioral skills associated with problem solving, coping, and interpersonal communication techniques. In addition, HIV prevention messages including condom instructions must be comprehensible to Hispanics with lower educational levels. In terms of channel factors, research reveals that Hispanics prefer certain nontelevision mass media channels—AIDS hotline, book, pamphlet—for credible HIV/AIDS information and interpersonal channels—like an older family member—for advice and motivation for the adoption of HIV risk reduction behaviors. Research on receiver factors suggest that Hispanics are less knowledgeable about HIV—especially in the area of transmission through casual contact. Moreover, Hispanics generally display strong homophobic attitudes and somewhat negative attitudes and beliefs regarding condom use. Research also indicates that Hispanics are less likely to use condoms during sexual activity. Finally, the spread of HIV in Hispanic populations seems to occur through both documented modes of transmission, that is, by needle sharing and by unprotected sexual contacts.

Although behavior change appears to be the major goal of HIV/AIDS prevention programs, McGuire (1989) suggested that there are a number of response steps mediating persuasive communication that campaign planners should take into account. Specifically, there are 12 response steps or output variables:

1. exposure to the communication (e.g., seeing/hearing an AIDS prevention message or commercial)
2. attending to the persuasive attempt (e.g., paying attention to the actual message or commercial)
3. liking and becoming interested in the communication (e.g., displaying a positive attitude toward the prevention message or commercial)
4. comprehending the persuasive communication (e.g., understanding the message or commercial about condom use)
5. acquiring the skills presented in the communication (e.g., learning how to use a condom properly)
6. yielding to the persuasive communication or changing attitudes (e.g., changing one's attitudes toward condoms)
7. remembering the content of the communication (e.g., remembering condoms as a method of HIV prevention)

8. retrieving the information acquired through the communication (e.g., remembering to use condoms)
9. making behavioral decisions based on retrieved information (e.g., deciding to use condoms during sex)
10. behaving in accord with decision or behavioral change (e.g., actually using a condom during sexual intercourse)
11. reinforcing the desired behavior (e.g., feeling that sex with a condom is rewarding)
12. consolidating such behavior for future use (e.g., continue using condoms whenever having sex)

Finally, McGuire noted that the goals of an educational campaign can be any of the above response steps.

McGuire's model demonstrates the complexity of the persuasive communication process in health education. In terms of HIV/AIDS prevention programs for Hispanics, health educators, public health officials, and researchers need to (a) determine the specific objectives—the output variables—of their intervention (e.g., increasing knowledge about HIV transmission), (b) manipulate the communication factors—the input variables—to produce optimal outcome (e.g., the combination of source, message, channel, and receiver characteristics leading to maximum changes in the target population), and (c) evaluate the program in terms of each objective during the course—as opposed to after the end—of the campaign so that adjustments can be made to input or communication variables to create the desired results.

For a program to be effective, a clear definition of output variables is necessary. Such outcomes will aid the campaign planner in determining how input variables are to be manipulated. More specifically, source, message, and channel characteristics related to the communication process would be decisively different if the objective of the campaign is to convince the target population to use condoms as opposed to simply increasing their knowledge about HIV transmission. In the first instance, the campaign may encourage the use of interpersonal channels—like older family members—to provide HIV prevention advice, such as condom use, whereas the content of the message focuses on teaching the audience the skills that are necessary to use condoms properly. In the second situation, to increase the audience's knowledge, the campaign may use mediated channels—such as pamphlets—and credible sources like medical professionals to disseminate accurate information about the disease and its transmission. As it is readily apparent, the combination of input characteristics is likely to change according to the specific outcome desired; therefore, it is important to evaluate the program at each stage of the process—for example, changes in cognition or knowledge, attitudes, or behavior.

In his response steps mediating persuasive communication, McGuire (1989) also points out that success at one stage (e.g., increase in knowledge) does not automatically lead to success in others (e.g., adoption of safer sexual behavior). Therefore, it is not surprising to find that successful HIV information dissemination programs have not produced much behavior change in their target populations (see, e.g., Baum & Nesselhof, 1988; Edgar, Freimuth, & Hammond, 1988). Moreover, McGuire (1989) notes that behavioral changes are preceded by proper modifications in cognitive (e.g., knowledge of safer sex guidelines) and attitudinal (e.g., feelings associated with the adoption of safer sex guidelines) components. This has important implications for the design of future programs: Strategies for knowledge and attitude change must be incorporated into the educational process as intermediate steps leading to health behavior modification. In addition, for preventive behaviors to be adopted they must also be acquired; specifically, two sets of skills are involved: (a) interpersonal—that is, knowing how to discuss and negotiate safer sex with an intimate partner—and (b) behavioral—that is, knowing how to wear and dispose of condoms properly. Finally, McGuire's model points out that persuasion does not terminate with behavioral change: The adoption of new behaviors must be reinforced, maintained, and consolidated to ensure their future enactment. For example, if the final goal of an educational campaign is to change a sexual behavior in Hispanic men (e.g., to use condoms during sexual intercourse), such program needs to consider (a) increasing their knowledge about HIV including transmission, prevention, and their own vulnerability to the virus; (b) changing their attitudes—from negative or neutral to positive—about condoms; (c) teaching them how to discuss condom use and safer sex with an intimate partner as well as how to wear condoms properly; (d) motivating them to change their behavior, in this case, to use condoms; and (e) reinforcing their adoption of the new health action so that they continue using condoms in future sexual interactions.

In sum, McGuire's communication/persuasion model not only informs us of the complexity of the process of educating Hispanics about HIV/AIDS but also provides guidelines for the design, creation, and evaluation of such preventative programs. Specifically, such programs for Hispanic communities need to be designed after careful consideration of how source, message, channel, and receiver characteristics interact to produce the best desirable outcome. In addition, the model describes 12 possible response steps—or outcomes—that may be achieved by manipulating the input—or communication—variables of the persuasion process. Finally, each one of the response steps provides an opportunity for assessment and evaluation of the effects of specific patterns of communication factors.

Although some studies have concentrated their attention on HIV/AIDS prevention in Hispanic communities (see, e.g., B. Marín & Marín, 1990a), much work remains to be done. Future research needs to (a) continue accumulating systematic knowledge about Hispanics and HIV/AIDS by concentrating on the testing of actual HIV/AIDS prevention models and evaluating the utility of current educational efforts; (b) analyze and investigate HIV/AIDS education and prevention as a complex persuasive communication process; (c) integrate and apply theories of social influence and persuasion techniques to HIV prevention programs for Hispanics; and (d) examine the interplay between communication—source, message, channel, and receiver—factors and persuasive effects by assessing the impact of communication on specific outcomes. As the HIV/AIDS epidemic enters its second decade, it is time for academic researchers, public health officials, service providers, and community leaders to come together to launch original education and prevention programs designed specifically to address the social and cultural realities of Hispanics in this country.

NOTE

1. The term "Hispanic" is employed as a label of convenience to refer to individuals whose ancestry can be traced to one of the Spanish-speaking Latin American countries or to Spain. It is a term used by the Bureau of the Census, the media, and social and behavioral scientists. Although members of this group share some fundamental cultural characteristics, it is also recognized that they have very distinct migrational and sociodemographic attributes.

14
♦

Impact of Poverty, Homelessness, and Drugs on Hispanic Women at Risk for HIV Infection

ADELINE NYAMATHI

ROSE VASQUEZ

As of March 1989, 1,681 Hispanic women had been diagnosed with acquired immunodeficiency syndrome (AIDS). The prevalence of AIDS among Hispanic women has led health professionals and community leaders to recognize the need for culturally sensitive education programs in the minority communities that would be effective in halting the spread of this deadly disease. Women in particular are fast becoming the focus of attention as AIDS has become the leading cause of death among women 25 to 34 years of age (Holmes & Fernandez, 1988). Women now account for 10% of all AIDS cases diagnosed; 20% of those women are Hispanic. Of children with AIDS, 23% are Hispanic; the majority of those are born to human immunodeficiency virus (HIV) infected mothers (Centers for Disease Control, 1989).

Although the incidence of AIDS among Hispanics is still relatively low, the number of AIDS cases among Hispanic women has been increasing more rapidly than among non-Hispanic women ("AIDS Among Hispanics," 1988). Although it may seem unimaginable that the threat of a deadly disease such as AIDS is insufficient to reduce high-risk behaviors, the reality of contending with homelessness, joblessness, starvation, and abandonment may become so overwhelming that the risk of AIDS becomes irrelevant. Yet relatively little is known about the crises women at risk may experience on a daily basis and the ways they deal with their most immediate concerns. Cultural and religious factors also present additional barriers that make it difficult, if not impossible, to reach minority women at risk for HIV infection in an effective manner. Because education programs that aim to motivate people to adopt risk-reducing behaviors, to eliminate misconceptions, and to inform about the modes of transmission remain the most important public health strategy for controlling the spread of AIDS, increased attention must be focused on developing realistic, culturally sensitive AIDS education programs for women at risk.

This chapter assesses the concerns and stresses of Hispanic women, coping responses commonly used, perceived feelings of self-esteem, locus of control, and emotional distress experienced. By understanding the special needs of these women and the motivating forces that might improve the delivery of health messages, a means to reach this vulnerable population may be developed.

HISPANIC WOMEN AND HIGH-RISK BEHAVIORS

There is almost universal agreement that intravenous (IV) drug use and unsafe sexual practices account for the disproportionate occurrence of AIDS in the Hispanic population. Among Hispanics, 42% of male cases and over 80% of female cases are IV drug related (Centers for Disease Control, 1989). Drug-related transmission is implicated in 77% of Hispanic pediatric cases, compared with 32% of cases among White children (Centers for Disease Control, 1989). Heterosexual Hispanic men using IV needles outnumber White male IV needle users 21.4 times. Moreover, Hispanic IV drug users (IVDUs) are 19 times more likely than White IVDUs to contract AIDS (Fullilove, 1988a).

Closer examination of needle use behavior, which often represents an activity born out of necessity rather than out of social bonding (Marín

& Marín, 1988), has shown that Black and Hispanic users are more likely to frequent "shooting galleries" (IVDUs' meeting places) than to engage in social sharing on a more personal level (Schoenbaum, Selwyn, & Hartel, 1988). Black and Hispanic IVDUs have been more likely to share their equipment used in drug injections (Des Jarlais, Friedman, & Hopkins, 1985; Friedman, Des Jarlais, & Sotheran, 1986). Moreover, Peterson and Marín (1988) contend that recent Hispanic immigrants have reused needles and syringes for vitamin and medication injections and may share their equipment with neighbors and friends.

In a review of several studies, Fullilove (1988b) reports that minority bisexual and homosexual men who engage in unsafe sex are less likely than White men to regard themselves at risk for HIV infection. Moreover, men who have sex with other men may not label themselves as homosexual whether it be because the male is playing the dominant masculine role or engages in both homosexual and heterosexual activities (Carrier, 1985).

Although it is clear that persons at risk become so as a result of underlying risk behaviors rather than as a result of their race/ethnicity, economic and cultural factors affecting differences in ethnic groups are still being appreciated. Low-income, urban Hispanic women who are homeless, use drugs, or are prostitutes may have concerns more immediate than the threat of infection. For women whose attention needs to be directed toward survival needs, such as shelter, personal safety, or financial assistance, AIDS may be of low concern (Mays & Cochran, 1988). When the disease of addiction is considered, often the need for a fix supersedes the need for practicing safe sex. Moreover, the use of other drugs, such as alcohol or marijuana, can cloud the sensorium and prevent one from taking the necessary precautions.

CONCEPTUAL ORIENTATION

The modified Lazarus and Folkman (1984) stress and coping paradigm serves as the guiding theoretical framework for this study. Within this paradigm, coping is defined as constantly changing cognitive and behavioral efforts made to manage specific demands that tax or exceed the resources of the person. As a process, coping is affected by a constellation of variables that include situational and personal factors, coping responses, coping resources, and adaptive outcome.

METHOD

Design

Focus group interviews were used to answer the research questions. This qualitative approach is a systematic process of observing, detailing, describing, documenting, and analyzing the social and cultural worlds of a particular group of people (Leininger, 1985; Omery, 1987). By using this research method, nurses become sensitized to the beliefs and customs of multiethnic clients so that health education programs are appropriately planned and utilized (Tripp-Reimer, 1980).

Focus groups represent a useful combination of participant observation of interaction and the individual interview in direct probing of informant knowledge (Morgan & Spanish, 1984). Because the researcher can challenge or probe for additional responses, supporters of this method claim that it yields more in-depth analysis than that produced by formal quantitative methods (Mariampolski, 1984). Through focus group interviews, the researcher creates an environment that nurtures the expression of different perceptions and points of view without pressuring participants to reach a consensus (Krueger, 1988). The interviews are conducted several times with similar types of participants to identify trends and patterns in perceptions. Careful and systematic analysis of discussions provides insights into the world in which these women live.

Subjects and Setting

The study discussed here is part of a larger project designed to provide counseling and HIV testing for at-risk minority women. Invited to participate were Hispanic females who were (a) homeless, (b) IVDUs or sexual partners of IVDUs, (c) diagnosed with a sexually transmitted disease, or (d) prostitutes.

There were seven focus groups. Conducted by Hispanic and Black nurse researchers, the sessions were held in private rooms in one of two homeless shelters or at one of two drug rehabilitation program centers. The nurse researchers were thoroughly trained to provide mild, unobtrusive control over the group and were comfortable with group dynamics. The participants signed informed consent forms and received $10 at the completion of the 2-hour session.

A convenience sample of 43 Hispanic women participated in the focus groups. They ranked in age from 17 to 67 years; 38 (88%) were under 50 years of age. Thirty-six (83%) were homeless, 6 (7%) were IVDUs,

6 (7%) were sexual partners of IVDUs, 1 (2.3%) was a prostitute, and 1 (2.3%) had been diagnosed as having a sexually transmitted disease. The women were predominantly Catholic (33, or 76.6%), unemployed (33, or 76.6%), and not in school (29, or 67%). Mean educational level was 7 years. In terms of relationship status, 17 (40%) were single and 15 (34%) were married. Eight (18.6%) were living with someone, 2 were separated, and 1 was divorced. Nearly half (21, or 49%) were born outside the United States. Twenty-five (58%) had an average of 2.6 children.

Data Collection

Based on the components of Lazarus and Folkman's (1984) stress and coping paradigm and a thorough review of the literature, a structured guide was developed to assess the concerns and stresses the women experienced, the coping responses used, perceived feelings of self-esteem and locus of control, and emotional distress. Table 14.1 presents a sample of the open-ended questions.

Validity of the interview guide was assured by a thorough review of the literature on minority populations, particularly those at risk for HIV infection. Moreover, content validity was well established by an expert panel composed of researchers and clinicians working with AIDS and minority populations. All focus group sessions were tape-recorded and later transcribed. A content analysis of the report transcripts, identifying major themes and categories, was performed. Consistency of identification of themes and categories was verified independently by two nurses involved in research on AIDS among minority groups.

RESULTS

Content analysis revealed that regardless of their life experiences, caring for family, particularly the children, was of critical concern to the women interviewed. To successfully perform as providers, these women would need to maintain good health, become and/or remain drug free, and be financially stable. The overwhelming focus of their lives thus became overcoming threats to their role as provider. The threats consisted of situational factors (potential loss of health, drug addiction, lack of social support, lack of information about the potential threat of AIDS, and a life of poverty), personality factors (low self-esteem, helplessness, and loss of control), and emotion-focused coping responses (drug use,

Table 14.1 Sample of Structured Interview Items

1. Thinking back over the last few months, what would you say have been your major concerns or problems?
2. Thinking back over the last few months:
   a. What are some ways you have dealt with these problems or concerns?
   b. Who/what did you find most helpful and least helpful in dealing with these problems or concerns? Probes:
      talking to others
      getting information
      going to the clinic
   c. Of all these activities, which did you use most often? How available was it to you?
3. Thinking back over the past few months, how important do you think it is to feel good about yourself?
4. Thinking back over the past few months, how important do you think it is to feel you have control over what happens in your life? Why?

withdrawal, and prayer). The adaptive outcome for the women was to be an adequate provider and to optimize the health and well-being of their children (see Figure 14.1).

Situational Factors

Potential Loss of Health

The potential loss of health represented a major concern to most of the women because they were responsible for caring for the family and supplementing, if not providing, the financial support for the household. If they were not healthy, they would be unable to provide care, pay the rent, and keep the family together. As one reported, "Most of us, since we don't have any disability, the only money we can get is welfare . . . and that's not enough."

Fears about AIDS were a reality for drug-using women. Many had heard about the dangers of sharing needles or having sex with an IVDU. One drug abuser said, "What worries me is getting AIDS. When you go out with someone or when you have a boyfriend, you don't know what sexual relations he has had. You don't know it, but he could infect you." What was immediately apparent, however, was not a fear of dying from AIDS but, rather, fear of the impact on the family if the provider could not perform her role. For many, the thought of their children being cared for by someone else was frightening.

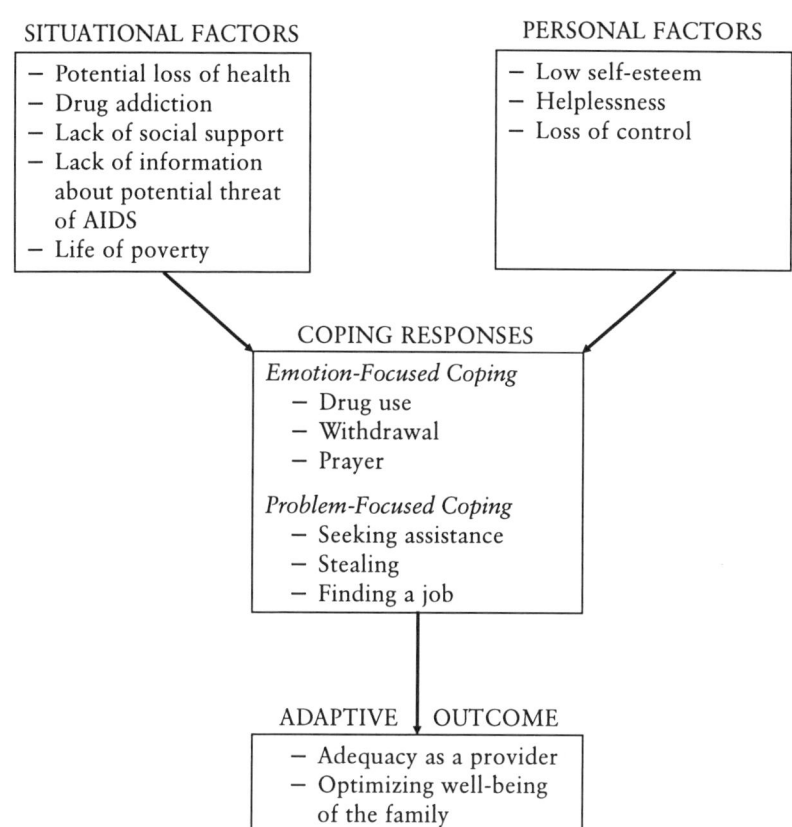

Figure 14.1. Factors Affecting Hispanic Women's Adequacy in the Provider

Drug Addiction

Women who abused drugs were keenly aware of the difficulty in being caring, warm parents while craving a drug high. For the drug-abusing mother, concern about her children's reaction to her drug use and to the abuse handed out left severe scars. One typical reaction was the following: "I was always worried about how my kids were when I came down, how they reacted when I was getting loaded, and what I did to them. I had a lot of pain inside me, hurt and anger towards myself for the things that I had done." Putting drugs before the family left many of the women angry and confused. They resented the fact that many of their babies would be born addicted. Although numerous obstacles made it difficult for them to end the drug cycle, there were positive influences, such as fear of imprisonment or the benefits of drug rehabilitation, which enabled some women to end their drug dependence. The most powerful influence of all was their children:

> What helped me to stop using drugs was my children. I realized I didn't want them to go through what I went through. I realized that if I was to continue to use drugs, my children eventually would probably end up using drugs themselves. And I know that there's more to life than drugs. What I want for my children is a good life.

Another commented,

> My son is the one that really made me open my eyes and made me realize I had something to live for. Here's this little 4-year-old kid crying when I come in loaded [at] 4:00 in the morning and he says, "Momma, I'm so scared you're gonna die." It was like a light went on. I went into a program 'cause I didn't have any other choice. I was so strung out. I learned how to deal with all the problems that I could never deal with before and get out all the anger I had, and that's how I did it.

Lack of Social Support

Many reported that drugs became their social support. As one described, "My only friend at the time I was involved with drugs was drugs. I couldn't care less if I had a close friend or if I was close to my family." While on drugs, being alone was an expected occurrence. Although many reported trying to quit, the failure rate was high. Moreover, many experienced a disturbing isolation because family members often lived out of the country and the women lacked the social and emotional support of close family ties. Perhaps even more distressing were the accounts of family members abandoning the family. For one woman, multiple losses of loved ones drove her to drug use:

> I was 14 years old. I had a sister who I was very, very close to; she was 12. And she died. You know, after that I became real rebellious. I didn't want to get close to anybody in my family. And I just kinda, just changed y'know. I started drinking. I started using pills and just went on from there. And it just carried on and on. A couple of times I stopped but then my grandfather who I was real close with, he died and that just took me down. You know it was like forget it, I'm not getting close to nobody. I

don't want God in my life. I don't want my parents in my life, that's it. All I want is the drug, 'cause that eased the pain.

Lack of Information About AIDS

When questioned about their concern over AIDS, several considered Hispanic women at little risk:

> I think that if you have a plan to make an investigation about AIDS among Hispanic women, then this thing that you're doing is pretty good. But I think that since none of us here probably have any of these illnesses, wouldn't it be better to do a program like this in some of the buildings where you have maybe hundreds of people? For example in the building where I live, there a lot of homosexuals.

Other women verbalized concerns regarding public restrooms, hotel beds, and being near men: "Well, I'd like to know if the AIDS infection is stuck on the toilets where you're going to sit down, or if it's a toilet where a lot of men go."

The idea of attending an AIDS education program where a Hispanic woman with AIDS would speak was agreeable to most. Fear of men who have prostitutes on the side was common. Most thought that being tested for the HIV would be useful.

Life of Poverty

Poverty was not a stranger to many of these women. Accounts of working in the fields instead of going to school were common and encouraged in them a desire to provide a better life for their children. One described this vivid remembrance: "When I was growing up we had to struggle a lot. We all had to work in the fields since we were very young children, just to be able to survive. So I didn't even have the opportunity to study through the first grade." Life was a daily struggle against inadequate resources and a double standard. Many complained about having the sole responsibility for cooking, cleaning, and caring for ill children whether or not they were employed. In view of the many situational obstacles that these women faced, it is not surprising that many reported crying and depression as common occurrences. Particularly distressful, however, was the combination of unfavorable situational factors and debilitating personal factors, such as low self-esteem, hopelessness, and loss of control.

Personal Factors

Low Self-Esteem

The effect of drugs on self-esteem was most damaging. The following passage describes one woman's feelings about herself:

> I was really worried because I wasn't able to concentrate on anything, because of my drug use. I always felt really dingy, and really dumb. Somebody would say something to me and I couldn't really compute it until after several minutes. Y'know in my brain I couldn't really understand.

Another woman with low self-worth hid from her well-dressed friends. About her appearance, she said, "I didn't give a shit about myself."

For drug-abusing women, perhaps even more distressing than low self-esteem was the disgust that family members felt toward them.

> It made me feel ashamed after I had the baby because my whole family found out that I was using drugs, and they kinda looked down on me about it. I'm trying to bring myself back up now, but to them they're always going to look at me as a person who used drugs and endangered my baby's life just to get high.

Hispanic women also experienced low self-esteem as a result of being unable to express themselves adequately. One woman shared the following comment: "I think that in this country you feel discriminated against because you can't speak English very well. And this is a complex that you get a lot in this country." Hispanic women described a multitude of moods which included feeling ashamed, helpless, confused, scared, jealous, humiliated, and angry.

Loss of Control

Addiction took away a woman's control over herself. As one explained, "You know I put myself in a lot of places where I shouldn't have been. You know I endangered myself. But I didn't give a shit. I didn't care about nothin'." While using drugs, women frequently experienced a profound sense of helplessness. Not only were they unable to help themselves when they craved a high but they were also unable to imagine that others could help them. During the time they were on drugs, women reported being aimless and lacking direction in their lives. They often expressed anger when they were unable to see a way out.

While several placed absolute control over events in the hands of God, or powerful others, some verbalized a strong sense of internal control. These comments illustrate this attitude: "If we get what we have it's because we work and we sacrifice ourselves"; "When I get what I want, it's not because of luck. It's because I worked for it."

Some women who abused drugs reported that under certain circumstances their children were taken away from them. Several of these women regained control of their lives in order to get their children back. One whose children were taken away reported the following experience:

> If it's important, you will do whatever you can to make it better. I first lost my kids because my boyfriend's sister-in-law called the social workers on me. I wanted to kill her. I went down to her house, I broke her windows, I threatened to kill her. At first I was mad, I was confused, I wanted to die. And I just kept getting high, and I started going crazy. Then I went to a drug place and now I think that was the best thing that could ever happen to me.

Coping Responses

The coping style of the women interviewed was predominantly emotion focused. The most common of these coping strategies were praying to God, drug use, and withdrawal through daydreaming. Selective problem-focused strategies included discussing the problem with others, obtaining more information, and attempting to control their lives.

Emotion-Focused Coping

Prayer. For the majority, God represented the only hope and salvation. For those who were particularly religious, confidence in God prepared them for "anything that could happen." For others, God gave them the patience to endure the situation, the poverty, and the worries, and the power to persevere. Several drug-abusing women were unable to find solace in God because drugs were their be-all and end-all.

For one woman, praying to God was not a helpful strategy for she resented the fact that God allowed her brother to be taken away: "I'm not into praying like I used to because I had a resentment towards God because he took my brother. Why did God let this happen? I would pray and I'd go to meetings. I tried to understand, why him?"

Drug Use. For several, drugs eased the pain of crisis, helped them forget the unfavorable situational factors confronting them, and alleviated some of their emotional distress. However, reality was never found to be at a comforting distance as the prospect of dragging the children into a life of drugs was unbearable. In fact, for many, recognizing the effect of their drug dependency upon the children was the first step in overcoming their addiction.

Withdrawal. Another common emotion-focused coping response was daydreaming. For one woman, daydreaming helped her live and provided some hope. For others, getting away or wanting to be alone seemed to serve a similar purpose. One explained, "There's times when I just say, 'God just take me away,' and I wish I could go like that, but it doesn't happen. There's times when I wish I could just snap my fingers and be off in a desert island with nobody around me. Snap my fingers and that's it."

Problem-Focused Coping

Another coping strategy used by many women was a problem-focused approach. Some sought assistance by talking over their problems with others. One found that explaining to her child what she was going through was beneficial for both of them. Others tried to acquire more information or accepted a particular situation. Some women cited finding employment or stealing as other means of coping. Very few reported prostitution as a means of survival.

DISCUSSION

Despite the growing AIDS crisis in the Hispanic community, culturally sensitive AIDS programs are woefully lacking. It is clear that cultural and socioeconomic factors must be taken into account by AIDS educators attempting to communicate with young Hispanic women. Mata and Jorquez (1988) show that Hispanic women today are often unemployed, have no health insurance, and have a long history of poor health. They contend that much of the published educational material is irrelevant to these women.

Hispanics from Mexico, Central America, and South America have value systems, life experiences, and communication patterns that are different from those of the dominant Anglo culture (Vargas, 1988).

When the distinct cultural and social values and beliefs of Hispanic women are integrated into a program implemented by bilingual Hispanic nurses, then nurses and other health professionals can begin to address the needs of this population, facilitate assimulation of information, and provide an environment in which acceptance, trust, and assistance are apparent (Martin, 1979; Valle & Vega, 1980).

The focus group interviews with Hispanic women at risk for HIV infection provided helpful insights into their concerns, coping responses, and feelings of self-esteem and control and underscored the importance to them of the family structure. Whether the family was defined as extended family, husband, or just the children, the women focused on the importance of success in the provider role.

The most serious situational factor which the drug-using women discussed was the grip that their addiction had on their lives. Drugs provided immediate gratification and distraction from hopelessness and pain. The high unemployment rate among Latinos in poor communities forces many into the world of drugs and thus provides not only an escape from the problems of poverty but also a means of obtaining additional income through dealing. For many, the series of unsuccessful attempts to abandon drugs was demoralizing and led to lower self-esteem and lack of self-confidence. For drug-abusing mothers, the thought of abusing or neglecting their children was devastating. Recognition of the effect of drugs on her children became the first step in letting go of drugs.

Women who were not identified as drug users reported that lack of financial security and social support threatened the security of their families. The level of interaction among Hispanic families is generally high, and the family is viewed as a source of support, security, and strength. Mata and Jorguez (1988) observed that even among IVDUs in the barrio there was widespread reliance on personal and social support networks for learning to use drugs, for obtaining drugs, for information and resource exchanges, and for coping with illicit drug use.

The majority of Hispanic women interviewed did not report the threat of AIDS as a common fear. Denial of the potential of this threat, or lack of knowledge of the potential threat, is, however, of serious concern to many, particularly because the topic of safer sex practices is a difficult one to discuss within a predominantly Catholic population whose values and beliefs hold that the female should remain innocent and unaware of sexual practices until her husband provides the education. The fact is, however, that heterosexual transmission is 15% higher among Hispanics than among Whites (Centers for Disease Control, 1989). Moreover, although Hispanics are intensely family oriented, heterosexual monogamy is often undermined by the "macho" male's abuse of his spouse and the classic double standard, under which men can frequently have affairs and visit prostitutes ("AIDS: The Crisis," 1987). Furthermore, Hispanics account for 42% of all U.S. AIDS cases among gay and bisexual men (Centers for Disease Control, 1989). Many of the female sex partners of these men are unaware of their partners' bisexuality or of their partner's current or past drug use. As a result, they are often unaware of the risk of HIV infection.

With respect to personal factors, the Hispanic women interviewed identified loss of control, low self-esteem, and helplessness as common experiences. These inadequacies diminished their ability to successfully carry out the parental role, and, in many cases, nurtured the drug habit. Loss of self-esteem was extremely difficult for these women to cope with because respect is a highly valued concept in Hispanic cultures.

Coping responses used by Hispanic women, particularly drug abusers, were primarily emotion focused. For many, the use of drugs was a convenient escape from reality, to a world without pain. Unfortunately, when the high disappeared, the realization of the effect of the drug dependency on the family was quite disturbing. Another emotion-focused strategy was turning to prayer and religion. For some women entrenched in years of drug abuse, religion became their only salvation. Problem-focused strategies were likewise reported. Particularly among non-drug-using women, holding down a job, seeking food and shelter, and stealing were methods of assuring family survival. Few reported prostitution as a means of survival.

Despite the serious obstacles to providing AIDS education to Hispanic women, overcoming cultural insensitivity is one way that nurses can assure effective service delivery and positive outcomes for this population. Those most at risk are young (one third of the U.S. Latino population is under 15; the median age is 23), poor (40% of the Latino families are female headed; 51.3% of these live below the poverty line), and have low educational levels (Giachello, 1985). Consequently, developing educational materials at the third- to fourth-grade educational level would be most practical. Moreover, as the family is the pivotal focus for Hispanic women, educational messages should take into account family and cultural values that might have an impact on both sexuality and drug use (Worth & Rodriguez, 1987). For example, to convince women that they need to educate their partners on the preventive aspects of condoms, an effective approach, which incorporates cultural values, might be to arrange an educational session with the woman and man. By ascertaining the role of the male in terms of protecting the family, and assuming that the children would be cared for by the mother, use of condoms would be critical in preventing HIV infection in the woman.

The results of the focus group interviews also point out the hierarchy of needs of Hispanic women who live in poverty, are poorly educated, and face language and cultural barriers. These women grossly underuse primary health care, family planning, and prenatal or pediatric care services (Worth & Rodriguez, 1987). Providing AIDS education to a population struggling for survival on a daily basis is anything but ludicrous. Nurses are in an ideal position to recognize the needs of women at risk and to communicate and network with community agencies to provide referrals, food and shelter, job training, and financial assistance. Trust and respect would be gained, thus opening the way for developing implementing AIDS education programs.

It is very clear that the best approach to ensuring cultural sensitivity is by training Latino health care professionals to provide more of the necessary education. Particularly when working with drug users, extensive background in the theories and practice of drug abuse is critical in developing a therapeutic relationship. Augmenting the health care team with well-trained lay personnel from the community who have experienced drug abuse, prostitution, or homelessness may also contribute to improving the delivery of the culturally relevant educational message and to slowing the spread of this deadly disease.

Health care agencies have an enormous task ahead to modify and expand their services to meet the needs of a distinct population. At this time, because education is the only strategy available to save thousands of lives, the educational messages must be appropriate and culturally relevant.

PART 5

Gender Studies Research

15

♦

Hispanic Masculinity: Myth or Psychological Schema Meriting Clinical Consideration

J. MANUEL CASAS

BURL R. WAGENHEIM

ROBERT BANCHERO

JUAN MENDOZA-ROMERO

*T*he construct of male gender identity as it exists among the more traditional Hispanic cultures and subcultures, popularly referred to as machismo, has not received the serious and in-depth attention that it merits from theoretically driven and empirically based social science researchers in the United States and, in particular, from researchers within the realm of applied psychology. Much of what is known about machismo is based on early descriptive studies conducted mainly by anthropologists and sociologists. With respect to the anthropologists (e.g., Madsen, 1964), their findings, obtained from traditionally oriented rural communities, have tended to be little more than a reiteration of the stereotypic characteristics that are popularly believed to be an inherent part of machismo. Relative to the sociologists (e.g., De la Cancela, 1986), the majority of whose work is much more recent, the tendency has been to provide psychodynamic, historical, and/or environmental interpretations vis-à-vis the prevalence of machismo. In all fairness, a few sociologists (e.g., Baca-Zinn, 1982) and psychologists (e.g., Cromwell & Ruiz, 1979) have conducted some research to more substantially validate and measure selective aspects of machismo among Hispanic subgroups. Unfortunately, their approach to studying machismo has tended to be atheoretical in nature and much too frequently simplistic in its conceptualization of the construct.

Our contention, reflected throughout this chapter, is that there is a tremendous need to reinvigorate research efforts among psychologists relative to the construct of machismo. The impetus for this position is strongly tied to research findings from studies conducted on males of European-American (Bem, 1981b) and/or Mexican ancestry (Díaz-Loving, Díaz-Guerrero, Helmreich, & Spencer, 1982; Lara-Cantú & Navarro-Arias, 1986) that empirically test the existence of a comprehensive male gender identity construct, or schema, that can impact all aspects of a man's life, as well as other studies, conducted predominantly on European-American males, that demonstrate a significant and positive relationship between level of male gender identity and social, mental, and physical well-being (Annandale & Hunt, 1990, Eisler & Skidmore, 1987). Given the focus of this chapter, these latter studies are so important from a clinical perspective that a brief and selective overview of recent research is here warranted.

Working from the "gender role stress" model proposed by Pleck (1981) that contends that men who fail to live up to the traditional demands of masculinity can experience conflict-related dissonance, Eisler and Skidmore (1987), in particular, have demonstrated a positive relationship between high male gender role stress and a strong propensity to engage in high-risk behaviors like high consumption of drugs and/or alcohol, outbursts of violence toward self and others, and promiscuous and unsafe sex that can have a detrimental if not lethal (i.e., contracting HIV infection) effect on one's overall well-being.

A handful of studies identified Type A disposition, lack of behaviors relevant to close relationships, and condom use and attitudes as correlates of masculinity ideology (i.e., the meaning that men ascribe to their behaviors) (Bunting & Reeves, 1983; Pleck, Sonenstein, & Ku, 1993a). Directing the attention to adolescents, Pleck, Sonenstein, and Ku (1993b) found that among adolescent males strong endorsement of masculinity ideology is associated with problem behaviors in four areas: school difficulties, substance use, delinquency, and sexual activity.

Anesthetization of the affective realm or restrictive emotionality, which certain researchers contend is a characteristic of men who strongly adhere to a traditional male gender identity, is believed to be a major factor in the development of psychosomatic symptomology (Flannery, 1978; Nemiah, 1977; Silverberg, 1986). Barefoot (1992), using a structured interview format, found a strong association between "indirect" expression of hostility and heart disease among males. Furthermore, there is a growing body of evidence (see Pennebaker, 1992, and Emmons, 1992, for reviews) that chronic repression of negative affect, including anger, may be related to a broader range of negative health consequences, such as cancer, asthma, excessive cholesterol levels, ulcers, irritable bowel syndrome, and insomnia. Sutkin and Good (1987) reported that men who are unable to communicate their feelings may be more comfortable seeking medical attention than mental health services. Complaints of chest, back pains, or headaches may be viewed by the traditional man as legitimate means for seeking attention; thus, for many men, illness may be the only escape from overbearing burdens.

Relative to violence, theoretical writings clearly point toward the cultural framework in which men are traditionally socialized to validate their masculinity through control, power, and competition (O'Neil, 1982), hence possibly encouraging or validating men's violence. In a review of men who batter, Koval, Ponzetti, and Cate (1982) summarized that these men typically (a) hold traditional patriarchal beliefs, (b) are emotionally inexpressive, (c) are isolated due to their difficulty in maintaining close relationships, (d) have low self-esteem that related to their using violence to achieve superiority, and (e) are unemployed or dissatisfied with their current employment (Good, Wallace, & Schuster, in press). From a comparative perspective of violence, and, in particular, spouse abuse, Finn (1986) found that men tended to hold more traditional sex role attitudes than women and as such were more likely to endorse the use of physical force in the marital relationship.

Focusing on the use of alcohol, Burda and Vaux (1987) found that men become more communicative with other men during social drinking. Hence men may use alcohol to overcome societal-based proscriptions against emotional expression, especially between men. According to Pasick, Gordon, and Meth (1990), addictive behavior is related in part to belief in the male gender-role need to feel omnipotent, which can be temporarily satisfied by alcohol, drugs, excessive gambling, or excessive sex.

Directing attention to help seeking, there appears to be a relationship between a strong male gender identity and unwillingness to seek help. For instance, the results of one study reveal that both gender and sex-role orientation significantly influenced help-seeking attitudes. Women were more tolerant of the stigma associated with seeking professional help, more willing to recognize a personal need for help, and more open to sharing problems with others (Johnson, 1988). The stigma that men associate with seeking help in general is greater when the problems for which help is being sought are of a sexual nature (Metz & Seifert, 1990).

Finally, capturing the total essence of the research, Sharpe and Heppner (1991) found that gender role conflict was negatively related to almost all the frequently used measures of psychological well-being. Given such a comprehensive finding, one can understand why Leafgren (1990) postulated that there is a paradox in that men who are successful in meeting the expectations of the culture may harm their own health in the process (e.g., become interpersonally isolated).

Given the strong clinical implications that emanate from the research, there is a pressing need, especially for the sake of generalizability, to conduct similar studies with men from diverse racial/ethnic groups. To this end, steps should be taken to tighten the design and methodological procedures that are used in such studies. More specific, it is of the utmost importance that the research be theory driven, methodologically sound, empirical in nature, and, given the evidences of "real life and death" problems associated with extreme male gender identity, have direct clinical application.

Working from the perspective that, for the reasons noted above, psychologically oriented research on machismo is necessary, a major purpose of this chapter is to provoke thought relative to the type of theory that could be used by psychologists to provide a more substantive and pragmatic understanding of machismo as well as give consistent shape and direction to the body of studies that might emanate from such research efforts. With this purpose in mind, we propose and exemplify a psychologically based theoretical model that could be used by researchers and practitioners to give shape and direction to their respective endeavors and that identifies, from a purely clinical perspective, how this theory can be used to better understand and in turn provide more effective treatment to men whose social, mental, and physical well-being is negatively affected by their staunch adherence to a rigid traditional male gender identity.

However, before addressing these two major objectives, we need to make clear that we do not focus on machismo within the Hispanic culture from the belief that such a construct exists only in this culture.

On the contrary, we take the approach that machismo is not now and may never have been solely Hispanic phenomenon. This position is in line with Gilmore's (1990) landmark cross-cultural study of masculinity that found that concepts of manhood similar to those inherent in so-called Hispanic machismo are nearly universal, in that they can be found in most—but not all—cultures worldwide. However, despite these commonalities, differences may exist in how the equivalent of the machismo construct is defined across cultures. Subsequently, although the term machismo may have become part of the English language, especially as a result of the women's movement, what this term connotes relative to the non-Hispanic English-speaking populace is not the same as what it implies to the Hispanic populace and, in particular, to Hispanics who continue to adhere to their traditional cultural beliefs and behaviors (Mirandé, 1988). Here we use the term machismo to suggest the broad specific beliefs, attitudes, and behaviors that have been traditionally ascribed to men and are addressed throughout this chapter. We also approach the study of machismo within the Hispanic culture because of our interest to understand comprehensively and in depth the complex sociopsychological makeup of this culture. It is our belief that only through such understanding will it be possible to effectively and sensitively address the human services, educational, and physical and mental health needs and problems that many individuals who comprise this diverse culture are confronting.

Finally, although this chapter focuses on U.S. Hispanics in general, we are very aware of the great diversity that exists within the Hispanic populace (race, ethnicity, nationality, socioeconomic status level, etc.). The reasons for focusing on Hispanics in general are twofold: the belief that no one ethnic or national Hispanic subgroup has a sole market on male gender identity, or in this case the construct of machismo, and the sparsity of studies on the prevalence and impact of machismo on any one of the respective subgroups that comprise the Hispanic populace.

THE PREVALENCE OF MACHISMO

There exists a variety of perspectives on the prevalence of machismo within the Hispanic culture. Although there are those who contend that the construct is very pervasive and as such plays an important and pivotal role in defining the traditional culture itself (Gonzalez, 1982; Mirandé, 1988; Peñalosa, 1968), there are others who believe it is nothing more than a stereotypic myth inaccurately ascribed to the Hispanic culture as a whole (Baca-Zinn, 1982). Others contend that machismo is much less ingrained than previously thought and as such has played a less determining role in defining the culture (Benavides, 1992). For example, according to Benavides (1992), Mexican culture is actually matriarchal. He also contends that the whole culture is oriented to respect for and love of the mother, who raises the children, cares for the household, and passes down the family history.

Still others would grant that although the construct has played a defining role vis-à-vis the traditional culture machismo is on the decline as a result of acculturation, modernity, and/or economic advancements (Cromwell & Ruiz, 1979; Gonzalez, 1982). The few studies that support this view have tended to limit their focus on assessing the prevalence of traditional family sex roles (Gonzalez, 1982), conjugal household decision making (Cromwell & Ruiz, 1979), and conjugal interaction (i.e., the sharing of household duties) (Baca-Zinn, 1980).

Despite disagreements relative to the degree of machismo that exists among Mexican Americans, substantive data show that differentiated gender identity exists across almost all cultures (Gilmore, 1990). Furthermore, based on available data it also appears that the degree and/or level of identity relative to the respective genders can vary across cultures and within subgroups of specific cultures (see Díaz-Guerrero, 1975). Given the growing body of literature that underscores the potentially negative impact that strong and strict adherence to one's gender identity (i.e., machismo) can have on one's mental and physical well-being in today's rapidly changing society, the construct of masculine gender identity appears differentially across cultures and begs to be systematically studied and understood.

GENDER SCHEMA THEORY

To more concretely understand and in turn effectively address machismo and the differential impact that it may have on the sociopsychological functioning and well-being of Hispanic men, and, for that matter, Hispanic women, it is necessary to identify psychological theories, constructs, and/or processes that will enable us to empirically capture, measure, and examine this complex psychological phenomenon. To this end, in this section we propose that serious consideration be given to the gender identity development theory proposed by Bem (1985). Although we could have chosen any of the other major personality and/or developmental theories that have been proposed to explain gender identity, such as psychoanalytic theory (Bronfenbrenner, 1960; Freud, 1914/1966), social learning theory (Mischel, 1970), or cognitive development theory (Kohlberg, 1966), we have opted for gender schema theory because we believe that it is much more comprehensive, interrelating the basic elements inherent in both social learning and cognitive development theory. It is our contention that by interlinking these two theories with their respective emphasis on environmental factors and individual cognitive processing, gender schema theory provides the opportunity to examine the impact of a macho gender identity from a social and individual perspective. Furthermore, it serves as an excellent vehicle from which to study gender identity development with persons from diverse environments and cultures. Finally, we believe that, unlike the other explanations that have been put forth to explain machismo, gender schema theory is the only one that adequately meets the basic criteria inherent in all "good" theories (Ryckman, 1989).

Given the limitations of this chapter, it is not possible to provide an in-depth presentation of gender schema theory; consequently, what follows are those aspects of the theory that can contribute to an improved psychologically based theory of machismo. To facilitate such understanding, after each part of the theory is addressed, brief comments pertaining to the relationship of the theory to the understanding of machismo are presented. A brief example is then presented to demonstrate how the theory can lend itself to understanding specific dynamics that might be observed in a Hispanic family. The chapter concludes with a discussionof the theory's applicability to clinical practice.

The basic assumption that underlies Bem's (1985) gender schema theory is that individuals become sex typed (i.e., they acquire sex-appropriate preferences, skills, personality attributes, behaviors, and self-concepts) very early in life. According to Bem (1981b), the process of sex typing begins when the child is cognitively ready to encode and to organize information, including information about the self, in accordance with the culture's definitions of masculinity and femininity. Working from this tenet with respect to machismo, one could expect that a child born into a traditional Hispanic family in which the male and female roles are strictly and differentially defined would very likely be socialized to assume his or her respective gender role.

From the perspective of gender schema theory, the definitions that underlie masculinity and femininity can be seen as a result of historical accident. More specifically, Hispanic culture and other cultures, have

> clustered a rather heterogeneous collection of personality attributes into two mutually exclusive categories, each category considered by the culture both more characteristic of and more desirable for one or the other of the two sexes. These cultural expectations and prescriptions are well known by

virtually all members of the culture. Individuals differ from one another in the extent to which they utilize these cultural definitions of gender appropriateness as idealized standards of masculinity and femininity. . . . In particular, sex-typed individuals are highly attuned to these definitions and are motivated to keep their behavior consistent with them, a goal they accomplish both by selecting behaviors and attributes that are consistent with their gender and by avoiding behaviors and attributes that are inconsistent with it. (Bem, 1981b, p. 355)

The comprehensiveness of the theory lies in the fact that its explanation of sex typing is compatible with both cognitive development and social learning theories. For instance, similar to cognitive development theory, gender schema theory proposes that sex typing is mediated by the child's own cognitive processing. With respect to social learning theory, gender schema theory works from the perspective that sex typing is a learned phenomenon; hence it is neither inevitable nor unmodifiable.

This emphasis on learning one's sex typing in gender schema theory is contrary to developmental theories of machismo, which have tended to be more predeterministic and give great emphasis to less tangible intrapsychic, historical, and/or socioeconomic forces to explain the development of an excessively strong male gender identity—machismo (e.g., Goldwert, 1985; Ingoldsby, 1991).

Furthermore, relative to the learning aspect of the theory, Bem contends that the child learns to evaluate his or her adequacy (i.e., self-esteem) according to a gender schema and as such begins to match his or her preferences, attitudes, behaviors, and personal attributes against the prototypes stored within this schema. It should be noted that the attitudinal and behavioral prototypes stored within the schema can vary significantly across ethnic cultures, subcultures, and communities. According to Bem (1985), as the gender schema becomes tied to one's self-concept and/or self-esteem an internalized motivational factor is engendered, which prompts him or her to regulate his or her behavior so that it conforms to the culturally defined and prescribed male and female norms.

Sex-typed individuals are seen to differ from others not in the degree of masculinity or femininity they possess but in the extent to which their self-concepts and behaviors are organized on the basis of gender rather than some other dimension (Bem, 1985). Working from this theoretical perspective that emphasizes a strong relationship between self-esteem and gender identity might help to explain why certain more traditionally oriented Hispanic men are so reluctant to relinquish extreme macho-oriented beliefs, attitudes, and behaviors that may be unconsciously contributing to the development of serious mental and health-related problems for themselves and/or their families.

Having described the theory, we present a brief example that demonstrates its use for understanding specific dynamics and subsequent problems that might be observed in a Hispanic family. To better understand such dynamics, background and orienting information is first provided. It is safe to say that schemas, in general, have a historical and developmental basis and are differentially affected by environmental and situational variables. There is some evidence that the traditional male gender schema may thrive in a more stable agrarian environment. Where the male head of the family is expected to maintain control of his emotions and provide a sense of security and stability. He is the final arbiter in all of the significant decisions within the family as well as the source of economic power.

The tight emotional control exhibited by such a male is usually not a problem as long as there are no major changes in his environment or direct challenges to his male schema. In this scenario, the woman is most frequently the one who takes care of the family, manages the household duties and responsibilities, and serves as the broker between the family and the rest of the community. The children are expected to be respectful of their parents and elders and, depending on their sex, are prescribed gender-specific roles and behaviors that they are expected to carry out without question. The division of gender-tied roles and behaviors in the family remains in balance and without question as long as the environment remains constant. However, if the environment changes, this tenuous balance can be altered rapidly. The type of environmental change to which we allude is that which takes place when a traditionally oriented Mexican family from Mexico immigrates to a U.S. city. This change of environment can significantly challenge male gender schemas that were adaptive in a previous setting but are now maladaptive in their present setting.

Having set the stage, direction is now given to a hypothetical family that three years ago immigrated to the United States from Mexico. The family in question is composed of mother, father, and four children, aged 6, 8, 11, and 14. The father works as an on-call laborer for a roofing company, and the mother has an entry-level assembling job at a small electronics company. The children are all in school, regularly watch English-language television programs, and as such are in constant contact with the dominant culture. Hence their traditional respective gender schemas are under constant challenge; however, given their youthfulness, their schemas may not be as staunchly ingrained and thus more malleable and adaptive to change. In some cases, the challenges that occur may lead to confusion and/or conflict with their parents whose schemas are more strongly rooted and less adaptive to change.

In this family, the mother finds it necessary to work outside the home for the family to remain financially solvent. Working gives her new opportunities and the ability to have a share in the wielding of economic power. New behaviors that are learned on the job and in her interactions with others may subtly influence and challenge aspects of her traditional female gender schemas.

Needless to say, all of the changes that occur in the children and the mother can affect the control and the prestige that are an integral part of the father's gender schemas. The children may now have to assume the role of broker and translator for the father in his interactions with the wider community. Having the children assume such a role may be humiliating because he is used to commanding a position of authority, power, and respect. Adding injury to insult, the mother is employed in a better-paying position that provides fringe benefits and that has greater stability and opportunities for job advancement. The father, adhering to his traditional male gender schemas may find himself greatly challenged, confused, and anxious vis-à-vis his previously unchallenged role as male head of household. Unfortunately, his gender-related schemas do not allow him to talk to someone about, or seek help regarding, his state of confusion and anxiety.

Having no expressive acceptable outlets, according to the research described earlier in this chapter, the resulting emotional turmoil may express itself somatically (e.g., ulcers, high blood pressure) or may lead to depression and/or violence directed toward self and/or others. In an attempt to reassert himself the father may exaggerate behaviors that had been adaptive in his previous environment (e.g., becoming more authoritative and exerting more control over his family) or may resort to high-risk behaviors such as excessive drinking or indiscriminate sexual activity. Of course, this dire scenario is not inevitable. The potentially negative outcomes for the father can be averted if he is willing and able to take steps to change his rigid gender schema (i.e., attitudes, beliefs) and his behaviors so that they are more accommodating to the new environmental and situational demands that he is forced to face on a daily basis.

IMPLICATIONS FOR CLINICAL INTERVENTIONS

Working from this example, we address the applicability of masculine gender-schema theory to clinical practice. To this end, the types of social, mental, and physical health problems associated with a strong adherence to a traditional male gender identity, and which were identified in the introductory section of this chapter, are used to differentially demonstrate the way in which male gender identity schemas may impact the affect, cognitions, and behaviors relative to varied aspects of the therapeutic process, from initial help seeking to presenting problems and, finally, to actual clinical and/or educational interventions.

From a help-seeking perspective, there is evidence showing that men with strong male gender identity schemas avoid all situations where they perceive themselves as helpless or weak. Therapy is seen by these men as an admission that they are no longer in control of the situation, and for this reason the need for therapy is often minimized or actively avoided (Heppner, 1981). To this point, Beck and Jones (1973) noted that when a male/female couple seeks therapeutic services it is usually the woman who initiates the process. Our own clinical experience with low-income, minimally acculturated Hispanic couples corroborates this. For males tied to a traditional gender schema, self-esteem is associated with the ability to cope and problem solve in an autonomous fashion (Heilbrun, 1961; Scher, 1981). In this light, therapy is looked upon as a humiliating and stigmatizing experience by such males (Johnson, 1988; Scher, 1979). Furthermore, because intimacy may threaten the male gender identity (O'Neil, 1981a, 1981b), the traditionally oriented male client is even less likely to view therapy as a solution to his problems (Carlson, 1981), tending instead to ignore them. From a complementary perspective, the focus of therapy on expressing feelings and emotions places these males at an even greater risk of feeling inadequate and thus denying help.

Given these findings, how can clinicians intervene in ways that remove some of these internalized barriers that impede the traditional male client's access to the therapeutic process? To this end, the therapist must begin to consider the wounded self-esteem and lack of motivation of the man who is forced to admit his inability to cope with his life and enlist the assistance of another to straighten things out (Heilbrun, 1961). Scher (1981) notes that men, conditioned to believe that autonomy is the highest good, can be adamant in their determination to face the world alone. The therapist can remove some of the barriers to treatment by reframing that a truly strong person is one who is able to acknowledge difficulties and obtain temporary assistance to surmount them and that it is in the client's and his family's best interests to do so (Silverberg, 1986).

From an intervention perspective, Robertson and Fitzgerald (1992) found that alternative helping formats (i.e., workshops, seminars, or classes) were rated far more favorably than personal counseling by men who were high in restrictive emotionality and high in success, power, and competition orientation, whereas for men with less traditional masculinity ideologies, both traditional psychological services (i.e., personal counseling) and alternative helping formats were viewed equally favorably. Complementing the work of Robertson and Fitzgerald (1992), the findings of McBride (1991) suggest that educational programs can help traditionally oriented men increase their interactions with others as well as help them take the first steps toward bridging the gap between cognition and affect. More specifically, McBride's study found that a child care program for fathers increased their involvement, accessibility, and responsibility for the care of their children. The fathers who participated in the study reported feeling more competent in their paternal role.

As noted in the introductory section of this chapter, masculine gender schemas may be dangerous to men's physical and psychological health in at least two ways. First, the adherence to the masculine gender role may lead to suppression or somatization of emotional problems. Second, men may not attend to physical symptoms or medical conditions because to do so would betray the schema of male strength and invulnerability. Addressing the first concern, Silverberg (1986) suggests that alexithymia is common in men and is an obstacle to psychotherapeutic progress. To overcome this obstacle, therapists need to convey to these clients that emotions rather than thoughts are causing them difficulty. In effect, therapists may need to take the time to teach male clients how to explore their emotions and/or inner life. To this end, therapists might consider using gestalt interventions to put men in touch with their feelings. However, every effort should be made to help clients understand the nature and purpose of the intervention.

This inability or difficulty in recognizing or describing one's emotions is implicated in the development of psychosomatic reactions (Flannery, 1978; Nemiah, 1977). There is a body of research suggesting that somatization of psychological distress may be more prevalent in Hispanic cultures (as reviewed by Angel & Guarnaccia, 1989). Moreover, some men may find that their medical condition serves as a means to compensate for their emotional inexpressiveness and male gender role rigidity. Being sick or injured may function as an emotional release from having to carry the weight of normal responsibilities and may fulfill affective needs as a result of talking about one's ailments and receiving attention from caregivers (Sutkin & Good, 1987). In dealing with Hispanic men who are not aware of their feelings or are unable to deal with them, it may be necessary to first address the physical symptoms. Toward this end we recommend that therapists work collaboratively with physicians and other practitioners involved in these male patients' health care.

With respect to the second concern, regardless of the psychological "advantages" of illness, many men do not seek medical attention until their condition has deteriorated as a result of their denial or inability to recognize their internal feelings, stress, strain, and medical symptoms (Meinecke, 1981; Silverberg, 1986). Given the evidence that individuals continuously monitor their health status and that this self-assessment is influenced by cultural and class factors (Angel & Guarnaccia, 1989), there is a need for clinicians to carefully examine the function that machismo might play in Hispanic men's failure or efforts to assess their health status and their willingness to access medical help, if necessary, and, in turn, to diligently follow a prescribed medical treatment.

From a personal health and societal perspective, given that the percentage of Hispanic men infected with HIV/AIDS itself is disproportionately higher than that of White males (Morales, 1990; Soriano, 1993), there is a pressing need for therapists to understand and in turn address the relationship between a macho orientation and high-risk behaviors, including the resistance to use condoms, that greatly increase the probability of acquiring the virus from both heterosexual and homosexual contacts. Furthermore, given the evidence that strong adherence to machismo values may hinder HIV-positive Hispanic men from revealing their HIV status to others, and as such prevent these men from seeking the emotional and social support they need to cope with the disease, it is urgent that more effective community-based outreach support systems be developed to reach these men.

With regard to violence, which is also a pressing societal concern, men who batter typically (a) hold traditional patriarchal beliefs, (b) are emotionally inexpressive, (c) are isolated due to their difficulty in maintaining close relationships, (d) have low self-esteem that appears to be related to their using violence to achieve superiority, and (e) are unemployed or dissatisfied with their current employment (Koval et al., 1982). When working with men who suffer from excessive anger and/or direct outbursts of physical violence directed against their spouses and/or others, therapists should consider such interventions as consciousness-raising groups, which explore the emotional inflexibility inherent in the masculine gender role, and role-plays and modeling as means of finding alternatives to violence when facing stress-related problems.

There is also a need for a close working alliance between practitioners and researchers to more closely examine the relationship between male adolescent endorsement of masculinity ideology and school difficulties, substance abuse, violence, delinquency, and sexual activity. To this end, clinicians and educators need to work together not only to understand but also to develop collaborative proactive and preventive programs to address problems in these four areas.

Finally from a comprehensive perspective, therapists need to take a more aggressive part in combating the stigma associated with personal and mental-health-related problems. Periodic and ongoing features in local newspapers and on radio and television would be a step in the right direction. Such reports should address the myths and stereotypes associated with mental-health-related problems, emphasize the importance of both men and women addressing their problems as soon as possible, and provide detailed information on the availability and accessibility of affordable community-based services.

CONCLUSION

As this chapter has shown, given the fact that recent literature shows a strong relationship between levels of male gender identity schemas and social, mental, and physical health well-being, there is a pragmatic clinical need to give serious and in-depth attention to the construct of machismo within diverse racial/ethnic groups and, given our own interest, the Hispanic populace in particular. To this end, we focused on the psychologically based gender schema theory, which in the past two decades has received quite a bit of attention from researchers studying gender identity primarily among the White majority. In focusing on this theory, our intention was to provide a rationale for why we believe it affords a solid theoretical base for clinical work relative to Hispanic male gender identity. Finally, we addressed how this theory can be used to better understand and, in turn, provide more effective clinical treatment to men whose social, mental, and physical well-being is negatively affected by their staunch adherence to a rigid traditional male gender identity. Having accomplished what we set out to do, we once more want to underscore the fact that our study of machismo in the Hispanic population should in no way be interpreted as meaning that this gender-related construct is found solely among Hispanics. As previously stated here, and supported by research (Gilmore, 1990), we know that this is not the case. Our interest in studying machismo is based on the belief that to effectively provide clinical services to any ethnic group it is necessary to carefully research and, in turn, understand any and all constructs, be they mythical or psychological in nature.

16

◆

Sex Role Identity Among College Students

A Cross-Cultural Analysis

BRUNILDA DE LEÓN

Although researchers have long recognized that issues of gender, race, and ethnicity are important variables in understanding similarities and differences in sex role development, cross-cultural studies on this topic are still scarce. Despite the fact that investigators have long argued in favor of the importance of the cultural, racial, ethnic, and social contexts, most research has focused on White middle-class women and also limited the inclusion or excluded Latino and Black women in their samples. The same can be said for Latino and African American males as well.

Researchers have begun to respond to the need for studying gender and ethnicity as status variables and to examine each variable (gender and ethnicity) both separately and in combination (Reid & Comas-Diaz, 1990; Salgado de Snyder, Cervantes, & Padilla, 1990; Vazquez & Gonzalez, 1981). In general, research studies have confirmed the importance of gender and ethnicity in understanding sociocultural and psychological characteristics, attitudes, and behaviors of ethnic minority individuals in our society.

Several researchers argue that although women are more inclined than males to reject traditional and stereotyped views of gender roles (Tucker, James, & Turner, 1985), both sexes in the United States are moving from traditional to more egalitarian sex role orientations (Tucker et al., 1985). Changes in the political, socioeconomic, and educational systems have brought changes in the family structure and marital roles (Davis & Chavez, 1985).

However, the literature indicates that in spite of societal and economic changes (e.g., industrialization, increased number of women working outside of the home, division of marital child-rearing tasks, household responsibilities) Blacks and Latinos still have a sex role system that is different from that of mainstream Americans (Reid & Comas-Diaz, 1990; Tucker et al., 1985). Blacks, for example, have been found to have more flexible family and gender roles and they share child-rearing duties to a greater degree than other racial/ethnic groups (Ho, 1987; Reid & Comas-Diaz, 1990). Furthermore, Black females with their long history of multiple roles as wives, mothers, providers (working outside of the home), and strong sources of social and emotional support to their families tend to exhibit more instrumental (positive masculine) qualities that facilitate the performance of these many roles (Gump, 1980; Reid & Comas-Diaz, 1990). In fact, most cross-cultural studies have found that Black women endorse more masculine qualities than Anglo women (Brown, Fee-Fulkerson, Furr, Ware, & Voight, 1984; Mason & Bumpass, 1975; Pugh & Vazquez-Nuttall, 1983). On the other hand, Black females tend to maintain traditional attitudes toward family and home behaviors (Gump, 1975, 1980; Reid & Comas-Diaz, 1990). Some authors also report that Black males have historically shared child-rearing responsibilities. However, they tend to hold traditional views about their child-rearing practices (Ho, 1987). Price-Bonham and Skeen (1982), for example, found that Black fathers tend to be significantly less androgynous (more traditional) in their attitudes toward their daughters and their sons than are White fathers. Other studies have found that Anglo, Black, and Latino males differ in their attitudes toward the roles of women (Wheeler, Wheeler, & Torres-Raines, 1977) and in their sex role orientations (De León, 1990; Price-Bonham & Skeen, 1982).

Because gender roles tend to be affected by cultural transitions and subsequent cultural adaptation (Comas-Diaz, 1987, 1988; Salgado de Snyder et al., 1990; Torres-Matrullo, 1980), when examining Latino populations, several other factors must be considered. Some of these factors are changes in traditional cultural values as a result of rapid socioeconomic changes, rapid transition into an industrialized society and educational institutions, migration, and related issues. Psychological stress and mental health status have been found to be highly correlated with generalized distress that is primarily related to gender and ethnic differences and to the process of adaptation of Puerto Ricans and other Latinos (Canino, 1982; Comas-Diaz, 1987; Salgado de Snyder et al., 1990; Soto & Shaver, 1982; Torres-Matrullo, 1980). However, several researchers have found that young, educated, and employed Puerto Rican and other Latino women in the United States with less traditional sex role orientation and higher levels of acculturation and socioeconomic status usually experience a more positive adaptation process and exhibit less adaptive and psychological stress (Espin, 1987; Rosario, 1982; Soto & Shaver, 1982; Torres-Matrullo, 1980).

Although research studies have mixed results, the literature also suggests that Puerto Rican and other Latino females are moving toward a more liberal sex role orientation. Research studies of Puerto Rican males have been neglected in the literature. Nevertheless, some researchers have begun to show some evidence that Puerto Rican males are also moving toward less traditional sex role orientation (De León, 1990; Del Valle, 1990; Ginorio, 1979; Ramos-McKay, 1977).

In spite of some mixed results, what appears to be fairly consistent in the literature is that there are differences in sex role orientation that can be attributed to race/ethnicity, gender, and social class for the cultural groups included in this study.

The main purpose of this cross-cultural study was to examine the sex role identity of male and female college students of four ethnic/racial groups; Puerto Ricans in Puerto Rico (PR-PR), Puerto Ricans in the United States (PR-US), Anglo Americans (Anglos) and Black Americans (Blacks). Ethnicity/race and sex were expected to be significant factors affecting self-attribution of masculine and feminine traits among the four cultural groups. Because migration to the United States and levels of acculturation of Puerto Ricans and other Latinos have been associated with changes in family roles and gender identity (Comas-Diaz, 1988; Salgado de Snyder et al., 1990), place of residence and degree of direct exposure to North American culture were also expected to affect the degrees of feminine and masculine qualities of Puerto Rican students. Similarly, Puerto Rican students were expected to have more traditional gender role identities (Canino, 1982; Ginorio, 1979; Rosario, 1982; Torres-Matrullo, 1980). A background questionnaire and the Bem Sex

Role Inventory (BSRI; Bem, 1974) were administered to all participants of the study.

METHODOLOGY

Subjects

Undergraduate male and female students attending a large university in Puerto Rico and students in six colleges from the northeastern part of the United States participated in this study. The sample of 763 students was divided into four ethnic/racial groups: 203 Puerto Ricans from Puerto Rico (126 females, 77 males), 197 Puerto Ricans from the United States (124 females, 73 males), 198 Anglo Americans (105 females, 93 males), and 170 Black Americans (80 females, 90 males). The ages of the sample ranged from 18 to 42 years for PR-PR, 18 to 52 for PR-US, 18 to 40 for Anglos, and 18 to 54 for Blacks. However, it is important to note that 88% of the total sample ranged in age from 18 to 25. The average age for each group was 21.10 for PR-PR, 25.08 for PR-US, 20.56 for Anglos, and 20.47 for Blacks. The results of the statistical data indicate that 58% of PR-PR had a family income of $19,000 or less, and 56% of the PR-US sample had that same family income. In contrast, 45% of Anglo students reported a family income of $50,000 or more, and only 7.4% of this group had an income of $19,000 or less. For Black students, 35% reported a family income of $50,000 or more, and only 12% had incomes of $19,000 or less. The marital status of the sample was as follows: single, 85.8%; married, 7.4%; and other, 4.1%. The level of education attained was distributed as follows: 20.4% freshmen, 31.3% sophomores, 27.4% juniors, and 20.8% seniors.

Procedure

Students were recruited through the cooperation of university officials. Those who volunteered were given a packet with the consent letter, instructions, a background questionnaire, and the short form of the BSRI. Students were interviewed in group sessions of approximately 20 to 25. Both the background questionnaire and the short form of the BSRI were administered to Puerto Rican students in English or Spanish, depending on their language proficiency.

Instrument

The BSRI was designed to study gender role identity and psychological androgyny. The original instrument consists of 60 items: 20 stereotypically feminine characteristics, 20 stereotypically masculine characteristics, and 20 neutral or socially desirable characteristics. The short, 30-item form of the BSRI, which includes half of the items of the original inventory (10 masculine, 10 feminine, and 10 neutral characteristics), was used for this study. On the BSRI, students are asked to give self-ratings on the feminine and masculine dimensions. The short form of the BSRI is considered not just a version of the original BSRI but an instrument that is psychometrically superior and a factorially purer index of "instrumental" and "expressive" traits (Mitchell, 1985). The person taking the BSRI is asked to indicate on a 7-point scale how well each of the items on the scale describes herself or himself. The scale ranges from 1 (*never or almost never true*) to 7 (*always or almost always true*). The BSRI treats femininity and masculinity as two independent dimensions rather than as two ends of a single dimension. It therefore allows a person to indicate whether she or he is high on both dimensions (androgynous), low on both dimensions (undifferentiated), or high on one dimension but low on the other (either feminine or masculine) (Bem, 1981a).

For the purpose of research, Bem (1981a) recommends that individuals be classified, on the basis of a median split, into four distinct sex role groups: feminine, masculine, androgynous, and undifferentiated.

The back translation method (Brislin, Lonner, & Thorndike, 1973) was used to prepare Spanish translations of the background questionnaire and the BSRI.

RESULTS

First, data from the BSRI were analyzed by the median-split method (Bem, Martyna, & Watson, 1976) and students were classified as androgynous, feminine, masculine, or undifferentiated. The categories on the BSRI by each ethnic/racial group in the sample are presented in Table 16.1. Frequency distributions show that a total of 51.4% of the sample ($N = 763$) was classified as androgynous. The remaining 48.1% was distributed as follows: feminine, 17.9%; masculine, 18.1%; and undifferentiated, 12.6%. The number of students in the androgynous category of

Table 16.1 Breakdown of Sex Role Categories on BSRI, by Group and Sex

Sex Role Group	PR-PR		PR-US		Anglos		Blacks	
	M	F	M	F	M	F	M	F
Androgynous								
n	44	75	48	57	36	43	47	41
Percentage	57.1	59.5	65.8	46.0	38.7	41.0	54.0	53.9
Feminine								
n	18	17	12	22	14	36	4	13
Percentage	23.4	13.5	16.6	17.7	15.1	34.3	4.6	17.1
Masculine								
n	9	22	7	23	27	12	23	15
Percentage	11.7	17.5	9.6	18.5	29.0	11.4	26.4	19.7
Undifferentiated								
n	6	12	8	22	16	14	13	7
Percentage	7.8	9.5	8.2	17.7	17.2	13.3	14.9	9.2

NOTE: BSRI = Bem Sex Role Inventory; PR-PR = Puerto Ricans from Puerto Rico; PR-US = Puerto Ricans from the United States.

the BSRI was equally distributed among both sexes: 50% of the females and 53% of the males. The highest percentage of students in the androgynous category was found among PR-PR (59%), followed by Blacks (54%), PR-US (53%), and Anglos (40%).

A comparison of the mean scores and standard deviations with the original normative sample of the short form of the BSRI (Bem, 1975) shows that males and females in this study have higher mean average scores on both femininity and masculinity scales. Table 16.2 presents means, medians, and standard deviations for the Femininity and Masculinity scales for the normative sample of the short form of the BSRI and for students in this study.

Females of the four ethnic/racial groups were compared on the BSRI Feminine Scale using an analysis of variance. Mean responses of the four groups of females were 5.98 for PR-PR, 5.97 for Anglos, 5.95 for PR-US, and 5.86 for Blacks. Ethnicity/race and place of residence (for Puerto Ricans only) proved to be nonsignificant, $F(3, 427) = .5602, p < .05$. Thus the hypothesis that the four groups of females students would significantly differ in self-attribution of feminine qualities on the BSRI was rejected.

When females were compared on the Masculine Scale of the BSRI, a significant difference in masculine traits was found, $F(3, 427) = 6.56$,

Table 16.2 Distribution of Means and Standard Deviations Among Respondents of the Short Form of the BSRI, by Ethnic/Racial Groups and Gender Compared to Bem's (1981b) Normative Sample

	Subgroups										
	PR-PR		PR-US		Anglos		Blacks		Norms		
BSRI Category	M	F	M	F	M	F	M	F	M	F	
Feminine											
Mean	5.83	5.98	5.98	5.95	5.22	5.97	5.42	5.85	5.19	5.57	
SD	.688	.648	.732	.792	.879	.652	.920	.770	.78	.76	
n	77	126	73	124	93	105	87	76	475	340	
Masculine											
Mean	5.37	5.32	5.41	5.17	5.22	4.89	4.89	5.38	4.88	4.78	
SD	.794	.798	.792	.925	.741	.779	.779	.917	.79	.81	
n	77	126	73	124	93	105	87	76	475	340	

NOTE: BSRI = Bem Sex Role Inventory; PR-PR = Puerto Ricans from Puerto Rico; PR-US = Puerto Ricans from the United States. The data from normative sample are from *Manual for the Bem Sex Role Inventory* (Bem, 1981b, p. 7).

$p < .001$. The mean scores for each group were 5.32 for PR-PR, 5.17 for PR-US, 4.89 for Anglos, and 5.38 for Blacks. Mean scores indicate that Black females obtained the highest scores and Anglo women obtained the lowest. As predicted, ethnicity/race was a significant factor in the degree of masculine traits that these women attributed to themselves. When the Scheffé test was applied, a significant difference was found between Anglos and Blacks and between Anglos and PR-PR but not PR-US.

Male of the four cultural groups were compared on the BSRI Masculine and BSRI Feminine scales. No statistical significance was found in self-attribution of masculine qualities for males of the four ethnic/racial groups in the analysis of variance, $F(3, 326) = 1.318, p < .05$. Mean scores for the group of males were quite similar (PR-PR = 5.31; PR-US = 5.41; Anglos = 5.22; Black = 5.43) and the hypothesis that the groups would differ in their BSRI Masculine scores was rejected. When males of the four cultural groups were compared on the BSRI Feminine Scale, however, ethnicity/ race had a significant effect. The results of the ANOVA revealed mean scores of 5.83 for PR-PR, 5.81 for PR-US, 5.22 for Anglos, and 5.42 for Blacks, and statistically significant differences were found among these groups, $F(3, 326) = 11.244, p < .01$. A post hoc test (Scheffé) indicates that Puerto Rican males of both groups (PR-PR and PR-US) were significantly different from Anglo and Black males in their BSRI Femininity scores. No statistical differences, however, were found between Anglos and Blacks. Puerto Rican students in the sample scored significantly higher than Anglos and Blacks on the BSRI Feminine Scale.

Additional statistical analyses reveal that Puerto Rican males had the highest percentage in the feminine category of the BSRI (PR-PR = 23.4; PR-US = 16.4; Anglos = 15.1; Blacks = 4.6) and the smallest percentage classified as masculine on the BSRI (PR-PR = 11.7; PR-US = 9.6; Anglos = 29.0; Blacks = 26.4).

The effect of age, marital status, and income on scores on the BSRI were analyzed using cross-tabulation and analysis of variance procedures. In each case, the relationship of the above demographic variables was examined. None of the relationships was statistically significant.

DISCUSSION

One of the most significant results of this study was that regardless of gender, ethnicity/race, income, and place of residence (for Puerto

Ricans), the majority of the students in the sample were more similar than different in sex role identity. As shown on Table 16.1, 51.4% of males and females of the four ethnic/racial groups were classified as androgynous on the BSRI, which indicates that these students scored high in both masculine and feminine traits. This finding implies a contemporary, ideal, and more liberal sex role preference and instrumental orientation (Bem, 1974, 1981a) among all groups. The fact that all the groups were selected from a college population with similar levels of education and other demographic characteristics—for example, age and marital status—might account for some of the similarities. The finding of no significant differences due to income, age, and marital status lends support to the findings of similarities within the sample.

The results of the study also revealed that women of the four ethnic/racial groups were significantly different from each other in their self-attribution of masculine traits, but no significant differences were found on these women's self-attribution of feminine qualities. The data revealed that Black women attributed to themselves the most masculine qualities, whereas Anglo women scored lowest on self-attribution of masculine traits. When the BSRI-Masculine scores of the four groups were further analyzed, interesting results were obtained. First, Puerto Rican females in Puerto Rico were not found to be significantly different from their Puerto Rican counterparts in the United States. Second, although the two groups of Puerto Rican females were not significantly different from each other, island Puerto Ricans obtained mean average scores that were close to those of Black females. Last, the responses of Puerto Rican females in the United States yielded mean average scores that are closer to those of Anglo females.

Although cross-cultural studies on gender roles are limited and the findings of recent research are inconsistent (Vazquez-Nuttall, Romero-Garcia, & De León, 1987), our findings are similar to those of Zeff (1982), who found Mexican American, Black, and White American females to be more similar than different with regard to sex role orientation, and the majority of the participants were androgynous. Our findings were also similar to those of Pugh and Vazquez-Nuttall (1983), who found Black women to be the most masculine, Hispanics next, and White women the least masculine. Several other researchers have also found Black females to hold more masculine/instrumental and androgynous attitudes and sex role behaviors than Anglos and/or other ethnic minority females (Brown et al., 1984; Mason & Bumpass, 1975). A long history of slavery, oppression, and participation in the labor force, and the need to be both employed workers and homemakers have forced

Black females to find instrumental ways to reconcile their many roles (Gump, 1980; Ho, 1987; Pugh & Vazquez-Nuttall, 1983; Reid & Comas-Diaz, 1990; Tucker et al., 1985). This experience is, to some extent, shared with other ethnic minority women.

Contrary to what is suggested in the early socioanthropological literature (Vazquez-Nuttall et al., 1987), and consistent with more recent psychosocial research (Canino, 1982; De León, 1990; Pacheco, 1981; Ramos-McKay, 1977; Rogler & Santana-Cooney, 1984; Torres-Matrullo, 1980), Puerto Rican women in the sample appear to have more positive masculine (instrumental) and contemporary gender roles and attitudes than previously described in the literature. Puerto Rican females in this study did not endorse high degrees of feminine attributes in their self-descriptions and did not perceive themselves as stereotypically feminine, passive, and submissive. Because no significant differences in self-attributed feminine traits were found among the two groups of Puerto Rican women (PR-PR and PR-US), the findings of this study do not support the hypothesis that Puerto Rican females in the island hold a more traditional gender role identity. Thus place of residence (Puerto Rico or United States), direct exposure to North American culture, and levels of acculturation do not appear to have a major impact in sex role development and self-attribution of feminine qualities of the Puerto Rican females in the sample.

The data on self-attributed masculine traits among males of the four ethnic/racial groups show a pattern that is consistent with that of females. No significant differences were found among the four groups of males on the masculine scale of the BSRI. The results did not show significant differences between the two groups of Puerto Rican males (PR-PR and PR-US). Puerto Rican males, regardless of place of residence are more similar than different, and they described themselves as very similar to Anglo and Black males. Nevertheless, when males were compared on the Femininity Scale, significant differences between Puerto Ricans (PR and US) and the two other groups of males (Anglos and Blacks) were found. Puerto Rican males in both samples described themselves as possessing the most feminine sex role orientation. Furthermore, Puerto Rican males in the sample had the highest percentage of males in the feminine category of the BSRI (PR-PR = 23.4; PR-US = 16.4; Anglos = 15.1; Blacks = 4.6), and the smallest number of males classified as masculine (PR-PR = 11.7; PR-US = 9.6; Anglos = 29.0; Blacks = 26.4). These findings are intriguing and unexpected for two reasons. First, they fail to support the stereotypes that describe Puerto Rican males as traditional, dominant, and extremely masculine and they question the myth of the superiority of the Puerto Rican male. Second, these findings provoke legitimate questions about intrinsic psychometric properties of the BSRI as an accurate and culturally sensitive measure of sex role identity for this group.

Lara-Cantú (1989; Lara-Cantú & Navarro-Arias, 1986) found that although the BSRI showed a factorial structure similar to other studies with English-speaking samples it may not be the most suitable inventory to assess the multidimensionality of personality traits of the sex role system of some ethnic/racial/cultural groups (e.g., Mexicans or Puerto Ricans). A multicultural understanding of the sex role attitudes and behaviors within Puerto Rican society may be helpful in explaining the unexpected results on the responses of Puerto Rican males. Puerto Rico, like other Latin American countries, has a markedly different cultural heritage, with greater emphasis on cooperation and affiliation. There is also a strong emphasis on a sense of familism, concern for others (especially for children and family members), strong belief in the extended family, and interpersonal relationships that involve a highly valued nurturance quality that is usually identified as a feminine characteristic. This nurturance component is present in everyday life events in Puerto Rican society. Therefore, it is possible to speculate that Puerto Rican men have endorsed many items on the BSRI that contain some of these positive feminine qualities.

Another interpretation of the results of the BSRI is that as women become less traditional in their sex role orientations (Tucker et al., 1985; Vazquez & Gonzalez, 1981; Williams, 1988) they will influence the behavior of males, and changes in the same positive direction will take place. As changes in the socioeconomic structure affect family and gender role expectations within a society, men and women have to negotiate their societal roles and accommodate into more appropriate lifestyles and problem-solving strategies that are necessary for social functioning. As many authors have argued (Acosta-Belen, 1986; Christensen, 1979), changes in Puerto Rican society are occurring as a result of technological and socioeconomic conditions that result in greater participation and power of Puerto Rican women in conjugal and family decision making, education, and sociopolitical life.

Additionally, there is evidence in the literature that indicates that women in Puerto Rican society had extraordinary importance, influence, and power under the island aborigines' (Taino) society, where family name and tribal leadership, for example, were inherited through the woman (Acosta-Belen, 1986; Sued-Badillo, 1975). Research literature suggests that women continue to have an important role in the family, society, economy, and political development in Puerto Rico (Acosta-Belen, 1986; Christensen, 1979; Pugh & Vazquez-Nuttall, 1983). As women gain more economic, educational, and political participation in the society, they will increase their influence in the family, particularly in the socialization of children and ultimately changing existing pervasive sex role stereotypes. A growing feminist movement in the island and increased levels of awareness about stereotyped sex role behaviors (Comas-Diaz, 1987; Valle-Ferrer, 1986) may also account for some of these unexpected findings. The male superiority within the Puerto Rican culture is a myth that needs to be reexamined from a more sensitive cultural perspective to understand its adaptive function and role in that society. In either case, the results of this study are encouraging and call for further research on cross-cultural sex role perceptions and attitudes of males and females.

This study is clearly limited in that it compared a sample of college students from four ethnic/racial groups. Therefore, caution should be exercised when interpreting and generalizing these results to other Latino, Anglo, or Black college and noncollege populations. Future studies should consider a developmental perspective that would reveal the ever changing structure of sex role development. Changing life situations (Abrahams, Feldman, & Nash, 1978; Feldman & Aschenbrenner, 1983), stage of family life (Feldman, Biringen, & Nash, 1981), and marital status (MacDonald, Ebert, & Mason, 1987) are all involved in the processes of sex role development. Future research should take into account status variables, such as race, ethnicity, class, and education, and also developmental stages, such as adolescence, adulthood, marriage, and old age. Because data collected primarily through self-report inventories (e.g., BSRI) is especially subject to social desirability factors, future studies should supplement self-report inventories with in-depth interviews and behavioral observations. This multiple-measures approach will facilitate the identification and the study of relevant variables and factors affecting the sex role development of culturally diverse populations.

The overall results of this investigation reaffirm the view that gender and ethnicity/race are important variables in the study of sex roles that should be studied both separately and combined. Further research in this area will help in understanding changing behaviors, attitudes, and personality factors from a cultural perspective.

17

◆

Hispanic Househusbands

SHARON KANTOROWSKI DAVIS

VIRGINIA CHAVEZ

This chapter is a study of Hispanic househusbands, men who challenge the norms of the larger American culture as well as the traditions of the Hispanic subculture and opt for a role that focuses on household maintenance and emotional family support. Have these men willingly relinquished the traditional male role of economic provider for the women with whom they live? What happens to their self-concept and self-esteem? How is the role reconciled with machismo? What do they tell their friends? What do they do with their time? Are they happy? These are the questions we attempted to answer in a qualitative field study of 22 househusbands in Southern California. Questionnaires and indepth interviews were used to probe these sensitive issues.

CONCEPTUAL BACKGROUND

Marital roles continue to change and to reflect the environment in which they exist. The trend toward egalitarianism in American society has been encouraged by economic as well as social factors; the declining gross national product, high unemployment rates, and recession are notable influences, as well as the women's movement, the trend toward dual-income families, and equal rights amendment issues.

Keith and Brubaker (1977) indicate that sex role attitudes and behavioral expectations have become less traditional, with more extrafamilial activities for females and greater participation in household activities for males. The wife's employment effects not only the amount of time she spends on household chores but also the extent to which the husband shares them.

Mason and Arber (1976), Arnott (1972), and Scanzoni (1978) address the effect of outside employment on attitudes. They find that females who have careers and who are the major source economic support for their families have greater expectations for the sharing of household tasks with their spouses.

The movement of women out of the home and away from traditional, sex-typed tasks has allowed for the emergence of the househusband role, As an extension of the role reversal, the househusband is defined as a male who spends the majority of his time and energies engaged in family life and household maintenance and who is economically dependent on an adult female with whom he has made a home. The househusband role has been discussed in numerous studies (Model, 1982; Pleck, 1976; Rapoport & Rapoport, 1976), which cover related issues ranging from the effects on the masculine self-concept to specific household task assumption by males. Several studies indicate that the greater the woman's economic contribution, the greater the man's domestic contribution.

These recent developments in the institution of the family find particularly strong resistance in the traditional Hispanic family, which Montiel (1973) defines as a stable one in which the father is the dominant figure and the mother assumes an inferior position. It is considered the father's failure not to provide adequately for his family; such neglect means a loss of status and respect. The traditional Hispanic family is founded on the supremacy of the father and the corresponding self-sacrifice of the mother (Senour, 1977); the father is still mainly responsible for the economic support of the family (Montenegro, 1973). Thus when the wife works outside the home the husband may view her employment as due to his own inadequacy as a provider rather than a role and a responsibility to be shared.

A major feature of traditional Hispanic culture is machismo, and the adult male may devote considerable effort to maintain and prove his manliness (Grebler, Moore, & Guzman, 1973). He should be stronger, more reliable, and more intelligent than the female and maintain her respect. His sense of manly honor may demand repayments of insults to himself and his family; revenge is usually physical and inevitable. Male supremacy and sexual prowess must be demonstrated.

The husband/wife relationship is frequently characterized by dominance-submission. The macho male may demand complete allegiance, respect, and obedience from his wife and children (Mirandé, 1977). Mexican American men have been reluctant to give up their machismo because it allows a retention of power in a society that has traditionally discriminated against them and dehumanized them (Murillo, 1971).

If the Mexican American family transcends the traditional family pattern and becomes more modern and egalitarian, it is usually accomplished through acculturation (Zinn, 1975). Universal evolutionary changes in the family structure occur with urbanization and industrialization and with increasing exposure to American culture. In addition, situational variables affect traditional family structure. Whether integrated into middle-class society or separated from that society by subcultural differences and barrio experiences, the Hispanic family is affected by societal, economic, and social conditions. Traditional values and practices may not meet the demands of the times; sometimes they must change.

METHOD

We examined 22 Hispanic families that opted to break with some elements of tradition. In all families, the female was employed outside the home and the male defined himself as a househusband; his major identity and work activities involved the maintenance of the home. In some families, the male was employed part-time outside the home, but the female was the major source of economic support.

An accidental sample was obtained initially through family and friends. Subsequently, a snowballing effect produced additional respondents of similar economic status or social circumstance. Husbands were chosen on the basis of their dependent economic status and their active participation and sharing in household duties.

A questionnaire was constructed with 17 open- and closed-ended questions. They were distributed with the help of a local Employment Development Department office. Interviews were conducted in private in the home of the subjects. The female was asked to remain in another room of the house during the interview with the male. After the interview's completion, she was invited by the researcher to share in private her thoughts and feelings about role transcendence. The interview lasted from approximately 20 to 90 minutes, depending on the subject's understanding of and willingness to respond to the questions.

The demographic characteristics of the sample were as follows: Fifteen couples were married, 4 were cohabitating, and 3 had other living arrangements. Their ages ranged form 20 to 53; median age was 32.7 years. Thirteen men were employed; 9 were not. Only 1 had become a househusband voluntarily—that is, without external and situational inducements. Of the 15 married couples, 10 had been married less than 10 years, and 5 had been married more than 15 years. Eleven men earned less than $10,000 per year, and 3 earned $25,000 or more. Most of the men stated that their religion was Catholic, with the remaining few simply stating that they believed in God. The majority of the men had a high school education, 3 had technical and vocational training, and 4 had attended some college. Only 1 had graduated from college.

FINDINGS AND DISCUSSION

Househusbands and Outside Employment

All of the 9 men who were unemployed stated that they were currently looking for work. The majority of these men had left the workforce because of the recession. Five were unemployed because of layoffs and 3 because of disability.

As reported by the interviewees, the majority of the female partners of the unemployed men did not object to the change from breadwinner to househusband as long as they were aware of his continuing search for employment. Five women did object to their partner's staying at home, which caused unhappiness and uneasiness between them. The spouse sometimes made life at home very difficult:

> My wife yells at me and she gives me a big headache. I get depressed and nervous being around her. I cannot sleep at night because she bitches at me all the time.

> My wife give me a lot of pressure to find work. She frustrates me, and get me mad. I tend to ignore her by spending more time in the garage working on the car with my friends. My whole day is ruined because she is so grouchy and hard to live with.

Males frequently reported stress and related physical problems as an effect of the role reversal. Some of their reactions were sleepless nights, headaches, nervousness, crying, sadness, and depression. The men did not report experiencing stress in their relationships with their children.

Whether employed or unemployed, many Hispanic househusbands have accepted the nontraditional division of labor and have adjusted well to their working partners. Most of these men saw their partners as independent and autonomous beings with the right to self-determination and participation in the workforce. The masculinity of these men did not appear to be threatened. The following comments reflect these views:

> I have no objections if my wife wants to go to work. If she wants to work I would not stand in her way. I would not care what other people say. Let her do what she wants to do.

> Latin women are in the 20th century now. It is a modern world and the economy is forcing them to become independent and career-minded. The divorce rates are extremely high and they are thinking twice about marriage and the person they marry. Women are on their own two feet, and don't have to depend on a man like they used to. More women are participating in the job market, and decisions are no longer left up to their husbands. There are different roads for women to choose nowadays. The Latina lady knows she has four or five kids to support and she knows she has to survive on her own if something happens to her man or marriage. We live in a materialistic world and we need money or a job to survive. Education is not important for the Latina. Traditionally, she was raised to be a good wife, and after the kids are gone, she then has to be prepared to be on her own for this changing, technological, materialistic world.

> It doesn't bother me that I'm not providing for my family. Housework is just as hard as working in the labor force. The bad point is that it's my responsibility to go to work, but I don't feel that I have to so I can keep my dignity. As for my wife, she can go to work if she wants to.

> I'm all for my wife working. She can be exposed to the true picture of the world. Why should I deprive her of this enrichment of life? I don't want to be selfish with her and I want her to be herself and become a person. That's what life is all about. I want her to have a career and meet people in the workforce. She can always spend time with the kids and be a wife to me.

On the other hand, some husbands still held traditional views; the male should be the provider and the female should stay in the home, especially if there are children:

> Men could always find work. He should go get a job. I'm an old-fashioned Mexican. I grew up thinking about progress, staying busy, going upward in mobility. I'd have a wife at home with my children. The children need both partners, and I feel I should go to work and my wife remain at home.

> I'd let my wife go to work if she had no children, but a mother of children should be home to care for them and to see them through school.

> I love my woman to be at home. I feel stupid when I stay at home. I look for work if I'm unemployed. The husband should go out and find a job and his wife stay at home with the children.

A few husbands were extremely traditional and maintained absolute power in the relationship. Their acceptance or nonacceptance of the woman working outside the home was the determining factor of her employment status. The strongest argument used by traditional Hispanic males invoked religion and the will of God to explain and maintain the role separation and differences. It also forms part of the base upon which machismo is built:

> The Christian life changed my marital relationship. Men are trained to be the boss of the house according to the Bible. This has been going on for centuries and it is written that men are the "boss."

> God made woman to please man, to take care of him, and fulfill all of his sexual needs and desires. Women are not supposed to be working because if they did, she would be too tired for her man. I don't like to see this happen.

These men perceived their roles as designated by God. Obviously, it is difficult to discuss, question, or challenge this argument. For some, tradition was immutable; for others, it was tempered by economic necessity:

> Ain't the place for a woman to be working. After all, the Bible says this. We work out our family problems together. In the workforce, the woman is considered weaker and men influence them and this tends to destroy a marriage through the husband's jealousy. I wouldn't allow my wife to work forever. If she keeps her job, she loses me.

> I would rather see my wife at home, but because of the economic situation both of us have to work.

The husbands were divided equally in their acceptance of their wives' employment. However, the husbands who were employed tended to be more traditional. The unemployed husbands tended to accept the working wife and househusband roles because of financial necessity. Although the playing of these roles brought many of them new insights, they did not appear to be roles that would continue and entail long-term commitments by these men.

Knowledge of the Househusband Concept

The men's awareness of the concept of househusband was explored to determine if they had prior knowledge indicative of insight into their situations. The majority of the Hispanic males interviewed did not know the meaning of the term. Those who attempted to define it gave the following responses:

Two adults who help with the housework. The adults do their own laundry.

Reversing the roles—the wife goes to work and man stays at home.

A 50-50 sharing of the household responsibilities.

The person who does his own duties and will help others in the house: for example, cleaning the walls, doing the dishes, fixing the faucet. The person also does the yard work and does the garden.

Sharing the chores between the spouses. The wife doesn't do all of the housework all by herself.

Those who were consciously aware of their participation in the household and had knowledge of the term responded more positively to the questions asked than the men who had no insight into their situation.

Household Responsibilities

It is general knowledge that when a woman is employed outside the home she is still responsible for many, if not most, of the household tasks she performed prior to her employment. It has also been documented (see, e.g., Blood & Wolfe, 1960) that certain tasks have been identified as sex-role linked and traditionally performed by members of one sex. We wondered if these observations would hold true in a study of Hispanic households in which role reversals had been affected. We found, in fact, that they did.

The results of the survey indicate that the participation of the husband and wife in household chores depended on the task (see Table 17.1). The working wife's traditional chores at home remained her major responsibilities and activities: for example: laundering, cooking, billpaying, and child care—feeding, clothing, and sending them to school. In contrast, the househusband's major activities were traditional male chores: yard work, taking out the trash, and gardening. When both husband and wife were equally responsible and shared tasks, it was recorded as both. Both engaged in shopping, vacuuming, and washing the car; each had equal responsibility for the activity. In these cases, the distribution of tasks depended on the availability of time and energy of the two partners. Unemployed househusbands participated in chores to a greater extent than their employed counterparts and helped their wives because they had more time at home. As a result, the relationship appeared more egalitarian.

Leisure Time Activities

A comparison was made between the working and nonworking househusbands regarding their leisure activities and hobbies. Employed men did not have the same amount of time as their counterparts to participate in social groups or recreational activities, so those husbands with free time mainly engaged in leisure activities. The majority of the husbands in both groups chose solitary activities in their spare time. These activities included watching television, sleeping, reading, and relaxing. Husbands also reported spending time with their families and doing things with them: for example, going to the movies, to the beach, camping, and fishing. The majority of the husbands who did not work spent their leisure time participating in outdoor sports like baseball, fishing, handball, softball, and tennis in order of choice. The husbands who were employed also enjoyed these sports, but the majority preferred to spend time with their families or chose solitary activities at home.

In addition, the husbands from both groups reported a number of hobbies during the hours when they were not with their families. The majority of the working husbands chose *individual* hobbies, and the majority of the nonworking husbands chose *social* hobbies. Individual hobbies included trains, artwork, coin collecting, painting, caring for animals, cabinet making, and kite flying. Social hobbies

Table 17.1 Household Responsibilities

	Husband	Wife	Both
Laundry	2	11	9
Dishes	3	9	9
Yard work	8	2	4
Shopping	2	9	11
Vacuuming	3	5	10
Dusting	2	9	6
Cooking	2	11	8
Gardening	7	3	6
Washing the car	9	3	6
Taking out trash	13	2	3
Paying the bills	5	11	7
Making sure the kids are fed, clothed, and sent to school	2	7	3

included participating in car shows, partying, church activities, and exercising at a spa.

In general, househusbands reported that their families were of central importance in their lives and that they preferred to spend leisure time with them. However, unemployed househusbands chose more social types of leisure activities, indicating that they needed to expand and develop their social contacts outside the family. Employed househusbands apparently did not have this need.

The Househusband's Friends

Understanding and acceptance of the role reversal by the househusband's peers and friendship groups were of critical importance to our respondents. Recognizing and seeking peer approval were central themes in their reported relations with others. They felt the need to explain and justify their role behavior to others, and when peer approval was not forthcoming they felt the need to defend themselves and their reputations. The househusbands' friends played an important role in their ability to maintain self-esteem and self-respect. The maintenance of a positive self-concept and personal dignity was important to the respondents.

To facilitate a better understanding of the role reversal, friends frequently received explanations for the living arrangement. The account usually incorporated mention of their economic status and external factors as temporarily being beyond their control. They were forced, by necessity, to become more active within the household. After some discussion, their friends adopted a similar understanding of the situation. There was a greater understanding between men in similar circumstances. The shared status allowed greater insight into and appreciation of the experience.

The majority of the husband's friends seemed to accept the role transcendence when the arrangement was explained as economically necessary. When economic circumstances were understood, the househusband maintained the respect of his friends:

> My buddies respect me, and they even help me around the house, too.

> My friends accept me, they understand the job situation, and the unemployment rate being so high. They know I'm seeking full employment.

Other friends could relate to the situation because it was described as temporary and the househusband role would change back to the breadwinner role when circumstances permitted:

> My friends understand my home situation because of my disability problem. They know it's not me—otherwise I would be working instead of being home with my wife.

Some househusbands reported having a positive effect on their friends' attitudes and activities in their own homes; the friends were more involved in home activities because of their association with a role transcender:

> My friends tell me that I am crazy, but since they see me help my wife and children, they have since changed their minds. I told them to help their wives and they did. The wives appreciated my encouraging them and expressing my feelings to help them at home.

The Hispanic male expects to be treated with dignity and respect by his friends and, as a warning to any who might malign his image, one interviewee aggressively stated,

> I would get pissed off if they would say anything bad about me. I do the housework because no one else will. I explained to them that my wife is sick and they understand. My friends do not make fun of me.

Because of the Hispanic traditions of role segregation and machismo, negative or derogatory comments from friends and acquaintances are encountered. Respondents reported being ridiculed, derided, and called *chavalas,* the Spanish word for women, or being feminine. An effective way of handling the derision was to react with humor and not to get angry or defensive when the insult occurred:

> I shined it on and laughed about it.

> I knew they were playing around and that they were teasing me. It was nothing serious, so we all laughed about it.

Yet some men did react negatively to the derision and reported responding with physical violence or verbal aggression:

> They called me "pussy whipped," and I ignored this comment, but I put him in his place. I told him off!

> After he called me a chavala, I kicked his ass. I then responded negatively by saying, "Fuck you!"

The husband's self-esteem was clearly enhanced by his friends giving him respect. Friends accepted and better understood the role transcendence when it was explained as being born of necessity. When the husband's masculinity and macho image were questioned or maligned by significant others; it had a deleterious effect on self-esteem.

Machismo and Role Transcendence

Machismo is being challenged by the present economic situation affecting the Hispanic adult male's role, social status, and marital obligations. Without full outside employment, his assistance with the household responsibilities and the children is requested by his wife. With her employment, his assistance becomes necessary. In becoming a role transcender, he modifies the traditional division of labor.

Upon acceptance of the role by family, friends, and the househusband himself, he receives positive reinforcement. This reinforcement enhances his self-acceptance and dignity, and he, in turn, gives more emotional support to his family and spends more time at home with them. He can develop a positive attitude toward his contribution in household affairs and this affects his family relations. He may help his wife with household chores and baby-sit children when needed:

> I really enjoy doing the housework. I try to have it done before noon so I can have the afternoon off to spend more time playing with my children.

The male Hispanic tradition of singular control of and responsibility for the family can be modified, if only temporarily. Sharing economic responsibility and household tasks may ease social pressures experienced by the traditional household head. In addition, he can better understand and empathize with his wife and her role performance as he begins to share the responsibilities in their home. One husband agreed that the role reversal helped him understand what his wife experienced on a daily basis:

> It doesn't bother me to stay home. Men should be home for 3 months and have their wives feed them bullshit. The men would change for the better.

In general, the househusbands in this study had a positive attitude toward their role transcending and regularly helped their spouses with the household chores. They shared the responsibilities and effected greater equality in their marriages. The strength of machismo may be slowly diminishing, if only as a result of temporary economic necessity giving rise to role reversals. Perhaps the understanding gained by these men because of increased activity in the home will not be forgotten entirely should economic conditions change.

Househusbands' Views of the Women's Movement

Since it has been suggested that the women's movement is, in part, responsible for the existence of role transcendence and is one of many situational variables affecting behavioral options, it seemed appropriate to include questions on the subject. Although we expected Hispanics, because of their traditions, to be less favorably disposed to the movement than the general population, we expected Hispanic househusbands to be more liberal because of their experiences and therefore as favorably inclined as the general population. Our expectations were supported by the data.

The majority of the husbands in our study had an awareness of the women's movement. Most held opinions on it: Some were in strong support of it; others were threatened and antagonistic. The following reasons were offered in support of the movement:

> The Mexicans take longer to change for the better. Younger women are affected more by the movement than older women due to the fact of marriage and it's harder for them to change. They are tied down to their traditional roles. For example, my mother and her mother practiced the roles of the male being the breadwinner and hers to stay home, but now the Chicana can go out into the world but they could not.
>
> The movement is a good idea. The older people can take care of kids. It's good for the women to help the community by working in progress for the kids. The women are finally coming out and intervening in the community. They can even fight against crime.
>
> Women are not slaves. They have the same rights as a man. If she wants freedom, let her.
>
> There are not enough women in the working force. Women do not have good jobs in general. The Black women are striving harder than Latinas. There are very few Mexicans in professional jobs for men and women.

Other husbands denied the movement or were negative and antagonistic toward it:

> I don't see any Latinas at my job. I feel women can't do the same job as a man and they can't handle it.
>
> There's not an effect on the community because there are not too many Chicanas in the women's movement.
>
> I don't pay any attention to the movement.
>
> There are not too many Chicanas in the movement because they grew up to be mothers and housewives. They need to be shown otherwise and need to change their environment. Chicanos are not into higher education and Chicanas prefer to take care of kids. Women are basically happy being wife and mother. The women in the movement take advantage of the situation and they have too much aggression.

Far from existing in a subcultural vacuum or culturally segregated barrio, the Hispanic community has felt the impact of the women's movement.

Although many see the movement as less relevant to the Latin community, they are aware that a movement exists and have definite opinions about it.

CONCLUSIONS

Our 22 respondents and their families allowed a closer look at change impacting the Hispanic community. Househusbands, role reversals, and role transcendence are concepts relating tot he evolution of the family. They are associated with current, external social factors such as the economic recession and the women's movement. We explored the impact of these major social changes at the individual level: the activities, experiences, and beliefs of persons to whom these concepts apply.

Most Hispanic househusbands view their situation as temporary and brought about by economic circumstances beyond their control. As househusbands, they have the opportunity to become more involved in family life and gain insight into their spouses' experiences. Many report closer relations with their spouses and children as a result.

The division of labor remains somewhat traditional; household chores are still more likely to be performed by members of a particular sex. Outside employment does not allow the Chicana to escape certain wifely duties. Time considerations are important mitigators; the spouse with the most free time is expected to perform the task. Leisure time activities are increasingly spent with the family. Househusbands who are employed prefer individual pursuits, whereas those who are unemployed tend to be more socially oriented.

The maintenance of a positive self-concept is enhanced through the acceptance of the househusband status by family and friends. When negativity is expressed, reeducation, joking, and physical conflict are reported to result. Although machismo is still a powerful influence, its strength may be weakening.

Hispanic males tend to deny or mistrust the women's movement. Many househusbands gave a qualified acceptance of the changes that have been effected by the movement and in their own experiences by viewing them as temporary. Because increased insight and understanding are gained by the househusband experience, it is anticipated that some of this knowledge will endure through changing economic and social conditions. The new empathy and identification between spouses may ensure that the traditional separation and role ascription between the sexes has decreased. Machismo and ascriptive sex role statuses in the Hispanic community, as indicated by the househusbands, may not be as immutable as they once were.

PART 6

Education and Academic Achievement

18

♦

Theoretical Assumptions and Empirical Evidence for Academic Achievement in Two Languages

KATHRYN J. LINDHOLM

Two-way bilingual/immersion education programs offer both native English- and Spanish-speaking children opportunities to become bilingual and biliterate in English and Spanish while studying the regular academic curriculum. Three important assumptions related to the theoretical relationship between language and thought underlie the two-way bilingual/immersion model: (a) High levels of proficiency in the two languages will facilitate cognitive processing; (b) there are two types of language proficiency, academic and communicative, and the extent to which one is proficient in these two types may vary; and (c) there is transfer of content across languages. This chapter addresses these theoretical assumptions in an examination of the Spanish and English language proficiency and academic achievement of second- and third-grade native English speakers and native Spanish speakers who had been enrolled in a two-way bilingual/immersion program for two to three years.

RELATIONSHIP BETWEEN LANGUAGE AND THOUGHT

Assumption 1: High Levels of Language Proficiency Facilitate Cognitive Functioning

Many early studies examining the cognitive functioning of bilinguals concluded that exposure of young children to two languages often had deleterious effects on their intellectual development, as measured by standard tests of intelligence (for a review, see Hakuta, 1986). However, careful examination of these early reports led to questions concerning the validity of this conclusion. Almost without exception, the monolingual control groups who gave significantly higher performances on standardized intelligence tests in these studies were speakers of a sociolinguistically dominant language, dominant in the sense that the language enjoyed greater prestige and greater communicative utility in the larger society from which the groups were selected. Moreover, in the majority of these studies the bilinguals, regardless of their proficiency in the dominant language, suffered from socioeconomic and environmental factors specific to their lower status in the community. Because of these and other shortcomings having to do with the tests themselves, many of these studies have been dismissed for their lack of valid scientific inquiry.

A number of studies have been conducted with bilingual children showing that, intellectually, bilingual children's experiences with two languages seem to result in mental flexibility, superiority in concept formation, and a more diversified set of mental abilities, whereas the monolinguals appear to have more unitary cognitive structures, which restricted their verbal problem-solving ability. Not all research is totally supportive of this position (for reviews, see Hakuta, 1986; Homel, Palij, & Aaronson, 1987). The important point is that there is evidence to suggest that bilingual development may facilitate cognitive and academic functioning.

Assumption 2: Levels and Types of Language Proficiency Affect Cognitive Development

The extent to which cognitive development may be influenced by language proficiency has been discussed by Cummins (1987) and by Toukomaa and Skutnabb-Kangas (1977). They speculate that there may be threshold levels of linguistic proficiency a child must attain to avoid cognitive disadvantages and to allow the potentially beneficial aspects of becoming bilingual to influence cognitive growth. This hypothesis assumes that a child must attain a certain minimum or threshold level of proficiency in both languages to enable bilingualism to exert a significant long-term effect and positively influence cognitive growth. However, if bilingual children sustain only a very low level of proficiency in either language the range of potential interaction with the environment through that language is likely to be limited and there will not be any positive affect on cognitive development.

In fact, Cummins and Toukomaa and Skutnabb-Kangas argue that there are two thresholds. Attainment of the lower threshold level of bilingual proficiency would be sufficient to guard against negative consequences of bilingualism. However, the manifestation of long-term cognitive benefits requires achieving the second threshold of a higher level of bilingual proficiency.

Thus the differential affects of bilingualism on cognitive development that have been reported in the literature have been explained by understanding the child's level of bilingual proficiency. In research showing negative affects on cognition, the threshold hypothesis would explain the negative influence by proposing that the bilingual children's proficiency in one or both languages was low enough to impede the interaction that occurred through that language in the school environment. Conversely, children who attained the upper threshold of bilingual proficiency, or high levels of skills in both languages, have demonstrated rapid academic and cognitive development. The threshold hypothesis predicts neither positive nor negative consequences on cognition of children who attain full native proficiency in their first language but develop only intermediate levels of proficiency in the weaker language.

The type of language proficiency is also important to examine because it influences our understanding of cognitive and academic functioning across languages. Cummins (1987), among others, has distinguished between two types of language skills: (a) academic language proficiency skills, or those skills necessary for cognitively demanding tasks that do not have contextual support (e.g., reading and writing tasks); and (b) basic communication skills, or those that require little cognitive attention and have considerable contextual support (everyday conversations).

The ability to succeed academically requires the acquisition of academic language skills that can be used in the abstract, to refer to things removed in time and space, particularly the kind of language required of reading tasks that enable a student to comprehend and critique text far beyond the contextualized picture-supported and simplistic vocabulary-supported stories given to beginning readers.

Research on children's and adults' acquisition of these types of language proficiency indicates that it takes about two years to master the basic communicative proficiency in a second language and five to seven years to develop adequate academic language proficiency in a second language (National Commission on Excellence in Education, 1983). However, the ability to access information in either of these types of language proficiency depends on how it is stored in memory.

Assumption 3:
Transfer of Content Occurs Across Languages

There are two major views of how bilinguals store and retrieve language. One view is that bilinguals develop the skills in each language independently and store them separately in the brain. According to this model, termed *separate underlying proficiency,* efforts to develop proficiency in one language do not facilitate development in another language and may, in fact, impede second language development because of limited storage space in the brain. The opposing view, labeled *common underlying proficiency,* proposes that there is a common storage space and that the development of skills and knowledge in one language is not independent of the acquisition of information in a second language. Rather, developing knowledge and proficiency skills in one language facilitates learning in the second language (Cummins, 1987).

Considerable research supports the common underlying proficiency viewpoint. Studies of academic skills in a bilingual's two languages typically show high relationships, with correlations in the .60 to .80 range (Cummins, 1979; Lindholm, 1991). Thus a bilingual who performs well in math in one language is very likely to perform well in math in a second language (Lindholm & Fairchild, 1989), even after only one or two years of schooling in the second language, once the student has the language proficiency skills for demonstrating that knowledge (Lindholm, 1991).

The specific objective of the present study was to address these three theoretical assumptions presented above by examining (a) the extent to which achievement in English (e.g., English math) is associated with achievement in Spanish (e.g., Spanish math; Assumption 3); (b) the relationship between communicative and academic language proficiency (Assumption 2); and (c) whether high levels of bilingual proficiency can facilitate academic achievement in both languages (Assumption 1).

METHOD

Program Design

The Washington Elementary School in San Jose, California, designed its bilingual/immersion program following the successful 10-year-old Spanish/English bilingual program in the San Diego city schools. According to the instructional design, both native English- and native Spanish-speaking second and third graders received 80% of their instructional day in Spanish. One teacher provided the Spanish instruction and used *only* Spanish. For 20% of the instructional day, teaching was carried out in English by nonbilingual/immersion teachers of the same grade who had been trained in second language acquisition. For the English instruction, each class moved to its English-speaking teachers' classroom. The instructional content was equivalent to that for students at the same grades not enrolled in the bilingual/immersion program. Reading instruction in English did not begin until third grade; prior to third grade, all reading instruction was carried out in Spanish (for further information on the bilingual/immersion model, consult Lindholm, 1990).

Subjects

A total of 168 students participated in the bilingual/immersion program evaluation research, but only the data for the second and third graders are discussed here (see Lindholm, 1989a, for a discussion of all students). Of the 66 second and third graders, 41 were second graders and 25 were third graders. In the second-grade class, 34 (83%) were native Spanish speakers and 7 (17%) were native English speakers. The third-grade class contained 21 (84%) native Spanish speakers and 4 (16%) native English speakers.

Also, English academic achievement data were collected from 118 second- and third-grade students who were attending the same school but were not enrolled in the bilingual/immersion program. Of these students, 32% were native Spanish speakers and 68% were native English speakers.

Testing Instrumentation and Procedures

Instrumentation

A number of testing instruments were administered to the students. The Comprehensive Tests of Basic Skills (CTBS), Form U was designed to measure achievement in English in the basic skills normally found in

U.S. state and district curricula. La Prueba Riverside de Realización en Español (La Prueba) consists of a series of progressive tests designed to measure academic achievement in reading and math in Grades K through 9 among native Spanish speakers. The Language Assessment Scale (LAS) tested the students' oral language proficiency in both English and Spanish. The Student Oral Language Observation Matrix (SOLOM), which is a rating scale developed by the California State Department of Education, assessed Spanish and English oral language proficiency in children in five domains: comprehension, fluency, vocabulary, pronunciation, and grammar. These instruments are described in greater detail in Lindholm and Fairchild (1990).

Procedures

All students were group administered the CTBS and La Prueba tests in March and May 1989, respectively, by their teacher. Students were also individually tested on the LAS in Spanish and English in May 1989 by the bilingual/immersion staff. Teachers completed the SOLOM in January 1989 in Spanish and English.

All of the achievement tests raw scores were converted to standard or scale scores, and to percentile ranks and normal curve equivalents.[1]

On the basis of students' English and Spanish scores on the LAS, students were categorized into one of three groups for the analyses: (a) dominant Spanish (i.e., FSP in Spanish, NEP or LEP in English), (b) dominant English (i.e., FEP in English, NSP or LSP in Spanish), or (c) bilingual (i.e., FEP in English, FSP in Spanish). Because there were only two Spanish-dominant and four English-dominant third graders, their scores must be interpreted with caution. The rationale for categorizing students as Spanish-dominant, English-dominant or bilingual was to determine whether students who became bilingual scored differently from the students who were still dominant in their native language. This information was necessary to address the first assumption previously stated regarding the advantages of bilingualism on achievement.

RESULTS

Academic Achievement in Spanish

Spanish Reading Achievement

Table 18.1 shows the students' mean percentiles from the La Prueba reading achievement subtest for each grade level (second, third) and language background (Spanish, English, bilingual). Students' mean performance was at or above average, with average defined as performance at the 50th percentile, for each of the second-grade groups and for the bilingual third graders. However, the percentiles for the Spanish-dominant and English-dominant third graders were well below average. At both grade levels, bilingual students' scores were all well above average and were higher than those for the Spanish- or English-dominant students. There was no significant difference at the second-grade level in the students' scores by language group (Spanish-dominant, English-dominant, bilingual), $F(2, 39) = 0.89$, $p > .05$, but there was a significant difference at the third-grade level, $F(2, 23) = 5.51$, $p < .05$, with the bilinguals outscoring the English dominants.

Another way of looking at Spanish reading achievement is to examine score distributions instead of averages, which tend to mask very high and very low performance. Table 18.2 presents the percentage of students who scored above the 50th and 75th percentiles. At least half of the students in each language group at each grade level (except for the English-dominant third graders) scored at the 50th percentile or higher. However, even more impressive, close to half of the bilingual students at both grade levels and the Spanish-dominant second graders also scored higher than the 75th percentile.

Spanish Math Achievement

Table 18.1 indicates that performance was close to average (48th percentile) for the Spanish-dominant second graders, slightly below average for the bilingual second graders, but above average for the English-dominant second graders. By third grade, for all groups, math performance was well above average.

Table 18.2 demonstrates how high the performance was on a more individualized basis. At both grade levels, over 25% of the students scored above the 75th percentile, and the majority of students scored at least above the 50th percentile. Thus, although it appears in Table 18.1 that the Spanish-dominant and bilingual second graders did not score at the 50th percentile according to their mean percentiles, Table 18.2 shows that in each of these groups about one fourth of the students scored at or above the 75th percentile.

There were no significant group effects in the performance of the Spanish-dominant, English-dominant, or bilingual students at either the second-grade, $F(2, 39) = 0.62$, $p > .05$, or third-grade level, $F(2, 23) = 0.04$, $p > .05$.

Table 18.1 Mean Achievement Percentiles, by Language and Content Area for Second- and Third-Grade Spanish, English, and Bilingual Students

	Spanish		English		
	Reading	Math	Reading	Language	Math
Second graders					
Spanish-dominant	65	48	4	8	36
English-dominant	59	67	36	22	36
Bilingual	76	43	21	22	36
Third graders					
Spanish-dominant	35	68	14	8	36
English-dominant	19	63	29	16	44
Bilingual	65	67	30	29	50

NOTE: The 50th percentile is average.

Academic Achievement in English

English Reading Achievement

As Table 18.1 indicates, the mean percentiles for all grades and language backgrounds were below average. Although the percentiles of the English-dominant students decreased from second to third grade, the percentiles of the Spanish-dominant and bilingual students increased from second to third grade. There was a significant group effect in the second grade, $F(2, 38) = 6.21$, $p < .01$, in which English dominants and bilinguals scored higher than Spanish dominants. By the third grade, however, this difference vanished, $F(2, 24) = 1.53, p > .05$.

According to Table 18.2, close to one fifth of the English-dominant and bilingual second graders and English-dominant third graders scored at or above the 50th percentile. Thus, although it appeared that the students received very low scores, certainly below-average performance, about 1 in 5 scored in the average to above-average range in three of the six groups. One bilingual second grader even scored above the 75th percentile, despite not having received any formal English reading instruction.

The performance of the two-way bilingual/immersion (BI) students was compared to the CTBS achievement of similar students in a non-two-way bilingual/immersion (NON) program. For this analysis, students' language background, as opposed to their bilingual proficiency, was used to assess group differences because proficiency data were not

Academic Achievement in Two Languages 281

Table 18.2 Percentage of Second- and Third-Grade Students Scoring Above the 50th and 75th Percentile

| | Spanish | | | | English | | | | | |
| | Reading | | Math | | Reading | | Language | | Math | |
	>50	>75	>50	>75	>50	>75	>50	>75	>50	>75
Second graders										
Spanish-dominant	75	58	50	25	0	0	8	0	25	0
English-dominant	71	14	72	29	17	0	17	0	67	17
Bilingual	86	52	48	29	24	5	19	10	54	5
Third graders										
Spanish-dominant	50	0	50	50	0	0	0	0	50	0
English-dominant	0	0	75	25	25	0	0	0	50	0
Bilingual	78	44	78	28	5	0	16	0	53	5

NOTE: The percentage at/above the 50th percentile includes the percentage at/above the 75th percentile.

available for the comparison group of students. At the second-grade level, the NON students scored higher than the BI students; this was a statistically significant result for the native Spanish speakers, $t(52) = 2.08$, $p < .05$, but *not* for the native English speakers, $t(39) = 1.85$, $p > .05$. In contrast, at the third-grade level, there was no statistically significant difference between the BI and NON students for either the native Spanish or English speakers.

English Language Achievement

In Table 18.1, as with English reading achievement, the mean percentiles for both grades and all language backgrounds were well below average. Although the scores of the Spanish-dominant speakers remained fairly constant from second to third grade, the percentiles for the bilinguals increased, and those for the English-dominant speakers decreased from second to third grade. In addition, as Table 18.2 shows, at least 15% of the bilinguals and English-speaking second graders scored at or above the 50th percentile. There were no statistically significant group differences at either the second-grade, $F(2, 38) = 1.58$, $p > .05$, or third-grade level, $F(2, 24) = 1.06$, $p > .05$.

In comparing the performance of the BI students with NON students, t tests showed that at the second-grade level the NON students outscored the BI students for both the native Spanish speakers, $t(52) = 1.92, p < .05$, and the native English speakers, $t(39) = 3.16, p < .01$. However, by third grade, the native Spanish-speaking BI students scored higher but not significantly so than the native Spanish-speaking NON students, $t(37) = .61, p > .05$, whereas the results were reversed for the native English-speaking students: NON students scored higher but not significantly so than the BI students, $t(48) = 1.49, p > .05$.

English Math Achievement

As Table 18.1 indicates, the mean percentiles for most language backgrounds at both grade levels were below average, with one exception. The only group whose average performance was at the 50th percentile comprised the third-grade bilingual students. There were no significant group differences at either the second-grade, $F(2, 38) = 0.23, p > .05$, or third-grade level, $F(2, 24) = 0.68, p > .05$. Overall, the performance of the students generally increased from second to third grade.

Table 18.2 displays the percentage of students who scored at or above the 50th and 75th percentiles. Only a few students scored above the 75th percentile. At the third-grade level, at least half of the students scored at or above the 50th percentile, and one bilingual scored above the 75th percentile.

Comparisons of the achievement of the BI students with NON students showed that at the second-grade level, the NON English and Spanish speaker scored higher but not significantly so than the BI English and Spanish speakers, $t(39) = .94, p > .05$ and $t(52) = 1.53, p > .05$, respectively. In third grade, the Spanish BI scored higher but not significantly so than the Spanish NON, $t(37) = 1.54, p > .05$, and there was no difference in the scores of the native English BI and NON students, $t(48) = .03, p > .05$.

Achievement Across Language and Content Areas

Several correlational analyses were run to try to better understand the relationships between achievement across languages and between language proficiency and achievement. In math achievement, findings revealed a positive and highly significant relationship across the two languages ($r = .58, p < .001$), indicating that math content that was learned in Spanish was also available in English. Spanish reading achievement was also highly correlated with English reading achievement ($r = .40$, $p < .001$).

There were also important relationships between content areas both across and within languages. For example, math achievement was highly correlated with reading achievement in both Spanish (Spanish math with Spanish reading: $r = .47, p < .001$) and English (English math with English reading: $r = .53, p < .001$). In addition, English math was highly correlated with Spanish reading ($r = .47, p < .001$). Also, English language achievement was as highly correlated with English reading achievement ($r = .44, p < .001$) as with Spanish reading achievement ($r = .41$, $p < .001$). Finally, oral English proficiency was highly correlated with English reading achievement ($r = .50, p < .001$) but not with English language achievement ($r = .24, p < .001$).

DISCUSSION

What the results collectively indicate is that the students were showing progress in demonstrating overall higher percentiles in third grade over second grade, and the performance of the students was similar to that of comparable native English- and native Spanish-speaking students in nonbilingual/immersion classes by third grade. In addition, the students' performance was analogous to that found in other bilingual/immersion programs (Lindholm, 1989b; Lindholm & Fairchild, 1989).

The major discrepancy between the results reported here and those from other studies was the low performance of the two Spanish-dominant and four English-dominant third graders. It is unclear whether the results of these few students are representative of other Spanish- and English-dominant third graders because of the small sample size. Furthermore, many analyses must be interpreted with caution as a result of the small sample. However, the results are suggestive of clarifications in the theoretical assumptions underlying bilingual/immersion education.

The first theoretical assumption considered the relation between language proficiency and achievement. Understanding this relationship requires elaboration of the role of language proficiency in achievement within the context of the threshold hypothesis (Cummins, 1987; Toukomaa & Skutnabb-Kangas, 1977). The threshold hypothesis, as indicated previously, states that there are cognitive advantages for bilinguals who have reached a higher level of proficiency in the two languages and neither advantages nor disadvantages for additive bilinguals who are proficient in one language but limited in proficiency in their second language.

Results showed that the second- and third-grade students who had developed the conversational skills to be rated as orally proficient in both languages scored higher, though not significantly higher, than students who were rated fluent in their first language but limited in their second language, in academic achievement tests in both English and Spanish. In examinations of the scores of the Spanish-dominant, English-dominant, and bilingual (who began school dominant or monolingual in Spanish) students from kindergarten through Grade 3, the gap between students dominant in their native language and bilinguals, which was minimal or nonexistent in the early grades, increased across the grades.

One interpretation of this result is that as the students received more instruction those who were proficient in the two languages developed better strategies for processing information, which led to their bilingual language proficiency. Of course, the alternative explanation is that more intelligent students acquired language faster and became bilingual, and these students, by virtue of their higher intelligence, also scored higher on achievement tests. Regardless of the interpretation, the results suggest a link between level of bilingualism and academic achievement. This relationship might have been much stronger had the sample been larger.

The findings also corroborate the distinction that various language education researchers have made between academic language and conversational language (e.g., Cummins, 1987). Analyses indicated that it was not enough for a bilingual to have high levels of conversational proficiency in the two languages to demonstrate advantages over students still dominant in their native language. If conversational proficiency were sufficient for an academic advantage in language and reading achievement tests in English, then English speakers, because of several years of conversational English in their homes, should have an advantage over bilinguals who were originally native Spanish speakers and only recently became classified as fluent in oral English. However, by third grade in the bilingual/immersion program, after only one academic year of reading instruction in English, bilingual students scored higher, but not significantly higher, than English-dominant students in language achievement, though equivalent in reading achievement. In addition, the bilinguals outperformed the English-dominant and Spanish-dominant students in English math achievement and in Spanish reading achievement.

To demonstrate the significance of academic language skills in academic achievement, we can look at the second graders who had received all of their instruction in reading and academic language in Spanish and had received only oral English prior to the testing. At this second-grade level, bilinguals outperformed the English-dominant students in Spanish reading achievement, showing a richer knowledge base in Spanish academic language skills. Although the scores of the English-dominant and bilingual students were comparable in English language achievement, the bilinguals scored much lower in English reading achievement. Thus, prior to their introduction to English academic language and reading, whereas English speakers had English oral proficiency advantages over bilinguals, the bilinguals performed lower in English reading. However, after one year of formal instruction in English reading and academic language, although the bilinguals scored equivalent to the English-dominant students in English reading, the bilinguals scored higher than the Spanish-dominant or English-dominant students in Spanish reading. These results suggest that the bilinguals had a better developed framework with the combination of Spanish reading, Spanish oral proficiency, and English oral proficiency skills from which to integrate the new reading and language skills in English.

Results from the correlation analyses were consistent with the distinction between academic and communicative language proficiency in showing that reading is highly dependent on academic language skills, oral English proficiency is not correlated with academic English proficiency, and both types of language proficiency are associated with English reading ability.

The Spanish and English achievement results also validate the achievement transfer assumption underlying the bilingual/immersion model in that the model assumes that content that is learned in Spanish will be available in English as well. The fact that the students were able to score as well as they did in English without content instruction in English (except one year of English reading for the third graders) demonstrates that the math, reading, and language concepts were available to them in both languages. These findings are consistent with previous research suggesting that there are interconnected pathways of content both within and across languages (e.g., Cummins, 1987) enabling transfer of content to occur.

However, it appears that the transfer of content across languages has its limitations. The major limitation is that students can only demonstrate transfer of content across languages once they have acquired sufficient language skills to do so, and the level of language sufficiency will vary depending on the language requirements of the subject matter. For example, although there was a high correlation between English and Spanish reading achievement, the correlation was much higher between

English and Spanish math achievement. Even math achievement was highly related to reading achievement in both languages, but English math achievement was also correlated with English academic language proficiency.

CONCLUSION

The results lend empirical validation to the three assumptions tested here regarding the relationship between language and thought. Findings indicating strong relationships of content across languages substantiated the transfer assumption. However, it was also suggested that there are language proficiency limitations imposed in transfer because some content areas (e.g., reading) require higher levels of language proficiency than others (e.g., math). It is not only the level of language proficiency but also the type of language proficiency that is important.

Results showed clear differentiation between academic language skills and communication skills, also confirming the assumption that there are two types of language proficiency skills. Finally, results were suggestive in showing that students who were rated as bilingual were beginning to show some advantages over the students still dominant in their first language. Because of the students' limited exposure to academic English, few cognitive or academic advantages could be expected. However, the trend toward such advantages is emerging and should become stronger over the next two years as students become more fully proficient in the two languages.

An important implication emerged from these results, which is that the two types of language skills, academic and conversational, need to be developed in both languages before one can expect to see high levels of achievement performance in language minority students. Developing both academic and conversational skills requires a considerable investment of time, which means that educators must be willing to wait patiently to see children performing at high levels of achievement in English. This is important because we often want to see instant success in both languages on the part of students in bilingual programs, and the results presented here show some compelling reasons why we do not see, nor could we expect to see, such academic success immediately. We are at an important crossroad in education, where our leaders are setting national educational goals to stimulate the problem-solving and second-language capabilities of our students and also closing the achievement gap between minority and majority students. Promoting programs that offer students opportunities to develop full bilingual proficiency may yield payoffs at both an individual level, through cognitive/academic achievement advantages, and at a societal level, in promoting dual language proficiency and achievement for *both* language-minority *and* language-majority students.

NOTE

1. Normal curve equivalents (NCEs) comprise an equal-interval scale ranging from 1 to 99, with a mean of 50 and a standard deviation of approximately 21. The use of NCEs allows meaningful comparisons between different achievement test batteries and between different tests within the same test battery.

19
♦

Academic Invulnerability Among Mexican American Students

The Importance of Protective Resources and Appraisals

SYLVIA ALATORRE ALVA

It has been widely documented that a number of sociocultural variables place Mexican American students at risk of academic underachievement, including the low educational and occupational attainment of parents, family income and composition, ethnic minority status, and the amount of learning materials in the home (e.g., Laosa, 1982; Rumberger, 1983; Steinberg, Blinde, & Chan, 1984). The assumption is generally held that these sociocultural variables influence or cause the disproportionate levels of academic failure and attrition found among Mexican American high school students (Brown, Rosen, Hill, & Olivas, 1980; Carnegie Council on Policy Studies in Higher Education, 1979; Hirano-Nakanishi, 1986; Pallas, 1987).

ACADEMIC INVULNERABILITY

Although it is evident that a constellation of sociocultural variables predispose Mexican American students toward academic failure, very little is know about the factors that mediate their academic success. Regrettably, there has been a tendency to focus almost exclusively on predictors of academic failure. There is very little empirical research available on Mexican American students who are academically successful or invulnerable to the detrimental conditions and events that place them at risk. Academically invulnerable students can be described as those who sustain high levels of achievement motivation and performance, despite the presence of stressful events and conditions that place them at risk of doing poorly in school and, ultimately, dropping out of school.

PROTECTIVE RESOURCES AND APPRAISALS

Several recent studies have linked a host of protective resources and appraisals to the successful adaptation and development of school-age children who are exposed to severe and/or prolonged psychological stressors (Clark, 1983; Compas, 1987; Gandara, 1982; Garmezy, 1981; Werner & Smith, 1982). Consistently, two generic types of protective factors have been identified as evident among invulnerable children: *personal* and *environmental* resources (Garmezy, 1981, 1983; Garmezy & Rutter, 1983; Rutter, 1979; Werner, Bierman, & French, 1971; Werner & Smith, 1982). Personal resources include the personality characteristics and attitudes that children possess, and environmental resources are external sources of information, support, and affective feedback. Although most of the work in this area has focused on children of clinically at-risk parents, there is empirical research to suggest that protective resources and appraisals also mediate the academic performance of educationally at-risk children.

Personal Resources

Several research studies indicate that a number of personal characteristics are typically evident among academically successful students. Academically successful students show a positive self-evaluation of their academic status at school (Wylie, 1979) and a sense of control over their academic success and failure (Dweck & Licht, 1980; Dweck & Wortman, 1982; Stipek & Weisz, 1981; Willig, Harnisch, Hill, & Maehr, 1983).

Environmental Resources

Academically successful students also appear to have a supportive network of family members, friends, neighbors, and teachers, which they rely on for counsel and advice in difficult or stressful situations. Mexican American parents, in particular, are mentioned by successful Mexican American students as an important source of support and encouragement (Alva, 1989; Gandara, 1982; Padilla & Alva, 1987). In Gandara's (1982) study of successful Mexican American professionals, she found that 93% of the professionals surveyed reported that the educational support received from their parents was the single most important factor affecting their high academic goals and expectations.

Although several studies support Gandara's finding that education is highly valued and encouraged by most Mexican American parents (Alva, 1989; Fleming, 1982), children also respond to the "beliefs" that school teachers and administrators have about their educational future. Ogbu (1983) argues that many Mexican American students fail to do well in school because in many ways the educational climate and teacher-student interactions communicate to students this weak link between academic success and social mobility.

In an effort to better understand the nature of teacher-student interactions involving Mexican American students, Buriel (1983) observed teacher interactions with Mexican American and Anglo fourth- and fifth-grade students who were matched on the basis of socioeconomic status, reading and writing ability, and English proficiency. Consistent with other studies in this area (Laosa, 1977), Buriel reports that teachers praised and encouraged Mexican American children less often, as compared to their Anglo classmates. Moreover, teachers interacted more positively with the students who were academically successful, irrespective of their ethnicity.

Subjective Appraisals

In addition to the presence of personal and environmental resources, subjective appraisals of stressful events in school and the social environment are also important mediators of achievement. Unarguably, there are vast individual differences in the interpretations and reactions of children who are exposed to potentially stressful events and social interactions. Moreover, the literature strongly suggests that the appraisal given to potentially stressful events determines the subsequent coping responses and behaviors of children who are exposed to stress (Compas, 1987).

With respect to Mexican Americans, research suggests that a host of sociocultural experiences related to the acculturation process are appraised as stressful (Cervantes & Castro, 1985). Using the Hispanic Children's Stress Inventory, Padilla and his colleagues (Padilla, 1986; Padilla, Cervantes, & Maldonado, 1988) have identified several events that are potentially stressful for Hispanic children and adolescents. Among the experiences commonly appraised as stressful by Mexican American children and adolescents are leaving relatives and friends behind when moving, feeling pressured to speak only Spanish at home, living in a home with many people, and feeling that other kids make fun of the way you speak English.

Kurtines and Miranda (1980) also suggest that differences in the Hispanic child's self and family role expectations can often lead to intrafamilial conflicts and stress. For instance, discrepancies in the values and practices of Hispanic children and their parents may create conflict and pressure in selecting which set of cultural norms and expectations to adhere to. Also, Hispanic children are often asked to interpret or translate the dominant language and culture for their parents, involving the child emotionally in the financial, legal, and social worries and concerns of the family.

The educational process can also be potentially stressful for many Mexican American students, with differences in their subjective appraisals accounting for important variations in their academic performance (Chavez, 1984; Minuchin & Shapiro, 1983). For instance, in a comparison study, Yamamoto and Brynes (1984) reported that Hispanic fourth, fifth, and sixth graders report a markedly higher incidence of school-related stressors as compared to majority group students. More specifically, Hispanic students reported significantly higher occurrences of stress for school events such as academic retainment (28% vs. 4%), a poor report card (62% vs. 39%), and being sent to the principal (63% vs. 48%).

Using *High School and Beyond* data, Wehlage and Rutter (1986) reported marked differences between high school graduates and dropouts in their appraisal of school events. Dropouts reported less favorable evaluations of their school's climate with respect to teacher interest in students and the fairness and effectiveness of discipline. Dropouts were more likely to report that teachers did not care for them and that they were treated in an unfair and arbitrary manner.

In a comparison of Mexican American students who received high versus low grades in high school, Padilla and Alva (1987) found that low-achieving students report significantly lower levels of satisfaction with school. Not surprising, the most commonly reported reason dropouts give for leaving high school is "I dislike school" (Savage, 1985).

Together, these findings point to the importance of examining the antecedents and correlates of invulnerability in school-aged children and adolescents who are at risk of failing in school. This chapter examines the role of protective resources and appraisals in mediating the academic achievement of at-risk Mexican American students. Furthermore, an examination of the effects of sociocultural risk factors, as well as the protective resources and appraisals on the academic achievements of Mexican American high school students, can provide information on their relative effects.

METHOD

Study Site

The study was conducted at a senior high school located in Los Angeles County. The school's ethnic composition was predominantly of ethnic minority background, with Hispanic students representing 78% of the total student body, Asian Americans/Pacific Islanders 14%, and non-Hispanic Whites 8%.

Respondents

The respondents were drawn from a cohort of 10th-grade students who met all of the following selection criteria: (a) of Mexican heritage, (b) currently enrolled in the 10th grade, (c) in the United States since at least the 7th grade, and (d) not currently in Special Education, Enrichment/Gifted, or English-as-a-Second-Language (ESL) programs.

Participants were 384 Mexican American 10th graders (163 males and 221 females), whose modal age was 16 years. The generational status of the sample was distributed as follows: 34.4% first generation (respondent born in Mexico), 41.1% second generation (respondent born in the United States and *both* parents were born in Mexico), and 22.1% mixed generation (respondent born in the United States, one parent born in Mexico and the other parent born in the United States).

Over two thirds (69%) of the respondents' fathers were employed, with most (47.9%) employed as skilled and semiskilled workers (e.g., carpenters, painters, and factory machine operators), as were 46% of the respondents' mothers, with most (19.0%) employed as semiskilled workers (e.g., seamstresses, hospital aides, and factory machine operators).

Procedure

The respondents were recruited from a required course for all 10th-grade students enrolled at the high school and asked to complete a paper-and-pencil survey, which required approximately 40 to 50 minutes to complete. From the entire pool of 10th graders, only those who met all of the selection criteria were included in this study. The grades and standardized test scores for the sample group were obtained from school records.

Measures

The measures used in this study were factor-analyzed to verify their construct validity (see Alva, 1989, for further information on the results of the factor analyses).

Survey Instrument

Sociocultural risk factors were measured using four independent variables: sex, father's occupation, generational status, and the respondent's language background. Occupational status was measured using a modified version of Hollingshead's (1965) Two Factor Index of Social Position. Although Hollingshead's occupational index is based on two characteristics, education and occupation, only the occupational standing of the head of household was measured. In families where there was no male head of household, the mother's occupational level was included in the analyses. Generational status was determined using a series of questions inquiring about the birthplace of the respondents, their parents, and grandparents. Language background was measured using a composite scale based on respondents' relative exposure to and usage of the English language in their daily lives (e.g., television, radio, and conversations with friends and family).

Personal resources were measured using two personality inventories. The Intellectual and School Status subscale (17 items) of the Piers-Harris

Self-Concept Inventory (Piers, 1984) was used to measure academic self-esteem. Clifford's Academic Achievement Accountability Scale (Clifford & Cleary, 1972) was used to measure the degree to which the respondents accepted personal responsibility for their academic performance.

Environmental resources consisted of three composite scales specifically designed to measure the educational support that respondents received from their parents, teachers, and friends. The respondents were asked to separately evaluate the educational attitudes and values of their parents, teachers, and friends. Some of the items in this scale were "They believe in the importance of getting a good education," "They encourage me to study hard," and "They value education highly."

The appraisal variables included two measures. First, the students' subjective appraisals of educational experiences were measured using three scales that each tapped a different dimension of the school's climate: respect and care, school involvement, and college preparation. The respect and care dimension of this measure included items such as "The teachers care about me," "Teachers treat me with respect," and "The teachers are fair." School involvement contained items such as "I participate in school activities," "The school's organizations and clubs are interesting and fun," and "I feel pride in my school." The school's college preparatory climate was measured using items such as "Someday, I will be a college graduate," "I feel encouraged to attend college," and "I am taught subjects that prepare me for college."

The second instrument used to measure the subjective appraisal of students was a modified version of the Hispanic Children's Stress Inventory (Padilla et al., 1988), which measured the degree of stressfulness of life events or situations in three domains: family concerns, intergroup relations, and conflicts involving language issues. The following is a sample of the items used to tap family concerns: "I have worried that my parents will not make enough money to pay all the bills," "A family member has been arrested," and "I have felt that I can't communicate well with my parents." The Intergroup Relations Scale included items such as "In certain situations at school, I have tried to hide my cultural background," "I have not been given the same opportunities as other students have." Last, conflicts with language issues were assessed using items such as "I have felt pressured to speak only English at school," "I have felt that other students make fun of the way I speak English," and "I have not understood some things when people explained them in English."

School-Based Information

From the original factor analysis, it was revealed that school grades and standardized test scores represent two separate constructs. Thus, from each respondent's records, the following academic outcomes were obtained: (a) a composite score of each respondent's reading, language, and math skills, based on the results of the Comprehensive Tests of Basic Skills (CTBS) taken during the 10th grade; and (b) a composite index of their grades received during two semesters of their 10th-grade year, excluding physical education classes.

RESULTS

Incremental Regression Analysis

A pair of regression analyses tested the proportion of variance incrementally explained by sociocultural risk factors and protective resources and appraisals. Academic outcomes were regressed on the predictor variables, which were blocked and entered in the regression equation in the following order: (a) sociocultural variables, (b) protective resources, and (c) appraisal variables. After each block was entered into the regression equation, the proportion of variance incrementally explained was calculated.

As summarized in Table 19.1, at Step 1, the sociocultural variables accounted for 8% of the variance of CTBS. At Step 2, the protective resources added 7% to the variance accounted for in CTBS performance. Last, the proportion of variance on CTBS scores that was accounted for by the appraisal variables was 13%, over and above the sociocultural and protective resources. In total, 28% of the variance on the CTBS measure was accounted for by a combination of sociocultural factors, protective resources, and subjective appraisals.

Following the same procedure for high school grades, the proportion of variance attributed to the sociocultural variables and the protective resources were negligible (1% and 8%, respectively) and statistically nonsignificant. However, the block of appraisal variables accounted for an additional 14% of the variance of high school grades, raising the total explained variance to 23%.

Stepwise Discriminant Analyses

A series of stepwise discriminant analyses was conducted to determine which variables best differentiated high- and low-achieving students.

Table 19.1 Incremental Partitioning of Variance

			CTBS[a]				Grades			
Step	Variable	df	Sum of Squares	F	R^2	R^2 Change	Sum of Squares	F	R^2	R^2 Change
1	Sociocultural	4	9.82	3.16*	.08	.08	1.68	.49	.01	.01
2	Protective resources[b]	9	18.04	2.68*	.15	.07	11.05	1.51	.09	.08
3	Appraisal	15	34.34	3.47**	.28	.13	28.84	2.68**	.23	.14

a. CTBS = Comprehensive Tests of Basic Skills.
b. Includes personal and environmental resources.
*$p < .01$; **$p < .001$.

From the total sample distribution ($N = 384$), only scores in the first and fourth quartiles of each academic outcome were selected. Students whose scale scores on each outcome measure fell within the bottom quartile were considered academically vulnerable, and students in the top quartile were considered academically invulnerable.

CTBS Performance

The stepwise discriminant analysis of academically invulnerable and academically vulnerable groups, based on CTBS performance scores, resulted in one underlying structure ($\chi^2 = 51.85, p < .0001$) that contained nine predictor variables (see Table 19.2). Moreover, the discriminant function had a canonical correlation of .66, indicating a strong relationship between the groups and the discriminant function. Stress involving language issues was the most powerful discriminator of high and low CTBS performance. Following in terms of relative discrimination power were self-concept, respondent's language background, family concerns, academic accountability, generational status, college preparation, involvement at school, and environmental support from friends. A classification matrix revealed that, overall, 85.71% of the cases were correctly classified, with 76.3% of the vulnerable cases (low performance on the CTBS) correctly classified and 92.5% of the invulnerable cases (high performance on the CTBS) correctly classified.

Socioculturally High-Risk Subsample

From the aforementioned discriminant analysis, it is evident that first-generation Mexican American students with limited English exposure

Academic Invulnerability

Table 19.2 Discriminant Function Coefficients

Variable	CTBS[a] High vs. Low	CTBS[a] High vs. Low (first generation)	Grades High vs. Low
Sociocultural			
Sex of respondent	—	—	—
Father's occupation	—	—	—
Language background	.62***	—	—
Generational status	.48***	—	—
Personal resources			
Academic accountability	.51***	—	—
Self-concept of intellectual and social status	.73***	—	—
Environmental resources			
Support from friends	.45***	—	.70**
Support from teachers	—	.61*	.72**
Support from parents	—	—	—
Appraisal			
Respect and care	—	—	—
Involvement at school	.46***	.72*	.82**
College preparation	.47***	.87*	.88**
Family concerns	.56***	.80*	.75**
Intergroup relations	—	—	.78**
Language issues	.83***	.66*	—

a. CTBS = Comprehensive Tests of Basic Skills.
*$p < .01$; **$p < .001$; ***$p < .0001$.

and usage are at most risk with respect to CTBS performance. To examine the factors that mitigate the CTBS performance of students in this particularly high risk group, only first-generation Mexican American students who scored below the median on the language background scale were included in the following discriminant analysis. Twenty-nine academically vulnerable and 17 academically invulnerable students were identified.

The stepwise discriminant analysis of a subsample of first-generation Mexican American students who had limited English exposure and usage resulted in one underlying structure ($\chi^2 = 42.57, p < .01$), with a canonical correlation of .62. As summarized in Table 19.2, five predictor variables significantly differentiated between the two high-risk groups.

The school climate college preparation subscale was the most powerful discriminator, followed by family concerns, involvement at school, language issues, and support from teachers. A classification matrix revealed that the five predictor variables included in the discriminant function correctly classified 82.6% of the cases, with 89.7% of the academically vulnerable group and 70.6% of the academically invulnerable group correctly classified.

High School Grades

Based on the distribution of grades for the entire sample, 54 academically vulnerable (low grades in the 10th grade) and 57 academically invulnerable (high grades in the 10th grade) students were identified. The stepwise discriminant analysis of academically invulnerable and vulnerable students based on grades resulted in one underlying structure ($\chi^2 = 25.26, p < .001$), with a canonical correlation of .55. The stepwise discriminate analysis identified six predictor variables that discriminated the groups (see Table 19.2). Again, college preparation was the most powerful discriminator of high and low high school grades. Involvement at school, intergroup relations, family concerns, and support from teachers and friends followed in relative importance. Overall, the six variables in the discriminant function correctly classified 72.07% of the cases.

DISCUSSION

The results of this study support the premise that a constellation of protective resources and appraisals can serve to buffer or protect at-risk students from the detrimental effects of sociocultural events and conditions that place them at risk of academic failure. An empirical examination of within-group differences in the personal and environmental resources and appraisals of at-risk students suggests that the prevailing research on risk factors may be theoretically and empirically restrictive. The results of the incremental regression analyses indicate that protective resources and appraisals cannot be ignored as important mediators of achievement, over and above the potentially detrimental effects that sociocultural risk factors have on academic performance.

Using discriminant analyses to identify the specific variables that differentiate academically successful students from their nonsuccessful classmates, the results of this study revealed that nine variables significantly distinguished between high and low CTBS performance with very high accuracy (86%). Of particular interest due to their central importance in the determination of risk groups were the two sociocultural variables that differentiated high and low achievers on the CTBS measure—generational status and respondent's language background.

Although it is not surprising that students who speak and are exposed to the least amount of English do not perform well on standardized tests, it is not clear why, when the dependent variable is school grades, language background does not differentiate between high and low achievers. Indeed, these findings raise several important issues.

First, it is important to reiterate that all the Mexican American students who were classified by the school as needing ESL instruction were excluded from our sample. The selection criteria also excluded students who had not been educated in the United States since at least the seventh grade. Thus, at the very least, we can assume that the English proficiency of our sample was above the ESL baseline.

It is not clear why the relative amount of English exposure and usage is important for CTBS performance and not for high school grades. One explanation is that performance on standardized tests like the CTBS requires a higher level of language proficiency. A comparison of the results of the stepwise discriminant analysis for high and low groups with respect to high school grades and CTBS performance suggests that high school performance is less dependent on the mediation of language than is standardized test performance. As Cummins (1979) points out, the linguistic competence of most bilinguals is based on several proficiency thresholds. Although these thresholds have not been defined in absolute terms, the notion of thresholds serves to underscore the importance of the contextual milieu in determining language proficiency. Even though all students in this study were beyond the threshold requiring ESL instruction, the attainment of a second, higher level of linguistic competence appears to be necessary for successful performance on the CTBS and other standardized tests. In contrast, the linguistic demands of the classroom setting require a lower threshold of linguistic competence in English.

Consistent with Cummins's notion of thresholds, there is growing evidence that teachers tend to modify and adjust their speech when communicating with students who are limited in English proficiency (see Fillmore & Valadez, 1986). Hatch (1983) reports that speech to second-language learners is characterized by a slower rate of speaking, clearer enunciation, shorter and less complex linguistic structures, and the increased use of gestures and extralinguistic cues that aid comprehension. Although the inclination to modify one's speech for the sake of language learners is a fairly natural process (see Snow & Ferguson, 1977, for "motherese" studies), it is produced interactively with the language learner strongly influencing the level of adjustments in form and content made by the teacher. Hence, in classrooms with many nonnative speakers of English, it is not surprising that teachers lower their linguistic demands, deliberately or unintentionally, making school grades less sensitive to differences in language background.

Turning to the discriminant analysis for high school grades, at the outset it should be noted that the results of the stepwise discriminant analysis did not reveal any significant sociocultural differences between the comparison groups. This is true for sex of respondent, father's occupational status, generational status, and respondent's language background. Although generational status and language exposure and usage effectively differentiated high and low performance on the CTBS measure, the comparison groups based on high school grades did not differ along any of these sociocultural characteristics. Nevertheless, it is important to recognize that the absence of sociocultural differences between the comparison groups based on high school grades is partially attributable to the sample's homogeneity, particularly with respect to parental occupation.

On the other hand, the results of the discriminant analysis for high school grades suggest that the comparison groups were most dissimilar in their environmental resources and appraisals. On environmental support, the academically invulnerable students reported higher levels of educational support from their teachers and friends. In contrast, the absence of parental support in predicting high school grades was surprising. The literature consistently suggests that the educational support from parents is strongly associated with achievement. However, the failure to find a strong relationship between parental sources of educational support and high school grades may be attributed to the limited range and high scores on the parental support measure. The median score on the parental support subscale was 49, from a possible total score of 50.

In terms of subjective appraisals, academically invulnerable students were more likely to (a) feel encouraged and prepared to attend college, (b) enjoy coming to school and being involved in high school activities, (c) experience fewer conflicts and difficulties in their intergroup relations with other students, and (d) experience fewer family conflicts and difficulties.

The primacy of the school's college preparatory climate in differentiating academically invulnerable and vulnerable students underscores the importance of a strong college preparatory climate. The results suggest that a positive college preparatory climate plays a critical role in encouraging students to succeed in high school. Overall, a student's appraisal of the school's college preparatory climate was the single best discriminator of academically invulnerable and academically vulnerable students.

Given that high school graduation and college admission depend largely on successfully completing a fixed number of courses and passing proficiency tests in basic skills, this study suggests that tenth graders are making important decisions that affect their educational future based largely on their appraised likelihood of attending college. Mexican American high school students who believed that they will someday graduate from college, and felt encouraged and prepared to attend college, were more likely to receive higher school grades.

Thus these results identify the need for early and continued contact between counselors and students, serving to motivate and encourage students to attend college. Studies have shown, however, that counselors typically do not assist high school students with their college plans until their junior or senior year. Lee and Ekstrom (1987), in a study based on the *High School and Beyond* data set, report that 50.4% of the high school sophomores reported no contact with a guidance counselor when making decisions about their school program. In a time when the college admission rate of Hispanic high school students is considerably lower than that of non-Hispanic Whites (Olivas, 1986), there is no doubt that greater attention needs to be focused on strengthening the link between high school and college for Mexican American students. In short, Mexican American students need early and positive contact with their counselors, teachers, and school principal, aimed at motivating and encouraging them to attend college. In order to build a strong college preparatory climate, schools can organize a series of workshops or retreats for school counselors and psychologists to assure that they are adequately prepared to work with Mexican American high school students and committed to the goal of increasing the representation of Mexican American students in colleges and universities. Schools can also build a strong college preparatory climate through school-sponsored activities for students such as college fairs, visits to local colleges and universities, information packets on colleges and financial aid, and visits from alumni students currently enrolled in college.

In summary, the results of this study suggest that the focus of research and policies for Mexican American students needs to shift away from school failure to school success. Indeed, the notion of invulnerability suggests that educational policies should be directed at building and expanding the protective resources and adaptive appraisals that promote academic success on the part of at-risk Mexican American high school students. As the study's results indicate, academically invulnerable students are markedly different from students who are academically less successful, with respect to their personal and environmental resources and adaptive appraisals.

20

♦

Educational Policy and the Growing Latino Student Population

Problems and Prospects

PEDRO REYES

RICHARD R. VALENCIA

A few public values have dominated educational policy in the United States: excellence, efficiency, and equity (Murphy, 1990). These values nonetheless have shifted in importance as American educators reform public schools. For instance, Callahan (1962) indicates that educational policies of the 1920s and 1930s were concerned with the efficiency with which schools were being conducted, and consolidation and reduction in expenditures were two of the most cited reforms. The policies in the 1960s and 1970s shifted their focus to equity as the dominant value. Lately, the reform movement has redirected its efforts to excellence as the dominant value in educational policy (Bacharach, 1991).

As these policy reforms have shifted in focus, the ideology and practice behind each movement have shifted as well. For example, in times of an efficiency mode all schoolchildren lose in terms of equity and excellence. Similarly, the ideology and practice driven by the excellence value affect students in many ways. The ideology is politically conservative, while the practice of excellence excludes many students, especially ethnic minority and economically disadvantaged students. The reforms seem to have a counteractive effect on ethnic minorities (Metz, 1990), especially the reforms of the 1980s and 1990s. With respect to Latino students and educational change, school reform efforts have neglected them as a group. In fact, the reform movement has exacerbated their ongoing educational plight.

A number of scholars have analyzed the school reform proposals, the first wave of which appeared with the publication of the report entitled *A Nation at Risk: The Imperatives for School Reform* (National Commission on Excellence in Education, 1983) made by different governmental and private entities (McDill, Natriello, & Pallas, 1985; Murane, 1986; Murphy, 1989, 1990; Sedlak, Wheeler, Pullin, & Cusick, 1985). Most analyses indicate that these reforms do not quite address the real problems experienced by schools and that much more needs to be done to improve education in general, especially when it comes to student performance (McDill et al., 1985). In making these pronouncements, reform analysts have ignored several critical questions: To what extent are race and ethnicity integral to the assumptions embedded in reform proposals? To what extent do such reform proposals, in practice, affect individuals of diverse racial/ethnic minority groups? In the context of this chapter, to what extent have reform proposals affected Latino students?

We argue that school reforms in the 1980s and 1990s have neglected the current demographic changes in the student population and that such disregard has marginalized and alienated a great majority of Latino and other racial/ethnic minority students. We analyze some of the consequences of school reform vis-à-vis Latinos and suggest policy changes.

THE CHANGING COMPLEXION OF PUBLIC SCHOOLS

The demography of this country has changed dramatically in the last decade and specific attention needs to be paid to those figures. Many demographers have pointed out again and again that changes have occurred in the age, socioeconomic, language, and racial/ethnic status of American youth (Hodgkinson, 1985, 1987; Yates & Ortiz, 1991). The

U.S. population is not only becoming older, poorer, more linguistically diverse, but it is also less White. People of other cultural backgrounds have increased dramatically during the past century, with Latinos being the fastest growing of this nation's large racial/ethnic minority groups (Chapa & Valencia, 1993).

Along with racial and ethnic status, we have the fact that many of these minority groups are bilingual (Omark & Erickson, 1983) and have a predominant language other than English (Yates & Ortiz, 1991). As discussed by Macías (1993) the Spanish-speaking is the fastest growing language minority group. The number of Spanish-speaking people is projected to increase to more than 22 million by the year 2000. Thus schools will face a student population that is mostly Latino and other racial/ethnic minority and who speak languages other than English. To further clarify this picture, we also have recent data showing that Latinos and other racial/ethnic minority groups comprise the *majority* of public school students in two of the nation's largest states. Latino and other minority K-12 students account for over 50% of the public school enrollments in California and Texas (Garcia, 1991; Valencia, 1991). These sharp growth patterns are not just restricted to the Southwest, but changes are occurring all over the country. For example, Chapa and Valencia (1993) point out that the metropolitan areas of New York/New Jersey, Miami/Fort Lauderdale, and Chicago/Gary have substantial concentrations of Latino schoolchildren. These major changes in Latino membership in the schools are the immediate future of public schools. To think that these changes are temporary would be a major flaw in any education and social policy directed to Latinos.

If one couples these Latino population growth trends with the current labor force in the public school systems, we see a shocking discrepancy between the makeup of educational staff and the makeup of the student body. For example, Valencia and Aburto (1991a) note that Latino teachers are the most severely underrepresented racial/ethnic group in the K-12 teaching profession. Based on 1986 data, "the national Latino school enrollment was about 10%, while Latinos comprised only 2.5% of the national teaching force—a disparity of 75% (underrepresentation)" (Valencia & Aburto, 1991a, p. 181).

As with the distribution of teachers, the number of Latino school principals appears the same. Out of 79,482, only 3% are Latino (National Center for Education Statistics, 1990). So the picture that emerges is quite clear: The great majority of the school personnel are White, monolingual English-speaking, with a professional training that considered little or nothing about the emergent demographic patterns and today's cultural diversity. When combined, these statistics are alarming and clearly necessitate changes in the educational system. As Valencia (1991) has underscored, the educational plight of Latino students is so severe that resources (both monetary and human) will be needed on an unprecedented scale to mount a workable offensive to promote school success.

EDUCATIONAL POLICY AND ITS ASSUMPTIONS

What has been the government's response to deal with the aforementioned trends and possible changes in the educational system for Latinos and other economically disadvantaged students? The government has initiated a series of educational reforms (see, e.g., Apple, 1990; Boyd, 1990; Chubb & Moe, 1986; Cooper, 1988; Kirst, 1988; Raywid, 1985, 1987). These reforms have taken on different configurations (Metz, 1988). In this section we only discuss what policy analysts have labeled "first wave reform."

When *A Nation at Risk: The Imperatives for School Reform* appeared, it unleashed hidden energies at the state and local levels to improve the quality of education. In fact, many states enacted legislation as a response to this call for education reform (Boyd, 1988). This first wave of reform proposed several avenues to increase student achievement such as raising the standards for student graduation, extending school time, aligning of curriculum with state mandates, increasing entry-level teacher salaries, and testing for teachers' levels of knowledge (Clark & Astuto, 1986; Doyle & Hartle, 1983; Finn, 1987a, 1987b). This preliminary reform effort, however, has been criticized from several perspectives. One of these perspectives has to do with the nature of the assumptions made by this report and related documents.

The reader may ask, why are we discussing the first wave of reform when the literature has already identified second and third waves of reform (see Elmore, 1990; Murphy, 1990)? Two reasons exist. First, the reality is that the majority of school districts around the country find themselves immersed in the first wave of reform. For example, many states still have policies (such as career ladders and entry-level testing for teachers) promulgated during the first wave of reform. Second, many of the assumptions embedded in the first wave are still present in the second and third waves of reform. Thus we revisit the assumptions of the first wave of educational policy.

Assumption 1: Schools Are Marketplaces

One of the major assumptions made by the first wave of reform was that schools need to be conceptualized as markets where competition and choice would somehow take care of the problems experienced in schools. The essence of this assumption is that markets are good for efficient allocation of resources and for motivating people (Cooper, 1988). To get this marketplace up and running, the government proposed a series of alternatives to fund an individual's education (Moore, 1989). For example, the government proposed ideas such as tuition tax credits, tuition transfers and vouchers—all of which are supposed to increase choice and make education competitive again (see, e.g., Apple, 1988; Boyd, 1988; Cooper, 1988).

One of the policies is that of tuition tax credits. Tuition tax credit deductions are financial incentives given to parents so that their children may attend any school, including private ones. That is, parents get to deduct educational expenditures from their taxable income. The idea of this policy is to promote school choice among parents and thus force public schools to improve their quality if they want to survive (or retain students). The tuition tax credit policy has not been embraced by many states in the country. In fact, Minnesota is one of the few states to enact this policy into law (Wolk, 1990). The law provides for parents to deduct from their income tax the costs related to textbooks, tuition, and transportation. To this point, however, there is no evidence that people are flocking out of public schools and enrolling in private or religious-affiliated schools. Moreover, there is little information on whether the quality of education in private or religious schools is better than that of the public schools. Finally, with respect to Latinos, there is little or no information on whether they have taken full advantage of such a policy. It is unlikely, however, that Latino parents have taken advantage of the policy given that most parents are economically disadvantaged (Chapa & Valencia, 1993; Hodgkinson, 1992; Pérez & De La Rosa Salazar, 1993).

Conceptually similar to the tuition tax credit, but different in approach, is the voucher policy. The voucher plan is an attempt to provide individuals with a redeemable "certificate" that entitles students to the right of education in any school of choice (Nathan, 1989). Again, the assumption is that the parent of the student has the "correct" information to select the best school for the child. Furthermore, this policy assumes that because of parental choice the public school would improve its quality

(Wise & Darling-Hammond, 1986). Several states are experimenting with this policy. For example, Wisconsin has recently approved a voucher program for 1,000 low-income students in Milwaukee (Martin, 1991). Preliminary findings indicate that the choice schools did not improve student scores any better than public schools and that student attrition was high in such schools (Witte, 1991). Witte reported that 86 of 249 students did not report to the choice schools again. Moreover, we have evidence that California experimented with a voucher program and the results were less than desirable. Most parents chose the local schools, did not have information about other schools, and found little differences among schools. Furthermore, there is the fear that given the widening gap between the economically advantaged and disadvantaged, poor Latinos will have even more inferior education. On top of these findings, students did not improve academically (Lieberman, 1986, 1989; Salganik, 1981). Vermont appears to have a more positive experience with the voucher program (McClaughry, 1987).

Similar to tax credit deductions, several states have adopted a policy named "tuition transfers" that allocates money to be used to pay tuition for those students who do not have access to a school. New England is an example of a region in which students may attend private academies if no local high school is available (Cooper, 1990). In some other cases, states such as Vermont and New Hampshire send their students across state lines to private schools if no local public schools are available. The popularity of this policy has not been explored in any detail up to now. Thus there is no way of measuring the effectiveness of the policy. We do not know how such a policy has affected different groups of individuals (such as minority students) nor do we know the cost-effectiveness of such a policy (Seldon, 1986).

Assumption 2: Schools Need Limited Change

A second major assumption of the first wave of reform proposals is that schools do not need to be dramatically changed (Kirst, 1990). That is, the current organizational structure, teacher incentive systems, authority relationships between teacher-administrator and student-teacher, and the organization of curriculum and knowledge are deemed acceptable. The major idea in this second assumption is to make "things harder" for students and for teachers. For example, many states enacted legislation to increase student graduation requirements. More math, more science, more "time on task" were needed to create this "new student" (see Kirst,

1988). To many politicians and reformers, it did not make any difference whether more math meant more of the same content, taught in the same way by the same unmotivated teacher. Politicians wanted change, but structural and systematic transformations were not part of the debate. Reformers and school administrators did not know how to start the change (Clark & Astuto, 1986).

On the other hand, some scholars of school reform have argued that Latino school failure—and its converse, school success—can be better and more fully comprehended by considering the full spectrum of systemic and institutional factors that drive and shape schooling. For example, Pearl (1991), in an analysis of Latino school failure, contends that such failure "can be fully understood only when analyzed in the broadest political, economic, and cultural contexts. Macropolicies establish the boundaries of possibilities" (p. 273). As Pearl underscores, the bottom line of workable school reform for Mexican Americans and other Latinos is to connect education with political action. He also admonishes that for policymakers not to pay attention to the linkages of schooling with a number of social issues, macropolicies, and the features of democratic schooling (e.g., students' rights, equal encouragement) will very likely result in the continuation of schooling problems for Latino students.

Assumption 3: Students Are Homogeneous

The third major assumption is that all students are alike and thus can meet and embrace all requirements imposed on them by others, such as state regulatory agencies (Kirst, 1990). As Metz (1986) points out, American students come from different socioeconomic backgrounds, thus implying diversity in values and aspirations. Not all children are the same; they have their own individual sets of values and ways of knowing. Therefore, to assume that uniformity works for everybody is to assume that cultural homogeneity exists in American society—an assumption that has no basis in fact. This uniformity assumption is questionable because it goes against the very essence of American society—a pluralistic society. Furthermore, as numerous scholars have emphasized, there is considerable heterogeneity within the general Latino population (e.g., Chapa & Valencia, 1993; Padilla, 1992; Valencia & Menchaca, 1992). Policymakers and school reformers need to comprehend and appreciate such diversity among Latinos in order to promote better schooling for this heterogeneous group.

Assumption 4: Schools Are Homogeneous

As with the third assumption, the reform movement also assumes that all schools are alike, driven by the same structures and technology, and have little or no ties to the local communities that support them (Metz, 1986, 1987, 1990). Of course, this assumption flies in the face of the American school reality. Schools are similar at the macrolevel but different within. These differences are determined by the community's ability to provide the structural and technological means for their operation. Some schools have inadequate facilities, lower quality of laboratories, fewer incentives to motivate teachers to perform at higher levels, and fewer human resources to enhance the quality of curriculum and instruction than other schools (e.g., regarding Mexican-origin students, see Donato, Menchaca, & Valencia, 1991). Moreover, the idea that schools have no ties with the local community also is a false assumption in light of the realities of American public schooling. To a large extent, communities shape what goes on in schools (Kozol, 1991). There is a value structure within the local community that is represented in the elected school board that most often molds curriculum, personnel, and financial policy. Thus each community has a unique set of inputs that makes schools definitely sui generis. For policymakers to ignore this fact is to display ignorance and lack of understanding of American public schooling.

Assumption 5: Schools Are Economically Uniform

The community value structure is not the only determinant of what goes on in schools. An even more powerful element is present in every school district in America: the socioeconomic status of the district. What goes on in one school may be totally different from what goes on in another nearby school district. The facilities, equipment, and quality of human resources available in any school are directly associated with the economic resources available in that community. Regarding Latinos, it is typical that the schools they attend are underfinanced compared to the schools that White students attend. A good case in point is the current legal and legislative struggles Latinos are experiencing in Texas in their attempts to gain equities in school financing (see Valencia, 1991). And again, no two communities are alike in American society. Consequently, this assumption of economic uniformity across schools is ill-founded and untenable. Thus a policy or set of policies that assumes uniformity is destined to fail (for details on outcomes of this face of the reform movement, see Honing, 1988; Kirst, 1990).

In sum, as its goal to renew education, the reform movement has generated a great deal of interest between and within different states. Several states have enacted legislation motivating school districts to improve teaching and student outcomes. This legislation, however, has been targeted to creating schools that look similar and to standardizing curriculum (Boyd, 1990). Most legislation has been directed to increase excellence in education at the expense of equity. Little effort has been devoted to increase the educational opportunities for Latinos and economically disadvantaged students or to develop curriculum relevant to Latino and other minority cultures within the mainstream of American education.

Apple (1990) notes that the urge for reform was generated for purely economic and ideological reasons rather than for egalitarian motives. The national economy has been slumping for some time and the budget deficit has only increased during the last decade. This economic crisis, in turn, has created massive unemployment and has forced hundreds of businesses to declare bankruptcy. This economic crisis has also affected many other individuals as indicated by the increase of poverty (Giroux, 1984). On the other hand, we also have had a political environment that is ideologically conservative and business oriented. Apple (1986) indicates that for the conservative right, "profits and production are not high enough; people are not competitive and do not work as hard" (p. 15). These (so-called) problems are perceived by powerful groups who are in key political and policy-making positions. They have criticized schools as the organizations responsible for not preparing citizens adequately for the world of work. Thus they have called for revitalizing schools and for a closer alignment of schools to the business community. Consequently, governmental policies have emphasized those values espoused by the conservative groups formerly in power (Apple, 1985; Reese, 1986).

Finally, the idea in these policy mechanisms of reform is to give parents and students the freedom to find a school of their choice that meets the child's needs and abilities. A voucher, for example, would allow parents to "buy at the marketplace" their child's education. Tuition tax credits, on the other hand, would allow parents to deduct money spent on their children for educational purposes, the idea being that parents would take their children to other educational centers such as private or public schools. The same idea is built into the tuition transfer proposal. Parents would have an opportunity to select a school suitable for their child's needs and it would make no difference whether the school be private or public. Somehow, this freedom to choose the "right" school would bring back excellence to schools (Doyle & Finn, 1984). Whether these policies have brought back excellence to schools or not, these proposals have propelled other changes for all students, specifically Latino and other minority students. What are some of the consequences of these reforms for racial and ethnic minorities? Specifically, what are the consequences of these reforms for Latino students concerning school failure and retention, stratification, and equity in schools?

EDUCATIONAL REFORM AND ITS CONSEQUENCES FOR LATINOS

School Failure and Retention

Implementation of the various reform commissions' prescriptions entails potential "school failure" for Latino students (see Valencia, 1991, for a sustained discussion on the nature of the construct of school failure). In raising academic standards, schools are likely to alienate further that student subpopulation that we frequently label "at risk," increasing dropout rates and related schooling problems (e.g., low academic achievement). Latino and other minority students are more likely than White students to possess one or more of the characteristics or situations associated with being at risk of dropping out (Natriello, McDill, & Pallas, 1986; Reyes, 1990; Velez, 1989). Some of these predictors are living with a single parent, having repeated a grade, having a disadvantaged socioeconomic background, being limited-English proficient, having disciplinary problems at school, having low levels of academic performance as measured by grades, and having irregular attendance patterns (excessive tardiness and unexcused absences).

The reform movement has called for curricular changes that require pursuing more demanding sequences of basic courses that can serve as prerequisites for college admissions. An immediate issue is that in many predominantly racial/ethnic minority schools such courses are not typically offered nor do students frequently enroll in them (Haycock & Navarro, 1990; Orum, 1986). Also, such curricular changes can result in fewer choices in selecting courses for students in those systems that adopt these recommendations. Other recommendations are the introduction of longer school days and longer school years. For Latino students who have had a hard time coping with the original set of curricular requirements—due to academic or personal problems—the raising of the ante in the middle of the game may be a strong inducement to simply give up and pursue other interests or avenues of mobility. As Alexander and Pallas (1984) suggest, students with relatively low grade point averages benefit very little from completing the kind of core requirements suggested by the school reform movement (Oakes & Lipton, 1990).

Student retention is a very serious problem currently being faced in our public schools. Latino students are hit particularly hard by this major schooling crisis. As Rumberger (1991) underscores in an analysis of Mexican American dropouts, "dropping out of high school is one visible form of educational failure. Although graduating from high school alone will not guarantee social and economic success, failure to graduate from high school will most likely deny it" (p. 85). Educators and policy makers have not yet been able to find a solution to remedy such a problem, and the current reform is likely to exacerbate dropout rates among Latino students. The reason for intensified dropout rates among these students is loud and clear. The current reforms encourage students to "buy out" better education at schools away from the local school. Students who have the means to do it will go, leaving behind only those who cannot afford to go. This creates a demoralizing effect among students, teachers, and parents because they are perceived as losers (Martin, 1991). When students (or teachers and administrators) receive constant negative messages about their status in a school, they tend to leave such organizations. With the current reform, however, it is very likely that Latino students—because of very limited economic resources—would be the ones to remain in schools where the quality of instruction and personnel is deemed inferior. Moreover, for Latino students with limited-English language skills and serious academic deficiencies, the logical choice is to drop out of school because of the constant negative experiences and frustrations. Thus the current policies are likely to increase further the inability of schools to retain Latino students, in general.

Stratification

Another set of reform recommendations emphasizes increased reliance on standardized tests of achievement at specified intervals. Although implementation of these recommendations has focused on testing for minimum levels of proficiency, minority communities and many academic researchers have often pointed to the adverse impact of these kinds of tests on minority students. Given that African American and Latino students fail the tests in substantially higher proportions than do Whites (Jaeger, 1982; Valencia & Aburto, 1991c), the minimum competency testing

(MCT) requirement is likely to have an adverse, disproportionate impact on minority students. Some critics contend that the diploma sanction will lower student's motivation to attend school, thus resulting in increased disciplinary and academic problems and higher dropout rates (Serow, 1984; Valencia & Aburto, 1991c). This gatekeeping mechanism can also result in the creation of a two-tiered certification process, as some schools have already moved in the direction of awarding two different kinds of high school diplomas: one for those who pass the MCT and another for those who complete all their courses but fail the exam. As Valencia and Aburto (1991c) describe, "This situation creates a new kind of dropout—students with a poor academic background who have the willingness to stay in school and graduate, but who will be denied a high school diploma because they do not meet the minimum standards" (p. 225). Above all, the major implication that emerges from MCT is that a stigma of failure for low-achieving students is reinforced, exacerbating stratification through a perpetuation of racial and economic inequality (Serow, 1984).

A second area of concern is that curriculum reform results in a single or uniform set of core courses to be taken by all students. This policy implication is that greater stratification will occur as lower-performing students will have fewer choices and will be forced into an unfair competitive situation with higher performing students. Forcing all students to work on similar tasks, without providing tutoring and other kinds of special help for the lower-achieving student, will result in "lower teacher and peer evaluations for lower ability students, lower self-evaluations, and ultimately lower performance" (McDill et al., 1985, p. 425; Natriello, McDill, & Pallas, 1990). Repeated experiences of such failure for Latino students can lead to frustration and increased probabilities of low achievement or leaving school prior to graduation.

Despite the fact that Latinos have faced historical racial oppression and subsequent social stratification (e.g., education, labor market; see, e.g., Longres, 1974; Menchaca, in press; Segura, 1984), there have been some gains over the decades. Compared to their parents and grandparents, Latino students have been more successful in completing high school and college, and thus have attained higher social status. Nevertheless, many racial/ethnic minority individuals continue to experience intensified stratification. For example, let us take Latinos as a case in point. Valencia (1991) notes that the national attention Latinos received in the late 1970s and early 1980s was accompanied by the frequently stated claim that the 1980s would be the "decade of the Hispanic." Within and outside the Latino community were expectations that Latinos would benefit from their growing presence. Gains along political, economic, and educational lines were anticipated. But, contrary to these improved "quality of life" expectations, many Latinos—particularly Mexican Americans and Puerto Ricans—were worse off as the decade of the 1990s began. In a report by the National Council of La Raza, *The Decade of the Hispanic: A Sobering Economic Retrospective* (Miranda & Quiroz, 1989), numerous trends were identified that captured the Latinos' dismal economic situation during the 1980s (e.g., increased rates of poverty, widening income disparity). In short, Latinos as a whole experienced increased stratification.

As we have been underscoring, current reform proposals seem to have a negative effect on Latinos and other economically disadvantaged racial/ethnic minorities. For example, it is likely that the already high dropout rate of secondary school Latinos will increase in the light of current reform efforts. This, in turn, has negative consequences because the odds of being unemployed will increase as well. It is widely known that there is a direct correlation between earnings and status attainment. Therefore, it is likely that Latinos will remain in the same low social status as they have been. Moreover, the labor market will steadily require employees to have college degrees in order to have a high-paying job (see Pérez & De La Rosa Salazar, 1993). What are the chances that Latinos will obtain a college degree given that they obtained a second-class instruction at second-class schools? The likelihood is that school reforms, as presently conceived, will increase the social gap between the haves and have nots, thus making more obvious than ever the social problems we observe in this country.

To sum, "school intensification" reforms seem to be designed for the more college-oriented student segment, with little attention being paid to the "at risk" population. It is almost an anticipation of what the labor market is beginning to look like: well-paid professional jobs at the top comprising no more than 20% of all new positions and semiskilled and unskilled jobs for the rest of the workers. The business and academic elites behind school reform movements anticipate little demand for factory and service positions requiring highly skilled labor. As many as 80% of today's youngsters (including many Latinos) may have been written off by the school reform movement (McDill et al., 1985).

Equity

Given the five questionable assumptions of school reform previously discussed here, it is not surprising, then, that one finds little attention focused on Latino and other minority students in the educational reform literature. For example, the National Commission on Excellence in Education (1983), which produced *A Nation at Risk,* completely ignored language minority students. Despite the tremendous population increase in language minority children (see Macías, 1993, for current data on the growing numbers of language minority Latino students), not one of the more than 40 reports commissioned by the National Commission was principally concerned with the problems faced by this subgroup.

Writing from a meritocratic perspective, and ignoring the historical role of American schools in reproducing class and racial/ethnic inequalities, the school reform literature assumes that language minority students are deficient. An example of this view can be found in Adler's (1982) *The Paideia Proposal.* In the section of the book devoted to "Overcoming Initial Impediments," we read that "the sooner a democratic society intervenes to remedy the cultural inequality of homes and environments, the sooner it will succeed in fulfilling the democratic mandate of equal educational opportunity for all" (p. 39). Ignoring the documented benefits of bilingual education (see Merino, 1991, for an overview of successful bilingual classrooms), the school reform movement basically takes an assimilationist approach, rejecting any possibility for cultural pluralism in American education. Once again, the focus and concern are on the middle-class White student, with potentially devastating consequences for the language minority student (Apple, 1987).

Another schooling condition that speaks to inequities in the educational experience of minority students is school segregation. Attending ethnically isolated public schools has been, and continues to be, a schooling reality for a substantial proportion of Black and Latino students (see Chapa & Valencia, 1993). An interesting development is that presently, Latino students now have the dubious distinction of being the most segregated of our nation's pupils (Orum, 1986; cited in Donato et al., 1991). In fact, Latino students in Texas and California are more segregated than Black students in Mississippi and Alabama (Orfield & Monfort, 1992). It has been well documented that segregation has adverse effects—such as lower academic achievement and higher dropout rates—on the schooling outcomes for Latinos (Donato et al., 1991). For example, in a more general overview, Levine and Havinghurst (1989), using 1984 data, wrote that

> Only about 10 percent of urban thirteen-year-olds attending disadvantaged urban schools with heavily poverty/minority enrollment have scores

as high as the average student in advantaged urban schools with lower minority/poverty enrollment, and only about 10 percent of 13-year-olds in advantaged urban schools relatively low in poverty/minority enrollment have scores below the average student in disadvantaged urban schools with high poverty/minority enrollment. (p. 53)

Undoubtedly, the beefing up of requirements has the potential of improving the academic preparation of college-bound students. There is enough evidence, however, that schools in large metropolitan areas continue the old practice of educational "triage," placing the best and the brightest in a small number of magnet or academically selective schools, and confining the vast majority of their students to dilapidated, mostly segregated schools. In Chicago, for example, which has a large Latino population, as recently as 1988 only about 18% of the city's 111,891 high school students were enrolled in the 12 selective high schools ("Chicago Schools," 1988). Interestingly enough, the major tactic the citizens of Chicago put in place to deal with their deteriorating school system has been to set up local school councils in every school that have the power to hire and fire principals.

Current reform legislation of choice encourages segregation and resegregation among students. It is clear that a few Latino students will be able to use vouchers or tuition tax credits for their education. On the other hand, it is likely that middle-class White students can make full use of those mechanisms to attend a better school. The net effect then will be that most middle-class students will go elsewhere for their education, leaving only Latino students and other less economically privileged students in the local school—not because these pupils do not want a better education, but because they do not have the means or the information to take full advantage of those programs. The likely outcome, then, is that segregated schools will increase. Compounding this problem of segregation, the schools of choice seem to have adopted exclusionary admission policies. It appears that magnet schools, for example, require high achievement scores for students to be considered for admission. This becomes problematic because many Latino students do not score as high on standardized tests as do White students (e.g., see Valencia, 1991). Therefore, most economically disadvantaged Latino students will be excluded from consideration for admission to a magnet school. To complicate the issue further, there is some research about magnet schools showing that (a) most parents do not know the admissions procedures, (b) these schools send frequently low-performing students back to their neighborhood schools, and (c) these schools do not provide services for handicapped students (Moore & Davenport, 1988).

In addition to equity issues related to language minority students and segregation, a third concern is the decline of minorities attending college. This decrease in college enrollment is seen in both Latino and Black student groups. The college enrollment rates among Black high school graduates declined in the 1980s (Hauser & Anderson, 1991). Regarding Latino students, evidence indicates that from 1976 to 1985 the Hispanic college attendance rate dramatically declined 28% (Orum, 1986, and Mingle, 1987; cited in Valencia, 1991). The overall picture appears to be not as encouraging as reformers would paint when equity is the point of discussion. In fact, the reform proposals aim to destroy the little equity that Latino students have enjoyed so far in public schools.

To summarize, the assumptions behind the school reform movement can be described as the decomposition of education into easily measured specific skills that enables meritocratic achievement for a select few. There is a perception of crisis, linked to images of undiscipline, disorder, and declining scores on standardized achievement tests. The solutions include changing the curriculum as well as marketing educational activities fueled by demands for accountability. The emphasis is on the individual student, without regard for any ethnic or racial-group origins. This trend is ultimately harmful to the mobility chances of Latinos, African Americans, and Native Americans because their oppressed minority status requires a curricular emphasis more in tune with their specific cultural histories (Natriello et al., 1990). In addition, their educational difficulties require group-specific interventions that are at odds with the assimilationist, individualist tone of the school reform movement. It is probably not a coincidence that as Latinos are gradually beginning to develop political muscle and a stronger presence in the administration of public educational systems, federal support for education has declined. An ideology of privatization has called for tax credit incentives for private schooling coupled with voucher plans (Moore, 1989). This model of educational reorganization, according to Wexler (1987), will create a "destruction of civic culture and public social relations; commodification of the education relation [and] . . . the conscious creation of educational markets" (p. 73). For Latinos, one can surmise that the notion of privatization is not in their best educational interests.

CONCLUSIONS

Implications for Policymakers

Given the rapidly growing Latino population and the current educational policy espoused by the government, there are two major implications for policymakers. First, a policy designed to achieve excellence at the expense of equity needs to be seriously questioned. The essence of social policy is to help the less fortunate and less powerful to achieve equity in society. It is clear that a major consequence of the current educational policy is not to attain equity but to further enhance the gap between those who have status, privilege, and power and those who do not. As a case in point, the current educational policy of school choice needs to be reconsidered by policymakers. An outcome of school choice policy is not to bring different cultural groups to acknowledge and celebrate multiculturalism but to segregate groups. The policy provides for groups of students to remove themselves from the local school that typically has diverse groups. At first glance, this reform effort seemingly provides an equal opportunity for all students to do the same, giving the impression that multiculturalism may be enhanced because many minority students usually trapped in poor quality schools may have the opportunity to go to a different school. The costs associated with moving to another school, however, were never considered by policymakers. A substantial proportion of school-aged Latino students are trapped in poverty in this country (see Pérez & De La Rosa Salazar, 1993, for current discussion of poverty trends among Latinos), thus eliminating the possibility of leaving the so-called poor school. For Latino students to make full use of choice, their parents need to understand how to define quality, know how to identify quality schools, know the admission procedures of other schools, and most of all have the money for transporting students to new locations. What are the chances that a poor Latino family will take full advantage of this choice policy? The answer is obvious. Moreover, policymakers do not understand that private or magnet schools cannot be forced to provide services equally well to all students. We know that in some cases private or magnet schools returned students to their local schools because of students' conduct or academic difficulties (Metz, 1986).

A second problem of current reform policy is that it assumes that all children are alike, speak the same language, and have very similar cultural expectations. This assumption of uniformity, of course, is not in line with the current and future reality of the public schools systems. Given the changing racial/ethnic demography, we know that the school population is and will be more diverse than ever. What works for one group does not necessarily work for another. Consequently, the policy's assumption of uniformity is ill-founded and is thus destined to fail as a good social policy. We need a policy that is theoretically sound and that reflects the current and future demographic changes of our country. We need a public policy embedded in multiculturalism with the help (monetary and otherwise) needed to revitalize the educational programs of those Latino and other ethnic minority students who presently have inadequate educational systems.

Implications for Administrators

The implications for policymakers are indeed important, but the implications for school administrators are of utmost importance. Administrators are what Lipsky (1986) called "street-level bureaucrats"—those who implement social policy and oversee its operation. This level is the most critical of all because the decisions taken at this level deeply affect all students. Given the current and future racial/ethnic demographic trends, there are several areas needing attention: administrator-teacher demographic concerns, preparation training, curricular issues, and staffing issues.

The administrator demographic reality is quite clear: The great majority of school administrators are mostly White, monolingual English-speaking, and with little or no knowledge of cultural diversity. Most administrators appear to lack cultural sensitivity and have a narrow perceptual lens that inhibits them from developing creative solutions to tackle the problems experienced by Latino students in school. This is especially problematic when Latino and other racial/ethnic minorities have become the majority in urban school districts. This change in student population also requires changes in the administrative structure. For example, more Latino administrators are needed, and thus energetic recruitment strategies must be in place to accommodate the necessary transformations of the administrative workforce.

Along with changes in the racial/ethnic makeup of administrators, changes must take place in the administrator preparation programs. With few exceptions, the current preparation programs for administrators do not include activities emphasizing ideas and concepts such as ethnicity, minority status, bilingual education, nonbiased assessment, second language acquisition, multiculturalism, and other issues that are germane to the current and future demographic trends of this country (Yates & Ortiz, 1991). Most of what takes place in administrator preparation programs include obsolete concepts of organization theory and the "nuts and bolts" type of courses in budget and fiscal management with a grand philosophy of survival. That is, administrators are taught how to play the game to survive in the local politics of the school.

This current curriculum hardly helps the administrator understand the problems experienced by White students, let alone those experienced by Latino students. Presently, most administrators are deficient because they do not have the knowledge to comprehend or the skills to deal with the academic and personal problems experienced by Latino students. Thus the solutions enacted to deal with Latino students by administrators typically fail. Preparation programs need to change in tune with the new reality of the public at large. For example, we need to provide perspectives on individual differences. Teachers, students, and administrators have unique learning styles. Preparation programs need to reflect that.

Moreover, preparation programs need to provide new conceptualizations of administration. We cannot rely on the dated philosophy of administration of bureaucracies—that people are basically lazy and that administrators are there to make sure employees get the work done. This philosophy has not worked and will never work in the school setting; it is counterproductive and reflects a dominant/dominated type of administration that does not work in schools (Reyes & Capper, 1991). Many education administration programs offer a 1920s philosophy of administration. It is time that educational administration programs provide new and different perspectives that are in tune with current thinking. For example, preparation programs should emphasize feminist, critical, and multicultural perspectives. These perspectives are likely to provide new conceptualizations to solve problems experienced by different groups such as teachers, students, and fellow administrators. Lack of substantive knowledge about how individuals work and think leads to incompetence for the most proficient administrator of operations.

The changes in the curriculum of administrator preparation programs are important; other changes, however, need to be made at the workplace. That is, we need to pay attention to the staffing patterns currently existing at the school district. As Chapa and Valencia (1993) emphasize, current demographic trends indicate that Whites are gradually becoming less and less of the K-12 public school population. Latino students are increasing at dramatic rates as are Latino students whose first language is not English (see Macías, 1993). Currently, the vast majority of public school teachers are White and monolingual English-speaking, most of whom have no training in English as a second language, bilingual language acquisition, or multicultural education. There is a great need for teachers who have the knowledge and understanding of their students, their parents, and their communities. Of equal importance is the need for the school labor force to reflect the diverse current and immediate future student population (see Valencia & Aburto, 1991a, 1991b, for a major, sustained analysis of the access problems Latinos have to the teaching profession; the authors also discuss proactive ways to increase Latino access to teaching).

Of equal significance as staffing is the curriculum that children are exposed to in schools. Most school curriculums are based on middle-class White values that emphasize individualism and competition as the essence of successful achievement. Furthermore, most of the curricular readings are written by White authors; there is little or no emphasis on the achievements of Latinos and different racial/ethnic minorities, nor is there any awareness that infusion of the Latino culture in the curriculum may help promote school success for alienated Latino students (e.g., see Apple, 1992, for a discussion of how "legitimate" knowledge in textbooks fails to include less powerful groups, such as women and people of color). Teachers and administrators often do not realize that much of the current curriculum has little personal or cultural meaning to Latino students, and thus these students frequently feel detached from the enterprise of schooling (see Pearl, 1991, for a provocative discussion of how curriculum changes can help bring about school success for Mexican Americans and other Latinos).

Given the enormous changes that are taking place and will take place in public schools, the significance of making internal changes in schools cannot be overemphasized. If the status quo continues, more and more Latino children in schools will feel as strangers in a school that emphasizes a curriculum based on the majority's experiences that have little to do with their own backgrounds. Moreover, if one couples the curriculum with the staffing patterns of schools, there will be little hope for Latino students. Most school personnel are part of the White majority and are trained with little understanding and knowledge of Latino cultures. Consequently, many Latino students are destined to fail in a system that has little understanding of their cultural outlook and backgrounds. So what are some actions that may be taken by policymakers and administrators?

Recommendations

First, we need a broader conceptualization of policy making in the educational field. That is, educational policy cannot be made based on the values of a single group. Theoretically, policy needs to be made within a multicultural context emphasizing the values of *all* the citizens of this country. We can no longer tolerate educational policies that ignore the needs of certain groups and help to perpetuate inequality in society. A good social policy is one that is designed to enhance the quality of life of all the citizens of the given society. The current educational policy—choice—only increases inequality for Latino and other minority students. Unless race, ethnicity, and cultural differences among groups are seriously considered in policy formation, any policy is certain to fail as a reform effort.

Second, it is clear that we need to recruit more Latino teachers at all levels of the educational system. The great majority of teaching staffs in public schools are White with little or no training in multicultural perspectives—which frequently renders them ineffective with Latino populations. This problem is of great concern, given the number of Latino students destined to be present in public schools. Thus administrators need to develop aggressive recruiting policies to address the need for Latino teaching personnel. For example, a school may develop a policy of partially funding Latino students to attend college, conditional that they would come back to the local school to teach for a certain number of years. Another alternative for the shortage of Latino teachers is to have institutions of higher education—working with local school districts—develop in-service programs to address the deficiencies of the majority of teachers. This suggestion does not imply a need to provide cursory in-service types of programs but, rather, to provide an ongoing training for extended periods until the individual is fully knowledgeable of minority cultures. This training must be associated with content on second language acquisition, bilingualism, and multiculturalism (see Valencia & Aburto, 1991b, for examples of other practical strategies associated with the identification, recruitment, diagnosis, and remediation of Latino teacher candidates).

Third, we need to engage in recruiting a larger number of linguistically diverse and racial/ethnic minority individuals into administrator preparation programs. This needs to be done in order to provide practitioners, researchers, role models, and the sufficient human resource power to address the changing demography of public schools. We can no longer afford to have public school leaders who have limited knowledge of a great number of students.

Along with recruiting Latino administrators we have to redesign our current preparation programs for administrators. We need to design programs and curriculum that not only take into consideration old concepts of administration but programs that consider new perspectives of administration (e.g., feminist, critical, and multicultural). We need to prepare a generation of administrators who will have the knowledge and skills to deal with the new challenges in a multicultural society.

We need to rethink, however, the content of the curriculum that all students are exposed to in school. This is especially true in years to come when the population of the public schools becomes more racial/ethnic minority and less White. The curriculum that once helped this nation become a world leader will need to change to meet the needs of a culturally diverse society. It is not the case that Latino students are deficient (as typically assumed), but the major problem lies in the relevancy of the curriculum and how that curriculum is delivered. A substantial number of Latino students see little connection between the curriculum and their immediate reality. Therefore, it is recommended that the curriculum taught in public schools be restructured to fit the needs of the students—restructured not to eliminate the concepts taught but to immerse those concepts in the context of cultural diversity. Only then will we see real interest and commitment to learning from all students, be they Latino, other racial/ethnic minority, or White.

In summary, it is clear that school choice as a policy is inherently appealing because it is based on freedom to choose. A democracy is not built, however, on liberty at the expense of equity. Both are important in a democracy (Boyd, 1990; Willie, 1991). The current approach for school reform does not consider the issue of equity as an important component to improve education. There seems to be a push for providing better education for those who already have a strong education program and for weakening the education program for those who already have inadequate programs. Would the current reform programs enhance equity for all students? Based on our analysis, the answer has to be "no." School choice, then, has little justification because it will increase inequity and stratification and will hamper social mobility for many individuals in society. Good social policy is intervention to provide for those in the weakest social condition. A good social policy would provide opportunities not available to them in a completely unregulated system (Willie, 1991).

In conclusion, we have enough evidence to be suspicious of the school reform movement of the 1980s. Given these proposals' virtual neglect of culturally diverse and economically disadvantaged students, we argue that school reform as envisioned in these reports will have very little positive impact on Latino communities. If anything, a case can be made that such policies can be potentially devastating to Latinos' educational chances. What seems to have worked in the more recent past to enhance the academic careers of Latino and other minority students is a mix of political power and more minorities staffing their schools (Apple, 1991). What minorities need, then, in addition to a more demanding course of studies, is more school board members, more administrators, and more teachers of their own racial/ethnic background (Meier, Stewart, & England, 1989) as well as comprehensive macrolevel school reform (Pearl, 1991). Only then will Latinos begin the long road to obtaining equity and a high quality of education in a multiracial, multicultural environment. The educational plight of Latino students has been persistent and pervasive. These stubborn schooling problems (e.g., segregation, limited access to higher education, diminished school achievement) coupled with the phenomenal growth of Latino students as well as the erosion of economic gains all point to the need for immediate and workable school reform. As Valencia (1991) notes, "When the schoolbell rings throughout the barrios in the 1990s, hopefully it will call us all to action" (p. 20).

References

Abrahams, B., Feldman, S. S., & Nash, S. C. (1978). Sex role, self-concept and sex role attitudes: Enduring personality characteristics or adaptations to changing life situations. *Developmental Psychology, 14*(4), 393-400.

Acosta, F. X. (1979). Pretherapy expectations and definitions of mental illness among minority and low-income patients. *Hispanic Journal of Behavioral Sciences, 1,* 403-410.

Acosta-Belen, E. (1986). Puerto Rican women in culture, history and society. In E. Acosta-Belen (Ed.), *The Puerto Rican woman: Perspective on culture, history and society* (pp. 1-29). New York: Praeger.

Adams, G. L., Dworkin, R. J., & Rosenberg, S. D. (1984). Diagnosis and pharmacotherapy issues in the care of Hispanics in the public sector. *American Journal of Psychiatry, 141,* 970-974.

Adler, M. (1982). *The paideia proposal: An educational manifesto.* New York: Macmillan.

Adler, P., Ovando, C., & Hocevar, D. (1984). Familiar correlates of gang membership: An exploratory study of Mexican-American youth. *Hispanic Journal of Behavioral Sciences, 6,* 65-76.

Adler, P. S. (1974). Beyond cultural identity: Reflections on cultural and multicultural man. In R. Brison (Ed.), *Topics in cultural learning* (Vol. 2, pp. 23-40). Honolulu: East-West Culture Learning Institute.

AIDS: The crisis in Latino L.A. [Special report]. (1987, October 30-November 5). *L.A. Weekly,* pp. 10-11.

Ajzen, I., & Fishbein, M. (1980). *Understanding attitudes and predicting social behavior.* Englewood Cliffs, NJ: Prentice Hall.

Alarcon, R. D. (1983). A Latin American perspective on *DSM-III. American Journal of Psychiatry, 140,* 102-105.

Albee, G. W. (1989). Primary prevention in public health: Problems and challenges of behavior change as prevention. In V. M. Mays, G. W. Albee, & S. F. Schneider (Eds.), *Primary prevention of AIDS: Psychological approaches* (pp. 17-20). Newbury Park, CA: Sage.

Alegria, D., Guerra, E., Martinez, C., & Meyer, G. (1977). El hospital invisible. *Archives of General Psychiatry, 34,* 1354-1357.

Alexander, K. L., & Pallas, A. M. (1984). Curriculum reform and school performance: An evaluation of the "New Basics." *American Journal of Education, 92,* 391-420.

Alpert, M., Kesselman, M., Marcos, L., & Urcuyo, L. (1973). The language barrier in evaluating Spanish-American patients. *Archives of General Psychiatry, 29,* 655-659.

Alva, S. A. (1989). Academic invulnerability among Mexican American high school students: A multivariate study. *Dissertation Abstracts International, 50,* 358B.

Alvarez, R. (1973). The psycho-historical and socioeconomic development of the Chicano community in the United States. *Social Science Quarterly, 53*(4), 920-942.

Amaro, H., Whitaker, R., Coffman, G., & Heeren, T. (1990). Acculturation and marijuana and cocaine use: Findings from HHANES 1982-1984. *American Journal of Public Health, 80*(Suppl.), 54-60.

American Psychiatric Association. (1980). *Diagnostic and statistical manual of mental disorders* (3rd ed.). Washington, DC: Author.

American Psychiatric Association. (1987). *Diagnostic and statistical manual of mental disorders* (3rd ed., rev.). Washington, DC: Author.

American Psychiatric Association. (1994). *Diagnostic and statistical manual of mental disorders* (4th ed.). Washington, DC: Author.

American Psychiatric Association. (1991). DSM-IV *options.* Washington, DC: Author.

American Psychiatric Association. (1994). *Quick reference to the diagnostic criteria from DSM-IV.* Washington, DC: Author.

American Psychiatric Association, Task Force on DSM-IV. (1993). DSM-IV *draft criteria.* Washington, DC: Author.

Andrade, S. J. (1982). Family roles of Hispanic women: Stereotypes, empirical findings, and implications for research. In R. E. Zambrana (Ed.), *Latina women in transition* (Monograph No. 7, pp. 95-106). New York: Fordham University, Hispanic Research Center.

Angel, R., & Guarnaccia, P. J. (1989). Mind, body, and culture: Somatization among Hispanics. *Social Science and Medicine, 28,* 1229-1238.

Angel, R., & Guarnaccia, P. J. (1989). Mind, body, and culture: Somatization among Hispanics. *Social Science and Medicine, 28,* 1229-1238.

Angle, J. (1976). Mainland control of manufacturing and reward for bilingualism in Puerto Rico. *American Sociological Review, 41,* 289-307.

Annandale, E., & Hunt, K. (1990). Masculinity, femininity, and sex: An exploration of their relative contribution to explaining gender differences in health. *Sociology of Health and Illness, 12,* 24-46.

Apple, M. W. (1985). *Education and power.* New York: Routledge & Kegan Paul.

Apple, M. W. (1986). *Teachers and texts: A political economy of class and gender relations in education.* New York: Routledge & Kegan Paul.

Apple, M. W. (1987). Producing inequality: Ideology and economy in the national reports on education. *Educational Studies, 18,* 195-220.

Apple, M. W. (1988). What reform talk does: Creating new inequalities in education. *Educational Administration Quarterly, 24,* 272-281.

Apple, M. W. (1990). Creating inequality: The political/economic context. In S. B. Bacharach (Ed.), *Education reform: Making sense of it all* (pp. 155-164). Boston: Allyn & Bacon.

Apple, M. W. (1991). The redefinition of equality in the conservative restoration. In W. Secada (Ed.), *The meaning of equity* (pp. 69-89). Philadelphia: Falmer.
Apple, M. W. (1992). The text and cultural politics. *Educational Researcher, 21,* 4-11, 19.
Applewhite, S. (Ed.). (1989). *Hispanic elderly in transition: Theory, research, policy, and practice.* Westport, CT: Greenwood.
Arce, C. H., Gurin, P., Gurin, G., & Estrada, L. (1976). *National study of Chicano identity and mental health: A proposal for research.* Unpublished manuscript, Institute for Social Research, University of Michigan, Ann Arbor.
Arce, C. H., & Santos, R. (1981). *Design and execution problems in a rare population sample survey.* Unpublished manuscript, Institute for Social Research, University of Michigan, Ann Arbor.
Arias, M. (1986). The context of education for Hispanic students: An overview. *American Journal of Education, 95,* 26-57.
Arnott, C. C. (1972). Husbands' attitudes and wives' commitment to employment. *Journal of Marriage and the Family, 34,* 673-684.
Arroyo, W., & Cervantes, R. C. (in press). The Mexican American child. In J. D. Nopshitz (Ed.), *Handbook of child and adolescent psychiatry.* New York: Basic Books.
Atkinson, D., Morten, G., & Sue, D. (1983). *Counseling American minorities.* Dubuque, IA: William C. Brown.
Au, K. H. (1980). Participant structures in reading lessons with Hawaiian children: Analysis of a culturally appropriate instructional event. *Anthropology and Education Quarterly, 11,* 91-115.
Baca-Zinn, M. (1982). Chicano men and masculinity. *Journal of Ethnic Studies, 10,* 20-44.
Bacharach, S. B. (1991). *Education reform: Making sense of it all.* Boston: Allyn & Bacon.
Bandura, A. (1977). *Social learning theory.* Englewood Cliffs, NJ: Prentice Hall.
Barefoot, J. C. (1992). Developments in the measurement of hostility. In H. S. Friedman (Ed.), *Hostility, coping, and health* (pp. 13-31). Washington, DC: American Psychological Association.
Baskin, D. (1984). Cross-cultural conceptions of mental illness. *Psychiatric Quarterly, 56*(1), 45-53.
Baskin, D., Bluestone, H., & Nelson, M. (1981). Ethnicity and psychiatric diagnosis. *Journal of Clinical Psychologist, 37,* 529-539.
Baum, A., & Nesselhof, S. E. A. (1988). Psychological research and the prevention, etiology, and treatment of AIDS. *American Psychologist, 43,* 853-858.
Baxter, M., & Bucci, W. (1981, June). Studies in linguistic ambiguity and insecurity. *Urban Health,* pp. 36-40.
Bean, F., & Tienda, M. (1987). *The Hispanic population of the U.S.* New York: Russell Sage.
Becerra, R. M., & Shaw, D. (1984). *The Hispanic elderly: A research guide.* New York: University Press of America.
Beck, D. F., & Jones, M. A. (1973). *Progress on family problems.* New York: Family Service Association.
Becker, M. H., & Joseph, J. G. (1988). AIDS and behavioral change to reduce risk: A review. *American Journal of Public Health, 78,* 394-410.
Bem, S. L. (1974). The measurement of psychological androgyny. *Journal of Counseling and Clinical Psychology, 42,* 155-162.
Bem, S. L. (1975). Sex role adaptability: One consequence of psychological androgyny. *Journal of Personality and Social Psychology, 31,* 634-643.
Bem, S. L. (1981a). Gender schema theory: A cognitive account of sex typing. *Psychological Review, 88,* 354-364.

Bem, S. L. (1981b). *Manual for the Bem Sex Role Inventory*. Palo Alto, CA: Consulting Psychologists Press.
Bem, S. L. (1985). Androgyny and gender schema theory: A conceptual and empirical integration. In T. B. Sonderegger (Ed.), *Psychology and gender* (pp. 179-226). Lincoln: University of Nebraska Press.
Bem, S. L., Martyna, W., & Watson, C. (1976). Sex typing and androgyny: Further explorations of the expressive domain. *Journal of Personality and Social Psychology, 34*(5), 1016-1023.
Benavides, J. (1992, October 17). Mujeres rule the roosters. *Santa Barbara News Press*, p. B1.
Berlin, I. (1987). Effects of changing Native American cultures on child development. *Journal of Community Psychology, 15*, 299-306.
Bernal, M. E., Knight, G. P., Garza, C. A., Ocampo, K. A., & Cota, M. K. (1990). The development of identity in Mexican American children. *Hispanic Journal of Behavioral Sciences, 12*, 3-24.
Berry, J. W. (1980). Acculturation as varieties of adaptation. In A. M. Padilla (Ed.), *Acculturation: Theory, models and some new findings* (pp. 9-25). Boulder, CO: Westview.
Berry, J. W., & Annis, R. (1974). Acculturative stress: The role of ecology, culture and psychological differentiation. *Journal of Cross-Cultural Psychology, 5*, 382-406.
Berry, J. W., Kim, U., Minde, T., & Mok, D. (1987). Comparative studies of acculturative stress. *International Migration Review, 21*, 491-511.
Berry, J. W., Kim, U., Power, S., Young, M., & Bujaki, J. (1989). Acculturation attitudes in plural societies. *Applied Psychology, 38*, 185-206.
Bertakis, K. (1977). The communication of information from physician to patient: A method for increasing patient retention and satisfaction. *Journal of Family Practice, 5*, 217-222.
Billson, J. M., & Terry, M. B. (1982). In search of the silken purse: Factors in attrition among first-generation students. *College and University, 58*, 57-75.
Bird, H. R., Canino, G., Rubio-Stipec, M., & Shrout, P. (1987). Use of the mini-mental state examination in a probability sample of a Hispanic population. *Journal of Nervous and Mental Disease, 175*, 731-737.
Blackwell, J., & Hart, P. (1982). *Cities, suburbs, and Blacks: A study of concerns, distrust, and alienation*. Bayside, NY: General Hall.
Blackwell, J. E. (1978). Social factors affecting educational opportunity for minority students. In *Beyond desegregation: Urgent issues in the education of minorities* [Monograph]. New York: College Entrance Examination Board.
Blood, R. O., & Wolfe, D. M. (1960). *Husbands and wives*. Glencoe, IL: Free Press.
Bochner, S., & Pendleton, D. (1980). The communication of medical information in general practice consultations as a function of patients' social class. *Social Science & Medicine, 14A*, 669-673.
Boreham, P., & Gibson, D. (1978). The information process in private medical consultations: A preliminary investigation. *Social Science & Medicine, 12*, 409-416.
Boxer, P. A., & Garvey, J. T. (1985). Psychiatric diagnosis of Cuban refugees in the United States: Findings of medical review boards. *American Journal of Psychiatry, 142*, 86-89.
Boyd, W. L. (1988). How to reform schools without half trying: Secrets of the Reagan administration. *Educational Administration Quarterly, 24*, 299-309.
Boyd, W. L. (1990). The national level: Reagan and the bully pulpit. In S. B. Bachrach (Ed.), *Education reform: Making sense of it all* (pp. 250-269). Boston: Allyn & Bacon.
Bravo, M., Canino, G. J., & Bird, H. (1987). El Dis en español: Su traducción y adaptación en Puerto Rico. *Acta psiquiátrica psiologico América Latina, 33*, 27-42.

Bravo, M., Canino, G. J., & Rubio-Stipec, M. (1991). A cross-cultural adaptation of a psychiatric epidemiologic instrument: The diagnostic interview schedule's adaptation in Puerto Rico. *Culture, Medicine and Psychiatry, 15*(1), 1-18.
Brewer, M. B. (1979). In-group bias in the minimal intergroup situation: A cognitive-motivational analysis. *Psychological Bulletin, 86,* 307-324.
Brigham, J. (1973). Ethnic stereotypes and attitudes: A different mode of analysis. *Journal of Personality, 41,* 206-223.
Brislin, R. W., Lonner, W. J., & Thorndike, E. M. (1973). *Cross-cultural research method.* New York: John Wiley.
Brody, D. (1979). An analysis of patient recall of their therapeutic regimens. *Journal of Chronic Disease, 33,* 57-63.
Brody, E. B. (1970). Migration and adaptation: The nature of the problem. In E. B. Brody (Ed.), *Behavior in new environments* (pp. 13-21). Beverly Hills, CA: Sage.
Bronfenbrenner, U. (1960). Freudian theories of identification and their derivatives. *Child Development, 31,* 15-40.
Brown, C., Rosen, N., Hill, S., & Olivas, M. (1980). *The condition of education for Hispanic Americans.* Washington, DC: National Center for Education Statistics.
Brown, D., Fee-Fulkerson, K., Furr, S., Ware, W. B., & Voight, N. L. (1984). Locus of control, sex role orientation, and self-concept in Black and White third- and sixth-grade male and female leaders in a rural community. *Developmental Psychology, 20*(4), 717-721.
Brown, G. H., Rosen, N. L., Hill, S. T., & Olivas, M. A. (1980). *The condition of education for Hispanic Americans* (NCES-80-303). Washington, DC: U.S. Government Printing Office.
Brunswik, E. (1952). The conceptual framework of psychology. In *International Encyclopedia of Unified Science, 1*(10). Chicago: University of Chicago Press.
Bunting, A. B., & Reeves, J. B. (1983). Perceived male sex orientation and beliefs about rape. *Deviant Behavior, 4,* 281-295.
Burda, P. C., & Vaux, A. C. (1987). The social support process in men: Overcoming sex-role obstacles. *Sex Roles, 40,* 31-44.
Buriel, R. (1983). Teacher-student interactions and their relationship to student achievement: A comparison of Mexican-American and Anglo-American children. *Journal of Educational Psychology, 75,* 889-897.
Burks, N., & Martin, B. (1985). Everyday problems and life change events: Ongoing versus acute sources of stress. *Journal of Human Stress, 11,* 27-35.
Burma, J. H. (1967). Spanish speaking children. In E. T. Keach, Jr., R. Fulton, & W. E. Gardner (Eds.), *Education and social crisis* (pp. 86-97). New York: John Wiley.
Burnam, M. A., Hough, R. L., Karno, M., Escobar, J. I., & Telles, C. A. (1987). Acculturation and lifetime prevalence of psychiatric disorders among Mexican Americans in Los Angeles. *Journal of Health and Social Behavior, 28,* 89-102.
Burnam, M. A., Karno, M., Hough, R. L., Escobar, J., & Forsythe, A. (1983). The Spanish Diagnostic Interview Schedule. *Archives of General Psychiatry, 40,* 1189-1196.
Callahan, R. E. (1962). *Education and the cult of efficiency.* Chicago: University of Chicago Press.
Canino, G. (1982). Transactional family patterns: A preliminary exploration of Puerto Rican female adolescents. In R. E. Zambrana (Ed.), *Work, family and health: Latina women in transition* (pp. 27-36). New York: Hispanic Research Center.

Canino, G. J., Bird, H. R., Rubio-Stipec, M., Woodbury, M. A., Ribera, J. C., Huertas, S. E., & Sesman, M. J. (1987). Reliability of child diagnosis in a Hispanic sample. *Journal of the American Academy of Child and Adolescent Psychiatry, 26*(4), 560-565.

Canino, G. J., Bird, H. R., Shrout, P. E., Rubio-Stipec, M., Bravo, M., Martinez, R., Sesman, M., & Guevara, L. (1987). The prevalence of specific psychiatric disorders in Puerto Rico. *Archives of General Psychiatry, 44,* 727-735.

Canino, I. A., Gould, M. S., Prupis, S., & Shaffer, D. (1986). A comparison of symptom and diagnosis in Hispanic and Black children in an outpatient mental health clinic. *Journal of the American Academy of Child Psychiatry, 25*(2), 254-259.

Cantwell, D. P. (1980). The diagnostic process and diagnostic classification in child psychiatry—DSM-III. *Journal of the American Academy of Child Psychiatry, 19,* 345-355.

Carlson, N. L. (1981). Male client-female therapist. *Personnel and Guidance Journal, 59,* 228-231.

Carnegie Council on Policy Studies in Higher Education. (1979). *Giving youth a better chance: Options for education, work, and service.* San Francisco: Jossey-Bass.

Carranza, M., & Ryan, E. B. (1979). *Language attitudes and other cultural attitudes of Mexican American adults: Some sociolinguistic implications.* Unpublished manuscript, Sociology Department, University of Nebraska, Lincoln.

Carrier, J. (1985). Mexican male bisexuality. In F. Klein & T. Wolf (Eds.), *Bisexualities: Theory and research* (pp. 75-85). New York: Haworth.

Carter, T. P. (1979). *Mexican Americans in school: A history of educational neglect.* New York: College Entrance Examination Board.

Centers for Disease Control. (1987a). Cigarette smoking among Black and other minority populations. *Morbidity and Mortality Weekly Report, 36*(25), 404-407.

Centers for Disease Control. (1987b). Human immunodeficiency virus infection in the United States: A review of current knowledge. *Mortality and Morbidity Weekly Report, 36*(Suppl. S-6), 1-48.

Centers for Disease Control. (1989). *HIV/AIDS surveillance.* Atlanta: Author.

Centers for Disease Control. (1991). *HIV/AIDS surveillance report.* Atlanta: Author.

Cervantes, R. C., & Acosta, F. X. (1992). Psychological testing for Hispanic Americans. *Applied and Preventive Psychology, 1,* 209-219.

Cervantes, R. C., & Castro, F. G. (1985). Stress, coping, and Mexican American mental health: A systematic review. *Hispanic Journal of Behavioral Sciences, 7*(1), 1-73.

Cervantes, R. C., Padilla, A. M., & Salgado de Snyder, N. (1991). The Hispanic Stress Inventory: A culturally relevant approach toward psychosocial assessment. *Psychological Assessment: A Journal of Consulting and Clinical Psychology, 3*(3), 438-447.

Chapa, J., & Valencia, R. R. (1993). Latino population growth, demographic characteristics, and educational stagnation: An examination of recent trends. *Hispanic Journal of Behavioral Sciences, 15*(2), 165-187.

Chavez, J. M. (1985). *Reliability scores for family environment scale,* Unpublished manuscript, Children's Hospital of Los Angeles.

Chavez, R. C. (1984). The use of high-inference measures to study classroom climates: A review. *Review of Educational Research, 54,* 237-261.

Chicago schools: Worst in America. (1988, April 28). *Chicago Tribune,* p. 2B.

Chrisman, N., & Kleinman, A. (1983). Popular health care, social networks, and cultural meanings: The orientation of medical anthropology. In D. Mechanic (Ed.), *Handbook of health, health care and health professions* (pp. 569-590). New York: Free Press.

Christensen, E. (1979). The Puerto Rican woman: A profile. In E. Acosta-Belen (Ed.), *The Puerto Rican woman* (pp. 51-63). New York: Praeger.

Chubb, J. E., & Moe, T. M. (1986). No school is an island: Politics, markets and education. *Brookings Review, 4,* 11-27.

Clark, D., & Astuto, T. (1986). The significance and permanence of changes in federal education policy. *Educational Researcher, 31,* 4-13.

Clark, M., Kaufman, S., & Pierce, R. C. (1976). Explorations of acculturation: Toward a model of ethnic identity. *Human Organization, 35*(3), 231-238.

Clark, R. M. (1983). *Family life and school achievement: Why poor Black children succeed or fail.* Chicago: University of Chicago Press.

Clifford, M. M., & Cleary, T. (1972). The relationship between children's academic performance and achievement accountability. *Child Development, 43,* 647-655.

Cohen, P., Streuning, E. L., Genevie, L. E., Kaplan, S. R., Muhlin, G. L., & Peck, H. B. (1982). Community stressors, mediating conditions and well-being in urban neighborhoods. *Journal of Community Psychology, 10,* 377-391.

Comas-Diaz, L. (1987). Feminist therapy with mainland Puerto Rican women. *Psychology of Women Quarterly, 11*(4), 461-474.

Comas-Diaz, L. (1988). Cross-cultural mental health treatment. In L. Comas-Diaz & E. H. H. Griffin (Eds.), *Clinical guidelines in cross-cultural mental health* (pp. 335-361). New York: John Wiley.

Community Service Society of New York. (1987). *Poverty in New York City, 1980-1985.* New York: Author.

Compas, B. E. (1987). Coping with stress during childhood and adolescence. *Psychological Bulletin, 101,* 393-403.

Cooper, B. S. (1988). School reform in the 1980s: The new right's legacy. *Educational Administration Quarterly, 24,* 282-299.

Cooper, B. S. (1990). An international comparison: Political forces for choice. In S. B. Bacharach (Ed.), *Education reform: Making sense of it all* (pp. 287-297). Boston: Allyn & Bacon.

Cope, R. G., & Hannah, W. (1975). *Revolving college doors: The causes and consequences of dropping out, stopping out, and transferring.* New York: Wiley Interscience.

Coreil, J. (1984). Ethnicity and cancer prevention in a tri-ethnic urban community. *Journal of the National Medical Association, 76,* 1013-1019.

Costantino, G. (1982). TEMAS: A new technique for personality assessment and psychotherapy for Hispanic children. *Hispanic Journal of Behavioral Sciences, 5*(4), 3-7.

Costanzo, P. R., & Dix, T. H. (1983). Beyond the information processed: Socialization in the development of attributional processes. In E. T. Higgins, D. N. Ruble, & W. W. Hartup (Eds.), *Social cognition and social development: A sociocultural prospective* (pp. 63-81). Cambridge: Cambridge University Press.

Costello, A. J., Edelbrock, C., Dulcan, M. K., Kalas, R., & Klaric, S. A. (1984). *Final report to NIMH on the Diagnostic Interview for Children.*

Cox, C. (1986). Physician utilization by three groups of ethnic elderly. *Medical Care, 24,* 667-676.

Crawford, I., & Robinson, W. L. (1990). Adolescents and AIDS: Knowledge and attitudes of African-American, Latino, and Caucasian Midwestern U.S. high school seniors. *Journal of Psychology and Human Sexuality, 3*(2), 25-33.

Crocker, J., & Major, B. (1989). Social stigma and self-esteem: The self-protective properties of stigma. *Psychological Review, 96,* 608-630.

Cromwell, R. E., & Ruiz, R. A. (1979). The myth of macho dominance in decision making within Mexican and Chicano families. *Hispanic Journal of Behavioral Sciences, 1,* 355-373.

Cromwell, V. T., & Cromwell, R. E. (1978). Perceived dominance in decision making and conflict resolution among Anglo, Black, and Chicano couples. *Journal of Marriage and the Family, 40*, 749-759.

Cross, W. (1978). The Thomas and Cross models of psychological nigrescence: A literature review. *Journal of Black Psychology, 4*, 13-31.

Cross, W. (1987). A two-factor theory of Black identity: Implications for the study of identity development in minority children. In J. Phinney & M. Rotheram (Eds.), *Children's ethnic socialization: Pluralism and development* (pp. 117-133). Newbury Park, CA: Sage.

Cuellar, I., Harris, L. C., & Jasso, R. (1980) An acculturation scale for Mexican-American normal and clinical populations. *Hispanic Journal of Behavioral Sciences, 2*, 199-217.

Cummins, J. (1979). Linguistic interdependence and the educational development of bilingual children. *Review of Educational Research, 49*, 222-251.

Cummins, J. (1984). *Bilingualism and special education: Issues in assessment and pedagogy.* San Diego: College Hill.

Cummins, J. (1987). Bilingualism, language proficiency, and metalinguistic development. In P. Homel, M. Palij, & D. Aaronson (Eds.), *Childhood bilingualism: Aspects of linguistic, cognitive and social development* (pp. 57-73). Hillsdale, NJ: Lawrence Erlbaum.

Davis, S. K., & Chavez, V. (1985). Hispanic househusbands. *Hispanic Journal of Behavioral Sciences, 7*(4), 317-332.

De la Cancela, V. (1986). A critical analysis of Puerto Rican machismo: Implications for clinical practice. *Psychotherapy, 23*, 291-296.

de la Zerda, N., & Hopper, R. (1975). Mexican-Americans' evaluations of spoken Spanish and English. *Speech Monographs, 42*, 126-134.

de la Zerda, N., & Hopper, R. (1979). Employment interviewers' reactions to Mexican-American speech. *Communication Monographs, 46*, 126-134.

Del Castillo, J. C. (1970). The influence of language upon symptomatology in foreign-born patients. *American Journal of Psychiatry, 127*, 242-244.

De Leon, B. (1990). Sex role perceptions and levels of acculturation of Puerto Ricans: A comparative study of Puerto Rican, Black and Anglo college students. *Dissertation Abstracts International, 50*, 3521A. (University Microfilms No. 90-01, 497)

Del Valle, M. (1990). Acculturation, sex roles and racial definitions of Puerto Rican college students in Puerto Rico and United States. *Dissertation Abstracts International, 50*, 3850A.

Derogatis, L. R. (1977). *SCL-90 (revised) version of manual-I.* Baltimore, MD: John Hopkins University School of Medicine.

Derogatis, L. R., Lipman, R. S., Rickels, K., Uhlenhuth, E. H., & Covi, L. (1974). The Hopkins Symptom Checklist (HSCL): A self-report symptom inventory. *Behavioral Science, 19*, 1-15.

Des Jarlais, D., Friedman, S., & Hopkins, W. (1985). Risk reduction for the acquired immunodeficiency syndrome among intravenous drug users. *Annals of Internal Medicine, 103*, 755-759.

Deuschle, K. W., & Diaz, M. (1981). The shortfall in Hispanic health manpower: The national and Mount Sinai-East Harlem picture. *Mount Sinai Journal of Medicine, 48*, 339-344.

Díaz-Guerrero, R. (1975). Interpretación de estilos de vida en distintos países a partir de diferencias en sexo y clase social. In G. Marín (Ed.), *La psicología social en Latinoamérica.* Mexico City: Editorial Trillas.

Díaz-Loving, R., Díaz-Guerrero, R., Helmreich, R. L., & Spence, J. T. (1981). Comparación transcultural y análisis psicométrico de una medida de nasgos masculinos (instrumentales) y femeninos (expresivos). *Revista de la Associación Latinoamericana de Psicología Social, 1*(1), 3-37.

DiClemente, R. J., Boyer, C. B., & Morales, E. S. (1988). Minorities and AIDS: Knowledge, attitudes, and misconceptions among Black and Latino adolescents. *American Journal of Public Health, 78*(1), 55-57.

Dohrenwend, B. P. (1966). Social status and psychological disorder: An issue of substance and an issue of methods. *American Social Review, 31*, 14-34.

Donato, R., Menchaca, M., & Valencia, R. R. (1991). Segregation, desegregation, and integration of Chicano students: Problems and prospects. In R. R. Valencia (Ed.), *Chicano school failure and success: Research and policy agendas for the 1990s* (Stanford Series on Education and Public Policy, pp. 27-63). Basingstoke, England: Falmer.

Dovidio, J., & Gaertner, S. (1986). *Prejudice, discrimination, and racism.* Orlando, FL: Academic Press.

Doyle, D. P., & Finn, C. E., Jr. (1984). American schools and the future of local control. *Public Interest, 77*, 77-95.

Doyle, D. P., & Hartle, T. W. (1983, December 6). President Reagan goes to school: The Reagan administration's first three years with the Department of Education. *Policy Week, 6*, 16-19.

Driedger, L. (1975). In search of cultural identity factors: A comparison of ethnic students. *Canadian Review of Sociology & Anthropology, 12*, 150-161.

Driedger, L. (1976). Ethnic self-identity: A comparison of ingroup evaluations. *Sociometry, 39*, 131-141.

Du Bois, W. E. B. (1971). *An ABC of color.* New York: International Publishing.

Dweck, C. S., & Licht, B. G. (1980). Learned helplessness and intellectual development. In J. Garber & M. E. P. Seligman (Eds.), *Human helplessness: Theory and application* (pp. 197-221). New York: Academic Press.

Dweck, C. S., & Wortman, C. B. (1982). Learned helplessness, anxiety, and achievement motivation: Neglected parallels in cognitive, affective, and coping responses. In H. W. Krohne & L. Laux (Eds.), *Achievement, stress, and anxiety* (pp. 93-125). Washington, DC: Hemisphere.

Dworkin, A. G. (1965). Stereotypes and self-images held by native-born and foreign-born Mexican Americans. *Sociology and Social Research, 49*, 214-224.

Edgar, T., Freimuth, V. S., & Hammond, S. L. (1988). Communicating the AIDS risk to college students: The problem of motivating change. *Health Education Research, 3*(1), 59-65.

Edgerton, R. B., & Karno, M. (1971). Mexican-American bilingualism and the perception of mental illness. *Archives of General Psychiatry, 24*, 286-290.

Edmunds, G. J. (1984). Needs assessment strategy for Black students: An examination of stressors and program implications. *Journal of Non-White Concerns in Personnel and Guidance, 12*, 48-56.

Eisler, R. M., & Skidmore, J. R. (1987). Masculine gender role stress: Scale development and component factors in the appraisal of stressful situations. *Behavior Modification, 11*, 123-136.

Ekstrom, R. B., Goertz, M. E., Pollack, J. M., & Rock, D. A. (1986). Who drops out of high school and why? Findings from a national study. *Teachers College Record, 87*, 356-373.

Elmore, F. (1990). *Restructuring schools: The next generation of educational reform.* San Francisco: Jossey-Bass.

Emmons, R. A. (1992). The repressive personality and social support. In H. S. Friedman (Ed.), *Hostility, coping, and health* (pp. 141-150). Washington, DC: American Psychological Association.

Erickson, F. (1987). Transformation and school success: The politics of educational achievement. *Anthropology and Education Quarterly, 18*(4), 313-334.

Erikson, E. H. (1968). *Identity: Youth and crisis.* New York: Norton.

Escobar, J. I. (1987). Cross cultural aspects of the somatization trait. *Hospital Community Psychiatry, 38,* 174-180.

Escobar, J. I., Burnam, M. A., Karno, M., Forsythe, A., Landsverk, J., & Golding, J. M. (1986). Use of the Mini Mental State Examination (MMSE) in a community population mixed ethnicity. *Journal of Nervous and Mental Disease, 174,* 607-614.

Escobar, J. I., Burnam, M. A., Karno, M., Forsythe, A., & Golding, J. M. (1987). Somatization in the community. *Archives of General Psychiatry, 44,* 713-718.

Escobar, J. I., Gómez, J. & Tuason, V. B. (1983). Depressive phenomenology in North and South American patients. *American Journal of Psychiatry, 140,* 47-51.

Escobar, J. I., Randolph, E. T., & Hill, M. (1986). Symptoms of schizophrenia in Hispanic and Anglo veterans. *Culture, Medicine and Psychiatry, 10,* 259-276.

Escobar, J. I., Rubio-Stipec, M., Canino, G. J., & Carno, M. (1989). Somatic Symptom Index (SSI): A new and abridged somatization construct. *Journal of Nervous and Mental Disease, 177,* 140-146.

Escobedo, L. G., & Remington, P. L. (1989). Birth cohort analysis of prevalence of cigarette smoking among Hispanics in the United States. *Journal of the American Medical Association, 261,* 66-69.

Espin, O. M. (1987). Psychological impact of migration on Latinas. *Psychology of Women Quarterly, 11*(4), 489-503.

Fabrega, H., Jr. (1989). Cultural relativism and psychiatric illness. *Journal of Nervous and Mental Disease, 177,* 415-425.

Fabrega, H., Ahn, C. W., Boster, J., & Mezzich, J. (1990). DSM-III as a systemic culture pattern: Studying intracultural variation among psychiatrists. *Psychiatric Research, 24*(2), 139-154.

Fabrega, H., Mezzich, J. E., & Ulrich, R. F. (1988). Black-White differences in psychopathology in an urban psychiatric population. *Comprehensive Psychiatry, 29,* 285-297.

Fabrega, H., Mezzich, J. E., & Ulrich, R. F. (1989). Structure of diagnosis in initial evaluation: Primary, auxiliary and rule out patterns. *Journal of Psychiatric Research, 23,* 169-186.

Fabrega, H., Pilkonis, P., Mezzich, J. E., Ahn, C., & Shea, S. (1990). Explaining diagnostic complexity in an intake setting. *Comprehensive Psychiatry, 31,* 5-14.

Falvo, D., & Tippy, P. (1988). Communicating information to patients: Patient satisfaction and adherence as associated with resident skill. *Journal of Family Practice, 26,* 643-647.

Fanon, F. (1963). *The wretched of the Earth.* New York: Grove.

Feldman, S. S., & Aschenbrenner, B. (1983). Impact of parenthood on various aspects of masculinity and femininity: A short-term longitudinal study. *Developmental Psychology, 19*(2), 278-289.

Feldman, S. S., Biringen, Z. C., & Nash, S. C. (1981). Fluctuations of sex-related self-attributions as a function of stage of family life cycle. *Developmental Psychology, 17*(1), 24-35.

Felice, L. G. (1981). Black student dropout behavior: Disengagement from school rejection and racial desegregation. *Journal of Negro Education, 50,* 415-424.

Félix-Ortiz, M., & Newcomb, M. D. (1992). Risk and protective factors for drug use among Latino and White adolescents. *Hispanic Journal of the Behavioral Sciences, 14,* 291-309.
Félix-Ortiz, M., & Newcomb, M. D. (1994). *The relationship between cultural identity and emotional distress.* Unpublished manuscript.
Fernández-Barillas, H. J., & Morrison, T. L. (1984). Cultural affiliation and adjustment among male Mexican-American college students. *Psychological Reports, 55,* 765-860.
Festinger, L. (1954). A theory of social comparison processes. *Human Relations, 7,* 117-140.
Fillmore, L. W., & Valadez, C. (1986). Teaching bilingual learners. In M. C. Wittrock (Ed.), *Handbook of research on teaching* (pp. 648-685). New York: Macmillan.
Finn, C. E., Jr. (1987a). Education that works: Make the schools compete. *Harvard Business Review, 65,* 63-68.
Finn, C. E., Jr. (1987b). Governing education. *Educational Policy, 1,* 315-320.
Finn, J. (1986). The relationship between sex role attitudes and attitudes supporting marital violence. *Sex Roles, 14,* 235-244.
Fisher, E., & Julius, N. (1987). *The elderly of East Harlem: People, resources, and service needs.* New York: City University of New York, Department of Community Medicine, Mount Sinai School of Medicine.
Fishman, J. A. (1968). Nationality-nationalism and nation-nationalism. In J. A. Fishman, C. A. Ferguson, & J. D. Gupta (Eds.), *Language problems of developing countries* (pp. 39- 51). New York: Wiley Interscience.
Fishman, J. A. (1972). *The sociology of language.* Rowley, MA: Newberry House.
Fishman, J. A. (1986). Bilingualism and separation. *Annuals of the American Academy, 487,* 169-180.
Fitzgerald, T. K. (1971). Education and identity—A reconsideration of some models of acculturation and identity. *New Zealand Council of Educational Studies,* pp. 45-57.
Flannery, J. G. (1978). Alexithymia, II. The association with unexplained physical distress. *Psychotherapy and Psychosomatics, 30,* 193-197.
Flaskerud, J. H. (1986). Diagnostic and treatment differences among five ethnic groups. *Psychological Reports, 58,* 219-235.
Flaskerud, J. H., & Nyamathi, A. M. (1989). Black and Latina women's AIDS related knowledge, attitudes, and practices. *Research in Nursing and Health, 12*(6), 339-346.
Fleming, L. (1982). *Parental influence on the educational and career decisions of Hispanic youth.* Washington, DC: National Council of La Raza.
Ford, K., & Norris, A. (1991). Urban African-American and Hispanic adolescents and young adults: Who do they talk to about AIDS and condoms? What are they learning? *AIDS Education and Prevention, 3*(3), 197-206.
Frances, A. (1990). DSM-IV: Work in progress. *American Journal of Psychiatry, 147,* 1439-1448.
Freud, S. (1966). On the history of the psychoanalytic movement. In A. Freud (Ed.), *The standard edition of the complete psychological works of Sigmund Freud, (Vol. 14).* London: Hogarth Press and Institute of Psycho-Analysis. (Original article published 1914)
Friedman, S., Des Jarlais, D., & Sotheran, J. (1986). AIDS health education for intravenous drug users. *Health Education Quarterly, 13*(4), 383-393.
Fullilove, R. (1988a). Minorities and AIDS: A review of recent publications. *MIRA* [newsletter], pp. 3-7.
Fullilove, R. (1988b). US minorities and the IVth International Conference on AIDS. *Multi-Cultural Inquiry and Research on AIDS, 2*(3), 1-2.
Gandara, P. (1982). Passing through the eye of a needle: High achieving Chicanas. *Hispanic Journal of Behavioral Sciences, 4,* 167-180.

Garbarino, J., Kostelny, K., & Dubrow, N. (1991). *No place to be a child: Growing up in a war zone*. Boston: Lexington Books.
Garcia, J. (1982). Ethnicity and Chicanos: Measurement of ethnic identification, identity, and consciousness. *Hispanic Journal of Behavioral Sciences, 4*, 295-314.
Garcia, J. E. (1991, September 7). Minorities in Texas' schools are majority. *Austin American-Statesman*, pp. A1, A6.
Garcia, M., & Lega, L. (1979). Development of a Cuban ethnic identity questionnaire. *Hispanic Journal of Behavioral Sciences, 1*, 247-261.
Garcia, M., & Marks, G. (1989). Depressive symptomatology among Mexican-American adults: An examination with the CES-D scale. *Psychiatry Research, 27*, 137-148.
Garmezy, N. (1981). Children under stress: Perspectives on antecedents and correlates of vulnerability and resistance to psychopathology. In A. I. Rabin, J. Arongy, A. M. Bavelay, & R. A. Zucker (Eds.), *Future explorations in personality* (pp. 43-84). New York: Wiley Interscience.
Garmezy, N., & Rutter, M. (Eds.). (1983). *Stress, coping, and development in children* (pp. 43-84). New York: McGraw-Hill.
Garrison, V. (1977). Doctors, "espiritista" or psychiatrist? Help seeking behavior in a Puerto Rican neighborhood in New York City. *Medical Anthropology, 1*, 164-185.
Garza, R. T., & Gallegos, P. I. (1985). Environmental influences and personal choice: A humanistic perspective on acculturation. *Hispanic Journal of Behavioral Sciences, 7*(4), 365-379.
Garza, R. T., & Lipton, J. P. (1982). Theoretical perspectives on Chicano personality development. *Hispanic Journal of Behavioral Sciences, 4*, 407-432.
Garza, R. T., & Lipton, J. P. (1984). Foundations for a Chicano social psychology. In J. L. Martinez, Jr. & R. H. Mendoza (Eds.), *Chicano psychology* (2nd ed., pp. 335-365). New York: Academic Press.
Giachello, A. (1985). Hispanics and health care. In P. Cafferty & W. McCready (Eds.), *Hispanics in the United States: A new social agenda* (pp. 160-176). New Brunswick, NJ: Transaction Books.
Gibson, M. A. (1987). The school performance of immigrant minorities: A comparative view. *Anthropology and Education Quarterly, 18*, 262-275.
Giles, H. (Ed.). (1977). *Language, ethnicity and intergroup relations* (European Monographs in Social Psychology). London: Academic Press.
Giles, H., Llado, N., McKirnan, D., & Taylor, D. (1979). Social identity in Puerto Rico. *International Journal of Psychology, 14*, 185-201.
Giles, H., & Powesland, P. F. (1975). *Speech style and social evaluation*. London: Academic Press.
Gilmore, D. D. (1990). *Manhood in the making: Cultural concepts of masculinity*. New Haven, CT: Yale University Press.
Ginorio, A. B. (1979). A comparison of Puerto Ricans in New York with native Puerto Ricans and native Americans on two measures of acculturation: Gender role and racial identification. *Dissertation Abstracts International, 41*, 983B-984B. (University Microfilms No. 78-18, 283)
Giroux, H. (1984). Public philosophy and the crisis in education. *Harvard Educational Review, 54*, 186-194.
Glaser, K. (1981). Psychopathologic patterns in depressed adolescents. *American Journal of Psychotherapy, 35*, 368-382.
Glazer, N. (1985). The political distinctiveness of the Mexican Americans. In W. Conner (Ed.), *Mexican-Americans in comparative perspective* (pp. 207-224). Washington, DC: Urban Institute Press.

Goffman, E. (1963). *Stigma: Notes on the management of a spoiled identity.* Englewood Cliffs, NJ: Prentice Hall.
Goldman, S. R., & Trueba, H. T. (Eds.). (1987). *Becoming literate in English as a second language.* Norwood, NJ: Ablex.
Goldwert, M. (1985). Mexican machismo: Flight from femininity. *Psychoanalytic Review, 72,* 161-169.
Gonzalez, A. (1982). Sex roles of the traditional Mexican American family: A comparison of Chicano and Anglo students' attitudes. *Journal of Cross-Cultural Psychology, 13,* 330-339.
Good, G. E., Wallace, D. L., & Schuster, T. B. (in press). Masculinity research: A review and critique. *Applied and Preventive Psychology.*
Gordon, B. (1980). *The self-concept of Black Americans.* Lanham, MD: University Press America.
Gozzi, E., Korsch, B., & Francis, V. (1968). Gaps in doctor-patient communication: Doctor-patient interaction and patient satisfaction. *Pediatrics, 42,* 855-871.
Grebler, L., Moore, J. W., & Guzman, R. C. (1970). *The Mexican American people.* New York: Free Press.
Grebler, L., Moore, J. W., & Guzman, R. C. (1973). The family: Variations in time and space. In L. I. Duran & H. R. Bernard (Eds.), *Introduction to Chicano studies* (pp. 309-331). New York: Macmillan.
Greenberg, M. A., Wiggins, C. L., Kutvirt, D. M., & Samet, J. M. (1987). Cigarette use among Hispanic and non-Hispanic White school children. *American Journal of Public Health, 77,* 621-622.
Grossman, B., Wirt, R., & Davids, A. (1985). Self-esteem, ethnic identity, and behavioral adjustment among Anglo and Chicano adolescents in West Texas. *Journal of Adolescence, 8,* 57-68.
Group on Culture and Diagnosis, Steering Committee. (1993). *Cultural proposals and supporting papers for DSM-IV, third revision.* Rockville, MD: National Institute of Mental Health.
Guarnaccia, P. J., Good, B. J., & Kleinman, A. (1990). *American Journal of Psychiatry, 147*(11), 1449-1456.
Guarnaccia, P. J., Rubio-Stipec, M., & Canino, G. (1989). Ataques de nervios in the Puerto Rican diagnostic interview schedule: The impact of cultural categories on psychiatric epidemiology. *Culture, Medicine and Psychiatry, 13,* 275-295.
Gump, J. (1975). A comparative analysis of Black and White women's sex-role attitudes. *Journal of Consulting and Clinical Psychology, 43,* 858-863.
Gump, J. (1980). Reality and myth: Employment and sex role ideology in Black women. In F. Denmark & J. Sherman (Eds.), *The psychology of woman* (pp. 349-380). New York: Psychological Dimensions.
Gurin, P., Miler, H., & Gurin, G. (1980). Stratum identification and consciousness. *Social Psychology Quarterly, 43,* 30-47.
Hahn, R. A., & Castro, K. G. (1989). The health and health care status of Latino populations in the US: A brief review. In O. Martinez-Maza, D. M. Shin, & H. E. Banks (Eds.), *Latinos and AIDS: A national strategy symposium* (pp. 66-84). Los Angeles: Center for Interdisciplinary Research in Immunology and Disease.
Hakuta, K. (1986). *Mirror of language.* New York: Basic Books.
Hall, W. S., Cross, W. E., & Freedle, R. (1972). States in the development of Black awareness: An exploratory investigation. In R. L. Jones (Ed.), *Black psychology* (pp. 156-165). New York: Harper & Row.

BARNES & NOBLE
Booksellers since 1873
105 Fifth Avenue New York, NY 10003
(212) - 807 - 0099

188196 200 46 34831

463680   0800
                PADILLA

25.50*

Sub Total   25.50
A - NYC 8.25% TAX Total   2.10

TOTAL   27.60**

Cash   27.60

13:39 03/10/97 Normal Sale

THANK YOU
*** RETURN WITHIN 7 DAYS ***
ACCOMPANIED BY RECEIPT

Garbarino, J., Kostelny, K., & Dubrow, N. (1991). *No place to be a child: Growing up in a war zone*. Boston: Lexington Books.
Garcia, J. (1982). Ethnicity and Chicanos: Measurement of ethnic identification, identity, and consciousness. *Hispanic Journal of Behavioral Sciences, 4*, 295-314.
Garcia, J. E. (1991, September 7). Minorities in Texas' schools are majority. *Austin American-Statesman*, pp. A1, A6.
Garcia, M., & Lega, L. (1979). Development of a Cuban ethnic identity questionnaire. *Hispanic Journal of Behavioral Sciences, 1*, 247-261.
Garcia, M., & Marks, G. (1989). Depressive symptomatology among Mexican-American adults: An examination with the CES-D scale. *Psychiatry Research, 27*, 137-148.
Garmezy, N. (1981). Children under stress: Perspectives on antecedents and correlates of vulnerability and resistance to psychopathology. In A. I. Rabin, J. Arongy, A. M. Bavelay, & R. A. Zucker (Eds.), *Future explorations in personality* (pp. 43-84). New York: Wiley Interscience.
Garmezy, N., & Rutter, M. (Eds.). (1983). *Stress, coping, and development in children* (pp. 43-84). New York: McGraw-Hill.
Garrison, V. (1977). Doctors, "espiritista" or psychiatrist? Help seeking behavior in a Puerto Rican neighborhood in New York City. *Medical Anthropology, 1*, 164-185.
Garza, R. T., & Gallegos, P. I. (1985). Environmental influences and personal choice: A humanistic perspective on acculturation. *Hispanic Journal of Behavioral Sciences, 7*(4), 365-379.
Garza, R. T., & Lipton, J. P. (1982). Theoretical perspectives on Chicano personality development. *Hispanic Journal of Behavioral Sciences, 4*, 407-432.
Garza, R. T., & Lipton, J. P. (1984). Foundations for a Chicano social psychology. In J. L. Martinez, Jr. & R. H. Mendoza (Eds.), *Chicano psychology* (2nd ed., pp. 335-365). New York: Academic Press.
Giachello, A. (1985). Hispanics and health care. In P. Cafferty & W. McCready (Eds.), *Hispanics in the United States: A new social agenda* (pp. 160-176). New Brunswick, NJ: Transaction Books.
Gibson, M. A. (1987). The school performance of immigrant minorities: A comparative view. *Anthropology and Education Quarterly, 18*, 262-275.
Giles, H. (Ed.). (1977). *Language, ethnicity and intergroup relations* (European Monographs in Social Psychology). London: Academic Press.
Giles, H., Llado, N., McKirnan, D., & Taylor, D. (1979). Social identity in Puerto Rico. *International Journal of Psychology, 14*, 185-201.
Giles, H., & Powesland, P. F. (1975). *Speech style and social evaluation*. London: Academic Press.
Gilmore, D. D. (1990). *Manhood in the making: Cultural concepts of masculinity*. New Haven, CT: Yale University Press.
Ginorio, A. B. (1979). A comparison of Puerto Ricans in New York with native Puerto Ricans and native Americans on two measures of acculturation: Gender role and racial identification. *Dissertation Abstracts International, 41*, 983B-984B. (University Microfilms No. 78-18, 283)
Giroux, H. (1984). Public philosophy and the crisis in education. *Harvard Educational Review, 54*, 186-194.
Glaser, K. (1981). Psychopathologic patterns in depressed adolescents. *American Journal of Psychotherapy, 35*, 368-382.
Glazer, N. (1985). The political distinctiveness of the Mexican Americans. In W. Conner (Ed.), *Mexican-Americans in comparative perspective* (pp. 207-224). Washington, DC: Urban Institute Press.

Goffman, E. (1963). *Stigma: Notes on the management of a spoiled identity*. Englewood Cliffs, NJ: Prentice Hall.
Goldman, S. R., & Trueba, H. T. (Eds.). (1987). *Becoming literate in English as a second language*. Norwood, NJ: Ablex.
Goldwert, M. (1985). Mexican machismo: Flight from femininity. *Psychoanalytic Review, 72*, 161-169.
Gonzalez, A. (1982). Sex roles of the traditional Mexican American family: A comparison of Chicano and Anglo students' attitudes. *Journal of Cross-Cultural Psychology, 13*, 330-339.
Good, G. E., Wallace, D. L., & Schuster, T. B. (in press). Masculinity research: A review and critique. *Applied and Preventive Psychology*.
Gordon, B. (1980). *The self-concept of Black Americans*. Lanham, MD: University Press America.
Gozzi, E., Korsch, B., & Francis, V. (1968). Gaps in doctor-patient communication: Doctor-patient interaction and patient satisfaction. *Pediatrics, 42*, 855-871.
Grebler, L., Moore, J. W., & Guzman, R. C. (1970). *The Mexican American people*. New York: Free Press.
Grebler, L., Moore, J. W., & Guzman, R. C. (1973). The family: Variations in time and space. In L. I. Duran & H. R. Bernard (Eds.), *Introduction to Chicano studies* (pp. 309-331). New York: Macmillan.
Greenberg, M. A., Wiggins, C. L., Kutvirt, D. M., & Samet, J. M. (1987). Cigarette use among Hispanic and non-Hispanic White school children. *American Journal of Public Health, 77*, 621-622.
Grossman, B., Wirt, R., & Davids, A. (1985). Self-esteem, ethnic identity, and behavioral adjustment among Anglo and Chicano adolescents in West Texas. *Journal of Adolescence, 8*, 57-68.
Group on Culture and Diagnosis, Steering Committee. (1993). *Cultural proposals and supporting papers for DSM-IV, third revision*. Rockville, MD: National Institute of Mental Health.
Guarnaccia, P. J., Good, B. J., & Kleinman, A. (1990). *American Journal of Psychiatry, 147*(11), 1449-1456.
Guarnaccia, P. J., Rubio-Stipec, M., & Canino, G. (1989). Ataques de nervios in the Puerto Rican diagnostic interview schedule: The impact of cultural categories on psychiatric epidemiology. *Culture, Medicine and Psychiatry, 13*, 275-295.
Gump, J. (1975). A comparative analysis of Black and White women's sex-role attitudes. *Journal of Consulting and Clinical Psychology, 43*, 858-863.
Gump, J. (1980). Reality and myth: Employment and sex role ideology in Black women. In F. Denmark & J. Sherman (Eds.), *The psychology of woman* (pp. 349-380). New York: Psychological Dimensions.
Gurin, P., Miler, H., & Gurin, G. (1980). Stratum identification and consciousness. *Social Psychology Quarterly, 43*, 30-47.
Hahn, R. A., & Castro, K. G. (1989). The health and health care status of Latino populations in the US: A brief review. In O. Martinez-Maza, D. M. Shin, & H. E. Banks (Eds.), *Latinos and AIDS: A national strategy symposium* (pp. 66-84). Los Angeles: Center for Interdisciplinary Research in Immunology and Disease.
Hakuta, K. (1986). *Mirror of language*. New York: Basic Books.
Hall, W. S., Cross, W. E., & Freedle, R. (1972). States in the development of Black awareness: An exploratory investigation. In R. L. Jones (Ed.), *Black psychology* (pp. 156-165). New York: Harper & Row.

Hammond, K. (1955). Probabilistic functioning and the clinical method. *Psychological Review, 2,* 255-262.
Harrison, D. F., Wambach, K. G., Byers, J. B., Imershein, A. W., Levine, P., Maddox, K., Quadagno, D. M., Fordyce, M. L., & Jones, M. A. (1991). AIDS knowledge and risk behaviors among culturally diverse women. *AIDS Education and Prevention, 3*(2), 79-89.
Harter, S. (1983). Developmental perspectives on the self-system. In E. M. Hetherington (Ed.), *Handbook of child psychology: Socialization, personality, and social development* (Vol. 4, pp. 275-386). New York: John Wiley.
Harwood, A. (1977). *RX: Spiritualists as needed.* New York: John Wiley.
Hatch, E. M. (1983). *Psycholinguistics: A second language perspective.* Rowley, MA: Newbury House.
Hauser, R. A., & Anderson, D. K. (1991). Post high school plans: An aspiration of Black and White seniors. *Sociology of Education, 64,* 263-277.
Haycock, K., & Navarro, M. S. (1990). *Unfinished business: Fulfilling our children's promise.* Oakland, CA: Achievement Council.
Hayes-Bautista, D. E. (1974). Becoming Chicano: A "disassimilation" theory of transformation of ethnic identity. *Dissertation Abstracts International, 34,* 5332A.
Hazuda, H. P., Stern, M. P., Gaskill, S. P., Haffner, S. M., & Gardner, L. I. (1983). Ethnic differences in health knowledge and behaviors related to the prevention and treatment of coronary heart disease. *American Journal of Epidemiology, 117,* 717-728.
Heilbrun, A. B. (1961). Male and female personality correlates of early termination in counseling. *Journal of Counseling Psychology, 8,* 31-36.
Heller, C. (1966). *Mexican American youth: Youth forgotten at the crossroads.* New York: Random House.
Helzer, J. E., & Canino, G. J. (1989). The implications of cross-national research for diagnostic validity. In L. N. Robins & J. E. Barrett (Eds.), *The validity of psychiatric diagnosis* (pp. 247-260). New York: Raven Press.
Helzer, J. E., Canino, G. J., Yeh, E.-K., Bland, R. C., Lee, C. K., Hwu, H.-G., & Newman, S. (1990). Alcoholism in North America and Asia. *Archives of General Psychiatry, 47,* 313-319.
Heppner, P. P. (1981). Counseling men in groups. *Personnel and Guidance Journal, 59,* 249-252.
Hirano-Nakanishi, M. (1986). The extent and relevance of pre-high school attrition and delayed education for Hispanics. *Hispanic Journal of Behavioral Sciences, 8,* 61-76.
Ho, M. K. (1987). *Family therapy with ethnic minorities.* Newbury Park, CA: Sage.
Hodgkinson, H. L. "Bud." (1985). *All in the system: Demographics of education—kindergarten through graduate school.* Washington, DC: Institute for Educational Leadership.
Hodgkinson, H. L. "Bud." (1987). Changing society: Unchanging curriculum. *National Forum, 67,* 8-11.
Hodgkinson, H. L. "Bud." (1992). *A demographic look at tomorrow.* Washington, DC: Center for Demographic Policy, Institute for Educational Leadership.
Hogg, A., Abrams, D., & Patel, Y. (1987). Ethnic identity, self-esteem and occupational aspirations of Indian and Anglo-Saxon British adolescents. *Genetic, Social and General Psychology Monographs, 113,* 487-508.
Hohman, A. A., Richeport, M., & Marriott, B. M. (1990). Spiritualism in Puerto Rico: Results of an island-wide community study. *British Journal of Psychiatry, 156*(1).
Hollingshead, A. B. (1965). *Two factor index of social position.* Unpublished manuscript, Yale University, New Haven, CT.

Hollingshead, A. B., & Redlich, F. C. (1958). *Social class and mental illness*. New York: John Wiley.
Holmes, V., & Fernandez, F. (1988). HIV in women: Current impact and future implications. *The Female Patient, 13,* 48-52.
Homel, P., Palij, M., & Aaronson, D. (Eds.). (1987). *Childhood bilingualism: Aspects of linguistic, cognitive and social development*. Hillsdale, NJ: Lawrence Erlbaum.
Honing, B. (1988). The key to reform: Sustaining and expanding upon initial success. *Educational Administration Quarterly, 24,* 257-271.
Houston, L. (1984). Black consciousness and self-esteem. *Journal of Black Psychology, 11,* 1-7.
Hu, D. J., Keller, R., & Fleming, D. (1989). Communicating AIDS information to Hispanics: The importance of language and media preference. *American Journal of Preventive Medicine, 5*(4), 196-200.
Humble, C. G., Samet, J. M., Pathak, D. R., & Skipper, B. J. (1987). Cigarette smoking and lung cancer in "Hispanic" Whites and other Whites in New Mexico. *American Journal of Public Health, 75,* 145-148.
Hurtado, A., & Arce, C. H. (in press). Mexicanos, Chicanos, Mexican Americans, or Pochos... Que somos? The impact of language and nativity on ethnic labeling. *Aztlan: International Journal of Chicano Studies*.
Hurtado, A., Hayes-Bautista, D., Valdez, R. B., & Hernández, A. C. R. (1989). *California Identity Project survey materials*. Los Angeles: Chicano Studies Research Center.
Ingoldsby, B. B. (1991). The Latin American family: Familism vs. machismo. *Journal of Comparative Family Studies, 22,* 57-62.
Jaeger, R. M. (1982). The final hurdle: Minimum competency achievement testing. In G. R. Austin & H. Garber (Eds.), *The rise and fall of national test scores* (pp. 223-246). New York: Academic Press.
Jenkins, J. H. (1988a). Conceptions of schizophrenia as a problem of nerves: A cross-cultural comparison of Mexican-Americans and Anglo-Americans. *Social Science and Medicine, 26,* 1233-1243.
Jenkins, J. H. (1988b). Ethnopsychiatric interpretations of schizophrenic illness: The problems of nervios within Mexican-American families. *Culture, Medicine and Psychiatry, 12,* 301-329.
Jenkins, J. H., Karno, M., Selva, A., & Santana, F. (1986). Expressed emotion in cross-cultural context: Familial responses to schizophrenic illness among Mexican-Americans. In M. J. Goldstein, I. Hand, & K. Hahlweg (Eds.), *Treatment of schizophrenia* (pp. 35-49). Berlin: Springer-Verlag.
Jensen, J. V. (1962). Effects of childhood bilingualism, I. *Elementary English, 39,* 132-143.
Johnson, M. E. (1988). Influences of gender and sex role orientation on help-seeking attitudes. *Journal of Psychology, 122,* 237-241.
Jones, R. C. (1948). Ethnic family patterns: The Mexican family in the United States. *American Journal of Sociology, 53*(6), 450-452.
Jordan, C., & Jacob, E. (1987). Afterwards: Where are we now? *Anthropology and Education Quarterly, 18,* 365-367.
Jue, S. (1987). Identifying and meeting the needs of minority clients with AIDS. In C. G. Leukefeld & M. Fimbres (Eds.), *Responding to AIDS: Psychosocial initiatives* (pp. 136-155). Silver Spring, MD: National Association of Social Workers, Inc.
Kagan, S. (1984). Interpreting Chicano consciousness: Methodological and theoretical considerations. In J. L. Martinez, Jr. (Ed.), *Chicano psychology* (2nd ed., pp. 289-328). New York: Academic Press.

Kanner, A. D., Coyne, J. C., Schaefer, C., & Lazarus, R. S. (1981). Comparison of two modes of stress measurement: Daily hassles and uplifts versus major life events. *Journal of Behavioral Medicine, 4,* 1-39.

Karno, M., & Edgerton, R. G. (1969). Perception of mental illness in a Mexican-American community. *Archives of General Psychiatry, 20,* 233-238.

Karno, M., Jenkins, J. H., Selva, A., Santana, F., Telles, C., Lopez, S., & Mintz, J. (1987). Expressed emotion and schizophrenic outcome among Mexican-American families. *Journal of Nervous and Mental Disease, 175,* 143-151.

Kaye, K. (1985). Toward a developmental psychology of the family. In L. L'Abate (Ed.), *The handbook of family psychology and therapy* (Vol. 1, pp. 38-72). Homewood, IL: Dorsey Press.

Keefe, S. E. (1980). Acculturation and the extended family among urban Mexican Americans. In A. M. Padilla (Ed.), *Acculturation: Theory, models and some new findings* (pp. 85-110). Boulder, CO: Westview.

Keefe, S. E., & Padilla, A. M. (1987). *Chicano ethnicity.* Albuquerque: University of New Mexico Press.

Keith, P., & Brubaker, T. H. (1977). Sex role expectations associated with specific household tasks: Perceived age and employment differences. *Psychological Reports, 41,* 15-18.

Kelly, G. (1955). *The psychology of personal constructs* (Vols. 1-2). New York: Norton.

Kim, J.-O., Nie, N., & Verba, S. (1977). A note on factor analyzing dichotomous variables: The case of political participation. *Political Methodology, 4,* 39-42.

Kim, J.-O., & Rabjohn, J. (1980). *Sociological methodology.* San Francisco: Jossey-Bass.

Kirmayer, T. (1991). The place of culture in psychiatric nosology: Taijin Kyofusho and DSM-III-R. *Journal of Nervous and Mental Disease, 179*(1), 19-28.

Kirst, M. W. (1988). Recent state education reform in the United States: Looking backward and forward. *Educational Administration Quarterly, 24,* 319-328.

Kirst, M. W. (1990). The crash of the first wave. In S. B. Bacharach (Ed.), *Education reform: Making sense of it all* (pp. 234-258). Boston: Allyn & Bacon.

Kleinman, A. (1979). *Patients and healers in the context of culture.* Berkeley: University of California Press.

Kluckhohn, F. R. (1953). Dominant and variant value orientations. In C. Kluckhohn & H. A. Murray (Eds.), *Personality in nature, society, and culture* (pp. 342-357). New York: Alfred A. Knopf.

Kluckhohn, F. R., & Strodtbeck, F. L. (1961). *Variations in value orientations.* Evanston, IL: Row, Peterson.

Kohlberg, L. A. (1966). Cognitive-developmental analysis of children's sex-role concepts and attitudes. In E. E. Maccoby (Ed.), *The development of sex-role differences* (pp. 82-173). Stanford, CA: Stanford University Press.

Koop, C. E. (1987). Surgeon general's report on acquired immune deficiency syndrome. *Public Health Reports, 102*(1), 1-3.

Korsch, B., Negrete, V., Freemon, B., & Davis, M. (1971). Gaps in doctor-patient communication: Doctor-patient interaction analysis. *Pediatric Research, 5,* 298-311.

Kovacs, M. (1985). The natural history and course of depressive disorders in childhood. *Psychiatric Annals, 15*(6), 387-389.

Koval, J. E., Ponzetti, J. J., & Cate, R. M. (1982). Programmatic interventions for men involved with conjugal violence. *Family Therapy, 9,* 147-154.

Kozol, J. (1991). *Savage inequalities: Children in America's schools.* New York: Crown Publishing Co.

Krause, N., & Carr, L. G. (1978). The effects of response bias in the survey assessment of the mental health of Puerto Rican migrants. *Social Psychiatry, 13,* 167-173.
Krear, S. (1969). The role of the mother tongue at home and at school in the development of bilingualism. *English Language Teaching, 24,* 2-4.
Kreisman, J. J. (1975). The curandero's apprentice: A therapeutic integration of folk and medical healing. *American Journal of Psychiatry, 132,* 81-83.
Krener, P. G., & Sabin, C. (1985). Indochinese immigrant children: Problems in psychiatric diagnosis. *Journal of the American Academy of Child Psychiatry, 24*(4), 453-458.
Krueger, R. (1988). *Focus groups: A practical guide for applied research.* Newbury Park, CA: Sage.
Kurtines, W., & Miranda, M. (1980). Differences in self and family role perceptions among acculturating Cuban American college students. *International Journal of Intercultural Relations, 4,* 167-184.
Lang, J., Munoz, R., Bernal, G., & Sorenson, J. (1982). Quality of life and psychological well-being in a bicultural Latino community. *Hispanic Journal of Behavioral Sciences, 4,* 433-450.
Laosa, L. M. (1977). Inequality in the classroom: Observational research on teacher-student interactions. *Atzlan: International Journal of Chicano Studies Research, 8,* 51-67.
Laosa, L. M. (1982). School, occupation, culture, and family: The impact of parental schooling on the parent-child relationship. *Journal of Educational Psychology, 74,* 791-827.
Lara-Cantú, M. A. (1989). A sex role inventory with scales for "machismo" and "self-sacrificing woman." *Journal of Cross-Cultural Psychology, 20*(4), 386-398.
Lara-Cantú, M. A., & Navarro-Arias, R. (1986). Positive and negative factors in the measurement of sex roles: Findings from a Mexican sample. *Hispanic Journal of Behavioral Sciences, 8,* 143-155.
Lazarus, R. F., & Folkman, S. (1984). *Stress, appraisal, and coping.* New York: Springer.
Leafgren, F. (1990). Men on a journey. In D. Moore & F. Leafgren (Eds.), *Problem solving strategies and interventions for men in conflict* (pp. 3-10). Alexandria, VA: American Association for Counseling and Development.
Lee, V. E., & Ekstrom, R. B. (1987). Student access to guidance counseling in high school. *American Educational Research Journal, 24,* 287-310.
Leininger, M. (1985). Nature, rationale, and importance of qualitative research methods in nursing. In M. Leininger (Ed.), *Qualitative research methods in nursing* (p. 9). New York: Grune & Stratton.
Leon, C. A. (1990). Actitudes de psiquiatras Latinoamericanos hacia la clasificacion de trastornos mentales. In H. Roselli (Ed.), *Psiquiatria en la America Latina* (pp. 278-301). Bogotá, Colombia: Tercer Mundo.
Levine, D. U., & Havinghurst, R. J. (1989). *Society and education.* Boston: Allyn & Bacon.
Levine, E. S., & Bartz, K. W. (1979). Comparative child-rearing attitudes among Chicano, Anglo, and Black parents. *Hispanic Journal of Behavioral Sciences, 1*(2), 165-178.
Lewin, K. (1935). *The dynamic theory of personality.* New York: McGraw-Hill.
Lewis, O. (1949). Husbands and wives in a Mexican village: A study of role conflict. *American Anthropologist, 51,* 602-610.
Ley, P., & Spelman, M. (1965). Communications in an out-patient setting. *British Journal of Social Clinical Psychology, 4,* 114-116.
Lieberman, M. (1986). *Beyond public education.* New York: Praeger.
Lieberman, M. (1989). *Privatization and educational choice.* New York: St. Martin's.
Lin, K., Lau, J. K., Yamamoto, J., Zheng, Y., Kim, H., Cho, K., & Nakasaki, G. (1992). A community study of Korean Americans. *Journal of Nervous and Mental Disease, 180*(6), 386-391.

Lindholm, K. J. (1989a). *The Washington Elementary School bilingual immersion program: Student progress after three years of implementation.* Unpublished report prepared for Washington Elementary School, San Jose Unified School District.
Lindholm, K. J. (1989b). *The Windsor Elementary School bilingual immersion program: Student progress after three years of implementation.* Unpublished report prepared for Windsor Elementary School, Windsor Union School District.
Lindholm, K. J. (1990). Bilingual immersion education: Criteria for program development. In A. M. Padilla, H. H. Fairchild, & C. Valadez (Eds.), *Bilingual education: Issues and strategies* (pp. 91-105). Newbury Park, CA: Sage.
Lindholm, K. J. (1991). Two-way bilingual/immersion education: Theory, conceptual issues, and pedagogical implications. In R. V. Padilla & A. Benavides (Eds.), *Critical perspectives on bilingual education research* (pp. 195-220). Tucson, AZ: Bilingual Review/Press.
Lindholm, K. J., & Fairchild, H. H. (1989). *Evaluation of an "exemplary" bilingual immersion program* (Tech. Rep. No. 13). Los Angeles: University of California, Center for Language Education and Research.
Lindholm, K. J., & Fairchild, H. H. (1990). First year evaluation of an elementary school bilingual immersion program. In A. M. Padilla, H. H. Fairchild, & C. Valadez (Eds.), *Bilingual education: Issues and strategies* (pp. 126-136). Newbury Park, CA: Sage.
Lipsky, M. (1986). *Street-level bureaucracy.* New York: Russell Sage.
Lloyd, D. N. (1978). Prediction of school failure from third-grade data. *Educational and Psychological Measurement, 38,* 1193-1201.
Longres, J. F. (1974). Racism and its effects on Puerto Rican Continentals. *Social Casework, 55,* 67-75.
Lopez, S., & Hernandez, P. (1986). How culture is considered in evaluations of psychopathology. *Journal of Nervous and Mental Disease, 176,* 598-606.
Lopez, S., & Hernandez, P. (1987). When culture is considered in the evaluation and treatment of Hispanic patients. *Psychotherapy, 24,* 120-126.
Lopez, S., & Nuñez, J. A. (1987). Cultural factors considered in selected diagnostic criteria and interview schedules. *Journal of Abnormal Psychology, 96,* 270-272.
Lopez, S. R. (1989). Patient variable biases in clinical judgment: Conceptual overview and methodological considerations. *Psychological Bulletin, 106,* 184-203.
Los Angeles Unified School District, Information Technology Division. (1993). *Number of total LEP and FEP students by region, by school, and by language classification.* Los Angeles: Author.
Low, S. M. (1981). The meaning of nervios: A sociocultural analysis of symptom presentation in San Jose, Costa Rica. *Culture, Medicine and Psychiatry, 5,* 25-47.
Low, S. M. (1985). Culturally interpreted symptoms or culture-bound syndromes: A cross-cultural review of nerves. *Social Science and Medicine, 21,* 187-196.
Lubin, B., Natalicio, L., & Seever, M. (1985). Performance of bilingual subjects on Spanish and English versions of the Depression Adjective Checklist. *Journal of Clinical Psychology, 41,* 218-219.
Luther, G. H., & Dukes, F. (1982, May). *A study of selected factors associated with the prediction and prevention of minority attrition.* Paper presented at the annual meeting of the Association for Institutional Research, Denver, CO.
MacDonald, N. E., Ebert, P. D., & Mason, S. E. (1987). Marital status and age as related to masculine and feminine personality dimensions and self-esteem. *Journal of Social Psychology, 127*(3), 289-298.
Macías, R. F. (1993). Language and ethnic classification of language minorities: Chicano and Latino students in the 1990s. *Hispanic Journal of Behavioral Sciences, 15,* 230-257.

Madrid-Barela, A. (1977). Pochos: The different Mexicans: An interpretive essay, Part I. *Aztlan: International Journal of Chicano Studies, 7*(1), 51-63.

Madsen, W. (1964). *The Mexican Americans of South Texas.* New York: Holt, Rinehart & Winston.

Magaña, A. B., Goldstein, M. J., Karno, M., Miklowitz, D. J., Jenkins, J., & Fallon, I. R. H. (1986). A brief method for assessing expressed emotion in relatives of psychiatric patients. *Psychiatry Research, 17,* 203-212.

Mahard, R. E. (1988). The CES-D as a measure of depressive mood in the elderly Puerto Rican population. *Journal of Gerontology Psychological Sciences, 43,* 24-25.

Maldonado, D. (1985). The Hispanic elderly: A socio-historical framework for public policy. *Journal of Applied Gerontology, 4,* 6-17.

Malgady, R. G., Rogler, L. H., & Costantino, G. (1987). Ethnocultural and linguistic bias in mental health evaluation of Hispanics. *American Psychologist, 42,* 228-234.

Mann, D. (1986). Can we help dropouts? Thinking about the undoable. *Teachers College Record, 87,* 307-323.

Manson, A. (1988). Language concordance as a determinant of patient compliance and emergency room visits in patients with asthma. *Medical Care, 26,* 1119-1128.

Marcia, J. (1966). Development and validation of ego-identity status. *Journal of Personality and Social Psychology, 3,* 551-558.

Marcia, J. (1980). Identity in adolescence. In J. Adelson (Ed.), *Handbook of adolescent psychology* (pp. 159-187). New York: John Wiley.

Marcos, L. R. (1976). Bilinguals in psychotherapy: Language as an emotional barrier. *American Journal of Psychotherapy, 30,* 552-560.

Marcos, L. R., Alpert, M., Urcuyo, L., & Kesselman, M. (1973). The effect of interview language on the evaluation of psychopathology in Spanish-American schizophrenic patients. *American Journal of Psychiatry, 130,* 549-553.

Marcos, L. R., Urcuyo, L., Kesselman, M., & Alpert, M. (1973). The language barrier in evaluating Spanish-American patients. *Archives of General Psychiatry, 29,* 655-659.

Marcus, A. C., & Crane, L. A. (1985). Smoking behavior among U.S. Latinos: An emerging challenge for public health. *American Journal of Public Health, 75,* 169-172.

Mariampolski, H. (1984). The resurgence of qualitative research. *Public Relations Journal, 40,* 21-23.

Marín, B., & Marín, G. (1988). Attitudes toward AIDS: Prevention strategies. *MIRA, 2*(3), 5-7.

Marín, B., & Marín, G. (1990a). Introduction. *Hispanic Journal of Behavioral Sciences, 12,* 107-109.

Marín, B., & Marín, G. (1990b). Effects of acculturation on knowledge of AIDS and HIV among Hispanics. *Hispanic Journal of Behavioral Sciences, 12,* 110-121.

Marín, B., Marín, G., & Juarez, R. (1988, April). *Strategies for enhancing the cultural appropriateness of AIDS prevention campaigns.* Paper presented at the 68th Annual Convention of the Western Psychological Association, Burlingame, CA.

Marín, B., Marín, G., & Juarez, R. (1990). Differences between Hispanics and non-Hispanics in willingness to provide AIDS prevention advice. *Hispanic Journal of Behavioral Sciences, 12,* 153-164.

Marín, B. V., Pérez-Stable, E. J., Marín, G., Sabogal, F., & Otero-Sabogal, R. (1990). Attitudes and behaviors of Hispanic smokers: Implications for cessation interventions. *Health Education Quarterly, 17,* 287-297.

Marín, G. (1986). Attributions for tardiness among Chilean and United States students. *Journal of Social Psychology, 127,* 69-75.

Marín, G. (1989). AIDS prevention among Hispanics: Needs, risk behaviors, and cultural values. *Public Health Reports, 104*(5), 411-415.
Marín, G., & Marín, B. (1990). Perceived credibility of channels and sources of AIDS information among Hispanics. *AIDS Education and Prevention, 2,* 154-161.
Marín, G., & Marín, B. (1991). *Research with Hispanic populations.* Newbury Park, CA: Sage.
Marín, G., Marín, B. V., Otero-Sabogal, R., Sabogal, F., & Pérez-Stable, E. J. (1989). The role of acculturation in the attitudes, norms, and expectancies of Hispanic smokers. *Journal of Cross-Cultural Psychology, 20,* 399-415.
Marín, G., Pérez-Stable, E. J., & Marín, B. (1989). Cigarette smoking among San Francisco Hispanics: The role of acculturation and gender. *American Journal of Public Health, 79,* 196-198.
Marín, G., Pérez-Stable, E. J., Otero-Sabogal, R., Sabogal, F., & Marín, B. V. (1989). Stereotypes of smokers held by Hispanic and White non-Hispanic smokers. *International Journal of the Addictions, 24,* 203-213.
Marín, G., Sabogal, F., Marín, B. V., Otero-Sabogal, R., & Pérez-Stable, E. (1987). Development of a short acculturation scale for Hispanics. *Hispanic Journal of Behavioral Sciences, 9,* 183-205.
Marín, G., & Triandis, H. C. (1985). Allocentrism as an important characteristic of the behavior of Latin Americans and Hispanics. In R. Diaz-Guerrero (Ed.), *Cross-cultural and national studies in social psychology* (pp. 85-104). Amsterdam: North-Holland.
Martin, M. (1991). Trading the known for the unknown: Warning signs in the debate over schools of choice. *Education & Urban Society, 23,* 119-143.
Martin, P. (1979). *La frontera perspective: Providing mental health services to Mexican Americans.* Tucson, AZ: La Frontera Center.
Mason, K. O., & Bumpass, L. L. (1975). United States women's sex-role ideology. *American Journal of Sociology, 80,* 1212-1219.
Mason, K. O. C., & Arber, J. L. (1976). Change in U.S. women's sex role attitudes. *American Sociological Review, 41,* 573-596.
Mata, A., & Jorquez, J. (1988). *Mexican-American intravenous drug users. Needle-sharing practices: Implications for AIDS prevention.* Unpublished manuscript.
Mata, A. G., Jr., & Jorquez, J. S. (1989). Mexican-American intravenous drug users' needle-sharing practices: Implication for AIDS prevention. In V. M. Mays, G. W. Albee, & S. F. Schneider (Eds.), *Primary prevention of AIDS: Psychological approaches* (pp. 329-344). Newbury Park, CA: Sage.
Matute-Bianchi, M. E. (1986). Ethnic identity and patterns of school success and failure among Mexican-descent and Japanese-American students in a California high school: An ethnographic analysis. *American Journal of Education, 95,* 233-255.
Matute-Bianchi, M. E. (1989). *Situational ethnicity and patterns of school performance among immigrant and non-immigrant Mexican-descent students* (Bilingual Research Group Rep. No. 89-05). Santa Cruz: University of California Press.
Mays, V., & Cochran, S. (1988). Issues in the perception of AIDS risk and risk reduction activities by Black and Hispanic/Latina women. *American Psychologist, 43*(11), 949-956.
Mays, V. M. (1989). AIDS prevention in Black populations. Methods of a safer kind. In V. M. Mays, G. M. Albee, & S. F. Schneider (Eds.), *Primary prevention of AIDS: Psychological approaches* (pp. 264-279). Newbury Park, CA: Sage.
Mays, V. M., Cochran, S., & Roberts, V. (1988). Heterosexual and AIDS. In A. Lewis (Ed.), *Nursing care of the person with AIDS/ARC* (pp. 313-319). Rockville, MD: Aspen.
McBride, B. (1991). Parent education and support programs for fathers: Outcome effects for paternal involvement. *Early Child Development and Care, 67,* 73-85.

McClaughry, J. (1987). *Educational choice in Concord*. Concord, VT: Institute for Liberty and Community.
McCool, A. C. (1984). Improving the admission and retention of Hispanic students—A dilemma for higher education. *College Student Journal, 18*, 28-36.
McDill, E. L., Natriello, G., & Pallas, A. M. (1985). Raising standards and retaining students: The impact of the reform recommendations on potential dropouts. *Review of Educational Research, 55*, 415-433.
McGuire, W. J. (1989). Theoretical foundations of campaigns. In R. Rice & C. Atkin (Eds.), *Public communication campaigns* (pp. 43-65). Newbury Park, CA: Sage.
McGuire, W. J., McGuire, C. V., Child, P., & Fujioka, T. (1978). Salience of ethnicity in the spontaneous self-concept as a function of one's ethnic distinctiveness in the social environment. *Journal of Personality and Social Psychology, 36*, 511-520.
McLaughlin, M., & Balch, P. (1980). Effects of client-therapist ethnic homophile on therapists' judgments. *American Journal of Community Psychology, 8*, 243-262.
Meier, K. J., Stewart, J., & England, R. E. (1989). *Race, class, and education: The politics of second-generation discrimination*. Madison: University of Wisconsin Press.
Meinecke, C. E. (1981). Socialized to die younger: Hypermasculinity and men's health. *Personnel and Guidance Journal, 60*, 241-245.
Memmi, A. (1968). *Dominated man*. Boston: Beacon.
Mena, F. J., Padilla, A. M., & Maldonado, M. (1987). Acculturative stress and specific coping strategies among immigrant and later generation college students. *Hispanic Journal of Behavioral Sciences, 9*, 207-225.
Menchaca, M. (in press). Chicano Indianism: An historical account of racial repression in the United States. *American Ethnologist*.
Mendoza, R. H. (1989). An empirical scale to measure type and degree of acculturation in Mexican American adolescents and adults. *Journal of Cross-Cultural Psychology, 20*, 372-385.
Mercer, N., Mercer, E., & Mears, R. (1979). Linguistic and cultural affiliations amongst young Asian people in Leicester. In H. Giles & B. Saint-Jacques (Eds.), *Language and ethnic relations* (pp. 15-26). New York: Pergamon.
Merino, B. J. (1991). Promoting school success for Chicanos: The view from inside the bilingual classroom. In R. R. Valencia (Ed.), *Chicano school failure and success: Research and policy agenda for the 1990s* (Stanford Series on Education and Public Policy, pp. 119-148). Basingstoke, England: Falmer.
Metz, M. E., & Seifert, M. H., Jr. (1990). Men's expectations of physicians in sexual health concerns. *Journal of Sex and Marital Therapy, 16*, 79-88.
Metz, M. H. (1986). *Different by design: The context and character of three magnet schools*. New York: Routledge & Kegan Paul.
Metz, M. H. (1987, August). *The impact of cultural variation on high school teaching*. Paper presented at the annual meeting of the American Anthropological Association, Chicago.
Metz, M. H. (1988). Some missing elements in the educational reform movement. *Educational Administration Quarterly, 24*, 336-460.
Metz, M. H. (1990). Hidden assumptions: Preventing real reform. In S. B. Bacharach (Ed.), *Education reform: Making sense of it all* (pp. 141-154). Boston: Allyn & Bacon.
Mezzich, J. (1987). *International diagnostic systems and Hispanic populations*. Paper presented at the Simon Bolivar Hispanic American Psychiatric Research and Training Program, Chicago.

References

Mezzich, J. E. (1989). International diagnostic systems and Latin-American contributions and issues. *British Journal of Psychiatry, 154*, 84-90.

Mezzich, J. E., & Rabb, E. S. (1980). Depression symptomatology across the Americans. *Archives of General Psychiatry, 37*, 818-823.

Miedzian, M. (1991). *Boys will be boys: Breaking the link between masculinity and violence.* New York: Doubleday.

Mingle, J. R. (1987). *Focus on minorities: Trends in higher education participation and success.* Denver, CO: Education Commission of the States and the State Higher Education Executive Officers.

Minuchin, P. P., & Shapiro, E. (1983). The school as a context for social development. In P. H. Mussen (Ed.), *Handbook of child psychology: Vol. 4. Socialization, personality, and social development* (pp. 197-274). New York: John Wiley.

Miranda, L., & Quiroz, J. T. (1989). *The decade of the Hispanic: A sobering economic perspective.* Washington, DC: National Council of La Raza.

Mirandé, A. (1977). The Chicano family. *Journal of Marriage and the Family, 39*, 747-756.

Mirandé, A. (1988). Que gacho es ser macho: It's a drag to be a macho man. *Aztlan, 17*, 63-69.

Mischel, W. (1970). Sex typing and socialization. In R. H. Mussen (Ed.), *Carmichael's manual of child psychology* (rev. ed., pp. 3-72). New York: John Wiley.

Mitchell, J. V., Jr. (Ed.). (1985). *The ninth mental measurement yearbook of the Buros Institute of Mental Measurements.* Lincoln: University of Nebraska Press.

Model, S. (1982). Housework by husbands: Determinants and implications. In J. Aldous (Ed.), *Due career families* (pp. 193-205). Beverly Hills, CA: Sage.

Montenegro, R. (1973). *Educational implications of cultural values of Mexican-American women.* Unpublished doctoral dissertation, Claremont Graduate School, Claremont, CA.

Montgomery, G. T., & Orozco, S. (1985). Mexican Americans' performance on the MMPI as a function of level of acculturation. *Journal of Clinical Psychology, 41*, 203-212.

Montiel, M. (1973). The Chicano family: A review of research. *Social Work, 18*, 22-27.

Moore, D. (1989). *School choice: The new improved sorting machine.* Chicago: Designs for Change.

Moore, D. R., & Davenport, S. (1988). High school choice and students at-risk. *Newsletter of the National Center on Effective Secondary Schools, 3*, 2-4.

Moore, J., & Pachon, H. (1985). *Hispanics in the U.S.* Englewood Cliffs, NJ: Prentice Hall.

Moore, J. W. (1988). Variations in violence among Hispanic gangs. In J. F. Kraus, S. B. Sorenson, & P. D. Juarez (Eds.), *Research conference on violence and homicide in Hispanic communities* (pp. 215-230). Los Angeles: UCLA Publication Services.

Moore, J. W., & Vigil, J. D. (1987). Chicano gangs: Group norms and individual factors related to adult criminality. *Aztlan, 18*, 27-44.

Moos, R. H., Insel, P. M., & Humphrey, B. (1974). *Manual for the Family Environment Scale.* Palo Alto, CA: Consulting Psychologists Press.

Morales, A. T. (1992). Latino youth gangs: Causes and clinical intervention. In L. A. Vargas & J. Koss-Chioino (Eds.), *Working with culture: Psychotherapeutic intervention with ethnic minority children and adolescents* (pp. 129-154). San Francisco: Jossey-Bass.

Morales, E. S. (1990). HIV infection and Hispanic gay and bisexual men. *Hispanic Journal of Behavioral Sciences, 12*, 212-222.

Morgan, D., & Spanish, M. (1984). Focus groups: A new tool for qualitative research. *Qualitative Sociology, 7*(3), 253-270.

Mulvihill, M., & Skovron, M. L. (1982). *East Harlem health data handbook.* New York: City University of New York, Department of Community Medicine, Mount Sinai School of Medicine.

Munoz, D., & Garcia-Bahne, B. (1978). *A study of the Chicano experience in higher education.* Final report for the Center for Minority Group Mental Health Programs, University of California, San Diego, and the National Institute of Mental Health.

Murane, R. (1986). Family choice in public education: The role of students, teachers and system designers. *Teachers College Record, 88,* 169-189.

Murillo, N. (1971). The Mexican-American family. In N. N. Wagner & M. J. Haug (Eds.), *Chicanos: Social and psychological perspectives* (pp. 106-130). St. Louis: C. V. Mosby.

Murillo, N. (1976). The Mexican American family. In C. A. Hernandez, N. N. Wagner, & M. J. Haug (Eds.), *Chicanos: Social and psychological perspectives* (2nd ed., pp. 15-25). St. Louis: C. V. Mosby.

Murphy, J. (1989). Educational reform and equity: A reexamination of prevailing thought. *Planning and Changing, 20,* 172-179.

Murphy, J. (1990). *The reform of American public education in the 1980s: Perspectives and cases.* Berkeley, CA: McCutchan.

Myers, H. F. (1982). Stress, ethnicity and social class: A model for research with Black populations. In E. Jones & S. Korchin (Eds.), *Minority mental health* (pp. 118-148). New York: Holt, Rinehart & Winston.

Nathan, J. (1989). *Public schools by choice.* Bloomington, IN: Meyer-Stone.

National Center for Education Statistics. (1989). *Dropout rates in the United States: 1988.* Washington, DC: U.S. Government Printing Office.

National Center for Education Statistics. (1990). *Digest of education statistics.* Washington, DC: U.S. Department of Education.

National Center for Health Statistics. (1989). *AIDS knowledge and attitudes of Hispanic Americans: Provisional data from the National Health Interview Survey* (DHHS Publication No. 89-1250, Advance Data No. 166). Hyattsville, MD: Author.

National Commission on Excellence in Education. (1983). *A nation at risk: The imperative for educational reform.* Washington, DC: U.S. Government Printing Office.

Natriello, G., McDill, E. L., & Pallas, A. M. (1986). A population at risk: Potential consequences of tougher school standards for school dropouts. *American Journal of Education, 94,* 135-151.

Natriello, G., McDill, E. L., & Pallas, A. M. (1990). *Schooling disadvantaged children: Racing against catastrophe.* New York: Teachers College Press.

Neff, J. A., Hoppe, S. K., & Perea, P. (1987). Acculturation and alcohol use: Drinking patterns and problems among Anglo and Mexican American male drinkers. *Hispanic Journal of Behavioral Sciences, 9,* 151-181.

Nemiah, J. C. (1977). Alexithymia: Theoretical considerations. *Psychotherapy and Psychosomatics, 28,* 199-206.

Newcomb, M. D., & Félix-Ortiz, M. (1992). Multiple protective and risk factors for drug use and abuse: Cross-sectional and prospective findings. *Journal of Personality and Social Psychology, 63,* 280-296.

O'Donnell, J. P., Stein, M. A., Machabanski, H., & Cress, J. N. (1982). Dimensions of behavior problems in Anglo-American and Mexican-American preschool children: A comparative study. *Journal of Consulting and Clinical Psychology, 50,* 643-651.

O'Neil, J. M. (1981a). Male sex role conflicts, sexism, and masculinity: Psychological implications for men, women, and the counseling psychologist. *The Counseling Psychologist, 9,* 61-80.

O'Neil, J. M. (1981b). Patterns of gender role conflict and strain: Sexism and fear of femininity in men's lives. *Personnel and Guidance Journal, 60,* 203-210.
O'Neil, J. M. (1982). Gender-role conflict and strain in men's lives: Implications for psychiatrists, psychologists, and other human-service providers. In K. Solomon & N. B. Levy (Eds.), *Men in transition: Theory and therapy* (pp. 5-44). New York: Plenum.
Oakes, J., & Lipton, M. (1990). *Making the best of schools: A handbook for parents, teachers and policymakers.* New Haven, CT: Yale University Press.
Oetting, E. R., & Beauvais, F. (1990). Orthogonal cultural identification theory: The cultural identification of minority adolescents. *International Journal of the Addictions, 25,* 655-685.
Offer, D., & Offer, J. B. (1975). *From teenage to young manhood.* New York: Basic Books.
Ogbu, J. U. (1978). *Minority education and caste: The American system in cross-cultural perspective.* New York: Academic Press.
Ogbu, J. U. (1982). Cultural discontinuities and schooling. *Anthropology and Education Quarterly, 13,* 290-307.
Ogbu, J. U. (1983). Minority status and schooling in plural societies. *Comparative Education Review, 27,* 168-190.
Ogbu, J. U. (1987). Variability in minority school performance: A problem in search of an explanation. *Anthropology & Education Quarterly, 18,* 312-334.
Olivas, M. A. (Ed.). (1986). *Latino college students.* New York: Teachers College Press.
Oliver, M., Rodriguez, C., & Mickelson, R. (1985). Brown and black in white: The social adjustment and academic performance of Chicano and Black students in a predominantly White university. *Urban Review, 17,* 3-23.
Olmedo, E. L. (1979). Acculturation: A psychometric perspective. *American Psychologist, 34,* 1061-1070.
Olmedo, E. L. (1980). Quantitative models of acculturation: An overview. In A. M. Padilla (Ed.), *Acculturation: Theory, models and some new findings* (pp. 27-45). Boulder, CO: Westview.
Olmedo, E. L. (1981). Testing linguistic minorities. *American Psychologist, 36,* 1078-1085.
Omark, D. R., & Erickson, J. G. (1983). *The bilingual exceptional child.* San Diego, CA: College Hill.
Omery, A. (1987). Qualitative research designs in the critical care setting: Review and application. *Heart & Lung, 16*(4), 432-436.
Orfield, G., & Monfort, F. (1992). *Status of school desegregation: The next generation.* Report to the National School Boards Association. Alexandria, VA: Council of Urban Boards of Education.
Orum, L. S. (1986). *The education of Hispanics: Status and implications.* Washington, DC: National Council of La Raza.
Pacheco, A. (1981). A study of sex role attitudes, job investment, and job satisfaction of women faculty at the University of Puerto Rico, Rio Piedras. *Dissertation Abstracts International, 42*(07), 3032A.
Padilla, A. M. (Ed.). (1980a). *Acculturation: Theory, models and some new findings.* Boulder, CO: Westview.
Padilla, A. M. (1980b). The role of cultural awareness and ethnic loyalty in acculturation. In A. M. Padilla (Ed.), *Acculturation: Theory, models and some new findings* (pp. 47-84). Boulder, CO: Westview.
Padilla, A. M. (1986). Acculturation and stress among immigrants and later generation individuals. In D. Frick, H. Hoefert, H. Legewie, R. Mackensen, & R. K. Silbereisen

(Eds.), *The quality of urban life: Social, psychological, and physical conditions* (pp. 100-120). Berlin: de Gruyter.

Padilla, A. M. (1988). Early psychological assessment of Mexican American children. *Journal of History of the Behavioral Sciences, 24,* 111-116.

Padilla, A. M. (1992). Reflections on testing: Emerging trends and new possibilities. In K. F. Geisinger (Ed.), *Psychological testing of Hispanics* (pp. 272-283). Washington, DC: American Psychological Association.

Padilla, A. M., & Alva, S. A. (1987, March). *Factors affecting the academic performance of Mexican American students.* Paper presented at the University of California President's Office, Linguistic Minority Conference, Los Angeles.

Padilla, A. M., & Lindholm, K. J. (1983). *Hispanic Americans: Future behavioral science research directions* (Occasional Paper No. 17). Los Angeles: University of California, Spanish-Speaking Mental Health Research Center.

Padilla, A. M., & Ruiz, R. A. (1973). *Latino mental health: A review of literature* (DHEW Publication No. 73-9143). Washington, DC: U.S. Government Printing Office.

Padilla, A. M., & Ruiz, R. A. (1975). Personality assessment and test interpretation of Mexican Americans: A critique. *Journal of Personality Assessment, 39,* 103-109.

Padilla, A. M., Ruiz, R. A., & Alvarez, R. (1976). Community mental health services for the Spanish-speaking population. *American Psychologist, 30,* 892-905.

Padilla, A. M., Cervantes, R. C., & Maldonado, M. (1988). *Psychosocial stress in Mexican immigrant adolescents.* Unpublished manuscript.

Pallas, A. M. (1987). *School dropouts in the United States.* Washington, DC: Center for Education Statistics, Office of Educational Research and Improvement.

Parham, T., & Helms, J. (1981). Influence of a Black student's racial identity attitudes on preference for counselor race. *Journal of Counseling Psychology, 28,* 250-257.

Parham, T., & Helms, J. (1985). Attitudes of racial identity and self-esteem of Black students: An exploratory investigation. *Journal of College Student Personnel, 26,* 143-147.

Parra, F. (1985). Social tolerance of the mentally ill in the Mexican-American community. *International Journal of Sociological Psychiatry, 31,* 37-45.

Parra, F., & Yiu-Cheong So, A. (1983). The changing perceptions of mental illness in a Mexican-American community. *International Journal of Sociological Psychiatry, 29,* 95-100.

Parsons, T. (1953). Age and sex in the social structure of the United States. In C. Kluckhohn & H. A. Murray (Eds.), *Personality in nature, society, and culture* (pp. 363-375). New York: Alfred A. Knopf.

Pasick, R. S., Gordon, S., & Meth, R. L. (1990). Helping men understand themselves. In R. L. Meth & R. S. Pasick (Eds.), *Men in therapy: The challenge of change* (pp. 152-180). New York: Guilford.

Patterson, A. M., Sedlacek, W. E., & Perry, F. W. (1984). Perceptions of Blacks and Hispanics in the campus environments. *Journal of College Student Personnel, 25,* 513-518.

Paul, M., & Fischer, J. (1980). Correlates of self-concept among Black early adolescents. *Journal of Youth and Adolescence, 9,* 163-173.

Pearl, A. (1991). Systemic and institutional factors in Chicano school failure. In R. R. Valencia (Ed.), *Chicano school failure and success: Research and policy agendas for the 1990s* (Stanford Series on Education and Public Policy, pp. 273-320). Basingstoke, England: Falmer.

Pearlin, L. I. (1983). Role strains and personal stress. In H. G. Kaplan (Ed.), *Psychosocial stress: Trends in theory and research* (pp. 3-32). New York: Academic Press.

References

Pearlin, L. I., Menaghan, E. G., Lieberman, M. A., & Mullan, J. T. (1981). The stress process. *Journal of Health and Social Behavior, 22,* 337-356.
Pearlin, L. I., & Schooler, C. (1978). The structure of coping. *Journal of Health and Social Behavior, 19*(2), 2-21.
Peñalosa, F. (1968). Mexican family roles. *Journal of Marriage and the Family, 30,* 680-689.
Pennebaker, J. W. (1992). Inhibition as the linchpin of health. In H. S. Friedman (Ed.), *Hostility, coping, and health.* Washington, DC: American Psychological Association.
Pérez, S., & De La Rosa Salazar, D. (1993). Economic, labor force, and social implications of Latino educational and population trends. *Hispanic Journal of Behavioral Sciences, 15,* 188-229.
Pérez-Stable, E. J. (1987). Issues in Latino health care—Medical staff conference, University of California, San Francisco. *Western Journal of Medicine, 146,* 213-218.
Peterson, J. L., & Marín, G. (1988). Issues in the prevention of AIDS among Black and Hispanic men. *American Psychologist, 43,* 871-877.
Petty, R. E., & Cacioppo, J. T. (1981). *Attitudes and persuasion: Classic and contemporary approaches.* Dubuque, IA: William C. Brown.
Petty, R. E., & Cacioppo, J. T. (1986). *Communication and persuasion.* New York: Springer-Verlag.
Phillips, S. (1972). Participant structures and communicative competence: Warm Springs children in community and classroom. In C. Cazden, D. Hymes, & V. J. John (Eds.), *Functions of language in the classroom* (pp. 370-394). New York: Teachers College Press.
Phinney, J. (1989). Stages of ethnic identity development in minority group adolescents. *Journal of Early Adolescence, 9,* 34-49.
Phinney, J. (1990). Ethnic identity in adolescents and adults: A review of research. *Psychological Bulletin, 108,* 499-514.
Phinney, J. (1991). *The multigroup ethnic identity measure: A new scale for use with adolescents and adults from diverse groups.* Manuscript submitted for publication.
Phinney, J., Alexander, S., & Chavira, V. (1991). *Ethnic identity issues of minority youth: Dealing with prejudice, discrimination, and culture conflict.* Unpublished manuscript.
Phinney, J., & Alipuria, L. (1990) Ethnic identity in college students from four ethnic groups. *Journal of Adolescence, 13,* 171-183.
Phinney, J., Lochner, B., & Murphy, R. (1990). Ethnic identity and psychological adjustment. In A. Stiffman & L. Davis (Eds.), *Ethnic issues in adolescent mental health* (pp. 53-72). Newbury Park, CA: Sage.
Phinney, J., Williamson, L., & Chavira, V. (1990, April). *Attitudes towards integration, assimilation, and separation among high school and college students.* Paper presented at the annual meeting of the Western Psychological Association, Los Angeles.
Pierce, R. C., Clark, M. M., & Kaufman, S. (1978). Generation and ethnic identity: A typological analysis. *International Journal of Aging & Human Development, 9,* 19-29.
Piers, E. V. (1984). *Piers-Harris Children's Self-Concept Scale: Revised manual.* Los Angeles: Western Psychological Services.
Pino, N. A. (1989). Educational strategies. In O. Martinez-Maza, D. M. Shin, & H. E. Banks (Eds.), *Latinos and AIDS: A national strategy symposium.* Los Angeles: Center for Interdisciplinary Research in Immunology and Disease.
Pleck, J. (1976). The male's sex role: Definitions, problems and sources of change. *Journal of Social Issues, 32,* 155-164.
Pleck, J. H. (1981). *The myth of masculinity.* Cambridge: MIT Press.
Pleck, J. H., Sonenstein, F. L., & Ku, L. C. (1993a). Masculinity ideology: Its impact on adolescent males' heterosexual relationships. *Journal of Social Issues, 49*(3).

Pleck, J. H., Sonenstein, F. L., & Ku, L. C. (1993b). Problems behavior and masculinity ideology in adolescent males. In R. D. Ketterlinus & M. E. Lamb (Eds.), *Adolescent problem behaviors* (pp. 165-186). Hillsdale, NJ: Lawrence Erlbaum.

Poma, P. (1983). Hispanic cultural influences on medical practice. *Journal of the National Medical Association, 75,* 941-946.

Powers, D. E. (1984). Differential trends in law grades of minority and non-minority law students. *Journal of Educational Psychology, 76,* 488-499.

Poznanski, E. (1985). Depression in children and adolescents: An overview. *Psychiatric Annals, 15*(6), 365-367.

President's Commission on Mental Health. (1978). *Report of the task panel on special populations: Vol. 3.* Washington, DC: U.S. Government Printing Office.

Price-Bonham, S., & Skeen, P. (1982). Black and White fathers' attitudes toward children's sex roles. *Psychological Reports, 50,* 1187-1190.

Prillerman, S. L., Myers, H. F., & Smedley, B. D. (1989). Psychosocial stress, academic achievement and psychological well-being of Afro-American college students. In G. L. Berry & J. K. Asamen (Eds.), *Black students: Psychological issues and academic achievement* (pp. 159-217). Newbury Park, CA: Sage.

Prince, R., & Tcheng-Laroche, F. (1987). Culture-bound syndromes and international disease classifications. *Culture, Medicine and Psychiatry, 3,* 3-19.

Pugh, C., & Vazquez-Nuttall, E. (1983, April). *Are all women alike? Reports of White, Hispanic, and Black women.* Paper presented at the annual meeting of the American Personnel and Guidance Association, Washington, DC.

Puig-Antich, J. (1982). Major depression and conduct disorder in puberty. *Journal of the American Academy of Child Psychiatry, 21*(2), 118-128.

Quesada, G. M. (1976). Language and communication barriers for health delivery to a minority group. *Social Science & Medicine, 10,* 323-327.

Ramirez, M. (1969). Identification with Mexican American values and psychological adjustment in Mexican American adolescents. *International Journal of Social Psychiatry, 11,* 151-156.

Ramirez, M. (1987). The impact of culture change and economic stressors on physical and mental health of Mexicans and Mexican-Americans. In R. Rodriguez & M. T. Coleman (Eds.), *Mental health issues of the Mexican origin population in Texas* (pp. 181-196). Austin: University of Texas, Hogg Foundation for Mental Health.

Ramirez, M., III. (1977). Recognizing and understanding diversity: Multiculturalism and the Chicano movement in psychology. In J. L. Martinez, Jr. (Ed.), *Chicano psychology* (pp. 343-353). New York: Academic Press.

Ramirez, M., III. (1983). *Psychology of the Americas: Mestizo perspectives on personality and mental health.* New York: Pergamon.

Ramirez, M., III, & Castañeda, A. (1974). *Cultural democracy, bicognitive development and education.* New York: Academic Press.

Ramirez, M., III, Cox, B., & Castañeda, A. (1977). *The psychological dynamics of biculturalism* (Technical report). Arlington, VA: Office of Naval Research, Organizational Effectiveness Research Program.

Ramirez, M., III, Garza, R. T., & Cox, B. G., (1980). *Multicultural leader behaviors in ethnically mixed task groups* (Technical report). Arlington, VA: Office of Naval Research, Organizational Effectiveness Research Program.

Ramirez, O., & Arce, C. (1981). The contemporary Chicano family: An empirically-based review. In A. Baron, Jr. (Ed.), *Explorations in Chicano psychology* (pp. 3-28). New York: Praeger.

Ramos-McKay, J. M. (1977). Locus of control, social activism and sex role among island Puerto Rican college and non-college individuals. *Dissertation Abstracts International, 38*(4B), 1957-1958.

Randolph, E. T., Escobar, J. I., Paz, D. H., & Forsythe, A. B. (1985). Ethnicity and reporting of schizophrenic symptoms. *Journal of Nervous and Mental Disease, 173,* 332-340.

Rapoport, R., & Rapoport, R. (1976). *Dual career families re-examined.* New York: Harper & Row.

Raywid, M. A. (1985). *Family choice arrangements in public schools: A review of the literature.* Washington, DC: National Institute of Education.

Raywid, M. A. (1987). Public choice, yes: Vouchers, no! *Phi Delta Kappan, 68,* 762-769.

Reardon, K. K. (1991). *Persuasion in practice.* Newbury Park, CA: Sage.

Reardon, K. K., & Rogers, E. M. (1988). Interpersonal versus mass media communication: A false dichotomy. *Human Communication Research, 15,* 284-303.

Reese, W. (1986). *Power and the promise of school reform.* New York: Routledge & Kegan Paul.

Reid, P., & Comas-Diaz, L. (1990). Gender and ethnicity: Perspectives on dual status. *Sex Roles, 22*(7-8), 397-408.

Remington, P. L., Forman, M. R., Gentry, E. M., Marks, J. S., Hogelin, G. C., & Trowbridge, F. L. (1985). Current smoking trends in the United States: The 1981-1983 behavioral risk factors surveys. *Journal of the American Medical Association, 253,* 2975-2978.

Reyes, P. (1990). Factors affecting the commitment of children at risk to stay in school. In J. Lakebrink (Ed.), *Children at risk* (pp. 18-33). Chicago: Anderson.

Reyes P., & Capper, C. A. (1991). Urban principals: A critical perspective on the context of minority student dropout. *Educational Administration Quarterly, 27,* 530-557.

Richwald, G. A., Schneider-Munoz, M., & Valdez, R. B. (1989). Are condom instructions in Spanish readable? Implications for AIDS prevention activities for Hispanics. *Hispanic Journal of Behavioral Sciences, 11,* 70-82.

Rickman, S. (1983). Stereotypes by Black college students revisited. *Papers in the Social Sciences, 3,* 21-28.

Riesman, F. (1962). *The culturally deprived child.* New York: Harper & Row.

Robbins, D. R., & Alessi, N. E. (1985). Depressive symptoms and suicidal behavior in adolescents. *American Journal of Psychiatry, 142,* 588-592.

Roberts, R. E. (1980). Prevalence of psychological distress among Mexican-Americans. *Journal of Health and Social Behavior, 21,* 134-145.

Roberts, R. E. (1987). An epidemiologic perspective on the mental health of people of Mexican origin. In R. Rodriguez & M. T. Coleman (Eds.), *Mental health issues of the Mexican origin population in Texas* (pp. 55-70). Austin: University of Texas, Hogg Foundation for Mental Health.

Robertson, J. M., & Fitzgerald, L. F. (1992). Overcoming the masculine mystique: Preferences for alternative forms of assistance among men who avoid counseling. *Journal of Counseling Psychology, 39,* 240-246.

Rodriguez-Scheel, J. T., & Arce, C. H. (1981, August). *Chicano identity and social change ideology.* Paper presented at the annual meeting of the American Psychological Association, Los Angeles.

Rogers, M. F., & Williams, W. W. (1987). AIDS in Blacks and Hispanics: Implications for prevention. *Issues in Science and Technology, 3*(3), 89-94.

Rogler, L. H. (1989). The meaning of culturally sensitive research in mental health. *American Journal of Psychiatry, 146,* 296-303.

Rogler, L. H., Malgady, R. C., & Rodriguez, O. (1990). *Hispanics and mental health: A framework for research.* Malabar, FL: Krieger.

Rogler, L. H., Malgady, R. G., & Costantino, G. (1987). What do culturally sensitive mental health services mean? *American Psychologist, 49,* 565-570.
Rogler, L. H., & Santana-Cooney, R. S. (Eds.). (1984). *Puerto Rican families in New York City: Intergenerational process.* New York: Hispanic Research Center.
Rosario, L. (1982). The self-perception of Puerto Rican women toward their societal roles. In R. E. Zambrana (Ed.), *Work, family and health: Latina women in transition* (pp. 95-107). New York: Hispanic Research Center.
Rosenberg, M. (1979). *Conceiving the self.* New York: Basic Books.
Rosenberg, M., & Simmons, R. (1972). *Black and White self-esteem.* Washington, DC: American Sociological Association.
Rosenthal, D., & Cichello, A. (1986). The meeting of two cultures: Ethnic identity and psychosocial adjustment of Italian-Australian adolescents. *International Journal of Psychology, 21,* 487-501.
Rosenthal, D. A., & Feldman, S. S. (1992). The nature and stability of ethnic identity in Chinese youth: Effects of length of residence in two cultural contexts. *Journal of Cross-Cultural Psychology, 23,* 214-227.
Rosenthal, D. A., & Hrynevich, C. (1985). Ethnicity and ethnic identity: A comparative study of Greek-, Italian-, and Anglo-Australian adolescents. *International Journal of Psychology, 20,* 723-742.
Ross, C. E., & Mirowsky, J. (1984). Mexican culture and its emotional contradictions. *Journal of Health and Social Behavior, 25,* 2-13.
Rubel, A. J. (1960). Concepts of disease in Mexican-American culture. *American Anthropologist, 62,* 795-814.
Rubio-Stipec, M., Shrout, P., Bird, M., Canino, G., & Bravo, M. (1989). Symptom scales of the Diagnostic Interview Schedule: Factor results in Hispanic and Anglo samples. *Psychological Assessment: A Journal of Consulting and Clinical Psychology, 1,* 30-34.
Ruble, D. N. (1983). The development of social-comparison processes and their role in achievement-related self-socialization. In E. T. Higgins, D. N. Ruble, & W. W. Hartup (Eds.), *Social cognition and social development: A sociocultural perspective* (pp. 134-157). Cambridge: Cambridge University Press.
Rugg, E. A. (1982). A longitudinal comparison of minority and nonminority college dropouts: Implications for retention improvement programs. *Personnel and Guidance Journal, 61,* 232-235.
Rumberger, R. W. (1983). Dropping out of high school: The influence of race, sex, and family background. *American Educational Research Journal, 20,* 199-220.
Rumberger, R. W. (1991). Chicano dropouts: A review of research and policy issues. In R. R. Valencia (Ed.), *Chicano school failure and success: Research and policy agendas for the 1990s* (Stanford Series on Education and Public Policy, pp. 64-89). Basingstoke, England: Falmer.
Rutter, M. (1979). Protective factors in children's responses to stress and disadvantage. In M. W. Kent & J. E. Rolf (Eds.), *Primary prevention of psychopathology: Social competence in children* (Vol. 3, pp. 49-74). Hanover, NH: University Press of New England.
Rutter, M., & Schaffer, D. (1980). DSM-III: A step forward or back in terms of the classification of child psychiatric disorders? *Journal of the American Academy of Child Psychiatry, 19,* 371-394.
Rychlak, J. F. (1968). *A philosophy of science for personality theory.* Boston: Houghton Mifflin.
Rychlak, J. F. (1977). *The psychology of rigorous humanism.* New York: John Wiley.
Ryckman, R. M. (1989). *Theories of personality* (4th ed.). Pacific Grove, CA: Brooks/Cole.
Sabin, J. E. (1975). Translating despair. *American Journal of Psychiatry, 132,* 197-199.

References

Sabogal, F., Marín, G., Otero-Sabogal, R., VanOss Marín, B., & Pérez, E. J. (1987). Hispanic familism and acculturation: What changes and what doesn't. *Hispanic Journal of Behavioral Sciences, 9*(4), 397-412.
Saenz, D. S. (1990). *Cognitive distinctiveness and problem-solving ability: A test for the generality of the token deficit effect*. Manuscript submitted for publication.
Saenz, D. S., & Lord, C. G. (1989). Reversing roles: A cognitive strategy for undoing memory deficits associated with token status. *Journal of Personality & Social Psychology, 56*, 698-708.
Saldaña, D. H. (1988). *Acculturation and stress: Latino students at a predominantly Anglo university*. Unpublished doctoral dissertation, University of California, Los Angeles.
Saldaña, D. H. (1994). Acculturation stress: Minority status and distress. *Hispanic Journal of the Behavioral Sciences, 16*(2), 116-128.
Salgado de Snyder, V. N., Cervantes, R. C., & Padilla, A. M. (1990). Gender and ethnic differences in psychosocial stress and generalization distress among Hispanics. *Sex Roles, 22*(7-8), 441-453.
Salganik, L. (1981). The rise and fall of educational vouchers. *Teachers College Record, 83*, 265-279.
Savage, D. G. (1985, February 5). Study shows 44% fail to finish high school. *Los Angeles Times*, pp. 1, 3.
Scanzoni, J. (1978). *Sex roles, women's work and marital conflict*. Lexington, MA: D. C. Heath.
Schepper-Hughes, N., & Lock, M. M. (1986). Speaking "truth" to illness: Metaphors, reification and a pedagogy for patients. *Medical Anthropology Quarterly, 17*, 137-140.
Scher, M. (1979). On counseling men. *Personnel and Guidance Journal, 57*, 252-254.
Scher, M. (1981). Men in hiding: A challenge for the counselor. *Personnel and Guidance Journal, 59*, 199-202.
Schinke, S. P., Botvin, G. J., Orlandi, M. A., Schilling, R. F., & Gordon, A. N. (1990). African-American and Hispanic-American adolescents, HIV infection, and preventive intervention. *AIDS Education and Prevention, 2*, 305-312.
Schinke, S. P., Moncher, M. S., Palleja, J., Zoyas, L. H., & Schilling, R. F. (1988). Hispanic youth, substance abuse, and stress: Implications for prevention research. *International Journal of the Addictions, 23*, 809-826.
Schoenbaum, E., Selwyn, P., & Hartel, D. (1988). HIV infection in drug users in New York: The relationship of drug use and heterosexual behavior and race/ethnicity. Abstract No. 8014, *IVth International Conference on AIDS*, Book 1.
Schwartz, I. M. (1989). *In justice for juveniles: Rethinking the best interests of the child*. Boston: Lexington Books.
Sedlak, M. W., Wheeler, C. W., Pullin, D. C., & Cusick, P. A. (1985). *Selling students short: Classroom bargains and academic reform in the American high school*. New York: Teachers College Press.
Segura, D. (1984). Labor market stratification: The Chicana experience. *Berkeley Journal of Sociology, 29*, 57-80.
Seldon, A. (1986). *The riddle of the voucher: An inquiry into obstacles to introducing choice and competition into state schools* (Hobart Paperback No. 21). London: Institute of Economic Affairs.
Seña-Rivera, J. (1976, August). *Casa and familia: An alternative model of the traditional extended family—A report on exploratory investigation*. Paper presented at the annual meeting of the American Sociological Association, New York.
Senour, M. (1977). Psychology of the Chicana. In J. L. Martinez, Jr. (Ed.), *Chicano psychology* (pp. 329-340). New York: Academic Press.

Serow, R. C. (1984). Effects of minimum competency testing for minorities: A review of expectations and outcomes. *Urban Review, 16,* 67-75.
Shapiro, J., & Saltzer, E. (1981, December). Cross-cultural aspects of physician-patient communication patterns. *Urban Health,* pp. 10-15.
Sharpe, M. J., & Heppner, P. P. (1991). Gender role, gender-role conflict, and psychological well-being in men. *Journal of Counseling Psychology, 38,* 323-330.
Shopland, D. R., & Brown, C. (1987). Toward the 1990 objectives for smoking: Measuring the progress with 1985 NHIS data. *Public Health Reports, 102,* 68-73.
Shweder, R. A. (1985). Menstrual pollution, soul lost and the comparative study of emotions. In A. Kleinman & B. Good (Eds.), *Culture and depression* (pp. 182-215). Berkeley: University of California Press.
Silverberg, R. A. (1986). *Psychotherapy for men: Transcending the masculine mystique.* Springfield, IL: Charles C Thomas.
Singer, M., Baer, H. A., & Lazarus, E. (1990). Critical medical anthropology in question. *Social Science and Medicine, 30,* v-viii.
Skilbeck, W. M., Acosta, F. X., Yamamoto, J., & Evans, L. A. (1984). Self reported psychiatric symptoms among Black, Hispanic and White outpatients. *Journal of Clinical Psychologist, 40,* 1184-1189.
Slaff, B. (1979). Adolescents. In J. Noshpitz (Ed.), *Basic handbook of child psychiatry* (Vol. 3, pp. 504-518). New York: Basic Books.
Slavin, R. E. (1983). *Cooperative learning.* New York: Longman.
Smedley, J., & Bayton, J. (1978). Evaluative race-class stereotypes by race and perceived class of subjects. *Journal of Personality and Social Psychology, 36,* 530-536.
Snow, C. E., & Ferguson, C. A. (1977). *Talking to children: Language input and acquisition.* Cambridge, England: Cambridge University Press.
Sole, Y. (1977). Language attitudes toward Spanish among Mexican-American college students. *Journal of LASSO, 2,* 37-46.
Soriano, F. I. (1993). AIDS and intravenous drug use among Hispanics in the U.S.: Considerations for prevention efforts. In R. Sanchez Mayers, B. L. Kail, & T. D. Watts (Eds.), *Hispanic substance abuse* (pp. 131-144). Springfield, IL: Charles C Thomas.
Soto, E., & Shaver, P. (1982). Sex role traditionalism, assertiveness, and symptoms of Puerto Rican women living in the United States. *Hispanic Journal of Behavioral Sciences, 4,* 1-19.
Spindler, L., & Spindler, G. (1967). Male and female adaptations in cultural change: Menomini. In R. Hunt (Ed.), *Personalities and cultured* (pp. 56-78). New York: National History Press.
Spitzer, R. L., Endicott, J., & Robins, E. (1975). Clinical criteria for psychiatric diagnosis and DSM-III. *American Journal of Psychiatry, 132,* 187-192.
Steele, S. (1990). *The content of our character.* New York: St. Martin's.
Steinberg, L., Blinde, P. L., & Chan, K. S. (1984). Dropping out among language minority youth: A review of the literature. *Review of Educational Research, 54,* 113-132.
Stipek, D., & Weisz, J. (1981). Perceived personal control and academic achievement. *Review of Educational Research, 51,* 101-137.
Stoeckle, J., & Waitzkin, H. (1972). The communication of information about illness. *Advances in Psychosomatic Medicine, 8,* 180-215.
Stoeckle, J., & Waitzkin, H. (1976). Information control and the micropolitics of health care: Summary of an ongoing research project. *Social Science & Medicine, 10,* 263-276.
Stonequist, E. V. (1935). The problem of the marginal man. *American Journal of Sociology, 41,* 1-12.

References

Stonequist, E. V. (1937). *The marginal man: A study in personality and culture conflict.* New York: Scribner.
Strunin, L. (1991). Adolescents' perceptions of risk for HIV infection: Implications for future research. *Social Science and Medicine, 32,* 221-228.
Suarez-Orozco, M. (1987). Becoming somebody: Central American immigrants in U.S. inner city schools. *Anthropology & Education Quarterly, 18,* 287-299.
Sue, D., & Sue, S. (1987). Cultural factors in the clinical assessment of Asian Americans. *Journal of Consulting and Clinical Psychology, 55,* 479-488.
Sued-Badillo, J. (1975). *La Mujer Indigena y su sociedad* [The indigenous woman and her society]. Rio Piedras, PR: Editorial El Gazir.
Sufian, M., Friedman, S. R., Neaigus, A., Stepherson, B., Rivera-Beckman, J., & Des Jarlais, D. (1990). Impact of AIDS on Puerto Rican intravenous drug users. *Hispanic Journal of Behavioral Sciences, 12,* 122-134.
Sutkin, L. F., & Good, G. (1987). Therapy with men in health-care settings. In M. Scher, M. Stevens, G. Good, & G. A. Eichenfield (Eds.), *Handbook of counseling and psychotherapy with men* (pp. 372-387). Newbury Park, CA: Sage.
Szapocznik, J., & Kurtines, W. (1980). Acculturation, biculturalism, and adjustment among Cuban Americans. In A. Padilla (Ed.), *Acculturation: Theory, models and some new findings* (pp. 134-160). Boulder, CO: Westview.
Szapocznik, J., Scopetta, M. A., Aranalde, M., & Kurtines, W. (1978). Cuban value structure: Treatment implications. *Journal of Consulting and Clinical Psychology, 46,* 961-970.
Tajfel, H. (1978a). *Differentiation between social groups: Studies in the social psychology of intergroup relations* (European Monographs in Social Psychology No. 14). London: Academic Press.
Tajfel, H. (1978b). Social categorization, social identity, and social comparison. In H. Tajfel (Ed.), *Differentiation between social groups* (pp. 61-76). New York: Academic Press.
Tajfel, H. (1981). *Human groups and social categories.* Cambridge: Cambridge University Press.
Tajfel, H. (1982). *Social identity and intergroup relations.* Cambridge: Cambridge University Press.
Tharp, R. G. (1989). Culturally compatible education: A formula for designing effective classrooms. In H. T. Trueba, G. Spindler, & L. Spindler (Eds.), *What do anthropologists say about dropouts?* (pp. 51-66). New York: Falmer.
Tharp, R. G., & Gallimore, R. (1989). *Rousing minds to life: Teaching, learning and schooling in social context.* Cambridge: Cambridge University Press.
Tharp, R. G., Jordan, C., Speidel, G. E., Au, K. H., Klein, T. W., Calkins, R. P., Sloat, K. C. M., & Gallimore, R. (1984). Product and process in applied developmental research: Education and the children of a minority. In M. E. Lamb, A. L. Brown, & B. Rogoff (Eds.), *Advances in developmental psychology* (Vol. 3, pp. 91-134). Hillsdale, NJ: Lawrence Erlbaum.
Torres-Gil, F. (1986). *Hispanics in an aging society.* New York: Carnegie Corporation.
Torros-Matrullo, C. M. (1980). Acculturation sex-role values and mental health among mainland Puerto Ricans. In A. M. Padilla (Ed.), *Acculturation: Theory, models and some new findings* (pp. 111-137). Boulder, CO: Westview.
Toukomaa, P., & Skutnabb-Kangas, T. (1977). *The intensive teaching of the mother tongue to migrant children of preschool age and children in the lower level of comprehensive school.* Helsinki: Finnish National Commission for UNESCO.

Tousignant, M. (1984). Pena in the Ecuadorian Sierra: A psychoanthropological analysis of sadness. *Culture, Medicine and Psychiatry, 8*, 381-398.

Triandis, H., Lisansky, J., Setiadi, B., Chang, B., Marín, G., & Betancourt, H. (1982). Stereotyping among Hispanics and Anglos: The uniformity, intensity, direction, and quality of auto- and heterostereotypes. *Journal of Cross-Cultural Psychology, 13*, 409-426.

Triandis, H. C. (1972). *The analysis of subjective culture.* New York: John Wiley.

Triandis, H. C., Marín, G., Lisansky, J., & Betancourt, H. (1984). Simpatía as a cultural script of Hispanics. *Journal of Personal Social Psychology, 47*, 1363-1375.

Tripp-Reimer, T. (1980). Clinical anthropology: Perspective from a nurse-anthropologist. *Anthropology Newsletter, 12*, 21.

Trueba, H. (1988). Culturally-based explanations of minority students academic achievement. *Anthropology and Education Quarterly, 19*, 270-287.

Tucker, C. M., James, L. M., & Turner, S. M. (1985). Sex roles, parenthood, and marital adjustment: A comparison of Blacks and Whites. *Journal of Social and Clinical Psychology, 3*(1), 51-61.

Turner, J. C. (1982). Towards a cognitive redefinition of the social group. In H. Tajfel (Ed.), *Social identity and intergroup relations* (pp. 15-40). Cambridge: Cambridge University Press.

Tzuriel, D., & Klein, M. M. (1977). Ego identity: Effects of ethnocentrism, ethnic identification, and cognitive complexity in Israeli, Oriental, and Western ethnic groups. *Psychological Reports, 40*, 1099-1110.

Uhlenhuth, E. H., Lipman, R. S., Balter, M. B., & Stern, M. (1974). Symptom intensity and life stress in the city. *Archives of General Psychiatry, 31*, 759-764.

U.S. Bureau of the Census. (1982). *Ancestry and language in the United States: November 1979* (Current Population Reports, Special Studies P-23, No. 116). Washington, DC: U.S. Government Printing Office.

U.S. Bureau of the Census. (1984). *The Hispanic population in the United States* (Current Population Reports, Series P-20, No. 431). Washington, DC: U.S. Government Printing Office.

Valencia, R. R. (1991). The plight of Chicano students: An overview of schooling conditions and outcomes. In R. R. Valencia (Ed.), *Chicano school failure and success: Research and policy agendas for the 1990s* (Stanford Series on Education and Public Policy, pp. 3-26). Basingstoke, England: Falmer.

Valencia, R. R., & Aburto, S. (1991a). Competency testing and Latino student access to the teaching profession: An overview of issues. In G. D. Keller, J. Deneen, & R. Magallan (Eds.), *Assessment and access: Hispanics in higher education* (pp. 169-196). Albany: State University of New York Press.

Valencia, R. R., & Aburto, S. (1991b). Research directions and practical strategies in teacher testing and assessment: Implications for improving Latino access to teaching. In G. D. Keller, J. Deneen, & R. Magallan (Eds.), *Assessment and access: Hispanics in higher education* (pp. 197-234). Albany: State University of New York Press.

Valencia, R. R., & Aburto, S. (1991c). The uses and abuses of educational testing: Chicanos as a case in point. In R. R. Valencia (Ed.), *Chicano school failure and success: Research and policy agendas for the 1990s* (Stanford Series on Education and Public Policy, pp. 203-251). Basingstoke, England: Falmer.

Valencia, R. R., & Menchaca, M. (1992). Demographic overview of Latino and Mexican-origin populations in the United States: Counseling implications. In G. M. Gonzalez, I. Alvarado, & A. S. Segrera (Eds.), *Challenges of cultural and racial diversity to counseling:*

Mexico City Conference Proceedings (pp. 27-35). Alexandria, VA: American Association for Counseling and Development.

Valle, R., & Vega, R. (1980). *Hispanic natural support systems: Mental health promotion perspectives.* Sacramento: Department of Mental Health.

Valle-Ferrer, N. (1986). Feminism and its influence on women's organizations in Puerto Rico. In E. Acosta-Belen (Ed.), *The Puerto Rican woman: Perspectives on culture, history and society* (pp. 75-87). New York: Praeger.

Vargas, R. (1988). *Dignity for Latinos with AIDS: Final report of minority AIDS need assessment.* Unpublished manuscript, Instituto Familiar de la Raza, Inc.

Vargas, W. G., & Cervantes, R. C. (1987). Consideration of psychosocial stress in the treatment of the Latina immigrant. *Hispanic Journal of Behavioral Sciences, 9,* 315-329.

Vasquez, M. J. (1978). *Chicano and Anglo university women: Factors related to their performance, persistence and attrition.* Unpublished doctoral dissertation, University of Texas, Austin.

Vazquez, M. J. T., & Gonzalez, A. M. (1981). Sex roles among Chicanos: Stereotypes, challenges, and changes. In A. Baron (Ed.), *Explorations in Chicano psychology* (pp. 51-70). New York: Praeger.

Vazquez-Nuttall, E., Romero-Garcia, I., & De Leon, B. (1987). Sex roles and perceptions of femininity and masculinity of Hispanic women: A review of the literature. *Psychology of Women Quarterly, 11,* 409-426.

Vega, W. A., Patterson, T., Salis, J., Nader, P., Atkins, C., & Abramson, I. (1986). Cohesion and adaptability in Mexican American and Anglo families. *Journal of Marriage and the Family, 48,* 857-867.

Velasquez, R. J., & Gimenez, L. (1987). MMPI differences among three diagnostic groups of Mexican-American state hospital patients. *Psychological Reports, 60,* 1071-1074.

Velez, W. (1989). High school attrition among Hispanic and non-Hispanic White youths. *Sociology of Education, 62,* 119-133.

Vigil, J. D. (1988a). Group processes and street identity: Adolescent Chicano gang members. *Ethos, 16,* 421-445.

Vigil, J. D. (1988b). Street socialization, locura behavior, and violence among Chicano gang members. In J. F. Kraus, S. B. Sorenson, & P. D. Juarez (Eds.), *Research conference on violence and homicide in Hispanic communities* (pp. 231-241). Los Angeles: UCLA Publication Services.

Vogt, L. A., Jordan, C., & Tharp, R. G. (1987). Exploring school failure and producing school success: Two cases. *Anthropology and Education Quarterly, 18,* 276-286.

Walsh, J. (1973). *Intercultural education in the community of man.* Honolulu: University of Hawaii Press.

Waterman, A. (1984). *The psychology of individualism.* New York: Praeger.

Wehlage, G. C., & Rutter, R. A. (1986). Dropping out: How much do schools contribute to the problem? *Teachers College Record, 87,* 374-392.

Welner, Z. (1978). Childhood depression: An overview. *Journal of Nervous and Mental Disease, 166*(8), 588-593.

Werner, E. E., Bierman, J. M., & French, F. E. (1971). *The children of Kauai: A longitudinal study from the prenatal period to age ten.* Honolulu: University of Hawaii Press.

Werner, E. E., & Smith, R. S. (1982). *Vulnerable but invincible: A longitudinal study of resilient children and youth.* New York: McGraw-Hill.

Werner, O., & Campbell, D. T. (1970). Translating, working through interpreters, and the problem of decentering. In R. Naroll & R. Cohen (Eds.), *A handbook of method in cultural anthropology* (pp. 398-420). New York: Museum of Natural History.

Wexler, P. (1987). *Social analysis of education: After a new sociology.* New York: Routledge & Kegan Paul.
Wheeler, E. E., Wheeler, K. R., & Torres-Raines, R. (1977, March). *Women's stereotypic roles: A replication and standardization.* Paper presented at the annual meeting of the Southwestern Social Science Association/Southwestern Sociological Association, Dallas, TX.
White, C., & Burke, P. (1987). Ethnic role identity among Black and White college students: An interactionist approach. *Sociological Perspectives, 30,* 310-331.
Williams, G. (1979). Language group allegiance and ethnic interaction. In H. Giles & B. Saint-Jacques (Eds.), *Language and ethnic relations* (pp. 57-65). New York: Pergamon.
Williams, N. (1988). Role making among Mexican American women: Issues of class and ethnicity. *Journal of Applied Behavioral Sciences, 24*(2), 203-217.
Willie, C. V. (1991). Controlled choice: An alternative desegregation plan for minorities who feel betrayed. *Education & Urban Society, 23,* 200-207.
Willig, A. C., Harnisch, D. L., Hill, K. J., & Maehr, M. L. (1983). Sociocultural and educational correlates of success-failure attributions and evaluation anxiety in the school setting for Black, Hispanic, and Anglo children. *American Educational Research Journal, 20,* 385-410.
Wise, A., & Darling-Hammond, L. (1986). Education by voucher: Private choice and the public interest. *Educational Theory, 34,* 29-47.
Witte, J. F. (1991). *First year report: Milwaukee parental choice program.* Unpublished manuscript, Robert M. La Follette Institute of Public Affairs, University of Wisconsin—Madison.
Wolk, R. (Ed.). (1990). Most Minnesota students transfer for convenience, survey shows. *Education Week, 36,* 2.
Wong-Fillmore, L. (1983). The language learner as an individual: Implications of research on individual differences for the ESL teacher. In M. A. Clarke & J. Handscombe (Eds.), *On TESOL '82: Pacific perspectives on language learning and teaching* (pp. 157-171). Washington, DC: TESOL.
World Health Organization. (1992). *International classification of diseases, 10th revision (ICD-10).* Geneva: Author.
Worth, D., & Rodriguez, R. (1987, January-February). Latino women and AIDS. *SIECUS Report,* pp. 5-7.
Wylie, R. (1979). *The self-concept: Theory and research on selected topics* (Vol. 2). Lincoln: University of Nebraska Press.
Yamamoto, K., & Brynes, D. A. (1984). Classroom social status, ethnicity, and ratings of stressful events. *Journal of Educational Research, 77,* 283-286.
Yates, J. R., & Ortiz, A. A. (1991). Professional development needs of teachers who serve exceptional language minorities in today's schools. *Teacher Education and Special Education, 4,* 11-18.
Ybarra-Soriano, L. (1977). Conjugal role relationships in the Chicano family. *Dissertation Abstracts International, 39,* 1140A.
Zak, I. (1976). Structure of ethnic identity of Arab-Israeli students. *Psychological Reports, 38,* 239-246.
Zapata, J. T., & Jaramillo, P. T. (1981). Research on the Mexican American family. *Journal of Individual Psychology, 37,* 72-85.
Zeff, S. B. (1982). A cross-cultural study of Mexican American, Black American, and White American women at a large urban university. *Hispanic Journal of Behavioral Sciences, 4*(2), 245-261.

Zinn, M. (1975). *Chicanas: Power and control in the domestic sphere.* Ann Arbor: University of Michigan Press.
Zinn, M. B. (1975). Political familism: Toward sex role equality in Chicano families. *Aztlan, 6*(1), 13-26.
Zippin, D. H., & Hough, R. L. (1985). Perceived self-other differences in life events and mental health among Mexicans and Americans. *Journal of Psychology, 149,* 143-155.
Zitzow, D. (1984). The college adjustment rating scale. *Journal of College Student Personnel, 25,* 160-164.

Index

Academic invulnerability, 288-302.
Academic language proficiency, 276, 284-285. *See also* Threshold levels of linguistic proficiency
Academic performance, xiii, 43, 80, 82, 87, 273-286
  academic achievement in English, 280-282
  academic achievement in Spanish, 278-280. *See also* Educational policy; School performance
Acculturation, ix, xi-xii, xiv-xvi, xvii-xviii, 3, 5-6, 11, 13, 15-18, 21-25, 26-29, 33, 35, 39-42
  environmental influences, 25
  family functioning, 15-25
  gang participation, 149
  gender roles, 236, 241, 259
  Maori, 6
  measuring, 26
  mental health, 126, 135, 138
  multidimensional model, 5
  process, 25
  smoking behavior, 185-188, 191, 194
  socioecological influences, 11-12
  stress, 291
  unidimensional model, 5, 26
Acculturative stress, xi-xii, 43-54, 291
Achievement orientation, 21, 23
Active recreational orientation, 21, 23

Adaptation, 71-72
Additive bilinguals, 283
Adolescents, xiv, 131-147, 148-165, 199, 202-203, 205
AIDS risk and/or prevention, 196-212, 213-227, 243
Alcohol and/or alcoholism, 109, 120, 145, 149-150, 160-161, 215, 232-233, 240, 244
Allocentrism, 201
American identity, 35-40, 96
Androgynous, 249-250, 253
Anxiety, 9, 115, 240
  separation anxiety, 141, 144
Assimilation, 25, 316
  assimilated individual, 69, 112, 115, 135
Ataques de nervios, 135

Back translation method, 249
Basic communicative proficiency, 276
  See also Threshold levels of linguistic proficiency
Bem Sex Role Inventory (BSRI), xvi, 247-255
Bicultural, xix, 8, 11, 13, 28, 35-38, 40
  biculturalism, 68
Bicultural affiliation, 44
Bicultural model, 24
  bicultural orientation, 69

362

Index

Bilingual/Immersion program:
   two-way bilingual/immersion education, xvi, 273-286, 316, 320, 322
Bilingualism, xiii, xvi, 89-90, 98-99, 101, 118, 275, 283-284, 323
Bisexual men, 196, 207, 215, 226
Black identity formation, 60
   Black racial identity, 63
   Black ethnicity, 111
Bolivians, 29
Brunswik "lens model," 6

California Proposition, 63
Castelike or involuntary minority, 76-78
Catholic(ism), 23, 206, 217, 225, 260
Central Americans, 78, 184, 224
CES-D Scale, 114, 120
Chicano(a), xii-xiv, 7, 9, 10, 13, 46-47, 78, 90, 92-96, 100, 111, 117, 148-165, 270
   Chicano movement, 102
Children, xiv, 131-147, 148-165, 220-223, 240, 291-292, 309
Chileans, 29
Cholo(s), 78, 92, 96, 163
Clifford's Academic Achievement Accountability Scale, 294
Cognitive functioning, 274-275
College preparation, 294, 297, 301
College related stress, 44-54
College students, xvi, 43-54, 245-256
Common underlying proficiency, 276
Communication/persuasion model, xv, 198-212
   channel factors, 203
   message factors, 200-203
   receiver factors, 204-208
   source factors, 199-200
   see also McGuire's communication/persuasion model
Comprehensive Tests of Basic Skills (CTBS), 277-283, 295-299
Condoms, 199, 201, 205-209. *See also* Safe sex
Coping responses, 78, 214-215, 217, 219, 223-224, 291
   drug use, 224

prayer, 223
withdrawal, 224
Cuban students, 74
Cubans, xii, 78, 90, 175, 195
Cultural awareness, 4, 27, 44
Cultural discontinuities, 75-80, 82-84, 88
Cultural identity, 28-30, 39-41, 74, 155
Cultural Identity Scale, 33
Cultural Information Scale (CIS), 47
Cultural mismatch theory, 75-76, 79-84, 88
Cultural psychiatry, xiv, 107
Culture-bound syndromes, 134-135, 141. *See also Ataques de nervios; Mal de ojo; Susto*

Daily hassles, 45
Demographic Index (DI), 47, 53
Depression, 114-115, 137, 152, 160, 162, 240, 260-261
   Depression Adjective Checklist, 116
Diagnostic Interview Schedule (DIS), 115-116, 119-121, 137
Diagnostic and Statistical Manual of Mental Disorders (DSM):
   cultural bias in use of, 140-146
   DSM-III-R, 108, 119, 120-122, 127, 134
   DSM-IV, xiv, 131-147
Discrimination, 62, 69, 75, 83, 149
Distress, 43, 45, 48-54, 114-115, 122, 214, 242, 247
Doctor-patient interactions, 170-181
Dominican, 171, 175
Drug use, 39-40, 145, 149-150, 160-161, 204-206, 214-220, 222-227, 232-233, 244

Ecuadorians, 29
Educational policy, 303-325
Educational reform movement, 303-304, 308-309, 311, 313, 315-325
English language achievment, 281-282
English math achievment, 282, 286
English reading achievment, 280-281, 283, 285
Environmental resources, 290

Epidemiology, 109, 113, 122, 126, 130
Equal educational opportunity, 311, 316-318
Erikson's theory of ego identity, 60
Ethnic identity, xiii, 27, 44, 57-72, 82-83, 85, 88, 91, 93, 95-96, 99-100
Ethnic loyalty, 4, 27, 44, 47, 53
Ethnic psychology, x
Euro-American culture or orientation, 17, 24, 232
Eurocentric paradigm, xi
European immigrant families, 17, 90

Familialism, 201-202
Families of schizophrenics, 123. *See also* Schizophrenia
Family dysfunction, 155-164
Family Environment Scale (FES), 18-19, 22
Family systems perspective, 15-16
Family therapy, 155-164
Feminism, 33, 39
Feminist orientation, xvi, 36. *See also* Women's movement
First-generation individuals, 43

Gang involvement, xiv, 148-165. *See also Locura; Vatos locos; Veteranos*
Gay men, 196, 226
  homosexuality, 205-207, 215, 221, 243
Gender differences in smoking behavior, 187, 189, 193
Gender identity, xv-xvi, 233-244, 245-256. *See also* Feminism; Machismo
Gender role reversal, 261-270
Gender role stress model, 232
Gender schema theory, xvi, 236-244
Generational differences, 60, 74, 297, 300
Group therapy, 157-164

High school and beyond data, 74, 291, 301
High school grades, 295, 297-298
Hispanic Children's Stress Inventory, 291, 294
HIV/AIDS epidemic:

HIV/AIDS prevention, 196-212, 213-226
Hollingshead Two Factor Index of Social Position, 293
Homelessness, 213, 216, 227
Hondurans, 29
Hopkins Symptoms Checklist, 48. *See also* Symptoms checklist 90-R
Househusbands, xvi, 257-270
Humanistic Interaction Model, 3
Humanistic perspective, 4

Immigration, 42, 69, 141
Institutional racism, 86
Intellectual-cultural orientation, 21, 23
International Classification of Diseases (ICD-10), 132, 134
Intrafamilial relationships, 18

Japanese Americans, 86

La Prueba Riverside de Realización en Español (La Prueba), 278-283
Language and thought, 274
Language Assessment Scale (LAS), 278
Language attitudes, 90-91, 98-99, 102. *See also* Bilingualism
Language barrier, 169-181
Language concordance, xv, 172
Language discordance, 172, 179
Latino identity, 35-40
Latino principals and/or teachers, 305, 323
Locura, 153

Machismo, xvi, 201-202, 226, 231-232, 257-259, 262, 267-268, 270
Magnet schools, 317
Mal de ojo, 135
Marginal identity, 88
Marginal person theory, 4
Marginalization, 68, 70, 150
McGuire's communication/persuasion model:
  channel factors, 203
  message factors, 200-203
  receiver factors, 204-208
  source factors, 199-200

Index

Mental health problems, 107, 110-111, 116, 124-126, 130
Mental health research, 107-130
Mental health services, xiv, 131. *See also* Family therapy; Group therapy
Mestizo(a), 92, 94, 96
Mexican American family, 15-25, 239
Mexican American students, 82, 288-302
Mexican descendants, 90, 92, 112, 120, 184, 224
Mexican-traditional identity, 96-97, 100-101
Minimum competency testing, 313-314
Minnesota Multiphasic Personality Inventory (MMPI), 119
Minority status, 43, 44, 48-54
Modal personality approach, 5
Moral-religious emphasis, 21, 23
Multiculturalism, 319-320, 322-323
Multiculturals, 8, 11

Negative stereotypes, 62
Nicaraguans, 78

Oppression, x-xi
Organic disorders, 114

Paraguayans, 29
Patient Interview Schedule, 176
Perceived discrimination, 32-33, 35, 39, 48, 54. *See also* Discrimination
Personal resources, 289-290, 293
Personal Resources Scale, 146
Personality development, 13
Piers-Harris Self-Concept Inventory, 293-294
Polish Americans, 58
Political consciousness, xiii, 93-94, 97-100, 102
Political identity, 96-97
Prejudice, 62, 69
Protective resources, 288-292, 296
Psychological Index (PI), 47
Puerto Rican children, 117-118, 137
Puerto Rican students, 74, 76
Puerto Rico, xi, xvi, 90-91, 109, 112, 114, 120, 171, 175, 184, 242-256

Raza, 92-93, 100
Reactive adaptation, 4
Respeto, 33, 35-36, 39, 201-202
Role strain, 45-54
Rosenberg Self-Esteem Scale, 66-67

Safe sex, xv, 201, 225. *See also* Unsafe sex
Salvadorans, 29
Schizophrenia, 113, 116, 119-120, 123, 145. *See also* Families of schizophrenics
School choice, 307-308, 319, 324
School dropouts, 73-88, 291, 312-313
School performance, 71, 74, 278-286
Self-concept, 81, 84, 257-258, 259, 296
Self-esteem, xiii, 27, 57-58, 61, 63-70, 84, 214, 217, 219, 221-222, 233, 241, 243, 257, 265, 267
Self-identification, 59, 95, 158
Separate underlying proficiency, 276
Sex role identity. *See* Gender identity
Short Acculturation Scale, 33, 35
Simpatia, 201-202
Smoking behavior
  consequences of quitting, 190-192
  consequences of smoking, 189-190
  situational antecedents of smoking, 187-189
  smoking prevention and attitudes toward smoking, xv, 182-195
Social identity theory, xiii, 80, 82, 86
  social identities, 78-83, 87, 91, 156-158, 163
Social support, 220, 243, 257, 297, 300
Somatization problems, 114-115, 120, 145, 242
Spanish language preference, 32
Spanish language proficiency, 32, 37
Spanish math achievment, 279-280, 286
Spanish reading achievement, 278-279, 282, 285
Spiritualists, 112
Stress, 44-54, 141, 147, 152-153, 215, 217, 247, 261, 289, 291
Stress-mediation-outcome model, 122
Student Oral Language Observation Matrix (SOLOM), 278

Subjective appraisals, 290-292, 296
Susto, 135
Symptoms checklist 90-R, 136-137

Threshold level of linguistic proficiency, 274-275, 283, 299
Tuition tax credits, 307-308, 311, 318

Unsafe sex, 197, 208-209, 214
Uruguayans, 29

Value orientations, 28, 38
Vatos locos, 153-155, 160, 163-164
Venezuelans, 29
Veteranos, 151, 160
Violence, xiv, 148, 150-164, 232, 240, 243-244. *See also* Gang involvement

White Americans, 59
Women's movement, 235, 256, 268-270

About the Editor

Amado M. Padilla received his Ph.D. in experimental psychology from the University of New Mexico. He is Professor of Psychological Studies in Education and chair of the Language, Literacy and Culture Program in the School of Education at Stanford University. Previously, he directed two national research centers, the Center for Language Education and Research and the Spanish-speaking Mental Health Research Center at the University of California at Los Angeles where he served as Professor of Psychology from 1974 to 1988. His current research interests include the social adaptation of immigrants and their children to American society and the acquisition and teaching of second languages to adolescents and adults. He was founding editor of the *Hispanic Journal of Behavioral Sciences*, which is currently in its 16th year of publication. He has published extensively in numerous areas, including bilingualism and Hispanic mental health. His books include *Latino Mental Health* (1973), *Crossing Cultures in Therapy* (1980), *Acculturation* (1980), *Chicano Ethnicity* (1987), *Introduction to Psychology* (1989), *Bilingual Education* (1991), and *Foreign Language Education* (1991).

About the Contributors

Sylvia Alatorre Alva is a Social Policy Fellow at the Center for Collaboration for Children at California State University at Fullerton. She received her Ph.D. degree in psychology from the University of California at Los Angeles, with a concentration in developmental psychology and social policy analysis and planning. She is Assistant Professor in the Department of Child Development at California State University at Fullerton. Her teaching and research focus on the educational attainment and psychosocial development of Mexican-American and minority group children and adolescents. She is a past Fellow at the Bush Center for Child and Family Policy Studies at the University of California at Los Angeles.

William Arroyo, M.D., is a Child and Adolescent Psychiatrist and Clinical Assistant Professor of Psychiatry at the University of Southern California and Director of the Child-Adolescent Psychiatric Clinic at the Los Angeles County-University of Southern California Hospital. He is a staff member of a private nonprofit organization, the Psychological Trauma Center, which provides psychological assistance to schools during the early aftermath of disasters and community violence. He has been honored by community organizations for his work with psychologically traumatized refugees. His publications are in the areas of psychological trauma and cultural issues related to mental health. He also served as an Advisory Group member to the *DSM-IV* Task Force.

Robert Banchero is a Ph.D. candidate in counseling psychology at the University of California at Santa Barbara from which he received a master's degree in education. His research interests focus on the relationship between theory and practice within the counseling process. After completion of his degree, he would like to work at fostering an ongoing dialogue between researchers and the counseling professionals in private practice.

Jerald Belitz is an Assistant Professor in the Department of Psychiatry and Clinical Coordinator of Programs for Children and Adolescents at the University of New Mexico School of Medicine. He received his B.A. from City College of New York and his M.A. and Ph.D. from the University of New Mexico. His areas of interest include ethics, multicultural issues and their relationship to child and adolescent development, affective and behavioral disturbances, and coping with trauma and abuse. For the past several years, he has specialized in working with gang-involved youths and other "high risk" adolescents.

Martha E. Bernal is Professor of Psychology in the Department of Psychology and Research Professor at the Hispanic Research Center at Arizona State University. She received her Ph.D. in clinical psychology from Indiana University at Bloomington and is a Fellow of the American Psychological Association and a Diplomate in Clinical Psychology of the American Board of Professional Psychology. Her research has focused on the development, socialization, and correlates of ethnic identity in Mexican American children. She has published numerous articles in this as and was coeditor with George Knight of *Ethnic Identity: Formation and Transmission Among Hispanics and Other Minorities* (1993) and with Phyllis Martinelli of *Mexican American Identity* (1993). Her parents emigrated from Mexico and she was raised in El Paso, Texas.

Raymond Buriel is Professor of Psychology and Chicano Studies at Pomona College, where he is also Associate Dean of Faculty. He received his Ph.D. in psychology from the University of California at Riverside. He did postdoctoral work at the Spanish-speaking Mental Health Research Center at UCLA on a Ford Foundation Fellowship and is a Scholar of the Tomas Rivera Center for Policy Studies in Claremont, California. He has served as a consultant to Project Follow Through, the National

Center for Bilingual Research, and the California State Department of Education. His research includes the acculturation and adjustment of Mexican immigrant families, with a special focus on the characteristics of immigrants that are conducive to success in the United States. His research has appeared in several book chapters and scholarly journals. He serves on the editorial boards of the *Hispanic Journal of Behavioral Sciences, Journal of Genetic Psychology,* and *Harvard Journal of Hispanic Policy.*

J. Manuel Casas is a Professor in the Counseling, Clinical and School Psychology Program at the University of California at Santa Barbara. He received his Ph.D. from Stanford University with a specialization in the areas of counseling and cross-cultural psychology. He has published widely in professional journals in the area of cross-cultural counseling and education. He is coauthor (with Joseph Ponterotto) of the *Handbook of Racial/Ethnic Minority Counseling Research.* He has served on the editorial board of *The Counseling Psychologist, Journal of Multicultural Counseling and Development, Hispanic Journal of Behavioral Sciences,* and numerous other publications. He consults on institutional interventions that contribute significantly to the success and/or failure of ethnic minorities in social, educational, and corporate settings.

Richard C. Cervantes is Assistant Professor of Clinical Psychiatry (Psychology) at the University of Southern California School of Medicine. He is Associate Director of the Clinical Psychology Internship Program and is a supervising psychologist in the Division of Child and Adolescent Psychiatry. He earned his Ph.D. in clinical psychology in 1984 at Oklahoma State University. He is a member of the USC Consortium for the Study of Youth Violence. He is a consultant to the Center for Substance Abuse Prevention and is a member of their Hispanic High Risk Youth Cluster Group. He is author of over two dozen journal articles and recently edited *Substance Abuse and Gang Violence* (Sage, 1992). His research is in the area of Hispanic children's mental health, with a special interest in psychological testing for youths.

Virginia Chavez is a student in the University of Utah graduate program in public administration, specializing in health administration. She is currently working at the Hispanic Research Center at Arizona State

University, where she conducts interviews with gang members and Latino youths who abuse inhalants. She has presented papers on Latino gangs in Arizona and on alcohol use among Latino youths at the annual meetings of the American Sociological Association.

Sharon Kantorowski Davis is Professor of Sociology at the University of La Verne in Los Angeles. She received her Ph.D. in sociology from the University of Southern California. Her research specialties are primarily in the sociology of deviance in the areas of crime, delinquency, and family violence. Her lifelong commitment to and involvement with issues of ethnicity and gender have resulted in the development of classes and of publications in *Ethnic Relations* and *Gender, Social Class and Ethnicity in Film*. In 1993, she was an invited speaker to an international conference in Sapporo, Japan on "Social Welfare in the 21st Century: An International Approach." During 1995 she will teach and do cross-cultural research in Athens, Greece.

Brunilda De León is Assistant Professor in the School and Counseling Psychology Program, School of Education at the University of Massachusetts in Amherst. She received an M.S.W. from the University of Puerto Rico, and an Ed.D. in school psychology from the University of Massachusetts. Her research has focused on the areas of bilingual, cross-cultural, and multicultural assessment, career opportunities for minority students, and cultural adaptation, gender roles, and issues in the mental health of ethnically diverse populations. She consults widely in the areas of school, family, and community mental health.

Horacio Fabrega Jr., M.D., is Professor of Psychiatry and Anthropology at the University of Pittsburgh. He received his M.D. from Columbia University in New York City and completed his psychiatry residency at Yale University. He has been involved in cultural psychiatry and medical anthropology for approximately 30 years, and has written two books and over 120 articles in peer-reviewed journals. He has done extensive cross-cultural work in Mexico and Peru and has conducted research with ethnic minorities in the United States, primarily with Hispanic Americans and African Americans. His work includes clinical, social psychiatric, and health services studies. His current interests involve theoretical aspects of psychiatry and medicine, and ways of increasing cultural sensitivity in international systems of psychiatric diagnosis. He is actively involved in caring for patients in the brain injury unit at the Western Psychiatric Institute and Clinic.

Judith Freidenberg received her Ph.D. in anthropology from the Graduate Center, City University of New York, where is she now a Senior Research Associate with the Center for Urban Research. Her teaching and research have focused on Latinos in the United States, with a particular interest in translating anthropological findings to policymakers. Her latest work is on elderly Latinos in East Harlem, New York City. This work was the subject of an anthropological exhibition of text and visual imagery at the CUNY Graduate Center, and of a book, *Growing Old in Spanish Harlem: 1948-1994*. At the time this chapter was written, she was Assistant Professor of Anthropology at Mount Sinai School of Medicine, CUNY.

María Félix-Ortiz de la Garza is an Assistant Professor in the Department of Psychology at the University of Southern California. Previously she was a Clinical Psychology Fellow at the University of California at San Francisco and conducted research and provided clinical services at Substance Abuse Services, Department of Psychiatry, at San Francisco General Hospital. Her research interests are in etiology and prevention of drug use and abuse, especially among Latino youths, and in the development of client-led support groups as adjuncts to structured addiction treatment. She was a Ford Predoctoral Fellow (1987-1991) and was awarded the Joseph A. Gengerilli Award for Most Distinguished Dissertation in the UCLA Department of Psychology in 1993. Her recent publications appear in the *Hispanic Journal of Behavioral Sciences* and *Journal of Personality and Social Psychology*.

Placida I. Gallegos is Vice President of Southwest Communication Resources, Inc., a consulting firm in San Diego, California, and is a consultant with the Kallel Jamison Consulting Group, the national diversity firm. She holds an M.S. in marriage and family counseling from Loma Linda University and an M.A. and Ph.D. in social psychology from the University of California at Riverside. She has done extensive research, training, and consulting in the area of cross-cultural relations and the influence of ethnic and gender diversity on interpersonal relations. She is on the faculty of the California School of Professional Psychology and teaches courses on gender and cultural diversity in the workplace.

Raymond T. Garza is Provost and Vice President for Academic Affairs and Professor of Psychology at the University of Texas at San Antonio. His prior academic appointment was with the University of California at Riverside where he also served in several academic administrative positions as Associate Dean of UC Riverside's Graduate Division, Director of the Social/Personality Psychology Program, and Distinguished Scholar of the Tomas Rivera Center. He has an M.A. in psychology from Texas A&M University and a Ph.D. in psychology from Purdue University. His areas of research and teaching expertise include intergroup relations, Hispanic personality development, research methods, and minority mental health. He is author or coauthor of 68 research articles, book chapters, and professional papers and has received major grants from the National Institute of Mental Health, the Office of Naval Research, and the Pew Charitable Trusts.

Henry Gomez is a Cardiology Fellow at the Long Island Jewish Medical Center in New Hyde Park, NY. He received his M.D. from the Mount Sinai School of Medicine in New York City and completed his internal medicine residency at Montefiore Medical Center, Bronx, NY.

Patricia Gurin is Professor and Chair of the Department of Psychology at the University of Michigan. She received her Ph.D. from the University of Michigan in 1964. She has published eight books and monographs as well as numerous articles on topics including personal and social identity, the relationship of self to reference groups and society, and political empowerment. The impact of her work has led to roles chairing advisory committees (e.g., the Rockefeller Foundation Committee on Minority Single-Headed Households) and several National Institute of Mental Health research panels on social problem research.

Aida Hurtado is Associate Professor of Psychology at the University of California at Santa Cruz. She received her M.A. and Ph.D. in social psychology from the University of Michigan. Her research focuses on the effects of subordination on social identity and is especially interested in group memberships, like ethnicity, race, class, and gender, that are used to legitimize unequal distribution of power between groups. Her expertise is in survey methods with bilingual/bicultural populations. She has published extensively on issues of language and social identity for the Mexican-origin population in the United States.

George P. Knight is Professor of Psychology and Director of the Graduate Program in Developmental Psychology at Arizona State University. He received his Ph.D. in social/developmental psychology from the University of California at Riverside. He is a member of the editorial boards for *Child Development* and *Merrill-Palmer Quarterly*. His research interests include the development and socialization of ethnic identity, cross-cultural developmental issues, the development of prosocial and cooperative behavioral styles, and developmental social cognition. He recently coedited, with Martha Bernal, *Ethnic Identity: Formation and Transmission Among Hispanics and Other Minorities* and edited a special issue of the *Hispanic Journal of Behavioral Sciences* entitled "Ethnic Identity and Psychological Adaptation."

Kathryn J. Lindholm is Associate Professor of Child Development at San Jose State University where she teaches courses on multicultural child development. She received her Ph.D. in developmental psychology from the University of California at Los Angeles. Her research interests include assessing the effectiveness of the two-way bilingual immersion education model to promote bilingualism, academic achievement, and true integration in the school setting among native speakers of other languages, particularly Spanish speakers. She serves as consultant to many school districts, the California Department of Education, and the Center for Research on Cultural Diversity and Second Language Learning and has authored or coauthored journal articles and book chapters on child bilingualism, two-way bilingual immersion education, and multicultural themes in child development.

Barbara VanOss Marín is Associate Adjunct Professor of Epidemiology and Biostatistics at the University of California at San Francisco. She holds undergraduate and graduate degrees in applied social psychology from Loyola University of Chicago and completed a postdoctoral fellowship at UC San Francisco in health psychology. Her primary interests over the past 15 years have been research and intervention to promote healthy behaviors among Hispanics/Latinos in culturally appropriate ways. She is currenting studying cultural issues related to AIDS prevention among Latinos. She has received funding from the National Institute for Mental Health to develop, implement, and evaluate a culturally appropriate sex education program for sixth and seventh graders in predominantly Latino schools. She lived in Bogota, Colombia for four years.

Gerardo Marín is Professor of Psychology at the University of San Francisco. A native of Colombia, he has been working recently on the development and evaluation of culturally appropriate community interventions for smoking cessation and alcohol abuse prevention among Hispanics. He is serving as Senior Scientific Editor for the 1995 *Surgeon General's Report on Smoking* and has published over 100 articles, book chapters, and books, one of which is *Research With Hispanic Populations* (Sage, 1991).

Juan Mendoza-Romero is working on his master's degree in counseling psychology at the University of California at Santa Barbara. He has extensive experience working as a counselor with Chicano adolescents who are at high risk of abusing drugs and alcohol, dropping out of school, and/or becoming involved in negative gang activities. Upon completion of his degree, he plans to return to his community and continue his work with Chicano adolescents.

Hector F. Myers is Professor of Psychology and Director of the Minority Mental Health Program at UCLA and Director of the Biobehavioral Research Center at the Charles R. Drew University of Medicine and Science. He received his Ph.D. in clinical psychology from the University of California at Los Angeles. He has been nationally recognized for his work on stress and physical and psychological adjustment of African American adults and families. His most recent work has focused on psychosocial and biobehavioral factors in mood disorders and on HIV/AIDS disease in this population. He is a Fellow in the Society for the Psychological Study of Ethnicity. He received the 1993 Ethnic Minority Mentorship Award from the Society for Community Research and Action and the 1993 Outstanding Contributions to Psychology Award given by the Los Angeles County Psychological Association.

Michael D. Newcomb is Professor of Counseling Psychology and chairs the Division of Counseling Psychology at the University of Southern California, and is a research psychologist and codirector of the Substance Abuse Research Center in the Department of Psychology at the University of California at Los Angeles. He received his Ph.D. in clinical psychology from UCLA and is a licensed clinical psychologist in California. He is principal investigator on several grants from the National Institute on Drug Abuse and has published over 150 articles and book chapters and written three books. His research interests include etiology and consequences of adolescent drug abuse; structural equation modeling, methodology, and multivariate analysis; human sexuality; health psychology; attitudes and affect related to nuclear war; and cohabitation, marriage, and divorce.

Adeline Nyamathi is Associate Professor of Nursing at the University of California at Los Angeles. Her research focuses on coping and health outcome of homeless and drug-addicted women of color in Los Angeles. She is currently principal investigator of two studies funded by the National Institute on Drug Abuse that assess the effectiveness of culturally competent AIDS education programs delivered by nurses and outreach workers to impoverished women. She is also coprincipal investigator with researchers from RAND Corporation, all of whom study the impact of health programs in the community. She serves on the editorial boards of several journals, is cochair of the UCLA Latino Advisory Board, is a Fellow of the American Academy of Nursing, and is the recipient of UCLA's 1994 Distinguished Lecturer Award.

Regina Otero-Sabogal is Assistant Research Psychologist in the Division of General Internal Medicine at the University of California at San Francisco. Her research is on smoking and cancer in Hispanic women and adolescents. She is the principal investigator of the American Cancer Society grant to evaluate cancer control interventions for Hispanic women, the National Cancer Institute breast and cervical cancer interventions for Hispanic women, and the State of California UCTRDRP Smoking Prevention for Pregnant and Nonpregnant Hispanic Adolescents. She is coinvestigator on two NCI studies to develop cancer control interventions for Hispanics. She received a distinction award from the California Health Department, Office of Tobacco Control for her contributions to the development of antismoking interventions and educational materials.

Eliseo J. Pérez-Stable, M.D., is Associate Professor of Medicine at the University of California at San Francisco School of Medicine. He holds an M.D. degree from the University of Miami, trained in primary care internal medicine at UCSF, and completed a Henry J. Kaiser Family Foundation fellowship in general internal medicine before joining the faculty at UCSF in 1983. His research has focused on risk factor reduction interventions for Latino populations. He directs the Programa Latino Para Dejar de Fumar, the Latino Project in the Pathways to Cancer Screening in Four Ethnic Groups program project grant, and the San Francisco site of the National Hispanic Leadership Initiative on Cancer. He is codirector of the UCSF Medical Effectiveness Research Center for Diverse Populations, which seeks effective medical interventions in African American and Latino populations, with a special emphasis on cancer and cardiovascular disease.

Jean S. Phinney is Professor of Psychology at California State University at Los Angeles. She received her Ph.D. from the University of California at Los Angeles. Her research interests focus on the social development of ethnic minority adolescents, with particular emphasis on ethnic identity, and has published numerous articles on the topic. With the support of a grant from the National Institute of Mental Health, she is currently studying ethnocentrism and intergroup relations among adolescents in ethnically diverse high school settings. She is collaborating on an international study of ethnic minority adolescents in six countries and has been an invited speaker at international conferences in New Zealand, Belgium, and Spain. She also serves as Assistant Editor for the *Journal of Adolescence*.

Erich J. Rueschenberg received his Ph.D. in applied social psychology from Clarement Graduate School in Pomona, California. He also completed doctoral training in social-clinical psychology at the Wright Institute in Los Angeles. For 14 years he worked as the director of an outpatient mental health program in the Los Angeles area and also served as a consultant for various residential treatment programs for adolescents and young adults. He is currently employed by the State of

California Department of Corrections in San Luis Obispo. His main research interests are in the areas of acculturation, social support, help seeking, and comparing different approaches in mental health service delivery.

Pedro Reyes is Associate Professor of Educational Administration at the University of Texas at Austin. He received his Ph.D. in Educational Policy from Wisconsin University. His research interests include the analysis of teacher work conditions and school-level policymaking. He also studies the effects of state policymaking on student outcomes. In 1992-1993 he held a National Academy of Education fellowship.

Fabio Sabogal is Assistant Research Psychologist in the Division of General Internal Medicine, the Center for AIDS Prevention Studies, and the Medical Effectiveness Research Center for Diverse Populations at the University of California at San Francisco. He is a Hispanic health psychologist who has conducted various studies in the Hispanic community, including cancer, smoking, tuberculosis, nutrition, and HIV transmission. He has also done extensive cross-cultural research in Colombia, Guatemala, and the United States. Currently, he is coinvestigator of several projects: Pathways to Cancer Screening; Cancer Interventions for Hispanic Women; NCI National Hispanic Leadership Initiative; AIDS Technology and Information Exchange; Increasing Compliance With Tuberculosis Appointments; and Family of AIDS Behavioral Surveys.

Delia S. Saenz is Assistant Professor of Psychology and an Assistant Research Professor in the Hispanic Research Center at Arizona State University. She received her Ph.D. in social psychology from Princeton University. Her research interests include tokenism, intergroup processes, social identity, and courtesy stigma. The primary focus of her work is on social differentiation, the process in which individuals perceive themselves as distinctive on an important dimension from others in the immediate social environment. She has taken her laboratory-based ideas and expertise into field settings, as in her National Institutes of Health supported work on token minorities in public school classrooms and her work on reduction of intergroup discrimination among college students belonging to rival groups.

Delia H. Saldaña is Clinical Assistant Professor of Psychiatry at the University of Texas Health Sciences Center at San Antonio. Her research has focused on stress, coping, and social supports in Mexican Americans. She is currently principal investigator of two studies funded by the South Texas Health Research Center and the National Institute of Mental Health that explore ethnic and urban/rural differences in caregiving among families of the severely mentally ill. She is a coinvestigator on a Hispanic Health Aging Center grant from the National Institute on Aging working on projects to develop culturally sensitive assessments of subclinical disability and depression in elderly Mexican Americans. She also directs the Office of Community Research at San Antonio State Hospital, which coordinates research and program evaluation of outpatient psychiatric services to a 16-county catchment area in South Texas.

Rosa Seijo is a Developmental Pediatric Fellow at the Rose F. Kennedy Development Center of the Albert Einstein College of Medicine. She received her M.D. degree from Mount Sinai School of Medicine in New York City, and completed her pediatric residency at the Montefiore/Einstein Affiliated Hospitals in the Bronx, NY. Her research focuses on bilingualism and the development of language in developmentally disabled children.

Diana M. Valdez is Assistant Professor of Psychiatry at the University of New Mexico School of Medicine, Division of Child and Adolescent Psychiatry, and is a staff psychologist at Programs for Children and Adolescents, University of New Mexico Mental Health Center. She received her Ph.D. in social psychology from the University of California at Riverside and completed postdoctoral training in clinical child psychology at the University of New Mexico. Her interests include cross-cultural issues in the assessment and treatment of minority children, forensic psychology, and cross-cultural training and consultation.

Richard R. Valencia is Associate Professor of Educational Psychology at the University of Texas at Austin. His major field of specialization is ethnic minority education (psychological and social aspects), with emphasis on Mexican American students. He has published extensively on test validity/test bias issues vis-à-vis Chicano students as well as on more recent work on school segregation, high-stakes testing, and Latino demographic trends. His 1991 edited book, *Chicano School Failure and Success: Research and Policy Agendas for the 1990s*, received CHOICE's 1993 Outstanding Academic Book award. He serves on the editorial boards of the *Journal of Educational Psychology, Hispanic Journal of Behavioral Sciences,* and *Review of Educational Research.*

Rose M. Vasquez, R.N., F.N.P., is Clincial Coordinator and Director of the Women's HIV Clinic at the AIDS Healthcare Foundation (AHF) in Los Angeles, which serves a large population base of indigent Latin and majority patients. She is a coinvestigator on several clinical trials on HIV with the Southwest Community-Based AIDS Treatment (ComBAT) Group. She has a master's degree in nursing from UCLA and has been certified as a Family Nurse Practitioner by the American Nursing Association. She is a member of the HIV Community Planning Working Group, which is sponsored and funded by the Centers for Disease Control and Prevention (CDC) and the California Department of Health Services, Office of AIDS.

Burl R. Wagenheim is a Ph.D. candidate in counseling psychology at the University of California at Santa Barbara and holds master's degrees in education and communication. He was formerly an officer with the World Health Organization where he was responsible for numerous health promotion projects in South America, the Caribbean, and North America. His dissertation research examines the relationship between health behavior, emotional health, and having a sense of meaning and purpose in life.

Gustavo A. Yep is Assistant Professor of Communication Studies and Associate Director of the Institute for Asian American and Pacific Asian Studies at California State University at Los Angeles. He received his Ph.D. from the University of Southern California. He is currently a member of the advisory board for the new Asian Pacific AIDS Intervention Team, the executive board of the Southern California chapter of the Society for Public Health Education (SOPHE), the Cultural Issues and Minority Health Committee of SOPHE, and the board of directors of Pacific Clinics. He chairs the AIDS Committee of SOPHE. His work has appeared in book chapters as well as articles in a number of scholarly publications, and he is recipient of several research grants and teaching and service awards.